SEARCHING

FOR

MEMORY

SEARCHING FOR MEMORY

ALUÍZIO PALMAR

AND THE SHADOW OF
DICTATORSHIP IN BRAZIL

JACOB BLANC

THE UNIVERSITY OF NORTH CAROLINA PRESS
CHAPEL HILL

© 2025 The University of North Carolina Press
All rights reserved

Designed by Lindsay Starr
Set in Calluna and Futura Now
by codeMantra
Manufactured in the United States of America

Cover art: Aluízio Palmar mugshot, 1969. Courtesy of Aluízio Palmar.

LIBRARY OF CONGRESS CATALOGING-IN-PUBLICATION DATA
Names: Blanc, Jacob, author.
Title: Searching for memory : Aluízio Palmar and
the shadow of dictatorship in Brazil / Jacob Blanc.
Description: Chapel Hill : The University of North Carolina Press, 2025. |
Includes bibliographical references and index.
Identifiers: LCCN 2024045104 | ISBN 9781469681023 (cloth) |
ISBN 9781469681030 (paperback) | ISBN 9781469681047 (epub) |
ISBN 9781469681054 (pdf)
Subjects: LCSH: Palmar, Aluízio, 1943- |
Human rights workers—Brazil—Biography. |
Torture victims—Brazil—Biography. |
Dictatorship—Brazil—History—20th century. |
Human rights advocacy—Brazil. | Brazil—History—1964-1985. |
Brazil—Politics and government—1964-1985. |
BISAC: HISTORY / Latin America / South America |
HISTORY / Modern / 20th Century / Cold War | LCGFT: Biographies.
Classification: LCC KHD304.P35 B36 | DDC 365/.45092 [B]—dc23/eng/20241009
LC record available at https://lccn.loc.gov/2024045104

This book will be made open access within three years of publication thanks to Path to Open, a program developed in partnership between JSTOR, the American Council of Learned Societies (ACLS), the University of Michigan Press, and the University of North Carolina Press to bring about equitable access and impact for the entire scholarly community, including authors, researchers, libraries, and university presses around the world. Learn more at https://about.jstor.org/path-to-open.

For product safety concerns under the European Union's General Product Safety Regulation (EU GPSR), please contact gpsr@mare-nostrum.co.uk or write to the University of North Carolina Press and Mare Nostrum Group B.V., Mauritskade 21D, 1091 GC Amsterdam, The Netherlands.

TO THE MEMORY OF THOSE STILL MISSING,
AND FOR THE COURAGE OF THOSE STILL SEARCHING.

CONTENTS

LIST OF ILLUSTRATIONS viii

ACKNOWLEDGMENTS ix

INTRODUCTION. Life, History, and Memory 1

CHAPTER 1. Childhood Visions 21

CHAPTER 2. A Shadow Descends 34

CHAPTER 3. Taking Up Arms 53

CHAPTER 4. Prison, Torture 85

CHAPTER 5. Prison, Waiting 109

CHAPTER 6. Exile in Chile 132

CHAPTER 7. Exile in Argentina 146

CHAPTER 8. Transitions 172

CHAPTER 9. The Search 194

CHAPTER 10. Memory in the Time of Impunity 213

CONCLUSION. Out of the Shadows 232

NOTES 245

BIBLIOGRAPHY 269

INDEX 277

ILLUSTRATIONS

FIGURES

0.1. Aluízio Palmar in his garden, Foz do Iguaçu, 2020 12
1.1. Luzia and Anízio Palmar, with their two oldest sons, late 1940s 22
2.1. Students on the Icaraí beach, early 1960s 42
3.1. Aluízio Palmar at a horse racing festival near Cascavel, Paraná, late 1968 or early 1969 57
3.2. Police sketch of alleged bank robber, 1969 74
3.3. Profile of MR-8, *Manchete*, 1969 77
4.1. Photos of MR-8 prisoners, *Jornal do Brasil*, 1969 104
5.1. National Truth Commission visits Ilha das Flores, 2014 110
5.2. Imprisoned militants prior to their release from Brazil, 1971 129
6.1. Aluízio, Florita, and Eunice in Chile, ca. 1971 138
6.2. Aluízio and Eunice at a rally in Santiago, Chile, 1971 140
7.1. Aluízio on a tea plantation, ca. 1972 151
8.1. Aluízio at a May Day event with the PDT, 1982 or 1983 189
9.1. Aluízio at a book signing, Porto Alegre, 2005 210
9.2. Aluízio at the excavation site in Iguaçu National Park, 2010 211

MAPS

1.1. Locations of Aluízio Palmar's upbringing and militancy in south and southwestern Brazil 20
6.1. Locations of Aluízio Palmar's exile in Chile and Argentina 135
9.1. Paraná borderlands and likely location of 1974 massacre 204

ACKNOWLEDGMENTS

MY FIRST AND DEEPEST WORD OF THANKS GOES TO ALUÍZIO PALMAR, who shared with me two of the most precious things a person can give: their memories and their time. This project ended up taking far longer than Aluízio had thought it would, but he always remained a generous and kind collaborator. I learned more from Aluízio than one book can convey—not just about his history and that of Brazil but about solidarity, dedication, and the importance of speaking out against injustice. Thank you, Aluízio, for trusting me with your stories.

My deep gratitude also extends to the dozens of people in Brazil, Argentina, and Bolivia who also opened their memories to me. Above all to Aluízio's children: Florita, Andrea, Alexandre, Ana Luzia, Janaina, and Amanda. Even in the best of cases, it is difficult to speak about one's family. The family histories in this book are often complicated and tense, leaving me even more grateful that the Palmar family received my interview questions if not enthusiastically, at least with an open mind. And to the rest of my interviewees—the militants, prisoners, survivors, activists, and dedicated community members—I hope you find that the stories in this book do justice to the memories you so graciously shared.

Most of the people I interviewed will be reading the Portuguese version of this book, and for that I thank Laiz Ferguson, a gifted translator with whom I have now worked on three projects. Laiz also gave excellent editorial comments and personal reflections about her own family's history during the turbulent years of Brazil's dictatorship. My research process was aided by three transcribers who typed up my interviews. The Portuguese interviews were transcribed by Gabriella Barrozo and Isabel Grassiolli (students at UNIOESTE in Paraná, introduced to me by Professor Carla Luciana Silva) and the Spanish interviews by David Sierra Márquez. And for the final production of the book, my thanks to Bridgette Werner for preparing the index, and Gabriel Moss for the maps.

I started this project while on a fellowship from the Arts and Humanities Research Council, ostensibly working on a different book. I put the other project on hold to throw myself into this biography, taking advantage of not having to teach to try and balance two books at once. Other institutional support came

ACKNOWLEDGMENTS

through grants from the British Academy and the Royal Society of Edinburgh. At UNC Press, I have been lucky to work with both Elaine Maisner, who first took on this project, and then Debbie Gershenowitz, as well as their excellent editorial assistants, JessieAnne D'Amico and Alexis Dumain, and the project editor, Valerie Burton. Many thanks to everyone at the UNC Press production, marketing, and design teams.

From colleagues, I benefited from feedback at all stages. Debbie Sharnak and Leigh Payne read an initial version of the book, and our conversations during a Zoom manuscript workshop were instrumental. Donald Bloxham and Julie Gibbings also gave early comments for a talk at the University of Edinburgh, as did Aidan Russell at the Geneva Graduate Institute. I discussed the book with several of my colleagues at McGill, who have welcomed me to a wonderful new academic home. Thanks also to Rachel Nolan for reading a final version of the book's introduction and encouraging me to think even more about how to set a scene. Additionally, the comments from two peer reviewers were truly generative. As always, I received steady support from my on-call family editors: my brilliant wife, Isabel Pike, and my nerd-in-crime brother, Eric Blanc. And to my son, Jonah, my heart, thanks for always inspiring me to see the world through your toddler eyes.

SEARCHING

FOR

MEMORY

INTRODUCTION

LIFE, HISTORY, AND MEMORY

ON DECEMBER 2, 2019, Aluízio Palmar was sued by his torturer, a retired army officer named Mário Espedito Ostrovski. At the time of the lawsuit, both men were well over seventy years old. They had not crossed paths since 1969, when Ostrovski subjected Aluízio to intense physical and psychological abuse. Yet fifty years later, Ostrovski resurfaced to threaten his victim once more.

In the 1960s, the two men were on opposite sides of a Cold War conflict that was steadily spreading across Latin America. Aluízio was an armed militant fighting against Brazil's dictatorship and Ostrovski was an army lieutenant and prison interrogator. Aluízio had become active in political movements in the early 1960s while working and studying in Niterói, the industrial port city across the bay from Rio de Janeiro. In the aftermath of the military's coup in 1964, Aluízio became more radical and eventually went underground to participate in revolutionary armed struggle. The regime captured Aluízio in 1969 while he was attempting to build a guerrilla insurgency along the Paraná border of southwestern Brazil, and within a few months he was placed under the control of Lieutenant Ostrovski. Like thousands of others under the military regime that

INTRODUCTION

ruled Brazil from 1964 to 1985, Aluízio suffered various forms of torture during his two years in prison, including simulated drowning, mock execution, solitary confinement, and the infamous "parrot's perch" where he was strung up on a pole with his hands and feet tied together, his crouched body dangling upside-down.

Half a century separated Aluízio's torture and Ostrovski's lawsuit. During that time, Aluízio remained a committed political activist. After a decade in exile in Chile and Argentina, Aluízio returned to Brazil and worked as a journalist and political organizer. In the late 1990s, he became a full-time human rights activist, galvanized by his search for the bodies of militants who had been killed by the dictatorship. As part of his activism, he established the Center for Human Rights and Popular Memory (CDHMP, Centro de Direitos Humanos e Memória Popular) in Foz do Iguaçu, the border city where he had met his wife while conducting guerrilla training and where he returned after exile to raise his family. Aluízio's human rights work focused largely on questions of justice and the legacies of Brazil's dictatorship—themes that would come to define 2019, for Aluízio and for Brazil as a whole.

At the beginning of the year, Brazil had inaugurated a new president, Jair Bolsonaro, whose far-right populism and open nostalgia for the violence of military rule threatened to undo the work that Aluízio and so many other activists had achieved in recent decades. During Bolsonaro's first year in office, as the new government unleashed a wave of attacks on the rights of Indigenous and LGBTQ people, the environment, and the rule of law, Aluízio and his collaborators devoted themselves to what felt like a relentless torrent of campaigns locally and in solidarity with larger national movements.

And in December 2019, Ostrovski filed defamation charges relating to a post that Aluízio had made on Facebook. The post was not recent. It came from 2013, when Aluízio had publicized a protest that drew attention to the abuses committed by Ostrovski, who had been living in relative anonymity as a lawyer in Foz do Iguaçu. Six years later, in a context of reemergent reactionary politics under Bolsonaro, Ostrovski dredged up the old Facebook post and sued Aluízio for nearly US$10 million in moral damages. A torture victim being sued by his torturer was almost unimaginably perverse. But the lawsuit reflected Brazil's contentious history of dictatorship, and the shadows that continued to haunt Aluízio and countless others.

LIFE HISTORY IN THE SHADOW OF DICTATORSHIP

As with other human rights activists who survived the violence of dictatorship, Aluízio's life story served as a form of legitimacy to help support new social movements. After being released from prison by the military government in 1971, he spent most of the 1970s living in exile, initially in Santiago, Chile, and then in various locations in northeastern Argentina. He did not return to Brazil until 1979. During the first decades after his return, he was extremely hesitant to share his story. He took part in mobilizations to end the dictatorship, but he never openly discussed his participation in the armed Left or his time in prison. Aluízio only began speaking about himself in the 1990s, when he undertook what was essentially a one-man search for the bodies of six militants who had been disappeared by the military regime in 1974—several of the disappeared had been in the same revolutionary group as Aluízio, and he had also nearly fallen into the trap that led to their deaths. Over time, the memories of his experience became an increasingly important part of his search for the disappeared: the more he became a public figure known for having fought against and survived the brutality of dictatorship, the more attention was brought to his efforts to locate the bodies and achieve a semblance of justice for their families. For Aluízio, the narration of his life story became a key part of his transition from armed militant to human rights activist.

As part of his search for the disappeared, Aluízio entered a near-constant mode of autobiographizing: he wrote a memoir, gave public speeches, led seminars with university and high school students, contributed to Brazil's truth commission, and sat for interviews with journalists and scholars. Bearing witness to the violence he had suffered in the twentieth century—at the hands of Lieutenant Ostrovski and other military perpetrators—became a biographic tool in his pursuit of justice in the twenty-first century. Unlike neighboring Argentina and Chile, which held criminal proceedings and issued truth commission reports in the 1980s and 1990s, Brazil had no human rights trials or truth commissions as part of its process of transitional justice. The lack of legal accountability stretched back to 1979, when as part of the military's negotiated transition out of power, the government passed an amnesty law that reinstituted certain political freedoms—including the return of exiles—but also gave full immunity for human rights abuses. Brazil did not have a national truth commission until 2013, making it one of the last countries in Latin America to do so.[1] The commission, moreover, was entirely investigative—it could only document, not prosecute, cases of torture, disappearance, sexual violence, and political repression. In the absence of legal justice, former victims of Brazil's dictatorship used their own life histories to challenge the legacies of the Amnesty Law. Sharing memories of torture and imprisonment served as a counternarrative wedge into the dominant culture of impunity. And it was Aluízio's propensity to discuss his past—magnified by the unleashing effect of Bolsonaro—that led to him being sued by his torturer.

INTRODUCTION

A biography of Aluízio Palmar can thus contain multiple layers of storytelling. Although this book is primarily a chronicle of Aluízio's life between his militancy in the 1960s and the Ostrovski lawsuit fifty years later, it does more than just recount his life story. It is also a story about stories: how Aluízio has told his own life history, why he has transformed some of his most private stories into a public narrative, and the meanings of memory in the shadow of dictatorship.

MEMORY SCRIPT

Through my biography of Aluízio Palmar, I develop the concept of memory script. By approaching memory as a process of self-narration, I explore why people share certain memories in certain ways, how different platforms of memory relate to each other, and what a person's narration of memory suggests about how they understand their place in history. Instead of focusing on a particular output of someone's memories—a book, or a social media post, or testimony to a truth commission—we can analyze a given memory as part of a person's self-initiated life history. For a biographer interested in memory, the challenge is to simultaneously tell the person's story and pay attention to how that person has told their own story. This is particularly important when the memories relate to trauma and violence. Scholars of memory in Latin America have already established a set of innovative analogies for understanding the aftermath of political violence. Chief among these are Elizabeth Jelín's notion of an *emprendedor de memoria* (memory entrepreneur) and Steve Stern's idea of a memory box.[2] Whereas the former elucidates the efforts of a range of actors involved in contemporary memory struggles, and the latter helps explain how individuals contribute to a collective process of remembering and forgetting, my hope is that the concept of memory script can offer a complementary framework for understanding the *process* of memory-sharing.

There are three main characteristics of a memory script: it is practiced, it is repetitive, and it is performative. As a practice, memory-sharing is built up over years and exhibited across different platforms. We see this throughout Aluízio's memory work, which began in the 1990s with his investigations into the fates of six disappeared militants, then spread to his writing, organizing, and public speaking. His practice of memory often revolved around his 2005 book, *Onde foi que vocês enterraram nossos mortos?* (Where did you bury our dead?). The book is primarily an account of his search for the bodies of the six militants, but with interwoven autobiographical sections, thus straddling the lines between memoir and investigative journalism.[3] As Aluízio's book went through several reprintings between 2005 and 2019, his practice also grew institutionally, through the human rights center that he established in Foz do Iguaçu and a website on which he posts digitized archival material he collected from the years of military rule.[4] Across these various memory initiatives, and influenced by similar campaigns that he observed in Brazil and across Latin America and globally, Aluízio learned and practiced his craft.[5]

The second characteristic of a memory script, its repetitive nature, means that the style and content of a person's self-narration tends to follow similar patterns. In postdictatorship societies like Brazil, where few, if any, perpetrators of human rights violations have been brought to justice, victims of state violence deploy their life stories to challenge the dominant narratives that have glossed over or ignored the full extent of a country's authoritarian past. As a recurring practice of bearing witness, the repetition of a story helps it gain power. Memory-sharing is flexible and context-specific, and as Adam Gaffey writes in his study of ceremonial memory, "Every moment of repetition is a new opportunity to refashion, reimagine, and reconstitute the meaning of public discourse."[6] When oriented toward political campaigns in the present, the patterned sharing of memory is not merely a ritualized repetition of suffering or the Freudian "acting out" of trauma.[7] Amid the shadows of dictatorship, the repetition of memory is a way to bring renewed attention to past experiences of repression and resistance.

The third quality of a memory script, of being performative, means that, like all scripts, it requires an audience. A memory script is meant to be performed and received—that is how it gets its power to shape a narrative. As Diana Taylor observes in her study of gender and human rights activism with the Madres de la Plaza de Mayo in Argentina, "Performance, as a carrying through, needs the audience to complete its meaning, tie the pieces together and give them coherence."[8] The performance of memory is a way to transform the personal into the political, and to exorcise one's demons toward a broader social goal—an outward performance of suffering that Ana Elena Puga and Víctor Espinosa describe as a form of pragmatic activism.[9] That the performance of memory also brings greater attention to the storyteller is an almost self-evident, but nonetheless vital, element in why a person chooses to publicize the details of their life.

A memory script framework also engages the question of how to write about trauma. This was among the most complicated aspects of my collaboration with Aluízio: how to avoid defining Aluízio by his trauma. And how to understand his memories both within and separate from his traumatic experiences. Like most scholars, I am unqualified to make anything resembling an official diagnosis of Aluízio's mental and emotional status. Yet it is evident enough that his experience of torture, compounded by the politically and personally tumultuous years before and after his imprisonment, left profound marks. These included suicidal thoughts, drinking problems, and, especially in the early years of his children's life, being an emotionally distant father. In our interviews, Aluízio used the term "trauma," though he did so sparingly—as with other "step-back" moments in my analysis of Aluízio's memories, I draw readers' attention to examples of his reflections on trauma as they arise in this book.

For Aluízio, as for countless political prisoners and torture victims across the globe, the process of sharing his memories cannot be disentangled from the pain of the memories themselves. As I noted earlier, for nearly three decades after his imprisonment, Aluízio refused to discuss this experience. He only began speaking about his torture in the early 2000s, once he had become a full-time human rights activist. It is now a fixture of his memory activism. Yet the fact that he is willing to talk about his trauma does not resolve a host of underlying ethical and methodological questions around writing about his life. For survivors of torture, being interviewed about their past can mimic the torture itself—the interviewers' questions recalling those of the interrogator.[10] Asking a person about their trauma, even someone like Aluízio who has chosen to speak repeatedly and publicly about their experience, requires careful attention.[11] For scholars of memory, grappling with a subject's trauma is both fundamental and deeply perplexing—such that an entire subfield known as trauma studies emerged in the 1990s to help make sense of something that is hard enough for survivors to understand, let alone anyone else.[12]

For a memory script analysis of Aluízio's life, a key question relates to the narrative characteristics that arise from trauma. Psychologists use the term "autobiographical memory" to explain how people integrate a complex range of single, recurring, and extended events (*episodic memory*) into "a coherent story of self that is created and evaluated through sociocultural practices."[13] A person's narrative of autobiographical memory is always subject to change, and this is especially true for survivors of torture, who, studies have shown, can have fragmented and inconsistent memory of the traumatic events.[14] Trauma disrupts a person's ability to construct a coherent narrative and can distort a person's perception of time. This means that even activists like Aluízio who publicize their experience for political purposes carry with them an impossibility of narrating their memories in a purely documentary way.

But how do we balance a scholarly inclination to provide readers with a consistent narrative path and a source base that can resist an entirely linear progression? There is no obvious solution, no way to reconcile the subjectivities of a person's memories—whether traumatic or not—with the exercise of objective narration. Instead, two elements will coexist in this book: the larger narrative will proceed chronologically across Aluízio's life, while the traumatic memories on which much of the book is based will occasionally present a narrative that, on the surface, may seem irrational or untruthful. And it is precisely in these moments of tension, and through the questions they elicit, that an approach of memory script can help make sense of the external factors that orient the expression of traumatic memories.

LIFE HISTORY ON THE PERIPHERY

At first glance, Aluízio's political trajectory follows a standard path. He became a student activist while a teenager in the early 1960s in Niterói and embraced revolutionary politics after the military's 1964 coup. He was eventually imprisoned and tortured before living in exile until the period of the 1979 Amnesty Law. Yet, at seemingly each phase, Aluízio took the less-common path. While hundreds of thousands of young people took to the streets to protest the dictatorship, Aluízio was one of some 5,000 Brazilians who took up arms.[15] Even then, his group, the October 8 Revolutionary Movement (MR-8, Movimento Revolucionário 8 de Outubro), was one of the few organizations in Brazil that sought to imitate the Cuban Revolution's guerrilla *foco* strategy of rural rather than urban resistance.[16] When he was released from prison and sent to Chile in early 1970, instead of enjoying his newfound freedom under Chile's democratic socialist president, Salvador Allende, Aluízio opted for a second round of armed resistance—he joined a small group of Brazilian exiles committed to overthrowing the dictatorship back home.

Even before the 1973 military coup that ousted Allende, Aluízio left Chile and went underground in Argentina, where a military coup in 1976 would extend the shadow of violent dictatorship even farther across the region. While living clandestinely in Argentina, Aluízio posed as a farmworker to gather intelligence along the border and coordinate the cross-border movement of militants. Aluízio was so off the radar that when his name somehow appeared on a list of those who had been killed by the dictatorship, his former comrades assumed that the news was true and that he was dead.

For Aluízio, his decade in exile was defined by loneliness and a fear of being caught. His seven years in Argentina (1972–79) coincided with the rise of Operation Condor, a pan-dictatorship collaboration to surveil, imprison, and disappear militants across the Southern Cone. His exile was even more challenging because he brought his family along for most of it: he had met his wife, Eunice,

INTRODUCTION

in 1968 while conducting guerrilla training in Iguaçu National Park; his first child was born while he was in jail; and his next two children were born while the family lived under fake names with falsified documents in northeastern Argentina. Aluízio's isolated and dangerous exile left him resentful toward other Brazilians who spent their exile in Europe. Because his fringe experience does not feature in the better-known narratives of Rio- and São Paulo–based revolutionaries who wound up as part of the exile community overseas, his life history illuminates the political and personal factors that led some militants to go even farther off the beaten path.

Aluízio's place on the periphery of history continued upon his return to Brazil in late 1979. Although he initially returned to Rio de Janeiro—a city that likely would have planted him in the middle of the national mobilizations for democracy—Aluízio followed his wife back to the border city of Foz do Iguaçu. His experience of democratization thus took place outside of the major urban arenas of the struggle to end Brazil's dictatorship. In Foz do Iguaçu, he helped establish an opposition newspaper that focused on local examples of injustice such as the displacement of rural communities and the corruption of military politicians. Aluízio remained in Foz do Iguaçu after the official return to democracy in 1985, and he continues to live there to this day. The region also shaped his human rights activism, which initially formed around his search for the bodies of six militants who, in 1976, had been killed by the dictatorship, most likely in nearby Iguaçu National Park.

For someone with Aluízio's militant pedigree, living in a border town allowed him to become well-known locally and have a deep impact on regional political struggles, but it perhaps kept him from becoming more prominent at a national level. (The city is far more famous for the Iguaçu waterfalls than it is for any local citizens or political movements.) This position at the margins, both politically and geographically, showcases the life history of a man who did most of his work in an area far less studied by scholars—and far less valued by left-wing intellectuals—who have written about the dictatorship. As such, it broadens our understanding of the fight for democracy and accountability beyond Brazil's traditional centers of power. Aluízio's position both in the middle and on the periphery of history has shaped his self-narration. To understand the life histories of people like Aluízio Palmar, whose memories also function as a form of political resistance, tracing when and why they share their memories becomes a powerful exercise not only for writing a biography but also for analyzing how people make sense of their place in history.

METHODOLOGY

I first met Aluízio Palmar in 2013, while researching my dissertation on the Itaipu dam and the displacement of local farmers, peasants, and Indigenous communities near Foz do Iguaçu. My fieldnotes from August 6, 2013, describe my first impression of him: "Met with Aluízio Palmar who is just fantastic, a really cool and almost crotchety older dude, super smart. He picked me up and we drove to the under-construction [Center for Human Rights and Popular Memory].... He also took me to a local journalist office, where they are digitalizing tons of old newspapers."[17] Aluízio had cofounded one of those newspapers, *Nosso Tempo*, in 1980, and it served as a key source of my dissertation research. I also interviewed him as a participant-observer of the farmers movement, and he put me in touch with other people to interview. At the time, I had only a general understanding of his larger human rights work. In the years after my fieldwork, we sporadically stayed in touch, mostly on Facebook: he would forward me campaigns he was involved with and I shared with him the progress of my book.

When I saw his 2019 Facebook posts about the Ostrovski lawsuit, and as I witnessed an outpouring of solidarity notes from other activists in Brazil, I asked Aluízio for an interview. He agreed, and in January 2020 I wrote an online essay about the lawsuit and the legacy of military rule in Brazil.[18] My piece was one of several dozen published in Brazil and internationally, and the public campaign seemed to work. By June of the following year, Ostrovski dropped the suit, a rare victory under Bolsonaro.

In the interim, the entire world was rocked by the COVID-19 pandemic. In the months after I first interviewed Aluízio, as the lawsuit was still pending and as we found ourselves sitting anxiously at home, I was scared for him. He was a seventy-six-year-old diabetic living in Bolsonaro's Brazil during a global health crisis, and especially in the early phases of the pandemic, whenever I logged onto Facebook, I worried that I would see his obituary. With both of us stuck at home, I saw an opportunity to conduct a series of virtual interviews. I emailed Aluízio with my proposal to write a biography, and he accepted. The still-pending Ostrovski lawsuit likely factored into his decision—a bigger global spotlight on him could only help his solidarity campaign.

In May 2020, Aluízio and I began recording interviews. For the first several months, the conversations took place weekly, and they became more spaced out with time. Over the course of two years, we did twenty-five interviews, totaling nearly forty hours. As described below, I also interviewed three dozen

INTRODUCTION

people from across Aluízio's life. All of the interviews, with Aluízio and the others, took place digitally, most often using the WhatsApp audio function, but also with video calls on various platforms. This methodology was not without drawbacks, including my own desire to connect more strongly with my interviewees. With a decade of research experience in Brazil, I knew these spaces well: the gardens in Foz do Iguaçu where we would sit on plastic chairs under the shade of guava trees, and the small, yellow-tiled kitchens in Rio de Janeiro, where former militants would serve coffee and share stories of their younger days. But for this project, at this time, researching at a distance would suffice.

In parallel with the interviews, I started this project by reading Aluízio's memoir and his testimony to Brazil's truth commission. I also pored through his online presence, which included an outdated WordPress blog and his still-active Facebook page. Aluízio often uses social media to situate himself within the arc of Brazil's recent history. When there is an anniversary of an important event—a famous protest in 1968, the passage of the 1979 Amnesty Law, or the murder of a militant—Aluízio posts about how he experienced that moment. And when a former comrade passes away, he eulogizes them and talks about their shared experiences and accomplishments.

Aluízio's storytelling on social media often blends past and present. In October 2018, for example, a week before the runoff election between Jair Bolsonaro and Fernando Haddad, the candidate of the leftist Workers' Party (PT, Partido dos Trabalhadores), he posted on Facebook in the form of a letter to his eight grandchildren. To link his own history of resistance and repression to the current fight to keep Bolsonaro out of office, Aluízio offered a summary of his life under military rule. Aluízio wrote in a style that was both performatively intimate—appealing to his grandchildren, most of whom were not old enough to be on Facebook—and retrospectively political: like many former militants in the years and decades after their vision of a socialist revolution had faded, Aluízio reframed the goals of the armed struggle not as an effort to construct socialism but as a fight for democracy. The post, which received almost 1,000 likes and was shared nearly 400 times, merits being quoted in full.[19]

> My dearest granddaughters and grandsons,
> Almost fifty years ago, your grandfather was subjected to the most terrible and barbaric tortures. I was twenty-six years old and Brazil was dominated by a military dictatorship, which arrested, tortured, and killed its opponents. The press, music, and theater were under censorship. The word freedom was forbidden.

And it was because of the fight for democracy that I was arrested. And after passing through torture centers in Paraná, I was taken to Rio de Janeiro, where new tortures took place. Months before, agents of the military dictatorship invaded my parents' house (your great-grandparents). They went in search of weapons and found my books. It was ten years—1969, the year I was arrested, and 1979, the year I returned to legal life with political amnesty—that marked the life of our family. Eunice, your grandmother, still bears the scars of those dark years.

Sorry for those sad words from grandpa. Sad yes, because I think we are going through a moment very similar to the one our family lived through, which I don't want you to experience.

But let's get straight to the point. I want you to know that in this election, your grandfather voted for Fernando Haddad. It is what's possible at this moment, to vote for the candidate who gives us more assurance that democracy will be maintained and respected.

Fernando Haddad is the necessary option for public education and health to be valued and for the development of the good side of his party's earlier governments. The good side, yes, because there were also bad things that we cannot accept.

So my grandchildren, whatever the outcome, let's wait for the day to dawn without hatred.

Grandpa Aluízio

Although most of Aluízio's online presence focuses on his human rights activism and his memories of militancy, it also has a lighter side, which helped me see deeper into his personality. He often shares his favorite music, mostly Brazilian protest songs from his youth like those of Sérgio Ricardo, Chico Buarque, and Geraldo Vandré, but also by artists from other countries like the Argentine singer Mercedes Sosa and the Chilean group Inti-Illimani. (Many of our interviews were also sprinkled with lyrics; for Aluízio, music seemed a useful filter for processing and giving shape to his memories.) Aluízio can also be funny, with an understated, wry sense of humor. On Facebook, he not infrequently posts photos of Vladimir Lenin holding cats.[20] Aluízio is not necessarily the biggest Lenin fan—he prefers Che Guevara—but he does like cats and has several in his home. He also has a large tortoise named Coquito that he brought back from the Chaco region of western Paraguay, who lives in Aluízio's backyard and has a dent in his shell from the time that Aluízio backed out of his driveway without noticing him.

INTRODUCTION

FIGURE 0.1. Aluízio Palmar in his garden, Foz do Iguaçu, December 9, 2020. Photo by author.

The tortoise story was one of the few anecdotes in this book that Aluízio told me in person (fig. 0.1). I traveled to Brazil at the end of 2020 to finish research on a different project, and I arranged to visit Aluízio in his garden. It was exactly one year and one week since Aluízio had been sued by Ostrovski, and despite our masks and social distancing, his mood was upbeat. We talked for nearly two hours, with almost no mention of the collaborative biography or the dozens of hours of interviews we had already recorded. It was nice to just chat. Before I left, he gave me a tour of his vegetable garden and introduced me to Coquito the tortoise—Aluízio chuckled as he told me about Coquito's dented shell, with a twinge of embarrassment but also amusement. Being a memory activist in the shadow of dictatorship requires the ability to laugh at oneself, and Aluízio, despite a stubborn streak for which he is also famous, has no problem finding humor.

Over the course of our interviews, as I read deeper into the archive of Aluízio's blog and social media posts, I also compiled his digitally available memories, which included a dozen YouTube videos of his old presentations and interviews. This iterative process was useful because in our conversations, his initial reaction to many questions was to tell me the same stories, with the same details, that he has told elsewhere. Knowing the general patterns of Aluízio's memory script allowed me to anticipate emblematic anecdotes and ask for more information than he had provided elsewhere. And in the instances when he gave dates or names that did not seem to align, I could ask for clarification in real time.

Whenever possible, I corroborated Aluízio's stories with archival documents from the military regime, most of which came from digitized databases. These drew from three main sources: the Brasil: Nunca Mais online repository, which originated as a groundbreaking investigation in the 1980s; the National Archive's digital holdings connected to Brazil's 2013 National Truth Commission report; and Aluízio's own website, Documentos Revelados (Revealed documents), which houses a vast range of materials related to the era of dictatorship, including a Fundo Aluízio Palmar dedicated to his own life and the digitization of documents that he personally consulted in police and military archives.

My research also included interviews with three dozen people from various stages of his life, including family members, colleagues, and former militants. These interviews corroborated, deepened, or challenged the memories that Aluízio shared with me—an analysis of Aluízio's memory script would thus need to account for the memories of other people, too. Aluízio provided me with the contact information for most of the people that I interviewed, a helpful if not uncomplicated collaboration, as those he wanted me to speak with were more likely to say positive things about him. I also made my own contacts and interviewed many people that Aluízio did not know about beforehand. On the whole, these respondents shared the same generally positive assessment, though in a few instances I learned of interpersonal tensions from those who thought that Aluízio was headstrong and did not always respect professional protocols. Two people I spoke with said that Aluízio published material on his website for which they had not given authorization. Even people who praised Aluízio—very much including those he had introduced me to—also shared stories about his stubbornness.

Aluízio gave me the phone numbers for all six of his children, five daughters and one son. Despite knowing the types of negative family stories that his children would likely share, Aluízio seemed to have no problem with my interviewing them. In the end, I was able to speak with five of the six children. Although I was in contact with Aluízio's fourth-oldest child, she stopped responding to my messages after I sent an example list of questions. After several follow-up attempts, I had to move on without the interview.

INTRODUCTION

The conversations with Aluízio's children were especially useful because his wife, Eunice, does not give interviews. Aluízio and several of his children told me that Eunice's refusal to share her memories is the product of her harrowing experience during Aluízio's imprisonment and their shared time in exile. The children told me about the impact that Aluízio's militancy had on their mother—for example, staying up late at night crying while the family lived clandestinely in Argentina. They also described a contradiction between a man who outside the home was a tireless warrior against injustice and the one who for much of his adult life was distant and chauvinist in the home. One daughter, Janaina, told me that Aluízio's machismo was the reason she considers herself a feminist. Another daughter, Florita, the oldest, who was born while Aluízio was imprisoned, said that it took years of therapy for her to finally have a decent relationship with her father. And although Aluízio's only son, Alexandre, tended to have more forgiving views on his father, he shared his sisters' sadness about a lack of fatherly love. Through these interviews I also learned about an extramarital affair in the 1990s, when Aluízio was over fifty years old, that led to the birth of his youngest child, a daughter named Amanda. In contrast to how Aluízio shared his memories about politics—a patterned narration that he could draw on almost absent-mindedly with extreme detail—his discussions about family were more sporadic and guarded. In these moments, I relied on the memories of his children to fill in the silences of Aluízio's memory script.

THE DYNAMICS OF A COLLABORATIVE BIOGRAPHY

Toward the middle of my interviews with Aluízio, as I was preparing to start my writing process, I asked if he wanted to coauthor the book with me. I was keenly aware of the power dynamics and at times contentious history of foreign scholars writing life histories of Latin American activists, and I wanted to discuss the possibilities of authorship.[21] He declined, telling me that he already had too much work on his plate.[22] Having written his own memoir nearly two decades earlier and now keen to be the subject of a professional biography, Aluízio seemed content to cede the authorial voice to me.

Aluízio's disinterest in coauthoring did not fully resolve potential ethical and methodological concerns. So, I proposed, and Aluízio agreed to, the following process for what became a collaborative biography: when I finished a chapter, I would translate it into Portuguese and share it with him, and he offered comments or corrections. He read every section of the book, including this introduction, and we discussed it afterward. Aluízio sometimes insisted on the inclusion of a particular anecdote—when reading my draft chapters, he called attention to stories that he had told me but which I had left out. Often, I stuck to my original choice and did not include the detail, though in key moments, when his insistence felt reflective of a larger theme in his memory script, I added it to the text. And in one case, after a lengthy dialogue with Aluízio, I removed certain details and rephrased parts of my analysis relating to the testimony of a former army soldier involved with the 1974 disappearances. In this book I always tell the reader when these changes happened, how Aluízio reacted to my initial draft, and why I ultimately included or removed something.

Once the full text was professionally translated, Aluízio reread the whole book. Along with offering a few minor factual and grammatical corrections, he also asked me to include something that he had not expressed during our four years of conversations—he wanted to thank his wife, Eunice. Twenty minutes after we signed off from a Zoom conversation in which we had reflected on the deeply personal contents of the biography, Aluízio sent me the following text message: "I forgot to say that I would like my eternal gratitude to Eunice to appear somewhere in the book. Thanks to her, we managed to overcome all the difficulties."[23] I told him that I would add it to the introduction.

More than any previous project I have undertaken, this book changed profoundly over the course of actually writing it. Initially, amid the chaos of a global pandemic, I did not think much beyond the immediate steps at hand: do a lot of interviews with Aluízio and write his life story. Once the first rush of interviews gave way to a more sustained approach, and as I brought in other sources and reflected more deeply on my exchanges with Aluízio, the project began to shift. I focused more not only on the question of memory and memory-sharing but also my own role as a biographer who actively collaborated with the book's protagonist. It took me a long time to get comfortable writing about my own exchanges with Aluízio and other interviewees. Writing in the first person felt clunky and self-indulgent. But with time, and with feedback from colleagues and peer reviewers, I came to realize that a collaborative biography required writing myself into the narrative. Even with that growing self-awareness, my work with Aluízio presented a special set of challenges.

What can make a collaborative biography so revealing—the proximity between writer and subject—also makes it very difficult to navigate. My analysis of Aluízio's memories required entering an uncomfortable space of studying, and at times complicating, the statements of a torture victim who dedicated the second half of his life to human rights activism. Writing a biography of someone who is still alive is tricky enough, and it can be even more complicated when you already know that person and respect them. When his children told me about the thornier parts of his character, I had to decide which, if any, of these details I would discuss with Aluízio. And when triangulating the various platforms of his memory script, I also discovered some discrepancies, in which he seemed to stylize his memories in ways that did not always align. As part of our collaborative biography, when I came across these moments of misaligned memories, I shared them with Aluízio. In the book, I describe his reactions to these discrepancies.

The mechanics of a collaborative biography lent the perception of possibly knowing everything there was to know. If I wanted more details or clarification, all I had to do was ask Aluízio. The digital nature of our work meant that he was always just a click away. But I was mindful of interview fatigue and of potentially frustrating or disrespecting him; as it should be, he retained the power to withdraw his consent and terminate the project whenever he wanted. Our collaboration was genuine, with our relationship built on mutual respect and solidarity, but I was always aware of our positionings: as part of Aluízio's storytelling about his life, I was his audience. So I had to pick and choose which follow-up questions seemed important enough to push for deeper answers. There were only so many times that I could ask him to go beyond his standard memory script for the sake of this book. Mostly, our back-and-forth exchanges yielded the details I was hoping for. At other times, certain stories remained fuzzy.

Some elements of Aluízio's life history also felt a bit taboo. Chief among these was his relationship with Eunice, his wife. As mentioned above, my interviews with his children helped round out the silences in Aluízio's storytelling about Eunice, which allowed me to avoid confronting the topic too bluntly in my conversations with him. An indirect workaround, perhaps, but one of an endless number of tricky choices I had to make throughout the project. Another taboo related to César Cabral, a person who pops up in various chapters of this book: he was a fellow militant in the 1960s, a brother-in-law (Aluízio and César married sisters from the same family), and he would end up playing a crucial, if complicated and perhaps illicit, role in Aluízio's investigation into the case of the six disappeared militants. Aluízio and I talked at length about César, but as we will see toward the end of this book, the exact progression of events remains a bit obscure. As much as I wanted to fill every gap and solve every puzzle, I came to terms with the fact that this was neither feasible nor necessary.

Readers of this book will undoubtably come across certain passages that leave them wanting more information. After having spent years immersing myself in the twists, turns, and minutiae of Aluízio's life, I can assure readers that if they want more details, so did I. My request to readers in those moments is to use the disorientation of unanswered questions to reflect on what it means to be invited into somebody else's memories. And, perhaps, the impossibility of ever fully knowing another person.

This collaborative biography can be understood as part of Aluízio's efforts to bring greater public attention to his memories. This was not a passive hope: Aluízio put a tremendous amount of time into our collaboration, including forty hours of interviews, introducing me to family and colleagues, and sharing photo albums and documents. A biography written in English, by a US scholar, would bring a global spotlight to his life story. And the Portuguese translation of the biography, set to be published in parallel with the English version, would also increase his status for Brazilian readers. This book's title, *Searching for Memory*, is more than just a nod to Aluízio's efforts to document the violent truth of Brazil's dictatorship—it also reflects Aluízio's personal search to be memorialized, to have his place in history acknowledged and commemorated. And he wanted to see this search come to fruition. During the two years of our interviews, and even afterward, he often asked me about the progress of the book. When I would tell him about its current stage of writing, drafting, or peer review, he almost always replied, only half-jokingly, that he hoped to still be alive when the book came out. At one point I asked Aluízio why he had agreed to our collaboration, and he said that "I was already used to talking, it's not like you got me when my mouth was shut. I had been making this speech for a long time. And it's always good to talk because in talking, you remember, too. Rescuing my memory, little by little, I build a story."[24]

BOOK STRUCTURE

This book has ten chapters, following Aluízio's life from his childhood in the 1950s all the way through the early 2020s. The first chapter opens with Aluízio's early years growing up as the son of a shopkeeper in São Fidélis, a small town in the interior of Rio de Janeiro state. When Aluízio was fifteen, his family moved to the outskirts of Niterói, a bustling port city across the Guanabara Bay from the city of Rio de Janeiro. It was in Niterói in the early 1960s that Aluízio threw himself into political activism, as a student activist and as a member of the Brazilian Communist Party (PCB, Partido Comunista Brasileiro). Chapter 2 traces Aluízio's radicalization in the aftermath of the military's 1964 coup, as he and a group of other students broke from the PCB and formed a clandestine group called the MR-8. Chapter 3 follows the MR-8's efforts in building a guerrilla insurgency to confront the dictatorship. This chapter also explores the internal dynamics of the MR-8, particularly the fact that, like other armed militants in Brazil, they were mostly white, middle-class men conditioned to the dominant gender norms of the era; this experience in the armed underground was central to their participation in—and later memories about—the activist world in which they operated. After nearly a year mobilizing with the MR-8, Aluízio was arrested in April 1969, when he got into a routine car accident and was found with subversive materials and weapons in his vehicle.

Chapters 4 and 5 chronicle Aluízio's two years in prison, during which time he was tortured and shuffled between various military detention centers. In early 1971, he was released along with sixty-nine other political prisoners in exchange for the kidnapped ambassador of Switzerland. The sixth and seventh chapters follow Aluízio's decade-long experience in exile. He first lived in Chile, where he and the other exchanged prisoners were granted residency, but he eventually moved to Argentina, where he stayed until 1979. Although he had been freed from prison, these years remained extremely tense. Eager to rejoin the armed resistance against Brazil's military regime, he joined the People's Revolutionary Vanguard (VPR, Vanguarda Popular Revolucionária), comprised at that point mostly of Brazilians living in exile. As part of the VPR, he moved to the Argentine countryside and lived clandestinely as a day laborer, working on yerba mate tea plantations as a cover for his militancy. After several close encounters with security forces—including a chance meeting with a double agent who would soon orchestrate the disappearances of six militants in 1974—Aluízio finally gave up his militancy and moved his family to the Chaco province, where he lived with false documents and ran a small soda business. By the end of the decade, as democratization was beginning to take shape back in Brazil, Aluízio returned with his family to Foz do Iguaçu. Chapter 8 follows Aluízio at a moment of great transition, both for himself (returning to "normal" life after a decade underground) and for Brazil, where the return of democracy was on the horizon.

Chapter 9 offers a summary of Aluízio's long and circuitous search for the bodies of the six militants disappeared by the military regime in 1974, which included three failed excavations along the Paraná border. The search had so many twists and turns that it feels like a detective novel, except that in this real-life crime story there was no reveal at the end. Even today, a definitive set of answers remains elusive. Although Aluízio did solve how the murders most likely happened, the bodies themselves have never been found. The tenth and final chapter charts the progression of Aluízio's memory initiatives in the 2010s. In many ways, this was his most active period of community organizing. Despite now being in his seventies, he expanded his website devoted to publishing archival material from the dictatorship, started the Center for Human Rights and Popular Memory, got involved in education programs across the country, and was a contributor to Brazil's truth commission. The chapter details the final attempted excavation, in 2018, for the six disappeared—which again yielded no results.

The conclusion opens with a discussion of the 2019 lawsuit by Aluízio's former torturer and ends with an extended reflection from Aluízio on his own life, offering lengthier direct quotes than elsewhere in the book. My biography of Aluízio Palmar thus closes with a largely unabridged example of his memory script. Telling the story of Aluízio's life, and the memory script in which it is told, reveals a series of overlapping searches—a search for the importance of history's periphery, a search for one's place in larger historical narratives, and a search for justice.

MAP 1.1. Locations of Aluízio Palmar's upbringing and militancy in south and southwestern Brazil. Courtesy of Gabe Moss.

CHAPTER 1

CHILDHOOD VISIONS

ALUÍZIO PALMAR was born on May 24, 1943, in São Fidélis, a medium-sized town in the northern interior of Rio de Janeiro state, 300 kilometers from the city of Rio de Janeiro (map 1.1). The closest big city was Campos, 50 kilometers to the southeast and linked by the Paraíba River that emptied into the Atlantic Ocean further downstream. São Fidélis had fewer than 30,000 inhabitants, and like most of the surrounding region—whose residents are known locally as *papa-goiabas*—it relied on the cultivation of two main crops: sugarcane and guava fruit.

Both of Aluízio's parents came from agricultural backgrounds. His mother, Luzia Pires Ferreira Netto, grew up on the outskirts of Recreio, Minas Gerais, where her father grew rice and served as the local notary. When her father—Aluízio's grandfather—died in 1930, Luzia was sent to live in São Fidélis with her uncle, who owned a large sugar plantation, the Fazenda da Casa Branca. Her relatively wealthy uncle sent her to a nearby school, providing Luzia with an education that many girls in rural areas did not have access to in the 1930s, and she developed an attachment to poetry and literature that she would later share with her children. While living on the Casa Branca estate, Luzia eventually met a young man named Anízio Palmar, the son of a tenant farmer, who would pass by on his way to work in the sugarcane fields.[1] The two eventually fell in love. Looking back on how his parents met, Aluízio chuckled and remarked that "[my mother's uncle] did not allow it. Can you imagine, a young girl living on the estate, going out with a poor guy from the interior? He was good-looking, with a trimmed mustache, but he had little education and no

CHAPTER 1

FIGURE 1.1. Luzia and Anízio Palmar, with their two oldest sons, José Amaro (*left*) and Aluízio (*right*), late 1940s. Courtesy of Aluízio Palmar.

money. My mother was from a good family. My father, the only thing he was good at was pulling weeds out of the ground."[2]

Despite the objections of Luzia's family, she and Anízio married and moved into the center of town, where they set up a small store at the corner of Faria Serra and Frei Ângelo Streets, just down the road from the local sawmill. The store sold a bit of everything, from salted beef to farming tools, and from kitchen supplies to grains, rice, and beans. Anízio and Luzia lived in a house behind the store, where they raised six children—five boys and one girl. Aluízio was the second-oldest child (fig. 1.1).

The family store was the center of Aluízio's childhood. "I was raised in that store, I worked in the store, we all did," Aluízio told me. "*Mamãe* made sweets to sell, cakes, snacks, things like that. Saturdays were the busiest, when people came in from all over. In the morning, townspeople came by, and in the

22

afternoon the farming families arrived. Most of them came into town on foot, but the better-off ones came on horse, which they tied up near the train station. Dad was a great storyteller and people stayed in the store until late at night, leaning on the counter, drinking cachaça, eating beef jerky with manioc flour, and listening to dad tell his tales."[3] Spending time at the store also allowed Aluízio to develop a special bond with his mother—as he wrote at one point on his Facebook page: "Anything that is good in me I owe to her.... She was my friend and confidant during some of the hardest moments of my life. To quote Gilberto Gil, she was my measuring stick and my compass."[4] Daily interactions at the family store exposed Aluízio to townspeople and farmers stopping by for provisions, discussions about issues in the community, and the routines of a dignified, if challenging, life in the rural interior. Aluízio was shaped by his upbringing in Brazil's interior, but when his family moved to the coast a decade later, his background became a source of his self-doubt among new classmates who grew up in cities and with relatively more money.

Aluízio attended a local Catholic school in São Fidélis, Ginásio Fidelense, and he chafed at the religious rituals, particularly having to recite prayers at the start and end of each class period. He disliked the Church from an early age, but religion was nonetheless a part of his upbringing. Two of his brothers were altar boys and his mother was a devout Christian.[5] In Aluízio's memories, "Mamãe never missed a single Sunday morning mass, and at Easter, she took command of the family. There we'd go, on a real religious tour. All of us well dressed ... walking in the procession, going through town."[6] As Aluízio grew older and more politically aware, he became increasingly resistant to the Church: "I didn't want to submit myself to its control. The Church really dominated the whole town, and that started to mess with my head."[7] The colonial-era church, the largest building in São Fidélis, was the hub of town life—as well as the seat of power for the conservative clergy who held great influence in the region. The bishop of São Fidélis, Dom Antônio de Castro Mayer, would later become a leading figure of Brazil's religious Right, writing several prominent essays against the liberalization of the Church, and joining the Tradition, Family, and Property movement that was a vocal ally of the military coup in 1964.[8]

Aluízio's childhood in São Fidélis followed a fairly consistent pattern. In his memoir, he describes a typical day of school followed by working at his family's store, with any downtime spent playing soccer, taking naps, playing in the street, or venturing with friends into the surrounding countryside. A favorite spot outside of town was the home of Zezé, an older woman who had worked as a nanny for him and his siblings, and whose house was often filled with the

CHAPTER 1

smell of fresh *quindins* (an egg and coconut custard).[9] During the soccer season, Aluízio often spent Sunday afternoons at the Amaral Peixoto municipal stadium to cheer on the local team, Clube Esportivo Fidelense, and his favorite player, the midfielder Azulão.[10] The team competed only in the regional league, and Aluízio remembers that Azulão often hung around his father's store. São Fidélis was not a big place, but for young Aluízio, it was his whole universe.

His initial understanding of politics came primarily through his father, who belonged to the center-left Brazilian Labor Party (PTB, Partido Trabalhista Brasileiro). The PTB was in power for many of Aluízio's formative years, under the presidency of Getúlio Vargas (1951–54). When PTB candidates campaigned in the interior, they stopped at the Palmar family store in São Fidélis, and Aluízio would listen to them talk with his father and other locals about the state of the country. Aluízio and his mother made a game out of eavesdropping on these debates: she would imitate the speeches of Vargas and he would raise his arms wide, a pantomime of the gestures he witnessed from the PTB candidates.[11] As he later described on Facebook, at the age of ten Aluízio's awareness of national politics accelerated when Vargas committed suicide on August 24, 1954. He and his classmates were allowed to stay home from school, and with his family he listened on the radio to the reading of Vargas's final note to the people of Brazil. He remembered his father crying. Later in life, Aluízio would say that Vargas's death had pushed him to think about the world around him, and what it meant to fight for a fair and democratic society.[12]

Exposed to a *trabalhista* tradition in his father's store, Aluízio also encountered communist ideas when a group of workers from Campos came to pave the roads of São Fidélis. It took several months for them to transform the town's dirt roads into layered cobblestone, and Aluízio talked with them when they shopped at his family's store.[13] Many of the workers belonged to the Brazilian Communist Party, and Aluízio asked them about their politics. On several occasions, Aluízio walked to the outskirts of town, where the workers lived in temporary canvas tents, to continue these conversations. During this same period, a math teacher had also given him a few political books, broadening the topics to discuss with the road workers. "I was anxious to learn things," he told me. "All young men are curious, no? I wanted to know what was happening, and why. Not a political consciousness yet, it was curiosity more than anything."

By the end of the 1950s, Aluízio's father decided to move the family out of the interior to live in a bigger city where his children could get the education that he never did. In 1958, he purchased a plot of land in São Gonçalo, an area on the outskirts of Niterói. In November of that year, once Aluízio and his brothers finished their school term, they traveled by train from São Fidélis to Niterói, and spent the next several months camping on the land where his father and a few hired workers built a house. This location on Rua Vicente de Lima would be the family's new home as well as its livelihood. Anízio set up a store in front of the house, which he named Armazen Fidelense, an homage to their roots in São Fidélis. During the months of construction, Aluízio was put in charge of the cooking, and he tried his best to replicate the *comida roça* (dishes from the countryside) that his mother had taught him, such as stewed fish or rice with beef jerky.[14] By February, the house was ready and they returned to São Fidélis to gather their belongings for the move to São Gonçalo.

Leaving his childhood home made an intense impression on Aluízio. He recalled that as the family loaded up the truck with all their belongings, a few neighbors sang them a goodbye: "Quem parte leva saudade de alguém que fica chorando de dor" (Those who leave take with them sorrows for someone left crying in pain).[15] For Aluízio, the sadness at leaving São Fidélis was offset, in part, by the excitement of moving to a new place. São Gonçalo was essentially a suburb of Niterói, which promised many of the things that a fifteen-year-old from the interior had never experienced: a big city, the beach, and a frenetic daily routine that would put him in contact with new social groups and political ideas.

NEW HORIZONS IN NITERÓI

The Palmars new home in São Gonçalo was twenty kilometers north of downtown Niterói, connected by several bus lines and an electric tramway that ran along the Guanabara Bay to the city's main artery, the Barcas ferryboat terminal on Avenida Visconde do Rio Branco. Niterói was the state capital, while the city of Rio de Janeiro across the bay was its own federal district, the state of Guanabara. Especially before the 1970s, when a new bridge connected the two, Niterói and Rio de Janeiro existed as closely connected though distinct spaces. Niterói, with its shipping industries and metalworking factories, had a reputation as the gritty neighbor across the water, a contrast to Rio's status as the national capital and center of cultural life. Aluízio and his family belonged to a wave of domestic migration into Niterói that was expanding the city and changing its demographics. Most of the new residents came from the northern interior of the state—like the Palmars—or from the northeastern regions of the country.[16] The Palmars' relocation in 1959 was also part of a national trend, as this was the period when more Brazilians began living in cities than in the countryside, pushed by a decline in key agricultural sectors and the allure of newly expanding urban industries, often on the periphery of large cities. In

CHAPTER 1

the 1940s and 1950s, when Aluízio was a child in São Fidélis, about a third of Brazilians lived in urban areas, but by the 1960s, this proportion had increased to more than half.[17] By growing up in the countryside and then coming of age in a city, Aluízio mirrored a changing Brazil.

One of Aluízio's first memories of Niterói was of the massive lines of people at the Barcas terminal who commuted to Rio de Janeiro. Each day, some 100,000 passengers took the ferries—nearly half of Niterói's population. The mix of people astounded the young arrival from the interior: among the multitude of workers and housecleaners were also doctors and lawyers in suits and ties, all waiting to cross the bay.[18]

What Aluízio did not know was that his new city was on the verge of social unrest. With a growing population straining the existing services, and with rampant inflation in Brazil making it even harder for workers to make ends meet, a vortex of economic stresses soon found an outlet at Niterói's ferry terminal. In early May 1959, only a few months after the Palmars arrived, Grupo Carreteiro, the company that ran the ferries, announced that it would not raise the salaries of its employees. In response, the ferry workers called a strike for May 22.[19] On the day of the strike, the lines of people waiting at the Barcas became far larger than usual. In an attempt to keep order, the military—which had been brought in to block the strike—began corralling the waiting passengers. When a shoving match broke out between an officer and some workers, a tense situation spiraled into what became known as the Revolta das Barcas. Striking workers mixed with frustrated passengers, and a mass of people stormed the Carreteiro company offices and set the building on fire. The military responded violently, and the resulting melee killed 6 people and injured 118.

More than the violence on display, or what it signaled about the inequalities that pervaded his new city, what most struck Aluízio about the Revolta das Barcas was the reaction of the state governor, Roberto Silveira, who in the aftermath of May 22 came out in support of the workers. Silveira, like Aluízio's father, was a *trabalhista* from the PTB, and Aluízio—who turned sixteen two days after the conflict at the ferry terminal—was inspired by what he described in his memoir as the governor's "democratic attitude and solidarity with the working classes."[20] Soon afterward, Aluízio wrote an essay about Governor Silveira for a writing competition at his new school that, as he was proud to share with his family, won first place.

Like in São Fidélis, Aluízio was required to work at his family's store, though he increasingly spent his time traveling to school and hanging out with new friends. In his first year in Niterói, Aluízio attended the Colégio Plínio Leite, a high school less than a kilometer from the Barcas terminal. But needing to help his family, and wanting a bit of pocket money for himself, Aluízio also worked in the human resources department of an insurance company in downtown Rio de Janeiro, where he helped process paystubs. Like many of Niterói's inhabitants, Aluízio now made a daily commute on the ferries into Rio and back each day. This was common for working- and lower-middle-class teenagers in Niterói, and after a year at the Colégio Plínio Leite, Aluízio switched to the Liceu Nilo Peçanha, a high school that held classes exclusively in the evenings for students who needed to balance work during the day and their studies at night. Working in Rio de Janeiro and studying in Niterói presented a demanding daily schedule: he left his parents' house in São Gonçalo by seven each morning, took a bus to the Barcas, then a ferry across to downtown Rio, and finally walked to the insurance company. At the end of the day, he would do the same commute in reverse and return to Niterói for classes at Nilo Peçanha. The ferry offered a rare moment of downtime, and he often slept on the thirty-minute rides across the water.[21]

At Nilo Peçanha, located only a few blocks from the Barcas, Aluízio befriended several student activists, most of whom belonged to the youth section of the Brazilian Communist Party. Although he did not yet officially join a political party, he did become active in youth movements by joining the *grêmio estudantil* (student association) and helping run a small student newsletter.[22] The more involved he became in the student movement, the more he was recruited to join one of the many Marxist groups with a presence in Niterói. Along with members of the PCB, Aluízio also spent time with those of two other radical groups, the Revolutionary Marxist Organization-Workers Politics (POLOP, Organização Revolucionária Marxista-Política Operária) and the Trotskyist Revolutionary Workers Party (PORT, Partido Operário Revolucionário Trotskista). POLOP formed in early 1961, when dissidents from several left-wing organizations (the PCB, the Brazilian Socialist Party, and the PTB) sought to create a radical alternative to the PCB, which at the time advocated a gradual, reformist platform.[23] POLOP established bases in Minas Gerais, São Paulo, and Rio; Dilma Rousseff, who in 2011 would become Brazil's first female president, was a POLOP militant. PORT, on the other hand, was a smaller organization, though it proved particularly appealing to Aluízio, for reasons both ideological and personal. A close friend and classmate, Helinho Ribeiro Pinto, was in PORT, and introduced Aluízio to Trotsky's theory of permanent revolution, particularly as it was formulated for the Latin American context by J. Posadas, the pseudonym of the Argentine militant Homero Cristalli.

CHAPTER 1

An added draw to PORT was a young female militant named Helena, who came to represent somewhat of a recurring trope in Aluízio's memory script: women who made brief appearances at key moments of transition in his life, a reflection of the normative masculinity that shaped his political trajectory.[24] Aluízio shared the anecdote about Helena across multiple platforms, including in our interviews, on his Facebook page, and in an essay that he contributed for a book about the generation of 1968, a chapter that he titled "A minha doce trotskista" (My sweet Trotskyist). In the chapter, Aluízio recounts in a self-mocking tone, "That cute Trotskyist scrambled all my emotions and almost recruited me to PORT!"[25] The anecdote goes that while preparing to hand out flyers at the shipyards, Aluízio summoned the courage to tell Helena his feelings. Likely annoyed by the unsolicited advance, Helena pointed her finger at Aluízio and told him, "Comrade, at this stage of the struggle, all of our energies must be focused on fighting against the bourgeoisie and we must avoid any and all class deviations." Helena does not feature again in Aluízio's memories, but other women characters make similarly flirtatious appearances over the course of his life story.

Aluízio ended up joining the Brazilian Communist Party. Most of his fellow student leaders at Nilo Peçanha were in the PCB, and he was drawn to its program of national development and its "united front" against fascism. When the PCB first emerged in force in the 1930s, it had advocated a more confrontational stance that included armed struggle, though in subsequent decades—during the intermittent periods when the party was not outlawed—it embraced collaborationism and participation in electoral politics. Aluízio recalled that the platform of the Partidão (or Big Party, as it was known) made the most sense to him at the time: "They formed this idea: Brazil is a backward country, so in some sectors the system of labor is basically feudal. . . . The country is a dependent country, its economy is dependent [on foreign capital], so to make the country more independent we need to nationalize the economy. What we need is to create a national ideology, a new national culture. That was the thing I wanted."[26] At the time, Aluízio was really drawn to the PCB's emphasis on gradual stages of reformism. But it was precisely the more incrementalist platform that would eventually lead to a major splintering that saw Aluízio and many members abandon the party and take up arms after the 1964 military coup—what the historian, and former armed militant, Daniel Aarão Reis has called "the utopia impasse."[27] But in the more open climate of the early 1960s, the PCB remained a vibrant home for Aluízio and scores of other militants.

Soon after he officially joined the PCB, Aluízio was also elected to the leadership of the Secondary Students Union (União Brasileira dos Estudantes

CHILDHOOD VISIONS

Secundaristas), and in the coming years his activities for the PCB and the student movement often overlapped: organizing protests and student strikes, leafletting, and writing graffiti on the walls of Niterói—he remembered having a special skill for graffiti, telling me that he "was the king of graffiti, I loved painting walls. At the time it wasn't with spray paint, it was with an actual brush and paint."[28] Like Aluízio, most of his friends worked during the day and studied at night. Such a nonstop schedule often left them feeling drained, but they were motivated by a feeling that they were making history.

Niterói was an ideal place for militant teenagers in the early 1960s. Aluízio and his friends mingled with workers at the docks and the factories, and they spent countless hours debating politics. Without much money to sit at a bar, they often hung out in front of the movie theaters on the Rua da Praia or under the awnings of the office buildings on Avenida Amaral Peixoto.[29] Although perhaps an exaggeration, Aluízio claimed that he barely slept during these years, when after work in the day and school in the evening, the long nights of politics left little time for rest.[30] To save time commuting, Aluízio, at the age of seventeen, moved out of his parents' house in São Gonçalo and shared a room with other students in a *pensão* (boardinghouse) in Niterói. Living away from his parents offered more freedom and time for politics, but having to pay rent also compounded his financial stress. A high school friend named Umberto Trigueiros Lima told me that even compared to other students in working-class Niterói, Aluízio was poor: "He was a young kid from a humble situation, so he really struggled, but that's how he was, and he didn't break. He was cheerful, and dedicated, and he always found a way to keep up his political activities."[31]

For Aluízio and his friends, there was a particular pride about living in Niterói. In his history of Niterói, Anderson Carlos Madeira de Carvalho describes the city prior to the dictatorship as a vibrant space of leftist politics, especially compared to the Cariocas across the bay in Rio de Janeiro: "Laborists [*trabalhistas*], nationalists, communists, and Trotskyists vied for the hearts and minds of students and professors. Ideas were also discussed in the shipyards of Ponta de Areia, Ilha de Conceição, and Barreto, in metallurgical plants, in businesses, public offices, bank branches, and union halls."[32] In the early 1960s, the competing identities on each side of the Guanabara Bay mapped onto their respective state governments: compared to Rio de Janeiro, which was under the conservative governor Carlos Lacerda, Niterói had a center-left administration and was seen as a more democratic place. A prime example was the 1963 Congress of Latin American Solidarity for Cuba. When Lacerda prohibited the conference from taking place in Rio de Janeiro, Niterói's governor allowed it to be held at the headquarters of the Dock Workers Union (Sindicato dos Operários

Navais), located in the Barreto neighborhood. Like most political events in early-1960s Niterói, Aluízio attended the Cuban solidarity congress. As a representative of the student association, he mingled with delegates from across the Americas, watched a speech from Carlos Marighella—the Marxist writer who later in the decade would lead a prominent armed movement against the dictatorship—and listened to messages read on behalf of international figures like Bertrand Russell, Nikita Khrushchev, and Lázaro Cardenas.[33]

Politics at the national level reverberated in Niterói and helped accelerate the radicalization of many young people like Aluízio. On August 25, 1961, Brazil's president, Jânio Quadros, abruptly resigned and nearly triggered a constitutional crisis. Quadros had hoped that Congress would refuse to allow the ascension of his vice president, the leftist reformer João Goulart, who had been the minister of labor under Getúlio Vargas. Demanding that the presidential succession occur, allies of Goulart launched a "legality campaign" to guarantee the lawful transition of power. As in many Brazilian cities, Niterói mobilized an outpouring of support, with workers and students gathering at the Dock Workers Union. The national legality campaign succeeded, and after two tumultuous weeks, Goulart was inaugurated as Brazil's new president. With a leftist now in power, Aluízio and other student leaders in Niterói felt emboldened to ratchet up their activities. "We were riding high," Aluízio said. "On the crest of the wave."[34] All the same, the circumstances of Goulart's rise to power hinted at the challenges for a leftist government in the Cold War context of the early 1960s. For the Brazilian Left, the Goulart presidency became a moment of great promise and, eventually, of great trauma.

The next few years passed in what seemed like a blur of activism, as Aluízio organized with the youth section of the PCB as well as the student movement. In both roles, he was tasked with recruiting new members, though he was aided in his PCB work by a veteran militant named Apolônio de Carvalho. Apolônio had fought with the international Red Brigades in the Spanish Civil War as well as the French Resistance in World War II—Jorge Amado famously called him "a hero of three countries"—and he was something of a legend to the Brazilian teenagers seeking to join the PCB.[35] For Aluízio and other student militants, Apolônio represented the type of older male PCB leader whose approval they initially craved but later turned against when a generational and ideological divide led younger cadres to break from the party in favor of armed insurrection.

Umberto Trigueiros Lima was one of the Niterói youth recruited by the tandem of Aluízio and Apolônio. Umberto met Aluízio in late 1963, when they were both involved in the student movement. Umberto was impressed with Aluízio's fluency in political language and his commitment to militancy: "He was a very active person, a strong activist; he was always doing something, always organizing something."[36] After some initial conversations between the two of them, Aluízio brought Umberto, sixteen years old at the time, to meet the fifty-two-year-old Apolônio. One night, the three of them met on the campus of the Federal University of Rio de Janeiro State, in front of the Mazzini Bueno School of Medicine. As part of the induction into the PCB, Apolônio wanted to give Umberto a codename, which he took from the patron of the building behind them. For the next several years, first in the PCB and then as part of the armed underground resistance, Umberto was known as Mazzini. In a chapter for the same book about the generation of 1968 for which Aluízio contributed his essay "My Sweet Trotskyist," Umberto wrote about the advice that Apolônio gave him upon joining the party: "He told me, 'You are a young man full of energy and dreams and now you have a much bigger responsibility for your life, and for history. You are now the Party, the Party walks with you, and you speak for the Party.' I left with my morale completely boosted, ready for anything, any challenge."[37] For students like Umberto and Aluízio, figures like Apolônio helped make the great struggles of the twentieth century seem pertinent to their lives, and gave them the confidence to pursue ever-larger ideals.

Toward the end of 1963, Aluízio was fired from his job at the insurance company. In his telling, this was retribution for wearing political buttons on his shirt at work.[38] A month later, he was hired to work for the National Literacy Plan (PNA, Plano Nacional de Alfabetização), one of the Goulart administration's newest—and shortest-lived—reforms. Modeled on the literacy programs of the education scholar and activist Paulo Freire, the PNA was launched in 1964 with the goal of teaching nearly 2 million adults to read, representing a sizeable portion of Brazil's estimated 20 million illiterate adults in the early 1960s, nearly a third of the national population.[39] Because only literate adults could vote, the PNA was not simply a charitable or compassionate effort to help the poor; it also represented a concerted political movement to bring as much as 10 percent of the country into the electoral system. If successful, the campaign held the potential to help shift the balance of power more decisively to the left.

As part of the PNA, Aluízio worked in the Baixada Fluminense, the impoverished region just north of Rio de Janeiro. Each day, Aluízio took the ferry into Rio, where he met with other members of the "mobile recruitment team" that drove through the Baixada to encourage adults to participate in the literacy program.[40] They coordinated with local leaders and went through each neighborhood with loudspeakers to announce the classes, which were held in any available public spaces—schools, Evangelical churches, Umbanda and Candomblé *terreiros* (houses). Aluízio worked in four specific areas of the Baixada: Nova Iguaçu, Caxias, Nilópolis, and São João Meriti.[41] "It was so well received," Aluízio said. "People would get home from work, take a shower, have a snack, and go to school. Everyone went. The little schools were full." Freire's pedagogy emphasized the need to teach people through their own vernacular and experiences, an approach that greatly impressed Aluízio: "It used words that people actually knew, it was people's everyday life, it was the universe of each student. Students learned to read through the understanding of their own reality."

Working with the PNA was a common route of political engagement for young left-leaning Brazilians. Another PNA worker was Iná Meirelles, who would soon join the same armed group as Aluízio (the MR-8) and be tortured in many of the same detention centers.[42] Iná's experience with the PNA was even shorter than Aluízio's. She had begun her teacher training in late March 1964, only a few days before the coup, but it left a lasting impression on her. As she later recalled in a documentary series on women militants, "We had to take a test, a big test, there was an entrance exam [*concurso*] to participate in the literacy program, and so many people tried to get in. It was something that made you feel really good, [making] a huge change for the country through adult literacy, ending illiteracy in Brazil. It was a shame [that the program ended so soon], because so many young people were involved, we had mobilized so much."[43] After the coup, the new regime labeled the PNA a "subversive" activity and shut it down. In their memories, Aluízio, Iná, and many others considered the PNA a successful model of social justice and solidarity.

Prior to the coup, a pressing question for militants remained how the Left could build—and maintain—power. In his two years in office, Goulart implemented several key reforms, including the nationalization of a foreign telecommunications company, and he was now eyeing even larger changes. To announce his new programs, Goulart organized a mass assembly on March 13 in front of Rio's main train station, the Central do Brasil. Over 150,000 people attended what became known as the Comício da Central (the Central Station speech). Aluízio and his comrades from Niterói were among the crowd of supporters eager to hear Goulart's proposals: "We left in a caravan, taking the ferry and then on foot. As a group we took the boat across the Guanabara Bay and walked from Praça XV to Central do Brasil to join the rally. There was a large crowd, a tense environment, but also an atmosphere of joy and hope."[44] Goulart took the stage at 8 p.m. and outlined a series of sweeping reforms, including a significant agrarian reform plan. Addressing the massive crowd, and with audiences across the nation following the live broadcast on radio and television, Goulart declared that within the next sixty days his government would begin to expropriate large sections of agricultural estates that abutted government property such as highways, railroads, and dams: "Workers in the countryside will then be able to see, at least partially, the realization of their most immediate and justified demand, one that will give them their own piece of land to cultivate. . . . Agrarian reform is not the mere whim of government or the program of a party. It is the reality of an urgent need for all people of the world."[45] Looking back on that day, Aluízio recalled the speech as "extremely coherent, strong, very strong and radical, considering that he went to the root of our national problems. It was a speech that answered the demands of the people, and the crowd vibrated, the people vibrated, they sang, they cried, this rally was a very important moment."[46]

Goulart's speech proved to be the final straw for conservative leaders who had been maneuvering against him throughout his time in office. Across Latin America at this moment, right-wing forces were in the early phases of mobilizing what would soon become a Cold War wave of military coups—in some countries, such as Paraguay in 1959, dictatorships had already overthrown democratically elected leaders and instigated reigns of violence. With varying levels of support from the US government under President Lyndon Johnson, right-wing groups and their political, financial, and military allies sought to eradicate any allegedly communist elements that were believed to be taking root across Latin America.

In the aftermath of Goulart's speech in Rio de Janeiro, several conservative and centrist parties called for the president's resignation. Carlos Lacerda, the governor of Rio de Janeiro, called Goulart's speech a subversive attack on the Constitution and the honor of Brazilians, and three days later, a counter-demonstration took place in Rio's Praça da República under the banner of the March for Family with God for Liberty (a Marcha da Família com Deus pela Liberdade). Not content to wait and see whether Goulart would indeed start his agrarian reform program, the military took action two weeks later. On March 31, 1964, Brazil's armed forces staged a coup that overthrew Goulart and plunged the country into a dictatorship for the next twenty-one years. Aluízio's life, and that of many Brazilians, would never be the same.

CHAPTER 2

A SHADOW DESCENDS

BRAZIL'S COUP did not start according to plan. As originally envisioned, the military would stage a coordinated intervention later in the month of April. But a general named Olímpio Mourão Filho—who had previously helped orchestrate an authoritarian takeover in the 1930s—jumped the gun. In the late morning of March 31, General Mourão, commander of the Fourth Military Region stationed in Juiz de Fora, Minas Gerais, ordered his troops to begin marching on Rio de Janeiro. Initially, the Juiz de Fora troops were the only forces in motion across the country, but over the course of the day other commanders dispatched their soldiers, including at a few key stations in Rio de Janeiro.

Upon hearing radio reports of the escalation, Aluízio and other PCB militants gathered at the party's Niterói office in the Ajax Building on Praça do Rink. As Aluízio recalled in one of our interviews, several of the older leaders refused to believe that the military could pull off a coup: "They told us, 'No, this is nothing, this is just a *quartelada* [military expedition], these military guys will go back soon to Juiz de Fora. Nothing's going to happen, the government is too strong.'"[1] Here, Aluízio's depiction of the PCB as soft in the face of a coup was likely influenced by his frustration with the party in the coming years. Yet his memory nonetheless hinted at how many people were caught off guard, including those on the left who had pinned their hopes on the reformist aims of Goulart's presidency.

From the PCB office, Aluízio joined a crowd of protestors who marched to the front steps of the Legislative Assembly, where Afonso Celso Nogueira, a state deputy and PCB leader, gave an impassioned speech about the need to protect democracy. A squadron of police showed up and shot their guns in the air to disperse the crowd.[2] Nobody was injured that day in Niterói, though military violence against street protests elsewhere in Brazil left seven people dead, a sign of the repression that would spread in the coming decades. President Goulart, who on the morning of April 1 had made a final effort to negotiate with commanders in the armed forces, was forced to leave. From Brasília, he flew with his family to Porto Alegre in his home state of Rio Grande do Sul, and, after deliberating with allies for a few days, on April 4 he boarded a flight to Uruguay. With Goulart's departure, the military now ruled Brazil.

On the night of March 31, when the coup was still in motion, Aluízio did not return to his room in the student *pensão*. After the demonstration, he stayed at the house of his friend Aquiles Reis, whose father, Geraldo Reis, was a local PCB leader. The following morning, after listening on the radio to news of the escalating situation, Aluízio and Aquiles went back into the streets. Assuming that other protestors would also find their way to Niterói's main hub of activism, the two took a bus to the Dock Workers Union. When they arrived, they saw soldiers occupying the shipyards and the workers housing. "I broke down in tears," Aluízio wrote in his memoir. "My chest hurt, seeing all our dreams crumble."[3] The occupation of the docks was part of Operation Cleanup (Operação Limpeza), the military's effort to "cleanse" the Brazilian body politic of the threat of communist subversion. In Niterói, the first wave of arrests included union leaders and known and suspected Marxists. Along with the detention of those who lived in the city, detainees were brought to Niterói from as far away as Cabo Frio, 100 kilometers east. Soon, Niterói's prisons were so full that the military used the Caio Martins soccer stadium as a temporary prison.[4] This repression stretched across Brazil, where within a few months nearly 50,000 people were arrested, many of whom were similarly detained in makeshift prisons, including Rio's famous Maracanã stadium and several navy ships anchored in the Guanabara Bay. With its euphemism of health and purity, Operation Cleanup reflected the Cold War lexicon that Brazil's military used to justify its seizure of power. Rather than calling its intervention a coup, the government branded it as the "Revolution of 1964." In this logic, the military had acted selflessly to save the country, and anyone who stood against the true patriots became enemies to be eliminated.

Correctly guessing that he might soon be targeted by the regime, Aluízio asked Aquiles to go with him to his parents' house in São Gonçalo, where he wanted to grab a few changes of clothes and say goodbye. When they arrived, his mother greeted them solemnly, her tears suggesting that she already knew why Aluízio had returned and why he had to leave. His father was not home at that moment. Aluízio and Aquiles sat down briefly for a coffee but could not stay much longer. Aluízio remembered that his mother did not say a word as she walked him to the door and gave him a hug.[5] In the coming years he only visited her on a few occasions. After he went underground in May 1967, he did not see her again until June 1969, when she visited him in prison at a navy torture center on an island off the coast of Rio de Janeiro.

From São Gonçalo, Aluízio and Aquiles hastily returned to Niterói. At the Reis house, they recounted what they had seen at the docks, which Geraldo seemed to minimize by telling the two younger militants, "Take it easy, guys, this shitty *quartelada* isn't going to last long."[6] Aluízio then changed houses again and stayed with a friend named Milton Gaia Leite—three years later, Aluízio, Milton, and five others would create the MR-8 revolutionary group. While at Milton's house for several days, bad news continued to arrive, both for Brazil (the ongoing arrests of dissidents) and for Aluízio. As he later described on Facebook, through neighbors Aluízio had learned that the police had come to his parents' house looking for him. Not finding Aluízio, the police went through the house and seized allegedly subversive materials, including foreign novels like Fyodor Dostoyevsky's *The Brothers Karamazov* and Arthur Conan Doyle's *A Study in Scarlet*.[7]

A few days after the coup, the PCB sent word that its leaders should go into hiding. This included those in the youth section, and Aluízio imagined that his best option was the northern interior of Rio de Janeiro state where his extended family still lived. Not wanting to put his parents at risk, though needing their help to arrange his trip to the interior, Aluízio had a friend go to São Gonçalo to coordinate with his family. His father borrowed a truck and drove Aluízio to his brother's farm on the outskirts of São Fidélis.[8] As an added precaution, Aluízio slept in a small shed at the edge of his uncle's farm, just behind the chicken coop. Aluízio never left the farm, and he followed news from the outside world on a small battery-powered radio that he had brought from Niterói. From one of the only stations he could pick up—Rádio Globo—he learned about the continued arrests, the cancellation of political mandates, the April 9 passage of an Institutional Act (what would later become known as AI-1, as the first of seventeen such acts) that significantly curtailed constitutional freedoms, and the April 11 appointment of Humberto de Alencar Castelo Branco as president, the first of a half dozen indirectly elected military presidents who would rule Brazil.

After two weeks on his uncle's farm, Aluízio returned to Niterói. When he arrived, the city felt like a ghost town. "I couldn't find anyone," Aluízio told me in one of our earliest interviews. "Everybody had disappeared, they were all in hiding, I guess they ran away."[9] Hearing rumors that the police had rounded up local activists and detained them on ships docked in the bay, Aluízio left almost as soon as he had arrived, making a brief stop at the student pensão to pick up a few additional supplies.

He again went inland, though rather than returning to São Fidélis to stay with his father's brother, Aluízio went to Minas Gerais, where many of his mother's siblings lived. After a series of bus rides, he arrived in Recreio and walked five kilometers out of town to Conceição da Boa Vista, where his mother had grown up and where several of her sisters still resided. Aluízio knew that his mother's side leaned conservative, but he hoped that family loyalty—arguably the most valued institution in Brazilian culture—would be enough to grant him some sympathy. In a sign of the anticommunist propaganda that flourished in the broader context of Latin America's Cold War, and even more so in the aftermath of Brazil's coup, when Aluízio arrived unannounced at an aunt's house, she eyed him coldly and accused him—not incorrectly—of being a communist: "You have to leave now," Aluízio remembers her saying. "I don't want any communists in my house. Leave or I'll call the police."[10] Aluízio, tired from the long day's journey, pleaded his case and his aunt allowed him to spend the night, but on the condition that he leave by dawn.

The next morning, he went to a second aunt's house and received a warmer welcome. For two months, he lived with her family, spending his days playing with his younger cousins and rereading the few books he had brought—perhaps unwisely—with him from Niterói, including *The Eighteenth Brumaire of Louis Bonaparte* by Karl Marx and *State and Revolution* by V. I. Lenin. A man who ran the local bakery allowed him to read his daily copy of the *Correio da Manhã*, one of Rio de Janeiro's main newspapers; although politics were never discussed explicitly, the baker intimated his displeasure at recent national events. Aluízio's only outlet to talk about the coup was a medical student also taking refuge in the area—the two had crossed paths in the student movement in Niterói, and they now occasionally met up for brief conversations. Nobody in his family talked about Aluízio's situation, but it was hardly a secret: "All of my aunts knew I was there for political reasons, everyone knew. That was a small town, very few people, and everyone knew why I was there. It was a conservative place and the whole world knew about my politics."[11]

At one point toward the end of his stay in Conceição da Boa Vista, his aunt hosted a big party, and although Aluízio tried to enjoy the event, the upbeat mood of the music clashed with how he felt. After a particularly festive song from the popular rock and roll musician Roberto Carlos, Aluízio swapped the disc for one of the two long-play records he had brought from Niterói, playing a tune by Sérgio Ricardo, "Enquanto a tristeza não vem" (While sadness is away). Aluízio wanted to feel immersed in something political again: "That was protest music, music from the favelas, music about sadness, and misery, music that spoke about the reality of Brazil."[12] Nobody else seemed to appreciate the change in music. "The dance stopped right there, man, nobody continued," Aluízio said. "That wasn't music for dancing. Everyone went and sat down, looking around at each other, and thinking I was crazy." For Aluízio, the party was a sign that despite the relative safety of staying with his aunt, he needed to find a way to rejoin the struggle.

In late June, he returned to the coast, taking several buses to Rio de Janeiro and then the ferry back across to Niterói. Compared to the repressive climate when he had returned from his first escape into the interior, things now seemed calmer. Aluízio recalled that "the dust had settled a bit after those first few months, after the initial arrests, and the raids, the lineups had mostly stopped, and the detentions seemed less arbitrary."[13] Yet Aluízio could not shake his paranoia, feeling that people on the street were looking at him, and that police officers were waiting around every corner. For housing, he stayed with a fellow PCB militant named Jonas, an economics student at the federal university whose leftist Jewish parents were willing to help. Having already missed a sizable chunk of his semester, Aluízio did not go to school for the remainder of 1964. He returned to his studies at the start of the following year, attending the Colégio Batista for a one-year "preuniversity" course, what was then called a *curso científico*.

At that point, life in many ways mimicked what it had been prior to the coup. Living in what he called "semiclandestinity," Aluízio and his fellow youth militants took classes, went to work, and mobilized to grow the student movement. Still fearing for the safety of his family, he rarely visited his parents in São Gonçalo, opting instead to maintain a lower profile in Niterói. Despite certain trappings of normality, the authoritarian climate of Brazil forced activists to hold some of their events in secret, making the riskiness of their actions feel more palpable.

FROM STUDENT ACTIVISTS TO ARMED MILITANTS

After the first wave of postcoup repression, militants cautiously began to organize against the military regime. The student movement confronted the challenge of how to build political momentum amid the dictatorship's new policies. In November 1964, the government passed the so-called Suplicy Law. Named after its author, Minister of Education Flávio Suplicy de Lacerda, the law prohibited student organizations in universities from taking part in political "actions, demonstrations, or propaganda" or from "inciting, promoting, or supporting collective absences from scholastic work."[14] The Suplicy Law also mandated the creation of *diretórios acadêmicos* (academic directorates). The directorates were placed under the purview of the Ministry of Education, and the military envisioned that these new organizations would replace the National Student Union (UNE), a body that existed since 1937 and, especially during the precoup years under Goulart, had been a center of student activism. The dictatorship did not outlaw UNE, but it did maneuver to control the influence of student activists.

In 1965, while Aluízio completed his curso científico at the Colégio Batista, the most hotly debated topic within Niterói's student movement was whether to participate in the recently mandated directorates. Those in favor of working within the directorates argued that even though the associations were governed by the dictatorship, if the Left did not take part, conservative students would take them over and steer universities toward the reactionary policies of the government. This stance, which several of Aluízio's comrades in the PCB advocated, sought to win control of the directorates to transform them from within. But others saw participation in the directorates as a capitulation; this included students in Popular Action (Ação Popular, a group founded in 1962 by various Catholic youth groups) as well as members of the PCB who would soon form official factions within the party and break away.

Though contentious, these debates helped accelerate the organizational capacity of the student movement. As Aluízio recalled, "Those discussions took place over days and nights, the student meetings were intense. And even though the country was under a military government, the student movement was active. We had to hold assemblies and congresses, but in secret, no? We had to find places to have these meetings in secret."[15] Whether in the meeting halls of sympathetic churches or the homes of students, these meetings helped build a network of allies and physical spaces through which the movement would grow. The student debates of 1965 did not resolve the directorate issue. Some groups ran candidates for the associations, and others refused, choosing instead to operate within UNE, despite the limitations imposed by the government. These tensions about how much to directly confront the regime foreshadowed further divisions on the left in the coming years.

Aluízio completed his curso científico and in 1966 he enrolled as a social sciences major at the recently renamed Federal Fluminense University (UFF, Universidade Federal Fluminense) in Niterói—until a year prior, it had been called the Federal University of the State of Rio de Janeiro. To him, the UFF "bubbled with ideas, debates, and a whole lot of militancy."[16] Many others at the UFF shared this feeling. One such classmate was Liszt Vieira, who would soon join the armed underground and eventually participate in one of Brazil's four diplomatic kidnappings; Liszt's militancy was cut short when the military arrested and tortured him.[17] Like Aluízio, in the early 2000s Liszt wrote a memoir about his experience as a militant, a political prisoner, and an exile.[18] Accustomed to telling stories about this period of his life, Liszt received my questions with eagerness and great attention to detail. When I asked him about how it felt to study at the UFF in the early years of the dictatorship, Liszt excitedly told me that the "UFF was a place of cultural and political effervescence. . . . There was the struggle against the dictatorship, [but] the Left was also very fragmented, several subgroups, each one with its theories and strategies and tactics—lots of them considered themselves the owner of the truth. So it was a very effervescent environment . . . with discussions and student assemblies that went from ten in the evening until one in the morning, sometimes even later, it was an environment of a lot of political energy."[19]

Among Aluízio's first-year cohort at the UFF, what he called "my class of dreams and struggles," were several students who went on to play key roles in the fight against the dictatorship.[20] This included a core base that, along with Aluízio, would help form the October 8 Revolutionary Movement (MR-8), such as Luiz Carlos de Souza Santos, Ziléa Reznik, and Umberto Trigueiros Lima. Other cohortmates who would join different armed groups included Ivan Motas Dias, a member of the People's Revolutionary Vanguard (VPR) who was killed in 1971 by agents of the Air Force, and Maria do Carmo Brito, one of the most important female commanders in the country, who was a leading member first of POLOP, then the National Liberation Command (COLINA, Comanda de Libertação Nacional), and eventually the VPR.

At the UFF, some student militants took their studies more seriously than others. Among this group, Aluízio had a reputation as more of an organizer than a student. Liszt Vieira told me that Aluízio rarely went to class, and Maria do Carmo similarly recalled that from the beginning of their time at university, Aluízio "was already more preoccupied with the revolution than the campus."[21] For Maria do Carmo, his eagerness to prioritize politics over his studies was a good thing: "He was unrelenting."[22] But at times, this same tireless quality also caused problems, particularly in moments when he disagreed with decisions that had been made collectively. As Umberto Trigueiros Lima told me, Aluízio "was a very active person, but he was also very strong-willed. Let's say the group decided one thing and he did something else, because he didn't think it was right. So, we would fight about it, we would argue."[23]

A SHADOW DESCENDS

Like he had prior to the coup, Aluízio worked during the day in downtown Rio de Janeiro, this time at a shipping company in the Santo Cristo neighborhood. His days again followed a similar routine of an early-morning ferry ride across the water, a bus ride from the Rio terminal to the office building, and then back to Niterói for evening classes. When he arrived back at Barcas, he usually ate a quick snack of a fried pastry and sugarcane juice, and perhaps had time to return home to change his shirt before going to class. Most nights, he gathered with other students for political events. By this point, he had moved into a new pensão closer to the university, sharing a room in a converted townhouse on Rua Presidente Pedreira, in the Ingá neighborhood. The accommodation had the added benefit of being within walking distance of the Barcas, helping cut down on his transbay commute between work and classes.

The pensão also became the base for one of Aluízio's main activities in the student movement: printing a clandestine newsletter, *Resistência*. In the small room that he shared with another student, Antônio Carlos Pinto—known as Carlitos—Aluízio set up a silkscreen mimeograph, called a *reco-reco* for the sound it made. With a nylon canvas stretched tightly over a wooden frame, a cutout of text or images would be placed on a layer of paint, and one-by-one each piece of blank paper would get imprinted with the stenciled design. Each leaflet would then be left to air on a clothesline strung up near the ceiling.[24] Because of the clunk-clunk noise of the silkscreen, Aluízio tried to mostly do the printing at night when his roommate was out with friends. Carlitos was also a militant in the student movement, so he appreciated the purpose of the machine, but according to Aluízio, Carlitos often complained about the smell of the paint. When I asked Aluízio whether he was afraid to run a clandestine printing press out of his room, he said that he was mostly worried about the woman who ran the pensão: "I was afraid of the head of the boardinghouse, Dona Anita. What if one day she decided to come clean the room and found all the pamphlets hanging up on the line?"[25] Once dried and ready for distribution, the leaflets became a vehicle for the student movement to spread its message across the city. Umberto recalled that they would throw the copies from the roofs of buildings or leave them behind on buses. In addition to the leaflets, they also painted slogans on walls and bus stops, calling for students and the population at large to take a stand against the regime.[26]

Despite the repressive climate—and perhaps as a way to persevere in such a setting—the student movement organized parties to have fun and recruit new members. The student association at the UFF had a sixteen-millimeter film projector, and on the weekends the students would show movies and host other parties, sometimes charging a small cover fee to help raise funds. Looking

CHAPTER 2

FIGURE 2.1. Students on the Icaraí beach, early 1960s. Photo by Manoel Fonseca. Courtesy of Divisão de Documentação e Pesquisa da Fundação de Arte de Niterói.

back on his experience as a student militant, Umberto stressed the importance they placed on both dimensions of that identity: "We were always serious, twenty-year-olds always take themselves seriously. But it wasn't all frowns, no way. We liked to have parties, go out on dates, all those things."[27]

Umberto and Aluízio entered the university in 1966, and in both of their memories, their first year stood out as a lighter period before the conflicts that led them to abandon the student movement and take up arms. For Aluízio, this period of relative levity was facilitated by a new job. His roommate Carlitos worked at a branch of the Pareto bank near the main ferry terminal in Rio de Janeiro, and perhaps wanting to alleviate the nocturnal printing schedule, Carlitos helped get Aluízio a job. This meant that although he still needed to commute to Rio, Aluízio no longer had to take an additional bus after the ferry. Living near the Barcas in Niterói and working close to the terminal in Rio significantly cut down on his commute.[28] The new job also paid more, and for the first time since his family moved to São Gonçalo, he had a bit of extra time and money. When not working at the bank in Rio, his life in Niterói stayed within a small radius: his apartment in Ingá, the university a few blocks away, and the kilometer-long Icaraí beach (fig. 2.1). Increasingly during this period, Icaraí beach was the main meeting point for him and his comrades, and many of the late-night conversations on that beach formed the basis of the Niterói group that would soon break away from the PCB.

Prior to the schisms within the PCB, Aluízio and many of his fellow militants remained active in the party's youth section. Because the student movement was given a bit more freedom compared to the adult leaders of the PCB, the party often relied on its younger members. As Umberto recalled, "We were less impacted in that first phase, so the party sort of used the youth to help organize in the interior of the state, and to make contact with comrades that had fallen off the map a bit."[29] Because the PCB was officially illegal, one of the tasks for the youth section was to deliver communications between the various cadres spread across the region, as well as coordinating the party's internal elections. Aluízio also helped produce *Avante*, the PCB newspaper of the Niterói branch. Unlike the student leaflets printed in Aluízio's student accommodation, *Avante* required a higher level of security precautions: the designs were made in São Cristóvão, a northern neighborhood of Rio de Janeiro, and, once they were finished, Aluízio traveled at night to pick up lead matrices that he brought back to a safe house in Niterói, where they were used in a linotype press to print the final product.[30]

Aluízio enjoyed the work he did for the PCB. The party had been his first organized space of militancy, and he gained new insights about capitalism and class struggle from conversations with his fellow members and party leaders. He held older militants like Apolônio de Carvalho in particularly high esteem. But several years into Brazil's dictatorship, Aluízio, like other members in Niterói and elsewhere, began to feel frustrated by the PCB's approach to confronting the military regime. By the end of 1966, long-simmering tensions within the PCB and across other militant groups came to a boil, and the already dispersed Left soon splintered further.

THE PCB SPLITS

From the very first days of the dictatorship, leftists argued among themselves about who was to blame for the coup and why there had been no concerted resistance against it. Many of these conflicts focused on the PCB, the oldest and most influential party on the Brazilian Left. Splits within the party long predated the 1964 coup—the most recent schism had taken place in 1958, leading to the creation of the Maoist-leaning Communist Party of Brazil (PCdoB, Partido Comunista do Brasil)—though the military's recent seizure of power accelerated the theoretical and tactical scope of the debates. Those within the PCB who defended Goulart's reforms argued that more radical demands had ignited the conservative backlash. Others in the party attacked the PCB's leadership for having made alliances with centrist groups, a form of collaborationism that left the party unable to mount any serious response when the military staged its coup.[31]

The new regime moved quickly to arrest several party leaders. On April 2, barely two days after the coup, the main Communist leader in the Northeast, Gregório Bezerra, was captured in Pernambuco. In May, Carlos Marighella was arrested in Rio de Janeiro, and others soon followed, including Mário Alves, Ivan Ribeiro, and Leivas Otero. The targeting of PCB militants was aided in no small part by the military's seizure of nineteen notebooks kept by Luís Carlos Prestes, the party's secretary-general, which chronicled all major meetings and contacts since 1961.[32] From these so-called *cadernetas*, the military arrested almost 100 militants and suspended the political rights of 60 elected politicians. As such, the internal debates about strategy took place amid a spiraling crisis of leadership and organizational capacity.

In 1965 and 1966, as Aluízio continued to organize with both the student movement and the PCB, he began to think that what had originally attracted him to the Brazilian Communist Party—the stage theory of national development—was ill-suited for an authoritarian context. Perhaps, he thought, such a program could work in a democratic system, but under a dictatorship where elections were proscribed and dissidents were repressed, it felt as though much more needed to be done. The student movement provided a large network of other activists having similar doubts. By this time, UNE, the National Student Union, was essentially outlawed and its gatherings were held in secret. The UNE assemblies put Aluízio in contact with militants from Minas Gerais, various states in the Northeast, Rio Grande do Sul, and São Paulo, many of whom also belonged to one of the four main leftist organizations at the time: the PCB, the PCdoB, POLOP, and Popular Action. All these groups, it seemed, were debating how to confront the military regime.

It was through this network of youth militants that Aluízio was introduced to two texts that shaped his evolving views. The first book was theoretical: *A revolução brasileira* by the Marxist historian Caio Prado Júnior. Published in 1966 and influenced by Prado's visits to China, the Soviet Union, and Cuba, the book offered a stinging critique of the PCB by arguing that because national capitalism and imperialism are intertwined, any alliance with the bourgeois—as the PCB had done—was intrinsically counterrevolutionary.[33] And especially in the context of Brazil's dictatorship, which made it difficult to pursue traditional mass organizing (agitating for better working and living conditions), Prado's book envisioned a more direct path to socialism. The second text was tactical: *Revolution within the Revolution?* by Régis Debray, a French Marxist who went to Cuba in the 1960s. During that decade, the example of the Cuban

Revolution had become a source of great inspiration for young radicals across the hemisphere, and Debray's 1967 book became seen as a handbook for how to replicate guerrilla warfare. Debray's book was so instantly influential, among militants and intellectuals alike, that within a year of its publication, the New York–based *Monthly Review* dedicated an entire issue to "Régis Debray and the Latin American Revolution."[34]

Published first in Cuba, *Revolution within the Revolution?* quickly disseminated outward. Aluízio recalled that it arrived among his group when POLOP militants from Minas Gerais gave them a copy that someone had translated into Portuguese using a mimeograph printer. Having already learned about the Cuban Revolution through the writings of Che Guevara, student militants read Debray's book as an operational template for armed struggle. "Régis Debray opened the path to new forms of struggle," Aluízio told me. "First, that to make a revolution you don't need a party. That fit us like a glove. What a powerful idea! And second, the party emerges at the tip of a gun."[35] Particularly for younger militants frustrated by having to work within the systems of political parties, it was revelatory to read about guerrilla insurgency, through which small groups of armed cadres could foment a revolution. Umberto Trigueiros Lima, who had been the one to initially receive the copy of Debray's book from comrades in Minas Gerais, said that "we came to the conclusion that enough was enough, the regime was closing off the spaces of legal opposition and we decided that we needed to organize an armed struggle against the regime. So, we started to organize, to build an organization for armed struggle in the city and the countryside."[36] This desire to take up arms spread across various milieus in Brazil. The coming years saw the formation of three dozen groups dedicated to armed insurgency.[37]

Prior to forming an independent group, Aluízio and his comrades in Niterói first established a *dissidência* within the PCB, meaning that they remained within the party but as a dissident offshoot. Beginning in 1967, they were one of two local dissidências, both of which were mostly student-run. Their dissidência in Niterói was the Dissidência–Rio de Janeiro (DI-RJ, for the state of Rio de Janeiro) and the other was the Dissidência-Guanabara (DI-GB, based in the city of Rio de Janeiro, in the state of Guanabara). Dissidências existed across Brazil, including in Rio Grande do Sul, São Paulo, and Minas Gerais.[38] The DI-RJ was founded in early 1967 and over the course of the next year and a half transformed from a faction within the PCB to its own group, the October 8 Revolutionary Movement (MR-8), named in honor of the date, October 8, 1967, when Che Guevara was murdered in Bolivia. As we will see in the following chapters, the group that Aluízio helped create was not the only MR-8, nor was it the most famous: after Aluízio and most of his comrades were captured in 1969, another group of militants would adopt the name MR-8 as a way to counter the regime's statements about having dismantled the organization. It was this second MR-8 that helped orchestrated the September 1969 kidnapping of the US ambassador in Rio de Janeiro. And whereas Aluízio's original MR-8 group had little fame outside of Brazil, the second MR-8's kidnapping of the US ambassador was later dramatized as an Oscar-nominated movie, *O que é isso, companheiro?* (*Four Days in September*), loosely based on Fernando Gabeira's best-selling memoir of the same title.

Certain memories from this period feature centrally in Aluízio's memory script, even if, to me, they did not originally seem important enough to include in this book. My first draft of this chapter did not include an anecdote that he told me in one of our early interviews, about how the party, in an effort to undercut the dissidência, offered him a scholarship to study in West Germany.[39] When Aluízio gave comments on the drafted chapter, he noted that I left out the scholarship story. This particular memory seems to embody several themes that factored into his sense of self and his process of autonarration: an ability to take a stand against leaders in his own party, the missed opportunity to go abroad (something that would come up repeatedly when recounting his time in exile), and a desire to retain some authorial control, however subtly, in a biography about his life.

Along with interviews in subsequent decades with members of the DI-RJ/MR-8, what we know about the group's progression comes largely from the records of the dictatorship, most of which were compiled through violent interrogation after almost all its members were arrested within a span of five months in 1969. A navy surveillance folder from 1970 provides key details to the group's initial formation.[40] The DI-RJ started with seven founding members, two women (Ziléa Reznik and Iná Meirelles) and five men (Aluízio, Nielse Fernandes, Umberto Trigueiros Lima, Antônio Rogério Garcia Silveira, and Milton Gaia Leite).[41] They met at the apartment of either Milton or Nielse, where they planned events and held revolutionary study groups. Early on, the group sought to maintain its cover of being student organizers and encouraged members to attend classes as regularly as possible. If members had to miss meetings or actions, they were encouraged to offer material support by donating clothes, medicines, or money.

As the group moved forward, the question of funds became particularly important. To break away from the PCB, they needed to become financially autonomous. Along with the small donations given by the group's own members and sympathetic friends, some of the first funds were raised by stealing statues from public spaces around Niterói and pawning the stone and metal. This money then went to hosting parties and dances that, in turn, raised more money.[42]

A year and a half before the group switched to bank robberies to fund the purchase of weapons, cars, safe houses, and plots of land, its first big purchase was a printing press. On February 27, 1967, the DI-RJ hosted a carnival party fundraiser, what became known as the skeleton dance (*baile do esqueleto*).[43] As a cover for the dance's true beneficiaries, it was officially hosted by UFF's Student Union—Aluízio and several other DI-RJ members maintained their roles as student leaders—and held at the hall of the Dock Workers Union. The dance was packed, with almost 300 students from the UFF and high schools in Niterói and across the bay in Rio. For most of the night, the party was a great success, and there was little that could be considered political or subversive. It was only later in the evening that the singing of a particular song incited a police raid. In advance of the party, the Student Union had printed fliers with lyrics that parodied Máscara Negra, a popular song at the time by Zé Keti. The original chorus of the song was as follows: "So much laughter, oh so much joy. More than a thousand clowns in the hall. Harlequin is crying for the love of Colombina. In the middle of the crowd." The students parodied Zé Keti's uplifting, playful song with protest lyrics: "So many shots, oh so many cops! A thousand police in action. Students demonstrating in the streets. Screaming for freedom."[44] With the lyrics distributed across the party, most of the partygoers broke out in song, repeating the protest chorus over and over. Police soon arrived and detained dozens of students. Luckily for the DI-RJ, Nielse Fernandes, who had been in charge of collecting money at the door, managed to get away and rendezvoused later that night with Aluízio.

The dance had met its fundraising goals and Nielse gave the money to Aluízio. A few hours later, Aluízio took the first morning bus to the city of Campos, where a contact in the PCB had arranged for the sale of a printer. Aluízio discovered that buying a press was easier than transporting it: the press was heavy and needed to be dismantled into several pieces. Over the next month, Aluízio and other members of the DI-RJ took turns traveling to Campos to bring back the press a few pieces at a time.[45] When the printer was eventually reassembled in Niterói, the group began producing its own pamphlet, with tracts from communists like Mao Zedong and Régis Debray. According to Zenaide Machado, she and Umberto Trigueiros Lima oversaw production of the pamphlet, and when it came time to designing a symbol for its header, they chose an abbreviation for *Movimento Revolucionário 8 de Outubro*.[46] It was from this newsletter that the armed group MR-8 soon took its name.

CHAPTER 2

Three months after the skeleton dance, an incident at the UFF campus led Aluízio to withdraw from his studies. On the evening of May 15, 1967, Aluízio and Sebastião Velasco Cruz, another student activist and PCB militant from Niterói, were in the geography department putting up posters against the Vietnam War. As Sebastião recounted to me in our interview, a professor had previously warned them to be careful in the building, as it was rumored that the government often surveilled the geography and history departments. Sure enough, as the two of them walked up the stairwell and entered the fourth floor—home to the geography department—two students started pushing them, yelling to take down the posters.[47] Sebastião said that "as soon as we stepped foot on the fourth floor, two guys . . . were all over Aluízio. And it was like an automatic response, I didn't even think, I just saw what was happening and I jumped in to defend Aluízio." The ensuing commotion brought a crowd of other students.[48] What worried Aluízio was less the confrontation itself, and more the feeling that his attackers were not students, but "arapongas" (spies) from the government's Department of Political and Social Order (DOPS, Departamento de Ordem Política e Social). Although archival evidence does not explicitly say that the two students were spies, records from DOPS indeed show that Aluízio was under surveillance that evening. An entry at 8:10 p.m. states that "Aloísio and another were placing posters in the classrooms, they were in the department of Geography; confronted by Luiz Rogério and Ribamar; Ribamar was then beaten by blows from Aloísio. There was some shoving, but no major consequences."[49] Whether the two students were spies or had simply reported the incident to DOPS, Aluízio was clearly on the dictatorship's radar. Although the police had raided his parents' home just after the 1964 coup, his gradual move toward armed struggle made him an even greater target.

After the fight on May 15, Aluízio decided to stop attending classes and go "underground." He moved out of the student pensão and into the apartment of a fellow militant named Getúlio Gouveia. Having left his job at the bank earlier in the year, he now focused entirely on building the dissidência. For Aluízio, being underground felt liberating; he compared it to when he left his parents' house to live on his own in Niterói. "Being clandestine was a moment of freedom," he said. "It's a paradox, it's such a contradictory thing. Yes, you're clandestine under a damn dictatorship. But we were free because we didn't have to tell anyone what we're doing, where we're going. We were free, we weren't tied to anyone, we all dated everyone. A really magical moment. We weren't afraid of being arrested, dying, nothing like that."[50] This genre of recollection reveals the nostalgic undertones of Aluízio's memories. Even if he tends to criticize his time as a militant for being young and naive, in certain moments he also speaks longingly about this phase of life. His definition of freedom, moreover, is about politics but also about sex—his comments about being able to date anyone seem to reflect a sexualized vision of himself as a revolutionary. However much Aluízio would come to reject the more extreme politics of his militancy, he continued to draw validation from the personal memories of his younger days before taking up arms, before getting married, and before his arrest, torture, and exile.

Throughout the second half of 1967, he spent little time in the state of Rio de Janeiro, where he presumed the government was following him. Instead, Aluízio traveled throughout southern Brazil to make contacts with other groups and dissidências who might want to combine forces. With the writings of Régis Debray and Caio Prado Junior "bouncing" in his head, he became like "a traveling salesman, almost as if I was a preacher, I went out to defend the thesis of guerrilla warfare."[51] He spent extended time in São Paulo, staying in student housing at the University of São Paulo. There, the student militants Jeová de Assis Gomes and Fernando Ruivo organized meetings with leaders from several states, including Rio de Janeiro, São Paulo, Paraná, and Rio Grande do Sul. At some of the most intense periods of deliberation, the students had as many as five meetings per day, each lasting several hours. Following these initial gatherings in São Paulo, Aluízio traveled to Porto Alegre in Rio Grande do Sul, where he continued to advocate for building an armed insurgency in the countryside.

In the end, the various organizations could not find common ground. Although the groups agreed broadly about the need for direct action against the regime, they disagreed about the strategy and timespan for such a goal. The dissidência in São Paulo disagreed with Niterói's goal of guerrilla warfare, saying that it was too early to "ir pro mato" (go to the forest); later in the year, the São Paulo group would follow Carlos Marighella, the former PCB militant, and his newly created National Liberation Action (ALN, Ação Libertadora Nacional). The gaúchos from Rio Grande do Sul also went their own direction, joining the Communist Workers Party (POC, Partido Operário Comunista), and many in POLOP joined COLINA.[52] Even the DI-RJ's neighboring dissidência, the DI-GB across the bay in Rio de Janeiro, took a different approach: although the dissidência in Rio also defended the goal of revolution, its vision was for an urban front, rather than a rural-based foco insurgency. This left Aluízio's DI-RJ as one of the only remaining groups in Brazil seeking to pursue a Cuban-style guerrilla insurgency.

Despite the Left's inability to unify the armed struggle, Aluízio and his fellow militants in the DI-RJ remained undeterred. They also tried to recruit new members from within the wide network of PCB contacts. This included various labor unions in Niterói, as well as PCB members in cities like Cabo Frio, Campos, Friburgo, and Volta Redonda. In each case, Aluízio would locate people he thought might be sympathetic to the DI-RJ, and pitch them on the need to build a rural armed resistance. In Aluízio's recollection, the results almost never changed: "The same problems we had in Niterói with the workers, it was the same with the PCB members in the interior, and with the metalworker comrades, and the printers, and the bank workers. They would say 'look, we're against the dictatorship, we're communists, but we can't leave for the forest, take to the hills. Because we have families, kids, a job, a salary. We can't abandon that.'"[53] In hindsight, Aluízio called his reaction to these conversations a major error: "We would just pat them on the back, those who wouldn't go to the hills with us, and say, 'Bye-bye!' We would just break off contact. For us, the only useful people were the ones who joined us. If not, bye-bye. That was such a mistake to abandon everyone else." The idealism of youth thus mixed with the ego of inexperience.

In late 1967, an initial catalyst for armed struggle came not from the younger militants but from older leaders in the PCB. Carlos Marighella, who had taken part in underground struggles under Getúlio Vargas in the 1930s, became the most notable militant to break from the PCB and take up arms.[54] An early advocate of more direct action against the dictatorship, Marighella attended the Organization of Latin American Solidarity (OLAS) held in Cuba in August 1967. Because the Cuban government and OLAS promoted the need for armed revolution across the Americas—a stance the Brazilian Communist Party opposed—the PCB refused to endorse the 1967 OLAS summit. When he returned from Cuba, Marighella and several other members were expelled from the PCB.

The growing split within the PCB came to a head four months later, in December 1967, at the party's Sixth Congress. Still a leader of the party's youth section, Aluízio attended the Congress and witnessed the lengthy debates about the recent expulsion of Marighella. Ultimately, the party voted to denounce the strategy of armed struggle. The Congress's official resolution declared that proponents of insurgency "want to revive, with 'new' guerrilla clothes, the idea that a revolution can be made by adventurous foco insurgents, disconnected from the real movement of the masses."[55] The Sixth PCB Congress represented the final breaking point between the party's leadership and its various factions. Marighella formed the National Liberation Action (ALN), while other expelled members established the Revolutionary Brazilian Communist Party (PCBR, Partido Comunista Brasileiro Revolucionário). The party's two main dissidências, the DI-RJ and DI-GB, soon broke entirely with the party.

Other groups were undergoing similar schisms: by 1968, the four main leftist groups at the start of dictatorship (PCB, PCdoB, POLOP, Popular Action) had split into fourteen clandestine organizations.[56] According to the sociologist Marcelo Ridenti, the schisms within the Brazilian Left at this time centered on three fundamental debates: the particular character of revolution in Brazil, the method of struggle to seize power, and the type of organization needed to lead the movement.[57] The splintering and reshuffling of organizations did not resolve these three disagreements, and militants continued to agitate among themselves about the best path forward.

Of the various armed groups now proliferating across Brazil, the one that had shown the greatest interest in collaborating with the DI-RJ was the dissidência of Paraná, based in its state capital of Curitiba. Like the DI-RJ in Niterói, the leadership of the dissidência in Curitiba also belonged to the student movement, and the Federal University of Paraná had a strong base of support for building an armed struggle. Throughout his travels in 1967, Aluízio remained interested in establishing a base of guerrilla operations in Paraná. This was partially because militants in Paraná had been some of the few willing collaborators but also because an older militant named Oswaldo Soares had spoken to Aluízio at length about the region.[58] Soares was a former sergeant in the Air Force who had joined the Nationalist Revolutionary Movement (MNR, Movimento Nacionalista Revolucionário), an insurgent group with a strong presence of leftist members in the military. Régis Debray's book on guerrilla insurgency had stipulated a few key criteria for how to choose an area to launch the movement, including that it should be covered in dense forests (necessary to provide cover), and it should have a population with at least a small level of political consciousness (prior struggles in the region would make local communities more likely to collaborate). Soares helped convince the DI-RJ of the suitability of Paraná's western frontier, a region known mostly as the home of the Iguaçu waterfalls but which also had a history of militant rural struggles in the 1940s and 1950s.[59] The area was both relatively close (1,500 kilometers from Rio de Janeiro) and relatively isolated, and the militants hoped that the regime's surveillance and security systems would be less effective in the borderlands. Moreover, the area was a triple frontier, sharing a border with Argentina and Paraguay, where numerous transborder routes could facilitate the movement of people and weapons.

For Aluízio, the prospect of moving to western Paraná was thrilling, if also an unknown: "I had no clue what the west was, I thought it was like the shoot 'em up American Wild West. In my mind it was a lawless place. . . . I had no clue what the frontier was. I was a kid from Niterói."[60] For most of the first

CHAPTER 2

two months of 1968, the DI-RJ deliberated the merits of building a guerrilla base in western Paraná. In the end, the group approved the plan and set about designing a structure that would include a rural operation in Iguaçu National Park and an urban operation in Niterói and Rio de Janeiro that could rob banks to finance the guerrilla activities along the border.

Around the time that the group chose western Paraná, it also changed its name from the DI-RJ to the MR-8. No longer a dissidência, it now broke officially from the Brazilian Communist Party to pursue armed struggle. The MR-8 chose Aluízio to conduct the first reconnaissance mission to Paraná. The goal for this first visit was to establish contacts, scout out potential areas near the border for a guerrilla training camp, and then return to Niterói to debrief and organize the next steps. From there, the group planned to follow the lessons of Che Guevara and the template of Régis Debray to build a guerrilla insurgency and, eventually, a revolution.

Although the members of the MR-8, most of whom were students, were committed to armed struggle, few of them considered the full implications of what such a campaign entailed. When Aluízio left for Paraná in March 1968, he was twenty-four years old. Only recently had he ever left the states of Rio de Janeiro and Guanabara, and he had no experience with weapons or any type of armed fighting. When I asked him fifty years later whether he was afraid to take up arms against a violent dictatorship, Aluízio sighed and, in a softened voice, reflected on his decision to take to the hills in 1968: "To tell you the truth, we never thought about that, about the dangers. We thought we would never be imprisoned or killed. We thought we were invincible. Pretty crazy, isn't it?"[61]

CHAPTER 3

TAKING UP ARMS

ON MARCH 7, 1968, Aluízio took a bus to Curitiba, the capital of Paraná, almost a thousand kilometers from Niterói. There he got in touch with Berto Luiz Curvo, the president of the Paraná Student Union. Aluízio's main goal was to establish contacts in the border region, and Berto introduced him to Teresa Urban, a member of Popular Action. Teresa lived in Curitiba, but her boyfriend, a fellow militant named Fábio Campana, was currently in Foz do Iguaçu.[1] Once he had communicated with Fábio, Aluízio took a long bus ride west to Foz do Iguaçu. At the time, the main highway from Curitiba was not paved, and Aluízio remembered the dirt roads of the Paraná countryside kicking up a reddish dust that filtered into the bus.[2] None of the other passengers seemed overly concerned about the tinge that coated their clothing, and he took it as a welcome sign from a region known for the *terra roxa* (red earth) that provided some of Brazil's most fertile agricultural lands.

In Foz do Iguaçu, Aluízio stayed with Fábio, and the two of them began making new contacts in the surrounding area. Perhaps the most important was an Argentine named César Cabral, whose father owned a butcher shop. César had been an economics student and activist at the Universidad Nacional del Nordeste, and when his family left Argentina and moved to Foz do Iguaçu, he became close with radical Paraguayan exiles. Four months later, it was through César's Paraguayan contacts that Aluízio and the MR-8 would receive guerrilla

CHAPTER 3

training inside Iguaçu National Park.³ For several weeks, Aluízio, Fábio, and César traveled through the municipalities around Foz do Iguaçu. Soon Aluízio was convinced of the area's suitability for building an armed struggle, and he returned to Niterói.

It did not take much effort from Aluízio to convince the MR-8. His description of western Paraná seemed to map onto the young militants' vision of guerrilla warfare, and the group voted in approval. The plan had two stages. First, Aluízio and Nielse Fernandes would travel to Foz do Iguaçu to begin building a rural base of operations. Second, once the work along the border was underway, MR-8 members in Niterói would stage bank robberies to finance the guerrilla campaign. Nobody in the MR-8 had any experience with armed struggle or bank heists, but with no shortage of youthful confidence they set the plans in motion.

As he recounted in a post on his Facebook page, Aluízio held a strong memory of his final night in Niterói. This anecdote is another occasion on which he insisted that I include a story that was not in an early draft of this book.⁴ Tinged with masculine nostalgia and a sexualized sense of the dangers that awaited him, Aluízio wrote about a student dance at the UFF, where he met a young woman named Jane Gonzaga:

> Her body moving and sweating, it was like a rite of departure at a student party in Niterói. Around midnight, as the party was ending, she asks me,
> "Are you driving?"
> "No, I live close to here."
> "Can I go back with you?"
> She looked at me as if it were the last time, she laid her head on my shoulder and suddenly I saw her eyes fill with tears.
> And, without really knowing why, I said,
> "Don't be sad, we can see each other again tomorrow."
> "Tomorrow?"
> It was almost like she knew that I was going to Paraná, as if the secret of the MR-8 had leaked out.⁵

Aluízio's anecdote about Jane—and his insistence that I include it in the book—is emblematic of the types of masculinity that shaped revolutionary politics in Brazil and globally, when the rugged persona of Che Guevara mixed with the veneer of 1960s sexual revolution, producing a climate in which political legitimacy was tied to a militant's ability to assume a masculine persona.⁶ And because Aluízio's Facebook page is part of his memory script, its stylized sexuality also reflects the performative gender role that features strongly in the broader genre of militant memoirs. In Aluízio's narrative, Jane serves a narrative device representing the freedom (whether sexual or political) that Aluízio was sacrificing by going underground. And anchored by the image of her sweating, dancing body, Aluízio's depiction of Jane, and her alleged eagerness to go home with him, serves as a romanticized sendoff for a young militant at the start of a dangerous unknown. That Aluízio did not bring Jane back to his apartment is also meant as a signal to his audience that even in such moments, he remained committed to the political task at hand.

For security reasons, Aluízio and Nielse did not travel together to Foz do Iguaçu. Aluízio went first, bringing a large leather suitcase filled with supplies, including books by Régis Debray and Che Guevara, maps of the border region, a .38-caliber revolver, a hunting rifle, and a small amount of ammunition. Prior to Aluízio's departure for Paraná, the MR-8 had acquired a few weapons, some of which were purchased and the others stolen.[7] Fábio Campana had arranged a place for Aluízio to sleep in a room at the back of a bakery. A few days later, Nielse arrived, bringing another pistol, medical supplies, camping equipment, and antidotes for snake bites.[8] After about a week of sharing the small room at the back of the bakery, Nielse moved to the house of a local contact named Israel, while Aluízio stayed at César Cabral's apartment, which served as their base for the next few months.

During this time, Aluízio and Nielse's main activity was to survey the region. Traveling on foot, but also hitchhiking and taking occasional buses, they explored the northern perimeter of Iguaçu National Park (a 150-kilometer stretch between Foz do Iguaçu and Cascavel) and they also went as far as Umuarama, several hundred kilometers further north.[9] They spent much of their time scouting the region's topography: mapping out rivers and streams, and also the back roads and bridges they would need for transporting supplies. Because the insurgency would require local collaboration, they also spoke with farmers and townspeople to orient themselves to the area's social conflicts, both historical and ongoing. And given the eventual goal of taking their fight out of the forests and into the surrounding cities, Aluízio and Nielse also surveyed police stations, army garrisons, and other public buildings. Aluízio recorded these observations in a diary that he maintained during his year in Paraná—when he was arrested the following April, the diary was among the items seized by the military, helping his torturers to eventually identify him and his activities.

Aluízio and Nielse initially did the reconnaissance on their own. But within a few weeks, Fábio Campana introduced them to an older militant named Bernardino Jorge Velho, a former army sergeant who had also been in the Brazilian Communist Party. A supporter of the Pernambucan militant Gregório Bezerra,

CHAPTER 3

Bernardino shared the MR-8's goal of building a rural front of resistance. After meeting the young MR-8 militants in Foz do Iguaçu, Bernardino helped them build relationships with local communities. As Aluízio explained, when he and Nielse initially went out on their own, many people in the border region correctly pegged them as outsiders: "We were seen as city people, but not Bernardino. He was from the countryside. So he became our guide, the person who took us around and introduced us to people. It was thanks to Bernardino that we built a network of support."[10]

Several elements helped the MR-8 earn the trust of local people. Outwardly, the young militants and the rural communities shared a common cultural and phenotypical profile. Aluízio and Nielse were from European-descendant families, meaning that they were white; so too were most of the non-Indigenous inhabitants of western Paraná, who tended to come from families that had immigrated to southern Brazil from Italy and Germany in the first half of the twentieth century. These rural farmers had then migrated to western Paraná in the 1940s and 1950s, and their roots in the South provided a second entry point for the MR-8. Many of the farmers retained political allegiances to the southern states, most notably to Leonel Brizola, the former leftist governor of Rio Grande do Sul who had been forced to flee the country after the 1964 coup. Especially in the border regions of the country, it was said that Brizola was organizing a resistance movement, and the MR-8 took advantage of these rumors. "Bernardino told the farmers that we were representatives of Governor Brizola," Aluízio recalled. "He said that Brizola was coming back and that we had come first to organize a support base. Basically, he lied, and we just stayed quiet. Otherwise, we couldn't just show up and say, 'Hi, how are you, we're communists, we're here organizing a guerrilla foco.'"

From this initial, if misleading, introduction, Aluízio and Nielse built relationships throughout the region. In later months, once the MR-8 began its training sessions in the national park, several families allowed the militants to stash books, guns, and other supplies on their property. MR-8 members would often bring a small token of thanks to the farmers, such as a bit of meat or a bag of rice. Aluízio would also socialize with locals, as a way to ingratiate himself in the community and to alleviate the stress of his militancy. Figure 3.1 shows Aluízio at a horse racing festival near the town of Cascavel. Seated among local men, while children mingle between them, Aluízio looks at the camera with what seems to be a genuine smile.

In their attempt to go "incognito" in the countryside, Aluízio and Nielse dressed in farmers' clothing, and rather than using a backpack, they carried all their supplies in an empty flour sack. On their scouting missions they mostly

FIGURE 3.1. Aluízio Palmar (*seated, second to left, with white hat*) at a horse racing festival near Cascavel, Paraná, late 1968 or early 1969. Courtesy of Aluízio Palmar.

slept outside, either in fields or at the edge of the forest. On rare occasions, they stayed on the property of sympathetic farmers, such as one location in Vera Cruz do Oeste, where an older couple, Astra and Artur Fruet, let them sleep in the barn.[11] When it rained, sleeping outside was a problem, though it also provided a ruggedness that conformed to their image of guerrilla life. Having spent the past decade in the bustle of Niterói, Aluízio often found himself moved by his new surroundings. In his memoir, he wrote nostalgically about this experience: "One time we were coming back to Foz do Iguaçu, a bit before Itacorá [and] it started raining. We stopped in the middle of a mint field. . . . That night, in our sleeping bags, with the zipper pulled up to my chin, I fell asleep to the sound of the rain and the soft smell of mint."[12] In moments such as these, rural militancy could bring a sense of calm.

Spending time among rural communities also meant witnessing the harsh realities of peasant labor. Although many families in the area were smallholder farmers who owned their land, others relied on a variety of precarious work, including as tenant farmers, day laborers, squatters, or *boias-frias* (itinerant farmhands). The abuses on large plantations shocked the MR-8 members, most of whom had lived their whole lives in dense urban settings. Having grown up in a small interior town, Aluízio was familiar with the demands of farming, but it was a new experience to see it up close—no longer a small child in São Fidélis, Aluízio now witnessed this exploitation through the eyes of a committed militant. One estate stuck in his memory, the Fazenda Rami in Matelândia, where many workers had lost fingers in the "parakeet," a machine that separated the stems of ramie, a fibrous plant used to make clothes and rope.[13] Aluízio and his comrades went at night to the derelict workers housing on the plantation and spoke with them about their working conditions. In hushed voices, the young militants from Niterói told the farmworkers how a revolution could help liberate rural Brazilians. These conversations, however, served mainly to add fuel to the MR-8's own sense of indignation. The militants made no serious effort to intervene on farms. In their view, such advancements would come later as part of the revolution. According to their program, now was not the time to lead local struggles. It was time to become guerrilla rebels.

MEMORIES OF 1968

A few weeks before the MR-8 entered the forest and began its insurgent training, the opposition movement in Rio de Janeiro staged its most important action to date. Throughout the early months of 1968, the military regime had increased the scale of arbitrary arrests, most often against students. The targeting of youth movements, in turn, spurred more protest. On March 28, a demonstration took place outside of the Calabouço, a student restaurant, to demand that university restaurants offer more affordable meals. Although nominally a protest against the poor quality of the food, it was also a pretext for making broader political critiques.[14]

Several hundred students, mostly teenagers from local secondary schools, assembled outside of the Calabouço. Soon after police arrived on the scene, officers began shooting. Several students were seriously injured, and one took a fatal bullet to the heart: Edson Luís de Lima Souto, a poor eighteen-year-old student from the northern state of Pará who had recently moved to Rio, and who worked, and sometimes lived, at the Calabouço. Edson was one of the first students killed by the dictatorship, and his death sparked a new wave of protests. This culminated three months later with the March of the 100,000—one of the largest demonstrations in Brazilian history, and part of a wave of global protests in 1968 that included Paris in May, the Prague Spring, and US demonstrations against the Vietnam War. In subsequent years, the march's symbolism drew not only from its size but also for its position as a hinge moment in the history of Brazil's dictatorship. For protestors, the outpouring of dissent represented a final attempt at peaceful protest before some groups would opt to take up arms. And for the dictatorship, the march served as a form of self-justification for becoming even more repressive, paving the way for a new set of laws at the end of the year that would usher in its most violent phase. For all involved, the protest served as a rationale for whatever came next.

Aluízio was not among the 100,000 protesters in Rio de Janeiro that day in June. In our interviews, he emphasized that except for a quick return to Niterói in early 1969 to visit his father, once he arrived in western Paraná in March 1968, he did not leave the region until being captured by the military the following year. Yet decades afterward, when speaking about the history of 1968, he placed himself not in Iguaçu National Park—part of a small band of ultimately unsuccessful rebels—but rather in the middle of the demonstration, taking part in arguably the most emblematic day in Brazil's fight for democracy.

In 2018, as part of the fiftieth anniversary of 1968, Aluízio was invited to speak at the State University of Ponta Grossa, a regional university in Paraná, 100 kilometers outside Curitiba. Across Brazil on that day, commemorations of 1968 took place with the 2018 presidential elections on the near horizon—the firebrand Jair Bolsonaro was already starting to top polls, and it was unclear if former president Lula would be allowed to run. In this context, the legacy of 1968, and the blending of past and present, was almost palpable. Perhaps Aluízio wished that he had been invited to deliver his remarks at the larger events in Rio de Janeiro or São Paulo. Or maybe he was happy to address a Paraná audience that would likely be more familiar with his stories. The day before his speech, he promoted the event on Facebook, writing a short post about his participation in the famous protest:

> On that June 26, 1968, I crossed the Guanabara Bay with a group of classmates from the UFF and some high school students. We were nervous.... At that time the dictatorship was using extreme violence, even killing protesters. Knowing that we could be victims of a massacre, we went [to Rio], carrying pamphlets we had printed the day before on our homemade mimeographs. We got off the ferry at the Praça XV and went to the front of the Legislative Assembly, where we joined the crowd.... In a few minutes, we were surprised by the strength of the momentum that swelled the march in another direction. Suddenly, the streets of Rio de Janeiro were overtaken by the massive political demonstration that would come to be known as the "march of the 100,000." The dictatorship suffered a great defeat. It was really something amazing.

CHAPTER 3

Soon, at 7 p.m., I will be in the main Auditorium of the State University of Ponta Grossa, talking about this and other events from those years of dreams and struggles.[15]

Why did Aluízio claim to have been somewhere he was not? And what insights do these misrepresentations shed on larger themes about identity and historical memory? I initially approached this discrepancy with trepidation. This was the first, and arguably the most glaring, of the discrepancies in Aluízio's memory script. Rather than call it out directly, I opted to pose a series of follow-up questions about his time in western Paraná. After our interviews about this period in his life, I asked him several permutations of the same question: Once you arrived in Foz do Iguaçu in March 1968, did you ever leave the region?[16] No matter how I phrased it, Aluízio was unwavering in telling me that aside from once visiting his father, he never left the frontier.

His public comments in 2018 suggest a parallel form of memory-making, one that echoes Alessandro Portelli's study of how inhabitants in a small town in Italy misremembered the death of a local man. As part of his landmark reflection on oral history, Portelli calls on scholars of memory to focus "not only [on] the mechanics of the material event, but the events of the remembering and the telling, the patterns of the remembering and the forms of the telling through which we are able to perceive the 'event' in the first place."[17] When the event in question is politically symbolic, the act of remembering it can take on even more meaning. Amid the layered meanings of memory, Aluízio projected himself onto an event that took place a thousand kilometers away.

I sat with this information for over a year, putting off what I knew I needed to do, which was letting Aluízio know about the discrepancy. This case helped push me to fully embrace a methodology that, until that point, I had tiptoed around. It was easy to have a close relationship with my research subject when the exchanges focused primarily on the memories that he provided me, but it would be trickier to point out parallel or even discordant stories that I discovered through my research. At later moments, I would share archival documents with Aluízio, showing him places where the historical record complemented or corrected part of his accustomed narrative. But here, I needed to show him where different versions of his own memories did not align.

When I told Aluízio about my findings, I was relieved that he was not upset. Admittedly, I chose to convey this information in a carefully worded email rather than our usual WhatsApp or Zoom conversations, so it is possible that his initial reaction was different to the measured reply he sent later that night. In my email, I used the words "discrepância" (discrepancy) and "discordância" (something at odds with), which I hoped would provide a softer landing. Aluízio, in his reply, used the word "contradições," which he explained were part of a "mental confusion" that he sometimes exhibited. In this case, he claimed to have mixed up the dates of two events.[18] Rather than describe the 1968 protest, he told me that he had mistakenly drawn from his memory of a progovernment rally in 1964, two weeks prior to the coup. Toward the end of chapter 1, I quoted our interview in which Aluízio similarly described taking the ferry with his classmates across the bay to hear João Goulart's famous Comício da Central speech, and all evidence suggests that Aluízio had indeed taken part in the 1964 assembly. Yet it appears that despite what he claimed on social media, he had not participated in the 1968 event.

This memory is the overlapping result of several potential themes, including the passage of time and the fact that all memories are liable to slippage. Fifty years after the event in question, Aluízio grafted details from his earlier political work (taking the ferry from Niterói, protesting with other students, the mimeograph printer) onto what it might have been like if he had attended in person. The stories and images of that day in Rio de Janeiro have become so ubiquitous that Aluízio could conjure the sights and feel of the protest. Because this moment became elevated as a collective memory in leftist folklore, it became a potent and invokable narrative, even for those who had not been there.

But there are other considerations as well. Namely, a desire to place oneself at an important historical moment. Given the purpose of his Facebook post—to promote his appearance at a commemorative event, which itself took place far from Rio de Janeiro—we can also understand Aluízio's memory as a legacy of his political trajectory. The MR-8's campaign of armed struggle, like that of the various revolutionary groups in Brazil, did not achieve its goal of overthrowing the dictatorship. In the end, it could even be argued that the insurgent campaigns did more harm than good, given that the regime used the existence of a small number of armed groups as justification to unleash a disproportionate amount of violence. As such, putting himself among the protestors in 1968 can also be read as an attempt to re-narrate his chronology. Participating in the March of the 100,000 would have meant that he took up arms only after the waves of repression that followed the demonstration, repositioning himself at the center of a large, collective final effort at peacefully confronting the military regime. At stake here are the contested memories and timelines of armed revolution. With a retrospective awareness of the violence to come—and the victim-blaming rationale deployed by the dictatorship—stories about 1968 were highly symbolic.

Another possible explanation relates to questions of identity, belonging, and trauma. In our interviews, Aluízio often referred to himself as part of the generation of 1968, and it is even the name of a WhatsApp group (Amigos e Amigas de 68) of former activists and militants in which he is an active participant. The name conjures a connection to the global youth counterculture of the 1960s—evoking student protests in Paris and Budapest—and it implies a shared trajectory: in the aftermath of 1968, when Brazil's dictatorship became even more authoritarian, many activists went into exile, often settling in Europe, where they maintained bonds of solidarity on foreign soil. Aluízio took a different path. As we will see, after two years in prison, he settled in Chile but almost immediately returned to clandestine organizing, a choice that eventually led him to live in rural Argentina with a fake name and under constant threat of arrest. As a result, his decade in exile was defined by isolation, loneliness, and political disillusionment, making him resentful toward others who spent their exile in Europe. Aluízio told me that he enjoys being in the Friends of '68 WhatsApp group, but when people on the thread discuss exile, he gets frustrated: "They always talk about their time in exile, in Germany, in Switzerland, Sweden, in Paris, Rome. I think to myself, and I tell them, 'Fucking hell, while you all were living it up in exile, I was God knows where.'"[19]

In this context, Aluízio's memory of having participated in the 1968 march in Rio de Janeiro can also be seen as an effort to connect with a foundational moment for his generation. Scholars of trauma and memory have traced similar examples of identity formation. Dominick LaCapra writes that "traumatic experience has dimensions that may threaten or even shatter identity and may not be 'captured' by history, recorded in written archives, or contained by conscious recall. . . . In an apparent paradox, the extremely disconcerting or traumatic may also be affirmed or embraced as the foundation of identity."[20] As such, and when filtered through Aluízio's narratives of trauma, his memories of 1968 reflect a desire to be included in the hinge moment of what propelled many, but not all, of his generation to take a common next step in their experience of Brazil's dictatorship. In June 1968, 100,000 Brazilians had taken to the streets, peacefully protesting for the return of democratic rule. Despite his claims fifty years later, Aluízio had not been there. Instead, he had embedded himself in the Paraná borderlands as a member of a small group that had opted to pursue an armed campaign.

INTO THE FOREST

After several months of reconnaissance in the region, the MR-8 felt ready to begin training. This required two things: a plot of land and an instructor. For the former, a small property—known as a *sítio*—would serve as a base of operations and as a cover for their activity in the region. For the latter, the MR-8 needed an experienced militant who could teach the young cadres how to shoot, how to live in the forest, and how to build a guerrilla foco. Without these two assets, the MR-8 would continue to be little more than a handful of young adults walking along the Paraná frontier.

In July 1968, the MR-8 secured both the land and the trainer. With money from fundraisers and donations back in Niterói, the group purchased a farm, called Boi-Piquá, about thirty kilometers from the northernmost tip of Iguaçu National Park. Located between the towns of Cascavel and Toledo, the Boi-Piquá sítio had a wooden house, a small rice field, a horse, and a few cattle.[21] The MR-8 purchased the farm for 3,197 cruzeiros novos (NCr$)—roughly US$1,000 at the time.[22] Over the previous year, as the DI-RJ dissidência transformed into the MR-8, the group had steadily recruited members in both Niterói and Curitiba; Boi-Piquá was bought in the name of one of these new members, Marcos Antônio Faria de Medeiros, whose Paraná driver's license simplified the process of acquiring the land deed. A rotation of members would stay on the farm to coordinate supplies for the trainees in the park and to take care of the animals and crops. Boi-Piquá allowed the MR-8 to hold meetings, host members when they arrived in the region, and organize the collection of food, weapons, and equipment. The group soon carried out these tasks with the help of a car, a Willys Aero jeep that César Cabral and Hélio Gomes Medeiro bought in Cascavel after the group's first bank robbery in late August.[23] On the farm, the MR-8 also maintained what the authorities would later describe as "an 'archive' with books and publications clearly of communist character."[24] In mid-July, while the MR-8 was setting up its base at the Boi-Piquá farm, the group also found its trainer.

Rodolfo Ramírez Villalba was a Paraguayan militant who belonged to the Popular Colorado Movement, a group that had been expelled from the Partido Colorado, Paraguay's largest political party. While organizing with the clandestine resistance to the violent dictatorship of Alfredo Stroessner—which by this point had already been in power for nearly a decade—Rodolfo had relocated to the Paraná borderlands. There, he eventually met César Cabral, who introduced him to the Brazilian militants looking for a guerrilla instructor. For the MR-8, it was a lucky twist of fate that Rodolfo was in the frontier at precisely that moment; he would later return to Asunción, where he and his brother, Benjamin, would be captured, tortured, and disappeared by Stroessner's security forces.[25] Rodolfo was not much older than the MR-8 cadres, but he had the main asset that the young militants did not: he had been trained in guerrilla warfare, having spent time in Cuba a few years

CHAPTER 3

earlier.[26] For the young Brazilians, Rodolfo's connection to Cuba made him an especially magnetic figure. "The Cuban Revolution was pretty recent," Fábio Campana recalled. "It still felt like it had just happened the day before.... We studied the positions defended by Che and by Fidel, the idea of creating two, three, many Vietnams. We threw ourselves into the idea that the only option was armed struggle."[27] Rodolfo helped transpose a veneer of the Cuban Revolution onto the frontier of western Brazil—Aluízio referred to him as "our Che Guevara, our trainer."[28]

With a base now established at the Boi-Piquá farm, Rodolfo organized a program for teaching the MR-8 to become guerrilla fighters. In early August, training began in Iguaçu National Park. Along with Aluízio and Nielse, the other MR-8 members chosen to participate were Milton Gaia Leite—one of the group's founding members in Niterói—and João Manoel Fernandes, a new recruit from the student movement in Curitiba. César Cabral and Bernardino Jorge Velho also took part, as did a scattering of other members who occasionally traveled to Foz do Iguaçu. Rodolfo secured the initial weapons used for training. Eventually, the MR-8's bank robberies would allow them to purchase more guns, but at the start, the trainees in the forest used the outdated guns that Rodolfo could secure from his contacts across the border in Paraguay. One of the machine guns was a relic from the Chaco War in the 1930s.[29]

Between August 1968 and February 1969, the MR-8 used Iguaçu National Park as its training ground. Led by Rodolfo, the group spent weeks inside the park to practice shooting, marching, and ambushing. They established several resupply points at the edge of the park, where members at the farm would leave food and medicine, and the trainees learned how to stash supplies within the forest. Rodolfo instructed them on the basics of wilderness survival: hunting, fishing, building a fire, and identifying edible plants. For the young militants, most of whom had gone directly from the university to the forest, this was a challenging, if motivating, experience. João Manoel Fernandes, the recruit from Curitiba, told me that his time in the park was "very hard. We would go into the forest and spend thirty days there.... We learned a lot about facing our fears, and how to be alone in the middle of the forest. Because we couldn't just go crazy, that's not what guerrillas are supposed to do."[30] Aluízio explained that they wanted to become human chameleons: "We learned how to be just another animal, to be like a wild animal in the forest. We smelled like animals, yeah, and we knew how to live in the forest as if we were part of nature."[31] On the Brazilian side of the border, Iguaçu National Park extends for 1,700 square kilometers of Atlantic rainforest, and for six months, the small MR-8 band roamed the park with visions of armed revolution.

Although framed by lofty goals of overthrowing Brazil's dictatorship, the actual experience in the forest was quite banal. More often than not, it was exhausting. To chronicle their time in the forest, Aluízio kept a logbook of the guerrilla training, part of the diary that would be seized from him when he was captured in April 1969. A few weeks after the arrest, military officers transcribed a portion of the diary and attached it to Aluízio's prison file.[32] This transcription is the only surviving evidence of the training log.

Covering a two-week period at the end of December 1968, this chronicle of rebel training in a forested borderland coincided with a pivotal moment in Brazil's dictatorship. On December 13, only a few days before Aluízio's first diary entry, hardliners in the military passed Institutional Act no. 5 (AI-5, Ato Institucional Número 5), a draconian national security law that gave the president the power to close Congress and strip elected officials of their mandates. This new law represented a "coup within a coup" and ushered in the most violent period of military rule, from 1969 to 1973. For militants like those in Iguaçu National Park, AI-5 was a double-edged sword: to them, the hardening of the regime offered further proof that only an armed struggle could overthrow the dictatorship, yet the law itself made such a strategy even more dangerous. With the passage of AI-5, the military regime redoubled its efforts to cleanse the country of subversion. Against the backdrop of an increasingly authoritarian state—and in the close shadow of the Paraguayan dictatorship just across the border—Aluízio and his fellow militants in the forest prepared for armed conflict.

As evident in Aluízio's diary, the gulf between the regime and the militants grew ever wider. While the military expanded its power to target its enemies, the guerrilla training had yet to evolve into anything close to a serious threat. The transcribed diary offers a window into guerrilla life: details about daily movements and interpersonal problems, the difficulties communicating with the outside world, and a range of observations on the weather, food, and the deteriorating state of their equipment. All members are referred to by their codenames: Fiat is Milton Gaia Leite, Ivan is Nielse Fernandes, Miguel is César Cabral, Santos is Bernardino Jorge Velho, and Roberto is the trainer, Rodolfo Ramírez Villalba. Aluízio did not refer to himself in the diary, but his codename was André. Along with the various insights on the stilted progress of their guerrilla foco, there are two further items of note. The first is an ongoing disagreement with Bernardino (Santos), who according to the diary, had soured on the strategy of rural insurgency. Like the feelings that pushed him to break with the PCB, Aluízio again grew frustrated by what he saw as the stubbornness of older comrades. Second, the diary reveals the grueling and unromantic realities

CHAPTER 3

of guerrilla insurgency that rarely feature in later-day reminiscences about the armed struggle. Rather than a heroic and inspiring tale of revolutionary action along the lines of Che Guevara's diaries, Aluízio's firsthand account shows a rain-soaked slog through the forest, with little food, unreliable supplies, no contact with the outside world, and dwindling morale.

Much of the diary follows the group's march to and from a particular spot within the forest where they had left a *depósito* (hidden stash) of supplies. Below are select entries from Aluízio's diary from December 17 to 31, 1968.

> Dec. 17. Fiat and Ivan leave at 4 hr. I enter. We're taking the supplies hidden in the forest and we'll go meet Roberto and Santos, who are at the camp. We left at 5 hr., stopped several times.... We arrived at 11 hr., used a password and made contact with the radio.... At night another conversation [words crossed out] me and [words crossed out] again. This time about the experiences of A.R. [Armed Struggle] in P[araná]. Later Santos made some criticisms to Fiat, we discussed them. Then I presented a series of criticisms to Santos, and I think I was very aggressive with them, Santos is still bad politically. ... Later we will sleep with everyone doing two hours of watch.

> Dec. 20. Friday. At 6 hr. we packed up camp. The hike this time was harder, as the path crosses two hills. [words crossed out] Around 9 hr. we arrived at Rio Tândia, Roberto saw some capybaras, shot and missed. We made a first camp, on the right banks of the Floriano, but we left because of the ants. We made a second [camp] on the left bank and spent the rest of the afternoon there and night. At night there was a rain shower.

> Dec. 21. Saturday.... We camped by a waterfall. The place is very beautiful.... Right after setting up camp and having lunch, we cleaned the guns thoroughly. We plan to always clean the guns. Later it rained again and very strong. Santos and Miguel made some lambari fish. Later a stray dog appeared and stayed in camp.

> Dec. 22. Sunday. Last night it rained nonstop. We spent the day at camp in the rain [words crossed out]. All our clothes got wet. That night I slept on the floor w/ Roberto, sharing the blanket. We made the fire, w/ wet wood.... Miguel and Santos went fishing, caught many lambaris. Good news. Butterflies and flies make great

bait. I went for a few rounds of hunting but found nothing. The dog is still with us. We did a basic cleaning of the guns. From one day to the next they all get rusty. . . . The food is at an end and the rain continues. I had a political discussion with Roberto.

Dec. 23. Monday. We began to march early, in the rain toward the stash. It was a very strained march, because even though we have few supplies, our wet equipment weighs double. We have always obeyed the Front, Center, and Rearguard scheme. When we stop for a rest, everyone stops in his place. . . . We found macado bananas on the floor and ate them, it's a delicious fruit. We also eat other fruits, like ingá and coconut of pitanga. At 16 hr., still raining, we arrived at the stash. . . . Santos talks a lot about going back to the city. We are worried. We did basic cleaning of the weapons. We set up a tent with the 3 tarps, which by the way are horrible. . . . At night we slept around the fire. We lined the mud floor with broken taquara and pindoba leaves. . . . The transistor radio receiver has stopped working. We have no news.

Dec. 24. Tuesday. We spent the day in the rain. When one piece of clothing dries another starts to get wet. We went to the stash to get a list of things. We still left behind some of the medicine.

Dec. 26. Thursday. Soon after waking up we left some things up in the trees. We'll take supplies for 3 days. . . . The plant life is quite different in these places. The path is all palm. We find several species of wild fruits, such as guaimbé banana; sertitiam, ingá and guapuriti. Others like the tanjanana, very abundant here, are not edible. . . . At 15 hr. we stop, our canteens are empty and the thirst is barbaric. . . . 5 days we are disconnected from the world. The transistor radio does not work.

Dec. 27. Friday. At 8 hr. we left, this time with full canteens. We left the backpacks hidden. . . . The noise of the cars gets closer and closer. Finally we reach the road, it is 12.30 hr. I left Roberto providing cover and did some reconnaissance of the road. At 13 hr. we came back. . . . Later we ate rice and beef jerky (for a change) and stayed in the same place as before.

Dec. 28. Saturday. Today, it rained again and we had a meeting. . . . We discussed 2 points: (1) Overview, (2) criticism and self-criticism.

We decided on: Permanent watch day and night every 2 hours the patrol always chooses where to camp. (At night, we don't even talk.) Cooking at dawn, not keeping the fire going during the day. After we arrived at the safe place, we started training at night walking, evacuation, etc. . . . Santos raised his problems again. . . . I think this case will be very serious. I have to be careful with that guy.

Dec. 29. Sunday. We spent the day at camp. We washed clothes, took care of the cartridges, we did lookout with two people every two hours. Whenever anyone goes to shit they take their weapon(s) and ammunition. We're in bad shape. Coffee, bacon, maggi, and sugar are finished. The lack of tarps remains a problem. All of the food is disintegrating. . . . At night I had a chat w/ Santos. We went to the roots of the problems he's having. The man wavers at every level.

Dec. 31. The heavy weight of the backpacks that were delivered with supplies shocked all of us. In the old camp, we are getting ready to open another path or build a stash. But everything okay.

GIVING VOICE TO PAINFUL MEMORIES

In their memories, collected in interviews half a century later, none of the once-eager guerrillas offered an entirely cheery view of their attempt to build an armed struggle. With the benefit of hindsight, and forever changed by the experience of imprisonment and torture, the former militants that I spoke with expressed varying levels of regret at the strategy they had pursued. Even while acknowledging the naivete of their actions, many still looked back at their time in the forest with a particular sense of nostalgia. Yes, their efforts eventually failed, and as a result, they—like thousands of others in Brazil—suffered the violence of military rule. But for many of the former militants, a romantic memory still remained from the period before their capture.

João Manoel Fernandes's experience reflects the complex legacies of armed militancy. He had grown up in a large, religious family in the countryside of Santa Catarina, and, as one of fourteen children, João Manoel felt stifled by the environment of his childhood: "My whole world was about religion . . . and eventually I began to expand my mind and I came to see that neither Jesus nor God were going to save me."[33] When he attended university in Paraná, he became absorbed in the student movement, feeling that he had finally found a space to think critically. Like many student activists in the early years of the military regime, João Manoel's political evolution accelerated in tandem with the increasing repression of the regime.

By 1968, when he was introduced to other MR-8 members in Curitiba, the idea of joining an armed struggle seemed a natural progression. As one of the youngest members of the MR-8, what he later understood to be naivete was, at the time, precisely what made the experience so exciting: "I didn't even know how big our enemy was. Or even how small our organization was." At four different moments of our interview, João Manoel mentioned that they did not know the size of their enemy. João Manoel spoke as if the MR-8 had tried to single-handedly take down the dictatorship: "The army had 600,000 men, we had 30. That can't work... 600,000 against 30 can't work. Even if you really want a revolution, you can't." But at the time, the challenge was itself the motivation—"That was the point.... We really believed in the things we did and said."

For João Manoel, his invocation of what he said as a young militant was more than just a turn of phrase. Barely a year after joining the MR-8, the dictatorship literally silenced him. On the night of July 3, 1969, João Manoel was sitting at a typewriter in one of the group's safe houses in Curitiba. Around 10 p.m., several police officers burst in. This was one of the final raids conducted on the MR-8—half of the organization had already been arrested. By the following month, with nearly all its members imprisoned, the group would collapse entirely. In the military's documentation of the raid on João Manoel's apartment, a DOPS report stated obliquely that when the police entered the home, "the subject ... reacted, during which time he was injured, and was quickly taken to the Army General Hospital."[34]

In our interview, the full story of what happened became clear—both in what João Manoel said and how he said it. That night in Curitiba, the police came into his apartment and shot João Manoel in the throat. When he collapsed in a pool of his own blood, the police assumed he was dead. Only after spending time searching the apartment did the agents discover that he was still alive. He survived, but the damage to his throat never healed. Even once he regained the ability to speak—which came slowly over his many years spent in various military prisons—his voice remained hoarse and strained. When we spoke on the phone, his wife Célia often helped finish his sentences.

Decades later, João Manoel discussed his past with sorrow, but also with pride. "I was never young," he said. "My youth was destroyed. I was only ever a political militant." Like many of his generation, João Manoel could not fully move on from the traumatic years of Brazil's dictatorship. Though despite the violence etched onto his body, he still looked back on his militancy with a sense of awe. Especially when talking about his training in the national park, João Manoel spoke as if it were his most unique memory—not quite a positive experience, but an exceptional moment in time. The uniqueness of that memory, however painful, was something that set him apart.

THE OCTOBER 8 REVOLUTIONARY MOVEMENT

It is useful here to step back and offer an overview of the MR-8's progression from mid-1968 onward. Although the guerrilla activities along the Paraná border were the group's larger focus, most of its membership—and all of its financing—was based elsewhere. From August 1968 through May 1969, the MR-8 was active in Niterói, Rio de Janeiro, and Curitiba, leading a series of bank robberies and car thefts. When the military regime finally caught up with the group, almost all its members were captured in a cascade of arrests between April and July. The regime violently interrogated the MR-8 militants. Even if not all the information was reliable, enough pieces of testimony under torture allowed the military to construct a fairly complete account of the group's actions. These records enable us to chart the rise and fall of the October 8 Revolutionary Movement.[35]

From its initial five founders in 1967, the group grew to over thirty people two years later—twenty-five fully active members plus another half-dozen collaborators who helped with tasks such as hiding money or guns, scouting out locations, or making introductions to other armed groups. The MR-8 was divided into three main sectors: leadership, recruitment, and expropriations. Most of the members were students from Niterói or Curitiba, and almost all were in their early and mid-twenties (though they ranged in age from nineteen to thirty-six). Every member had a codename, most of which were relatively innocuous—Lucas, Lúcia, Kátia, Gabriel—though a few chose names from the global revolutionary canon: Antônio Rogério Garcia Silveira went by the name Wladimir, and Fábio Campana was Zapata.

Of the twenty-five members, six were women, as were four of the collaborators. Zenaide Machado was the only woman on the leadership team. The MR-8's male-leaning membership was typical. According to one tabulation, of all the political prisoners charged by the military regime, 84 percent were men.[36] As it was for many women in leftist politics—in Brazil and globally in the late 1960s—being a woman in an armed group like the MR-8 was an empowering but complex experience. In my interview with her, Zenaide described her relationships with former comrades as "friendships that I maintain, with affection, to this day. So much affection, and respect for the young people we were ... so dedicated to that vision of the world."[37] But Zenaide also highlighted the challenges of being a woman in a clandestine revolutionary movement: "We had clashes with the really machista comrades. At the time there were some strong clashes.... [It was] in the way they spoke, or how, for example, the whole structure and decisions belonged to the men. The women were like soldiers-in-waiting, just standing in the back. As if they were tools to be used. They were not seen as equal partners." A similar sentiment was expressed by Iná Meirelles, who passed away in 2015 but who shared her memories in many interviews over the years. In a documentary about women political prisoners in Brazil, Iná spoke about her experience in the armed struggle. "The funny thing is that I didn't realize it [at the time]; I realize it much more retrospectively," Iná told an interviewer. "I notice it in the machismo of our group, because it existed, for example, when it came time to participate in armed actions. Men generally went, few women participated.... [The men told us] that they were better for this and that we were better for doing the 'legal' parts. There was a lot of strong debate. I, for example, argued a lot because I wanted to have a gun. I had to have a gun. After all, I could just as easily be captured as them."[38]

As gestured to by Iná, many insights about their time as young revolutionaries came in later years. Zenaide told me that questions around gender and feminism did not become a central issue until the mid-1970s, once the most violent phase of dictatorship had ended and exiles began trickling back to Brazil, many of whom had become more explicitly attuned to feminist ideologies while living in Europe. This view was also shared with me by other militants like Jessie Jane Vieira de Souza, a member of the ALN who was imprisoned and tortured after a 1970 plane hijacking.[39] Even while acknowledging that a more sustained engagement with internal group dynamics only occurred afterward, Zenaide did link the fight against military rule to a fight for social change more broadly.[40] "We were engaged in a struggle for a revolution in customs, in attitudes," she told me. "There was the whole issue of freedom of sexuality, the appreciation of freedoms as a whole. So we were all in that moment when the dictatorship was reactionary, moralistic; it was severe, extremely conservative. We were all in a fight against that conservative morality." Freedom, whether political, cultural, or sexual, was a central theme in militant memories of the late 1960s. Iná, who would go on to become a medical doctor specializing in the treatment of patients with AIDS, said that she "was lucky to belong to the generation after the pill but before AIDS.... We were a generation that lived through a moment of rupture for the role of women. There weren't many of us, only a few women militants at the time, and I think we were really bold."[41]

CHAPTER 3

In the MR-8, as across the various armed groups in Brazil, women like Zenaide and Iná experienced a full range of solidarity and frustrations.

For the MR-8, building an armed insurgency started with the basics—getting money and supplies. The group's first major action was a bank robbery in Niterói. Although the MR-8 would later graduate to armed robberies, the initial theft was an inside job that required no weapons. Mauro Fernando de Souza was one of the newer members of the MR-8, and he was also a teller at the Banco Mercantil in Niterói. It is not clear whether Mauro was recruited specifically because he worked at a bank, though it surely made him an appealing militant. On August 19, 1968, Mauro stepped away from his desk and went to the bank's main vault. He took NCr$60,000 (almost US$20,000) and, after pausing to make sure that nobody was watching, walked out the front door. The MR-8 had prepared a series of safe houses, and Mauro first stayed in São Gonçalo—incidentally, less than three kilometers from Aluízio's parents—and then at an apartment in downtown Niterói. After a few weeks of laying low, Mauro was driven to the MR-8's farm at Boi-Piquá in the Paraná borderlands. Umberto Trigueiros Lima drove part of the stolen money to Curitiba, though most of it went to the guerrilla training in the park, including NCr$4,000 (a little more than US$1,000) to buy the Willys Aero jeep.

This robbery provided the money and confidence to pursue larger campaigns. Throughout the final months of 1968, while the guerrilla training was underway in Iguaçu National Park, the MR-8 escalated its urban actions. At 11 p.m. on January 3, 1969, the group staged its first car theft: on Rua Campos Sales near the Maracanã stadium in Rio de Janeiro, four MR-8 members stole a blue Volkswagen. The heist was led by João Manoel Fernandes—who had recently returned from his training rotation at the border—and the driver was Reinaldo Silveira Pimenta. Less than six months later, Reinaldo would be shot by the dictatorship during a raid on an MR-8 safe house in Rio de Janeiro, the group's only member to be killed directly by the regime. After the car theft in Maracanã, they drove to the São Cristóvão neighborhood, swapped out the license plates, and returned to Niterói.

Three days later, the stolen blue Volkswagen was used as the getaway car to rob the Banco Lar Brasileiro in Ipanema. Three militants took part in the heist: Umberto Trigueiros Limo (the first to enter, wielding an INA submachine gun), João Manoel Fernandes (the lookout at the front door), and Sebastião Filho Medeiros, who confronted the cashier and took money from the safe, a total of NCr$10,000 (US$3,000). In our interview five decades later, Sebastião reflected on the experience of his first heist: "Look, in those days banks didn't have the structure they do now. . . . Now they have those big metal doors, a bunch of security. It was all easier then, you show up and say, 'This is a robbery!'"[42] Both at the time and in the years since, the militants believed that these armed actions were necessary. João Manoel described the robbery: "We would try to get as much money as possible. Because having money was important. That's when we learned how fundamental money was. Unfortunately, we couldn't do anything without money."[43] Umberto similarly recalled that holding up a bank "was a risk, but that's what it was like. At that moment it was a necessary risk. The money itself wasn't the goal, the goal was to raise money for . . . the activities of the armed struggle. But it was a risk because we had to expose ourselves."[44]

The day after the robbery in Ipanema, an article in the *Jornal do Brasil* gave an in-depth report on the heist. According to the newspaper, the thieves arrived at the bank ten minutes before closing time and were gone within four minutes.[45] The article detailed how the robbery took place: "Three assailants entered the bank normally. . . . One of the thieves, with a revolver hidden in a blue envelope, yelled from the middle of the lobby: 'Nobody move, this is a robbery.' Next, another thief, holding a machine gun, took the employees to a back room, forcing them to lie face down on the floor. . . . Meanwhile, two other thieves took all the money they could from the safe." The newspaper also quoted a witness who said that one of the thieves was "a short mulatto"—a term for a mixed-race person. The article printed a composite sketch provided to police, showing the alleged dark-skinned thief. That sketch formed the basis for a more detailed rendering, which the police distributed widely (fig. 3.2). Wearing a beret and dark sunglasses, the figure was racialized as Black both implicitly through facial characteristics and explicitly in its accompanying text: "Dark brown (mulatto)—northern type—height of 1.60 m to 1.62 m approximately—age 25 to 27 years—broad face—medium complexion—northern accent."[46] According to Umberto, although the MR-8 did have several members of Afro- and mixed-descent origins, none of them took part in the Ipanema robbery, and none were from northern Brazil.[47]

This racial distortion can be read as part of broader patterns. Not only was it a reflection of discrimination within Brazilian society—witnesses and newspaper editors alike defaulting to prejudice—but it also showed how the actions of militant groups could be discredited. The MR-8's first major robbery occurred as other armed groups in Brazil had already begun similar assaults, and mainstream news coverage often described these robberies as the work of "terrorists" rather than the actions of antidictatorship rebels. In the *Jornal do Brasil*, the MR-8 was referred to as "a terrorist gang" and "a band of terrorists." To be sure, the young militants also made discursive choices—for them, they

CHAPTER 3

FIGURE 3.2.
Police sketch of alleged bank robber, 1969. Brasil Nunca Mais Digital.

were not stealing, they were *expropriating*. Yet given the power imbalances between an authoritarian state and small groups of armed insurgents, discourse from the former was more influential than that of the latter. In news coverage of the Ipanema robbery, the ethnic misrepresentation of the MR-8 showed how a political movement could be depicted as a racialized menace, one that had formed in the northern countryside and was now trying to infiltrate the so-called civilized milieu of southern coastal society.

The MR-8 staged two more bank robberies: on March 14 at the Banco Aliança (seizing NCr$27,590) and on May 7 at the Banco Nacional Brasileiro (NCr$19,066), netting the equivalent, respectively, of about US$10,000 and US$7,000.[48] Both robberies took place in northern Rio de Janeiro, in the neighborhoods of Abolição and Piedade, and they used the same strategy of getting in and out within four minutes. With the money, the MR-8 purchased more weapons, including a Colt machine gun and several .38-caliber revolvers. The group also conducted a total of five carjackings, all of them late at night in Rio de Janeiro, yielding three Volkswagens and two Willys Aero jeeps. Along with the stolen vehicles, the MR-8 purchased five more cars. The fleet of ten cars were used to transport militants and supplies between their various safe houses—apartments they referred to as *aparelhos* (hide-outs).

At various times, the MR-8 had fifteen different aparelhos: six in Rio de Janeiro, one in Niterói, two in São Gonçalo, and six in Curitiba. The aparelhos offered a place for militants to lay low after a robbery. After a few weeks had elapsed, members would transport money between aparelhos and to the guerrilla fighters near the border. The women militants, whom it was assumed would draw less attention from the police, were often tasked with moving the money. Iná Meireles de Souza (codename Lúcia) made several trips to Foz do Iguaçu, driving a red Volkswagen that the group had purchased. On at least one occasion she was joined by Maria Cândida de Souza Gouveia (codename Kátia) on the drive to Curitiba, where the two women delivered NCr$5,000 (almost US$2,000) hidden in a cookie tin. Iná was a skilled linguist and translated many Marxist writings into Portuguese, using a small printer at an aparelho in Curitiba to prepare leaflets.[49] For their cover as being young Brazilians leading normal lives, five pairs of militants even got married and lived together in the apartments, pretending to be newlyweds. One of the older members, Milton Gaia Leite, who was already married, moved into the Curitiba aparelho on Rua Alfredo Polis with his wife and two young children.

Although the MR-8 never officially collaborated with other armed groups, it did communicate with different organizations, including the VPR, whose leadership included the former army captain Carlos Lamarca; COLINA, the group based in Minas Gerais that had also staged several bank robberies; and the ALN led by Carlos Marighella, which would later take part in the kidnapping of Charles Elbrick, the US ambassador to Brazil. In Foz do Iguaçu, César Cabral made contacts with armed groups in Uruguay and Argentina, though nothing came from those efforts. In Rio de Janeiro, two MR-8 militants, Porfirio Sampaio and Reinaldo Silveira Pimenta, arranged a meeting with the Syrian ambassador in Brazil, hoping to collaborate with Fatah, the Palestinian National Liberation Movement. The potential connection to groups in the Middle East also yielded no results.

The MR-8's most successful contact was not a member of an armed organization but a banker named Jorge Medeiros Valle. Newspaper headlines would later baptize Jorge Medeiros as the Bom Burguês—the Good Bourgeois.

CHAPTER 3

Though within the MR-8 his nickname was Setenta (Seventy), for the first donation of NCr$70,000 (over US$20,000) that he made to the group.[50] Jorge Medeiros was a manager at the Leblon branch of the Banco do Brasil, and he became the MR-8's main benefactor, donating approximately NCr$300,000 (US$100,000). He later claimed that he obtained this money by illegally wiring funds from his branch to an account in Switzerland, which he then funneled back to the MR-8.[51] Jorge Medeiros also financed the group's most adventurous expedition: the attempted liberation of political prisoners held on the island of Ilha das Flores. With a small boat and scuba equipment, two MR-8 members and a trained diver did reconnaissance off the southern coast of Rio de Janeiro. This excursion was soon abandoned, but the notion of an underwater prison escape provided a sensationalistic story that captured public attention.

In August 1969, several months after all members the MR-8 were captured or killed, one of Brazil's biggest magazines, *Manchete*, ran a six-page spread with glossy images of the detained militants.[52] Aluízio, who was imprisoned at that moment in Paraná, was not pictured among the MR-8 who had been caught in Rio de Janeiro, once again keeping him just beyond the public spotlight. Under the title "MR-8: The Weapons of Subversion," the exposé included a full-page photo of the assets seized by police during raids on the MR-8 safe houses (fig. 3.3). The supplies were arranged for a photo-op, with the guns and ammunition laid neatly in a circle on the table, knives in a row on the floor, and the scuba equipment hung up like a painting on the back wall. On the opposite page of the *Manchete* article, the arrested militants are led along a path, surveilled by an officer with a German shepherd in tow. These pictures reflect the arc of the MR-8's militancy. On the left, the debris of an unfulfilled armed struggle: an arsenal of supplies and weapons, most of which were never used. And on the right, the militants—looking like the young students they were—shuffle toward another detention center and the horrors that awaited them.

THE PERSONAL IN THE POLITICAL

Although Aluízio's stated purpose was to build a guerrilla insurgency capable of taking down the dictatorship, he soon found another reason for being in the Paraná borderlands. In early August, Aluízio met a young woman named Eunice Almeida. Their paths crossed thanks to the small world of clandestine politics along the Paraná border: Eunice's sister Adelaide was married to César Cabral—one of Aluízio's closest comrades in the region. On August 6, 1969, César and Adelaide hosted a party at their house in Foz do Iguaçu, which Aluízio attended along with Fábio Campana.[53] Aluízio met Eunice at this party,

FIGURE 3.3. Profile of MR-8 included seized weapons (*left*) and imprisoned militants (*right*). *Manchete*, August 16, 1969, 24–25.

and they soon began dating. Eunice had previously worked as a receptionist at the local office of the state telecommunications company, though by the time she met Aluízio, she had changed jobs, recently starting work as an elementary school teacher.[54] The life of a clandestine militant did not make dating easy, but the two began a whirlwind romance. Five months after meeting, they married.

When they met, Aluízio was just beginning his training in the national park, and the relationship consisted mostly of brief meetings in Foz do Iguaçu. During this initial period, Eunice knew him only by his codename, André. Eunice was aware that her new boyfriend had leftist politics, but she did not know the full extent of his militancy. In Aluízio's retelling, she only discovered his real identity while cleaning his room, where she saw his wallet hidden under the mattress: "She found my real documents under the bed, and she told me, 'I know your name isn't André, your name is Aluízio.' And that was tricky for me to explain because she figured out my name. . . . So it wasn't really a secret anymore, everyone [in the family] knew."[55] Eunice's mother, Flora, disapproved of the relationship, but she herself came from a political family—they were supporters of Leonel Brizola—and one of her daughters was already married to César Cabral, another militant. Flora eventually gave her blessing, provided that the couple get married.

CHAPTER 3

Here, as with the wider taboos relating to my interview questions about Eunice, we are left with unanswered questions. Why did someone in either Aluízio or Eunice's situation opt for legal marriage? For Aluízio, devoting so much time to his new romantic partner distracted from the armed struggle and put him and his comrades at risk—to say nothing of the danger to Eunice by bringing her into his orbit. And for Eunice, if we follow Aluízio's story above, this means she was willing to marry somebody whose real identity she only recently discovered. There were undoubtably strong social and cultural forces insisting on marriage, though my strategic choices as a collaborative biographer preclude a more precise discussion of courtship, marriage, and sexual norms.

Given that Aluízio was now living primarily in Iguaçu National Park, a normal wedding was not possible. Instead, he made plans with Eunice for a furtive ceremony at a local notary. On December 31, 1968, he left the forest and drove to São Miguel do Iguaçu, where Eunice had also traveled on her own.[56] This was the same date of Aluízio's final entry in his guerrilla diary. By this point, the MR-8 had sold its original farm at Boi-Piquá and relocated to a new sítio, named Banhadão, outside Matelândia, a move precipitated by a fear that their cover might be blown. Representatives of a local logging company, Pinho e Terra, had been asking neighbors about the new occupants at Boi-Piquá—the company was trying to acquire the land of some local farmers, and Aluízio had been one of the MR-8 members who tried to talk the families out of selling. This sequence of events showcased the deep challenges confronting the MR-8. Building a guerrilla insurgency required establishing a connection with local communities, but those interactions could also bring unwanted attention and risk.

The new Banhadão farm was much closer to the national park and thus more convenient to slip away and get married. Aluízio was able to travel quickly from the forest to the sítio, and then to the notary thirty kilometers away in São Miguel do Iguaçu. He picked up a clean shirt at the sítio but otherwise showed up for the wedding in his tattered guerrilla fatigues.[57] Using his falsified ID card as "André," he and Eunice were married. The two of them returned to Foz do Iguaçu for the night, and the next morning Aluízio went back to the forest. In the coming weeks, while still embedded in the national park, he seemed to have found ways to sneak back to Foz do Iguaçu: on September 16, about nine and a half months after getting married, Eunice gave birth to the couple's first child, a daughter named Florita.

Only after getting married did Aluízio tell his fellow militants about Eunice. Some of the MR-8, like João Manoel, remembered Aluízio's secret relationship as a harmless thing that made his comrade happy: "That Eunice, he was really in love with that girl."⁵⁸ Others were upset with Aluízio for his erratic behavior over the previous months, when he would disappear for several days. Sebastião Medeiros Filho said that "Aluízio was reckless . . . he went out and got married, man, without telling anyone. . . . We all thought, 'This guy is the leader of our organization, and he got married without saying anything?'"⁵⁹ Although the militants trusted Aluízio, the climate of dictatorship meant that unexplained absences inevitably caused fears that perhaps he was a spy. Umberto Trigueiros Lima remembered the moment when Aluízio finally came clean: "Everyone was a little suspicious at that time, but what happened? He said, 'No, I have to confess something to you all, I was dating a girl and I married her.' . . . That was a crisis, it was a crisis. . . . That was a difficult moment, because it was against all the rules, against the protocols of security and interactions with the local population. . . . It was a crisis, but we got over it."⁶⁰ At the very end of our interviews, when I asked for clarification about how he had first met Eunice, Aluízio offered a somewhat rare admission of fault: "My marriage really created some problems within the organization. Even though it was a semisecret wedding and done in a small-town notary in the interior of Paraná, I confess that I made a mistake. I broke the basic rules."⁶¹

Getting married in the middle of planning an armed insurgency brought risks not only for the group but for Eunice as well. Four months later, when Aluízio was arrested, the military wanted to know whether Eunice was an accomplice. An interrogation log from one of Aluízio's torture sessions concluded that Aluízio "is always insistent that his wife knew nothing of his activities." Security forces made several visits to Eunice's house in Foz do Iguaçu, though she was never detained, and the police mostly left her alone.⁶²

The same could not be said for Aluízio's family, whom the dictatorship monitored closely. Even before Aluízio was captured in 1969, the military regime sent agents to his parents' house on numerous occasions. This included a raid soon after the 1964 coup—when they seized copies of Dostoyevsky and Conan Doyle—as well as a few more visits in the early years of military rule. When Aluízio went underground in 1967, the military renewed its efforts to find him. In February 1968, the army issued a search warrant for his arrest, and in December of that year, DOPS agents in Niterói put out a surveillance alert for him.⁶³ As the wave of bank robberies and militant actions escalated across Brazil, Aluízio's family was caught in the crosshairs.

In January 1969, the dictatorship discovered a Niterói cell of the COLINA group, and the police found references to Aluízio. With that evidence, DOPS agents returned to the Palmar house in São Gonçalo. Aluízio's youngest brother, Ivan, was fifteen years old at the time, and his experience that day illustrated the reality of life under an authoritarian regime, where any association with suspected militants was grounds for surveillance and repression. Ivan and I exchanged several text messages, and he seemed keen to record an interview about his older brother. In the end, he opted to avoid speaking on the phone, choosing instead to write up his memories—not about Aluízio but about the day in January 1969 when he was detained by the police. In a lengthy series of WhatsApp messages, he sent me not only the story below but also a photo of three loose pages of handwritten text, which he then typed up for my benefit.

On the day in question, Ivan came home to find his parents seated nervously on the couch, with police agents searching the house for clues about Aluízio. Ivan was forced to sit down next to his parents. His mom pleaded with the police to allow Ivan to leave, so that he could return to school for afternoon classes. Eventually, the police let Ivan go. But when he was just a block away from school, a car pulled up and threw him into the backseat. "I was panicking," Ivan wrote. "They took me away, saying that they knew I was going to meet Aluízio to warn him about the situation. I denied it, so they took me to the police station."[64] Ivan was placed in a holding cell with other prisoners, and after four hours they transferred him to a DOPS building. On the drive, the officers harassed and threatened Ivan, telling him they were going to cut off his long hair, which, they said, "was a thing for fags." After a two-hour interrogation at DOPS, the police decided that he did not have any information about his brother. Ivan was released, and as he walked to the front door, the same officer harassed him again: "You're leaving so soon, you little fag?" At that, the exhausted and scared teenager called the officer a son of a bitch. Even though Ivan said this under his breath, the officer was close enough to hear and he slapped Ivan across the left side of his head. The force was so great that Ivan's ear started to bleed. Disoriented, he left the DOPS precinct and ran to the closest bus stop, not returning home until late at night.

THE INSURGENCY UNRAVELS

The first six months of the MR-8's armed struggle had gone relatively well. The group led a sustained training mission in Iguaçu National Park, it established a network of contacts and safe houses in three cities, and it pulled off several bank heists. An actual uprising was still a distant notion, but the initial efforts were encouraging.

The group confronted a wave of setbacks in the early months of 1969, starting with the departure of several key members, including Zenaide Machado, José Milton Barbosa, and Joseph Bartolo Calvert. As she recounted to me, Zenaide had felt frustrated with the group's small size as well as it focus on building a guerrilla foco: "We were in a process of intense discussion and debate, a political split within the MR-8. [Some of us] were looking for bigger organizations that had more structure, a more complex understanding of revolution, and the country, one which wasn't so tied to foquismo."[65] Prior to leaving the MR-8, Zenaide had argued with her comrades about the need to collaborate, or even merge, with other armed groups. But the MR-8 decided to maintain its goals—at least for the moment. After breaking from the MR-8, Zenaide joined the VPR, José Milton joined the ALN, and Joseph tried to leave Brazil altogether, though he was captured while attempting to sneak into Uruguay.

The archival record of the dictatorship offers an interesting twist to this story. Military interrogation logs state that Zenaide was among a handful of MR-8 members who had been expelled by Milton Gaia Leite, one of the group's founders.[66] Having consulted these sources prior to recording many of my interviews, when I eventually spoke with Zenaide, I asked her about being expelled from the group. She seemed confused, and not a little insulted, at the suggestion that Milton had expelled her. Why might this detail have ended up in the interrogation report? Perhaps Milton had made up the story to protect Zenaide and the others, giving them a cover of no longer being in the group. Or perhaps the violence of imprisonment triggered his anger at former comrades for leaving the group. There is no way to know for sure. I attempted to interview Milton, but, as his brother Benedito told me, Milton suffered several psychotic breaks in the years after his imprisonment and torture, and he was not stable enough to speak with me about this history.[67] Here, what matters less is the precise "truth" about why certain militants left the MR-8 than the goal of balancing multiple sources, and multiple memories, at the same time.

The first splintering of the MR-8, in which several members left voluntarily, was soon compounded by forces outside of the group's control: on February 15, the dictatorship arrested Umberto Trigueiros Lima. Fortunately for the MR-8, Umberto's capture was linked not to the bank robberies but to his ongoing involvement with the student movement.[68] All the same, the arrest of a leading MR-8 member was cause for alarm. Soon after Umberto's arrest, the group in western Paraná was put further on edge when late one night, while the members were at the rural sítio, a jeep pulled up to the house. Because the car's floodlights shined brightly, the MR-8 militants could not see who was inside. Fearing the worst, they grabbed their guns and prepared for a fight. After a brief time that felt like much longer, the jeep reversed and drove away.[69] Perhaps it had just been a random person who had gotten lost, but in the aftermath of Umberto's arrest, the mystery jeep pushed the MR-8 to change its plans.

CHAPTER 3

At the initiative of several of the remaining women militants, the group called an emergency meeting in Curitiba.[70] In early March, the MR-8 gathered at one of its safe house apartments to discuss the state of the armed struggle. In addition to Umberto, militants from other groups had also been captured. In early February, the dictatorship arrested several student leaders in Niterói, including Liszt Vieira and Vera Wrobel, as well as Clarice Chonchol, a member of the armed group COLINA. The MR-8 discussed how it could implement better security measures and, more important, whether it should even continue a guerrilla campaign.

Ultimately, the MR-8 decided to abandon western Paraná all together. The group did not renounce a rural-based campaign, but it came to a consensus that the original location along Iguaçu National Park was no longer safe. In the short term, they discussed whether other areas in southern Brazil might be better options. João Manoel was tasked with traveling to Santa Catarina, his home state, to locate other potential areas to build a rural foco.[71] Not all members were in agreement about leaving western Paraná. Aluízio was among those who wanted to stay—not only had he led the group's activities along the border, but he now had his wife there. "In that moment, I did not think the region was unsafe," Aluízio said. "I thought the area was still very good. Because we were at the vanguard there, no other leftist groups, nobody had the contacts we did. . . . I thought we just needed to be more careful, maybe sell the sítio, move to another city, but continue on. I wasn't in favor of [leaving], but that's what was decided."[72] From Curitiba, the group got to work dismantling its apparatus in western Paraná.

Trying to keep a low profile, they spaced out trips to the border, where they slowly packed up the Banhadão farm and retrieved the guns and equipment they had hidden at different locations in the park. Because the group had left supplies at the homes of various collaborators, they had to collect belongings and inform their allies of their departure. It was on one of these trips, when the MR-8 had almost finished clearing out of the region, that the military regime finally caught Aluízio. Given the dictatorship's efforts to locate Aluízio for many years, the irony is that his arrest was the result not of government surveillance but of an otherwise routine incident.

On April 4, 1969, Aluízio and another MR-8 member, Mauro Fernandes de Souza, were driving the jeep through western Paraná for some final steps to deactivate the group's presence in the region. Over the previous year, the young militants had become friends with several local families, and Aluízio and Mauro wanted to say goodbye to a farmer named Francisco. It happened to be Easter Friday, and Mauro thought to buy some fish and a bottle of wine for a farewell meal. With Mauro driving, they went to Cascavel. On the outskirts of town, near the bus station, Mauro looked around for a store that sold fish. Distracted, he crashed into the car in front of him.

The accident was not serious. Both cars had a few dents, and nobody was hurt. Mauro spoke with the other driver and the two of them went off in search of a mechanic. This left Aluízio in a predicament: "I stood there thinking to myself, 'If I run, the jeep is just here, full of our things, and what if Mauro comes back and I'm not there? That's more dangerous, I think I'll just stay.'"[73] A crowd began to gather. Eventually, someone recognized Aluízio and began shouting. As Aluízio quickly figured out, the man was Marins de Oliveira Bello, an employee at the logging company, Pinho e Terra, whose inquiries had scared the MR-8 into moving its operations to a new site. Bello pointed at Aluízio and shouted, "Communist, terrorist!"[74] The military police soon arrived and looked into the dented jeep, which contained a large green suitcase and several backpacks. Without telling Aluízio why he was being detained, the police put him and the bags into their car and drove to the local precinct. By the time Mauro returned with a mechanic, Aluízio had disappeared.

When they arrived at the precinct, Aluízio was taken to a small room. There, the police began to open the bags on a table in front of him. The official arrest report gives a full list of the seized items: two .38-caliber Taurus revolvers, both rusted, and several books, including *On Practice* by Mao Zedong, *The Unfinished Revolution* by Isaac Deutscher, the autobiography of Fidel Castro, *Homage to Catalonia* by George Orwell, and *Fundamentals of Dialectic Materialism* by Nelson Werneck Sodré.[75] In addition to the guns and books, the bags also contained eleven maps of the region, all marked with names and annotations, a black notebook diary, and various written reports outlining the group's "internal debates and ideas of revolutionary struggle." The police also discovered a wallet that contained NCr$450 (about US$150) and an ID card with the name José de Augusto Lima—a falsified document that Aluízio had been using as a recent alias.[76]

According to Aluízio, it was only at that moment, as the police began taking out each item one by one, that the full magnitude of the situation swept over him. When the police stepped outside to discuss the situation, Aluízio tried to escape. "I jumped up like a cat," he said. "I ran like crazy out of the precinct and took off. I ran like a little devil."[77]

The room where Aluízio had been kept was near the front of the building, and soon he was outside on the streets of Cascavel. As he sprinted away, police ran after him, yelling for people on the sidewalk to "catch that thief!"[78] The getaway did not last long. After a few blocks, the police caught up to him when he

CHAPTER 3

tried to climb over a wall. Aluízio was brought back to the police station, where he was bound and dragged into a room. Just a month shy of his twenty-sixth birthday, Aluízio now found himself on the inside of a system that he had been mobilizing against for half a decade. In the hours, days, and years ahead, he would experience firsthand the violence of Brazil's dictatorship.

CHAPTER 4

PRISON, TORTURE

AT FIVE IN THE AFTERNOON, officers threw Aluízio into a back room at the Cascavel police station. This was the first of what became nine detention centers in Paraná and Rio de Janeiro between which the dictatorship would shuffle Aluízio, several more than once. At the police station in Cascavel, his captors severely beat him. Aluízio's escape attempt likely did him no favors, and this time the police made sure he was unable to run, let alone walk. Aluízio was punched so hard in the stomach and kidneys that he coughed up blood, and he was also subjected to the so-called telephone—agents delivered simultaneous blows to both of Aluízio's ears, an extremely painful and disorienting blow that can rupture the eardrums.[1] Aluízio was now one of the thousands of Brazilians who would suffer physical abuse within the dictatorship's network of nearly 250 detention centers.[2]

When police in Cascavel apprehended Aluízio, they did not know his identity. Although the military had been looking for him, the surveillance searches had focused on Niterói and Rio de Janeiro. Until this moment, the MR-8 had largely maintained its secrecy, and the government seemed unaware that the string of bank robberies was connected to any guerrilla activities in the Paraná frontier. Between punches, the police tried to identify the young man in their custody. At first, Aluízio stuck to the story of his most recent alias and said that his name was José de Augusto Lima, the name on the ID card seized in his suitcase. Aluízio claimed that he worked for a boat construction company in Niterói, and that he had come to western Paraná to buy building materials. The police quizzed Aluízio about the lumber trade, asking him about the differences

CHAPTER 4

between types of pine trees and the cost of a cubic meter of wood.[3] Aluízio could not answer these questions, and his captors quickly figured out that his ID card, and his story, was fake.

Aluízio told me that in the early weeks of his imprisonment, he never revealed who he was. He claimed that each time he was sent to a new prison, he provided a new story, including that he was a university student doing survey research for a class project.[4] It is possible that he did tell different stories each time he was shuffled to a different detention center. Yet archival documents state that the police identified him on the first evening of torture. Records from DOPS suggest that at 8 p.m. on April 4, only a few hours after his arrest, police in Cascavel reported "the arrest in that city, of the individual Aluízio Ferreira Palmar, in whose possession was found a great quantity of subversive material."[5] In the prisoner report filed the next morning, the Cascavel police again stated that the person in their custody was Aluízio Palmar.[6] Here, it is possible that Aluízio revealed his name under torture. It is also possible that the statements of both Aluízio and the police were valid: the authorities might have known who Aluízio was, and Aluízio might not have known that *they* knew who he was.

As part of the balancing act of our collaborative biography, I opted not to pose a direct question. There was little to be gained by asking what, if anything, Aluízio remembered having said during the interrogation sessions. Instead, in later interviews I circled back to Aluízio's initial arrest, and I asked him how his full name appeared in military documents so soon after his capture. He told me that when he was arrested, along with the fake identity card, he was also carrying his real documents. I did not press Aluízio for any more details. We did have several other conversations, however, about his time more broadly as a political prisoner, and in these he often mentioned how naive he had been. When I asked if the MR-8 ever discussed what its members should do if arrested, he said that "nobody had undergone training in going to prison, or in resisting, or in how to behave during an interrogation. Nobody was prepared. We all went from living in our parents' house to being guerrilla fighters. We went from college, from school, straight to the armed struggle.... Our training was mostly intellectual, it wasn't practical.... Nobody was prepared for any of it. We were amateurs."[7]

After his initial interrogation in Cascavel, Aluízio was subjected to a form of torture that became the most perverse symbol of violence in military Brazil: the *pau de arara* (parrot's perch). As described in the groundbreaking 1985 report *Brasil: Nunca mais*—the first systematic account of torture in Brazil—the parrot's perch "consists of an iron bar wedged behind the victim's knees and to which his wrists are tied; the bar is then placed between two tables, causing the victim's body to hang some twenty or thirty centimeters from the ground. This method is hardly ever used by itself: its normal 'compliments' are electric shocks, the *palmatória* [a length of thick rubber attached to a wooden paddle], and drowning."[8] At 8 p.m., after the Cascavel police called the DOPS headquarters in Curitiba, officers placed Aluízio in the parrot's perch, with a wet cloth over his face and water poured on him as he hung upside down.[9] Aluízio stayed in that position for several hours, drifting in and out of consciousness. When finally released, he had lost all feeling in his limbs, and the police needed to massage his arms and legs so that he could walk on his own.

A RETURN TO FOZ DO IGUAÇU AND CURITIBA

Early the next morning, on April 5, 1969, Aluízio was driven to the compound of the army's Frontier Battalion in Foz do Iguaçu. The battalion was not far from the bus station where, thirteen months earlier, he had first arrived in the region. Although exhausted from the violence of the previous night, his transfer to Foz do Iguaçu seemed to jolt his senses awake and he took in his new surroundings with surprising clarity. Decades later, Aluízio still remembered the exact layout of the building: after entering through the main door, he was led down a hallway and through another corridor that had three small holding cells, which typically held smugglers and contraband runners who had been arrested along the border. He was placed in the last room, farthest from the entrance.[10] Soon, a group of army officers came to his cell, beating Aluízio and repeatedly shoving his head in a bucket of water.[11] It was at this point that Aluízio contemplated suicide for the first time.

In his cell in Foz do Iguaçu, Aluízio was questioned about the other members of his organization. It would take several more weeks for the military to piece together a fuller picture of the MR-8, but even from the initial torture sessions, it was evident that Aluízio had contact with other militants. In the throes of his abuse, Aluízio told his captors about a secret meeting in Rio de Janeiro. This was a lie. He claimed that he was scheduled to meet his contacts on the roof of the Avenida Central building in downtown Rio de Janeiro, an office skyscraper whose construction Aluízio had seen during his teenage years. He hoped that the military would take him to the top of the building, wanting to use him as bait to capture other militants. If that were to happen, his plan was to jump to his death. "I was already at my limit," he wrote in his memoir. "And fear seeped into my courage."[12] This suicidal plan never came to pass, as the military did not take Aluízio to Rio. At least not yet.

CHAPTER 4

While asleep in the middle of his second night in Foz do Iguaçu, Aluízio was taken from his cell at around 3 a.m. and put into an army vehicle. As he recounted in a letter to Eunice a few months later, he was driven straight to Curitiba, arriving a little before noon on April 7 at the state headquarters of DOPS, located downtown on Rua João Negrão. He was held at DOPS for several hours and subjected to more interrogations.[13] At night, he was transferred again, this time only a few blocks away to the army's Fifth Military Command, situated across from the city's main square, the Plaza Rui Barbosa.[14] Aluízio stayed at the army garrison in Curitiba for one week, where along with questions about his subversive activities, he also had to talk about Eunice.

A picture of Eunice had been among Aluízio's seized items on the day of his arrest, and army officers used the photograph to extract more information. According to Aluízio, when he was first shown the picture, he said that the woman was a girlfriend who lived in Rio de Janeiro. But when confronted with an address in his diary that appeared to belong to Eunice's family, he admitted that the photo was of his wife—he insisted that neither she nor her family had any awareness of his politics. The military police did a brief investigation and found nothing incriminating. But the situation caused great anxiety. In one of his letters from prison, Aluízio told Eunice that "they knew your name, and the agents of repression were given orders to find you. I was terrified they would hurt you."[15] Soon after the police investigation into Eunice and her family, she was fired from her teaching job at the elementary school, further straining her situation and sparking gossip within the community.[16] What Aluízio did not know at that moment in early April was that Eunice was a few months pregnant. This fact would bring him happiness in the dark moments of his imprisonment, but also guilt for being behind bars while his wife had to prepare to give birth and raise a child with no guarantee that her husband would ever return to help.

Aluízio recalled a constant threat of violence during his week at the Curitiba garrison. Specifically, he remembered officers taunting him by saying that he would be sent to São Paulo and handed over to Sérgio Fleury.[17] Fleury was a police chief at DOPS who organized the so-called *esquadrões da morte* (death squads) in São Paulo and who was notorious for personally being involved in the torture of prisoners.[18] Among Fleury's victims was a Dominican friar named Tito de Alencar Lima ("Frei Tito"), whom Fleury kept in brutal captivity for months. Frei Tito was eventually released as part of the same prisoner exchange as Aluízio—they flew together to Chile in January 1971. Although Frei Tito survived Fleury's torture in the short term, the psychological and physical trauma became too much to bear, and he took his life a few years later.

For Frei Tito, as it was for many others, being sent to Fleury in São Paulo was a life-altering event.

As with most testimonial evidence, it is difficult, if not impossible, to corroborate that the officers had mentioned Fleury. At this time, Fleury was still in the early stages of his counterinsurgency reign, and it is up for debate whether his activities were already common knowledge within the wider military system, let alone to young militants. By including the name of Fleury in our interviews, it is possible that Aluízio projected an after-the-fact awareness of the brutality being unleashed elsewhere at that same moment. And it is also possible that Aluízio's invocation of Fleury was tied to a somewhat perverse desire to have been considered an important enough prisoner to warrant being sent to São Paulo. In this blending of personal and collective experience, and framed by a retrospective sense of his own place in history, Aluízio's memory took shape amid the violence of torture and the fear of an uncertain horizon. Whether at an army prison in Curitiba or in a secret detention center in São Paulo, the possibility of more torture weighed heavily.

While in Curitiba, he again thought about taking his own life. Aluízio said that he found a piece of broken glass in his cell and that he lay awake scrapping the jagged edge of the glass against his left wrist. In the end, he was unable to press down hard enough to draw blood: "I tried to cut my wrists, but I didn't have the courage."[19] Like with his recollection about Sérgio Fleury, we cannot know whether Aluízio did find broken glass in his Curitiba cell. It is possible, if perhaps a bit unlikely, that military guards had not seen a shard of glass in the cell of a newly arrived prisoner. But it is not inconceivable that in the shuffle of detainees, a remnant of a bottle or a chipped utensil could have gone unnoticed. There is no way to know definitively, and perhaps that is the point. Death and despair became a daily reality for many prisoners, and for those fortunate enough to survive detention, trauma could manifest in countless ways. As Aluízio wrote in his memoir many decades later, whenever he looked down at his left wrist, it would "bring back the memories that still cause a pain that is not physical, but stirs the depths of my soul."[20] For Aluízio, his left wrist became an appendage of his own memory, a constant reminder of what the dictatorship drove him to consider. As with all questions of history, though perhaps especially for periods of violence, a precise chronicle of events—the *certainty* of a given moment—is often impossible to determine. In that space of suspended truth, we can focus instead on the meanings of the memories that formed amid the suffering.

The interrogation at the army garrison provided a growing amount of information. One report from Curitiba observed that "Aluízio F. Palmar, as far as we can observe, is a really dangerous element, committed to the organization of guerrilla movements, he has a deep knowledge of the western region of this state."[21] And a subsequent four-page prisoner file—which also included some initial details of the MR-8's activities along the border—stated that "throughout the interrogations to which he was subjected, Aluízio Ferreira Palmar proved to be deeply impregnated with Marxist doctrines, and willing to subvert the social order of the country, including through armed struggle."[22] The prisoner file noted that the army should open an official investigation to "ascertain the truth and implications" of what Aluízio had already divulged. This triggered the formation of a *inquérito policial militar* (military police investigation) or IPM.

On April 14, after a week in Curitiba, Aluízio was taken from his cell and put in an army truck. The soldiers did not tell Aluízio where they were going. Soon they arrived at an airstrip and Aluízio was made to board a small plane. Perhaps the threat of a transfer to São Paulo had not been a bluff.[23] Perhaps he was considered a big enough threat after all, and the dictatorship would now send him to a villainous figure like Sérgio Fleury. Aluízio could see out a window of the plane, and in the afternoon light he saw they were flying toward the sun on the horizon. This meant they were not going east toward São Paulo or Rio de Janeiro, but west, back toward Foz do Iguaçu and the Paraná border.

FOZ DO IGUAÇU, AGAIN

Ten days after his arrest in Cascavel, Aluízio was back in the Paraná borderlands. On the drive from the airport in Foz do Iguaçu, Aluízio passed by areas that he had known from his courtship with Eunice, including the M'Boicy River where they would sit and drink *chimarrão* tea. In a twist of fate, the car went directly by Eunice's house, which was located on Avenida das Cataratas, a main avenue extending from the southern section of the city out toward the waterfalls and the airport. When the car passed in front of Eunice's home, Aluízio happened to see her siblings out front. We cannot know whether this route was deliberate, as another form of taunting from his captors, or if the officers simply took the most direct route to the army battalion. Either way, the effect was profound. As Aluízio wrote in a letter three months later, "I was really depressed from all of my tortures, and even just seeing all these places that I learned to love with you, it was like a cool breeze in the hot sun. When the car passed in front of your house, I craned my neck hoping that somebody would see me. Cleide was playing in the yard and Carmen was getting water. I wanted to scream with all my might. But I couldn't."[24]

Aluízio was kept in complete isolation upon his arrival at the Foz do Iguaçu Battalion. Not even the guards could talk to him. He only left his cell to make official statements for the IPM case. The investigation was led by Captain Marion Joel Gralha and lasted several weeks.[25] In Aluízio's recollection, Captain Gralha sought to build a friendly rapport—during their first meeting, Gralha opened the conversation by talking about music, and they discussed a common love for the songs of Chico Buarque. Aluízio also remembered that in later interrogations, Gralha presented the IPM in a fairly banal manner: "He explained to me that the High Command of the Fifth Military District had decreed my preventative detention [prisão preventiva], and that according to military penal codes, I needed to answer to an inquiry. Blah, blah, blah, it was all really formal."[26]

Gralha's mention of preventative detention offers an interesting window into the bureaucracy of Brazil's military regime, which tightly controlled but did not eliminate electoral politics. As part of the dictatorship's veneer of legitimacy, the regime maintained a set of legal procedures for detainees. These rules were not always followed—Sérgio Fleury's death squads are one of the more notorious examples. But in theory, the steps through which an alleged subversive could be prosecuted included the declaration of preventative detention, which formalized a prisoner's status within the legal system. Preventative detention was essentially a middle phase after arrest and before an investigation could be launched. Aluízio was arrested on April 4, and one month later, on May 9, the authorities officially submitted a request for his preventative detention.[27] This process was a mixed blessing: on the one hand, it pushed Aluízio deeper into the regime's apparatus of detention and surveillance, but in line with the regime's veneer of legal transparency, it also served to make him an "official" prisoner and thus far less likely to be disappeared. The status also came with benefits. After the request was submitted on May 9, Eunice could visit Aluízio, and when the request was approved on May 22, he was allowed to send and receive letters from her and other family members. Small liberties thus coexisted with the incessant violence heaped onto political prisoners.

During the questioning in Foz do Iguaçu, Gralha focused on the names and activities that Aluízio had written down in the training diary. In our interviews, Aluízio told me that when confronted with the diary, he tried to make up a convincing story with invented names. An interrogation log of the IPM in Foz do Iguaçu—one of the only full records of his questioning in prison—confirms that Aluízio did gave a few fake names, such as his claim that he had been recruited by people named Anivaldo and Marisa. Because there were no members of the MR-8 who went by those two codenames, that appeared to be one of Aluízio's efforts to deflect attention onto made-up people.[28] Much of the IPM report also shows that Aluízio minimized the extent of the group's activities. When asked what methods they employed to "transform a capitalist society into a socialist society," Aluízio replied that they were still in the early stages of surveying the region and still debating whether an armed insurrection would be appropriate. The military asked repeatedly about plans for an armed struggle, and Aluízio said that the revolutionary books he read had offered a misguided template for changing Brazilian society. According to the IPM report, Aluízio "said that the reality on the ground proved to be very different from the theories he had studied; that one of the theories preached a violent transformation, but that the social reality exposed the cavalier nature of that preaching." Although Aluízio feigned ignorance on certain details—like claiming that they had only entered the national park "to experience a bit what life was like in the jungle"—the records show that he also divulged some concrete information, including details of the Boi-Piquá farm and how the group managed its supplies.

Portions of Aluízio's IPM testimony were soon made public. An article in the Curitiba-based *Tribuna do Paraná* reported Aluízio's arrest and included the address of his family in São Gonçalo, his activities in Iguaçu National Park, and quoted a military lawyer as saying that Aluízio "confessed to being part of a group formed and led by subversive elements seeking to implant in the country a socialist 'republic' through armed insurrection."[29] Although the news of Aluízio's detention and ongoing IPM investigation surely worried his family and his fellow militants still at-large, he later saw it as a blessing. By publicly naming Aluízio—rather than simply letting him languish secretly in prison, or worse, killing him—the military acknowledged his captivity, making it less likely that he could be disappeared.

In early May, Aluízio was released from isolation. He was given a book for reading and he was allowed to shower and shave for the first time since his arrest a month earlier.[30] A week later, after the submission request for his preventative detention, he received visitors. His father, Anízio, and older brother, Evaldo, came to Foz do Iguaçu, and he was also visited by his mother-in-law, Flora. Having feared the worst after his arrest, everyone was happy to see Aluízio alive. On May 15, guards told Aluízio that his wife had come to visit. This news brought him tremendous relief. As he later wrote to Eunice, "I would no longer have your presence only in a photograph, which I looked at every day. I would see you in person."[31] Eunice visited Aluízio every day for four straight days. Their time always included a guard in the room, making it difficult to speak openly. "There was so much that I wanted to tell you, so many feelings that had built up [but] the officer was always between us, disturbing everything," Aluízio wrote to his wife. "That 'honor guard' meant that all we could do was look at one another." During these visits, Eunice did not tell Aluízio that she was five months pregnant. Perhaps the baby bump was not yet obvious, or maybe she wore loose clothing to conceal it. Either way, her decision to keep that information from Aluízio suggests a deep worry about introducing more complexity into an already difficult situation.

While Aluízio was imprisoned in Foz do Iguaçu, the military also closed in on the rest of the MR-8.[32] First, on April 28, four militants were detained in the Paraná town of Laranjeiras do Sul, about 150 kilometers from Iguaçu National Park. The four men—Sebastião Medeiros Filho, Antônio Rogério Garcia Silveira, Ivens Marchetti do Monte Lima, and Marcos Antônio Faria de Medeiros—were driving to the group's sítio near Matelândia. After Aluízio's arrest, when the MR-8 had to quickly abandon the region, they had left the sítio under the care of a militant named Azizio Cordeiro da Fonseca, who had been a member of the Peasant Leagues (Ligas Camponesas) in northern Paraná. The four men were driving back to inform Azizio that he should leave. As Sebastião Medeiros Filho told me in our interview, it had been raining heavily that day and the dirt road toward the national park was too muddy to continue. The group stopped in Laranjeiras do Sul, where they left their car and went to have lunch. After eating, they took a taxi back to their car, but one of them had left his bag in the cab—the driver looked inside the bag, discovered a gun, and went to the police station to report the group. The police came and took all four militants to the local precinct. That night, federal police agents happened to be passing through town, and paid a visit to the four young men who had been detained with weapons and large amounts of money. Sebastião remembered that one of the federal agents "opened the cell and recognized one of us: 'That's the terrorist from Rio de Janeiro, that's Ivens Marchetti.'"[33] Ivens was then taken to a separate cell and did not return for two days.

A few days later, on May 1, and most likely acting on the new details obtained under torture from the four militants, the police raided an MR-8 safe house in Rio de Janeiro, detaining a member named Geraldo Galiza Rodrigues. The cascade then continued, and the next day three more militants—Ziléa Reznik, Luiz Carlos de Souza Santos, and Tiago Andrade de Almeida—were captured during a raid on another safe house in Rio. Within these few short days, eight MR-8 members were arrested, almost a third of the organization. In a repeating cycle of detention and interrogation, the seizure of one militant enabled the regime to gather new information and locate more members of the group. The MR-8 would collapse completely by the following month.

CHAPTER 4

Two weeks after the first wave of arrests, agents told Aluízio that he was being sent to Curitiba. Although he did not yet know the reason for his transfer, the information obtained from the other MR-8 militants had allowed the military to piece together how Aluízio fit into the armed actions taking place across several states. On May 18, Aluízio had one final visit with Eunice, though he could not bring himself to tell her that he was leaving Foz do Iguaçu—it had been a small blessing being detained in the city where his wife lived, and the uncertainty on the horizon saddened him.[34] In advance of his transfer, Aluízio was again placed in isolation and barred from receiving visitors. The guards even took away his picture of Eunice.

On the morning of May 20, he was driven to the Foz do Iguaçu airport. As with his arrival, the car went in front of Eunice's house. Aluízio hoped that she might be outside, allowing him to get one last look before leaving. But she was not there. In Curitiba, Aluízio was again held in the army headquarters downtown. During a week of interrogation, officers sought to triangulate the information recently obtained from the other arrested members of the MR-8. In these moments, Aluízio realized that the military regime knew a great deal of information about the MR-8. The circle was clearly tightening around them. Claiming no knowledge of the robberies in Rio de Janeiro and Niterói, Aluízio told his captors that he had already shared everything he knew during his IPM testimony in Foz do Iguaçu.[35] This did not satisfy the regime.

ILHA DAS FLORES

With an expanding base of information about the MR-8, the regime decided to open a second IPM investigation. Unlike the first case against Aluízio that was overseen by the army, the second IPM came under the purview of the navy. Whereas the first IPM was based in Paraná, the new case with the navy was based in Rio de Janeiro. This meant that in addition to now having to respond to two cases at the same time, Aluízio would also be transferred between two jurisdictions in two different states. And although the army in Paraná had already put him through brutal interrogations, a second IPM with the navy also represented the potential for new forms of torture: the naval surveillance branch, Cenimar (Centro de Informações da Marinha) was among the dictatorship's most notorious security forces.

On May 28, after eight days in the Curitiba Army Battalion, Aluízio was transferred to Rio de Janeiro. First, he was held at the headquarters of the First Naval District, located downtown on the Mauá Plaza. From Rio, he then went to Ilha das Flores, a small island located in the Guanabara Bay, just across the water from São Gonçalo—only a few kilometers from where Aluízio's family lived. In the late nineteenth century, Ilha das Flores had been a processing point for newly arrived immigrants, and the navy later established an operations center on the island. After the 1964 coup, it became a detention center. Between 1969 and 1971, Ilha das Flores housed almost 200 political prisoners.[36]

The Cenimar agents who ushered Aluízio onto a boat in Rio de Janeiro did not tell him where he was going. Uncertainty was a constant feature of prison transfers, and militants rarely knew the precise details of their next location. This was especially nerve-wracking for transfers to the regime's various island prisons. Other MR-8 members recalled the panic caused by the uncertain voyage to Ilha das Flores. João Manoel Fernandes told me that on his passage to the island, agents handcuffed him to an anchor in the boat: "They pretended they were going to throw me overboard. So I told them to shoot me in the head, so I wouldn't suffer and drown. I was afraid of drowning. . . . They took me out to sea then turned around and dropped me off at Ilha das Flores, I didn't know if this was saving my life or killing me even more. These were terrible moments."[37] On the surface, Ilha das Flores was beautiful, a welcome change for those who had just come from bleak concrete prisons. In an interview with the historian Maria Fernanda Scelza, another prisoner remembered the island as a "really pretty place, idyllic, with flowering trees, the sea lapping on the shore, and it had a little white house on the ridge."[38] Aluízio soon became all too familiar with that small house on the island.

For his first several days on Ilha das Flores, Aluízio was kept in solitary confinement, locked in a windowless bathroom, and forced to sleep in the small space between the toilet and the wall. During this time, he was visited by a navy captain, Alfredo Magalhães, who beat him with the telephone method, smacking both ears simultaneously. Aluízio remembered that Captain Magalhães carried himself "like he was royalty," and focused on whether Aluízio had more information about the MR-8's activities in Rio de Janeiro and Niterói.[39] Aluízio later testified that while confined to the bathroom, he lost consciousness three times.[40] He was eventually moved to a prison cell that had more ventilation.

In the new cell, an officer named Clemente José Monteiro took over the interrogations, beating him with a cane and saying that Aluízio's previous experience in prison was nothing compared to what would now take place: "He told me that, 'you can't lie to us here, this isn't Paraná, this is Rio de Janeiro, you understand? This isn't the army, this is the navy. . . . This is the center of hell, if you don't know hell yet, you'll know it here.'"[41] On Ilha das Flores, hell seemed to concentrate in the little white house on the ridge known as the Ponta dos

CHAPTER 4

Oitis, a reference to the *oiti* trees clustered on that part of the island. In a room within the small building, Aluízio was stripped naked and placed in the parrot's perch. Officers harangued him with questions about the MR-8 in Rio de Janeiro. Along with the pain of being suspended upside down, Aluízio remembered the powerlessness that came from being tortured while naked: "When someone doesn't have clothes, in front of somebody who does, the person with clothes becomes superior to the person without. You feel submissive. You're in a position of submission. So that's what they did first, take off your clothes, then tie your legs, tie your arms, and hang you in the parrot's perch. That was a way to break a person, to show someone, 'you're in my hands now.'"[42]

One day while Aluízio sat in his cell, he heard a voice from a vent in the wall. To his surprise, it was Ziléa Reznik, one of the recently arrested members of the MR-8. Many of the MR-8 had been brought to Ilha das Flores, including Ziléa and Umberto Trigueiros Lima. Talking to Ziléa through the small hole between their cells was the first time that Aluízio had interacted with another prisoner since his arrest two months earlier. The two shared news of their arrests and treatment in prison. Aluízio spoke about his time in Paraná and Ziléa told him about her tortures on the island, which included being stripped naked and given electric shocks. According to Brazil's National Truth Commission, Ziléa was the first woman imprisoned by the dictatorship on Ilha das Flores.[43] Aluízio had not yet known of women being tortured. "I thought that most Brazilians saw women as something really special," he recalled. "We had respect for women, no? So I was shocked to know they were torturing women."[44] Six months later, Ziléa would help write a document about the torture of women on Ilha das Flores—the statement would get smuggled out of Brazil and become one of the first global calls for attention to the violence of Brazil's dictatorship.

After two weeks of isolation and abuse, the navy placed Aluízio and several other prisoners in a common cell. As he later wrote in a letter to Eunice, "It was a rush of greetings, hugs, and endless conversations. We invented lots of games, things like charades. Time went by quickly and things were less tense."[45] For two months, Aluízio had not interacted directly with other prisoners. Now, he not only shared living space with other people, but several of them were his friends and fellow militants. A week later, they were also allowed to receive visitors. On June 20, Aluízio's father, mother, and three siblings made the short trip from São Gonçalo across the water to Ilha has Flores. From a letter he would later write to Eunice, it seemed that a major topic of conversation during the forty-minute visit had been Eunice herself. In the month since his transfer from Foz do Iguaçu, Aluízio's parents had gone to meet Eunice for the first time. Aluízio recounted to Eunice what his mother had said: "She told me that she really likes you. That you're perfect for me, calm, thoughtful, etc." Aluízio said that his family maintained their composure during the visit, and that his mother cried only when saying goodbye.

"A PING-PONG" BETWEEN RIO AND CURITIBA

On June 24, Aluízio was called into the commander's office and told he was being transferred back to Curitiba to continue the army's IPM trial in Paraná. As he later wrote to Eunice, "There are two IPMs, and because I have to be processed in both of them, I think they'll do a ping-pong with me. Rio to Curitiba and back again."[46] On Ilha das Flores he had to go straight to the boat waiting outside, unable to first retrieve the food and clothes that his family had given him. Aluízio was taken across the bay to a military airport and flown to Curitiba. Rather than the army garrison where he had previously been detained, he was now placed in the city's Prisão Provisória (Provisional Prison) on Avenida Anita Garibaldi, in the Ahú neighborhood. Locally, this was known as the Ahú prison, and it became one of the regime's main detention centers in southern Brazil.

Upon his arrival at Ahú, Aluízio was placed in solitary confinement, a small windowless room in the basement that he later called "a hideous dungeon."[47] It was nearly winter in Curitiba—a cold city, by Brazilian standards—and the cell did not have a mattress or even a blanket. He was still dressed in the short-sleeved shirt he had been wearing when transferred from Ilha das Flores. He remembered watching his hands turn blue from the cold. After six days in solitary, Aluízio was transferred above ground and placed in a larger cell with other prisoners. To Aluízio's surprise, he would now share a cell with student activists who had already been in Ahú for nearly half a year.

On December 17, 1968, police in Curitiba had raided a secret meeting of the Paraná branch of UNE (the National Student Union) on the Chácara Alemão farm, arresting forty-two students. The raid occurred two months after the regime had repressed another UNE summit in the São Paulo town of Ibiúna. Six months since its apex at the March of the 100,000 in Rio de Janeiro, the student movement was succumbing to the tightening grip of military rule. Of the forty-two students arrested in Curitiba, fifteen were imprisoned at Ahú, thirteen men and two women. Three of them were studying medicine, and they tried to help the other prisoners after torture sessions. One of the students, João Bonifácio Cabral, told me that when Aluízio was first brought up from solitary, "he was really sad, shaken, you know? He told us all the details about his torture."⁴⁸ Beth Fortes, another one of the arrested students, said that "the first time I saw Aluízio he was really thin, with sunken eyes, hunched over as if he were an old person. But he told us that he'd just been tortured for several days. He had suffered a lot. Just seeing his physical condition, that's hard to forget."⁴⁹

The students welcomed Aluízio into their cell with solidarity and supplies, giving him a towel, bed linens, a coat, shirts, and cigarettes. Especially in the aftermath of Aluízio's initial experience of torture and solitary confinement, the camaraderie in the student cell of Ahú helped buoy his spirits. In his memoir, Aluízio wrote that, "honestly, those guys saved my life."⁵⁰ The cell was a converted classroom measuring thirteen meters by eight meters, much larger than anything he had encountered in prison, each person had their own bed, and there were also several desks and chairs. The students had also been allowed to equip the room with amenities brought by their families. As Aluízio recounted in a letter to Eunice, the room had an electric stove where they made coffee and small snacks, four radios, a small collection of books, two guitars, a chessboard, a set of dominoes, and four typewriters.⁵¹

The students had established a daily routine, which Aluízio happily joined. As he described in a letter to his younger brother, each day followed a similar pattern: wake up by 8 a.m., breakfast and time outside on the patio until 10:30 a.m.; followed by lunch and more recreation; quiet time and study in the early afternoon; coffee and exercise at 2:30 p.m.; more quiet time until dinner; leisure time until 9 p.m., including listening to the radio and discussion groups; and silence and reading before sleeping. One of the students, Vitório Seratiuk, recalled that keeping a strict schedule helped everyone persevere: "[We asked ourselves,] 'how are we going to get through this?' So we divided each day into twenty-four hours and we made a schedule for everyone. . . . We transformed our time in prison into a system to take care of ourselves."⁵² The prisoners also played soccer games on Wednesdays and Saturdays.⁵³ There were enough teams inside the prison to hold a tournament. Aluízio's team was called the Libertadores—the Liberators.⁵⁴ They also found ways to maintain a festive atmosphere: among the imprisoned students was a chemistry major who used a pressure cooker and pipes from the shower to make alcohol from pineapples.⁵⁵

Every Sunday was visitation day at Ahú, and prisoners sat with their family members for lunches that stretched well into the afternoon.⁵⁶ For Aluízio, his most frequent visitors were his father, Anízio, and his older brother, Evaldo, who drove from São Gonçalo to Curitiba. On the weeks when his family did not come, he spent time with the students and their families. During one of these visits, Beth Fortes was visited by her younger sister, who had recently given birth to a daughter named Dora, and she invited Aluízio to hold the newborn. In my interview with her, Beth said that "Aluízio's eyes sparkled, and [Dora] was really calm, she didn't cry at all. Aluízio's calmness, his sweetness, it must have had a calming effect on the baby.... Despite all his suffering, Aluízio was a good person."[57] The prisoners were also visited by clergy members, and Aluízio remembered his conversations with Sister Tereza Araújo, a Catholic nun from the Northeast who had moved to Curitiba in 1964.[58] Sister Tereza helped Aluízio by mailing many of his letters to Eunice in Foz do Iguaçu.[59]

Eunice herself never visited. She was very pregnant and decided against taking the daylong drive to Curitiba. It was likely during one of his family's initial visits at Ahú that Aluízio learned of Eunice's pregnancy. In his first letter to her from Ahú, on July 6, he said, "Don't worry about me, take care of yourself and our child. Look after him, it's so important."[60] And a week later, he wrote that "we will (as you say) have a new member of the tribe. He or she, I will love them profoundly."[61]

While imprisoned in Ahú, Aluízio also encountered someone who would shape the rest of his life: Alberi Vieira dos Santos. Alberi was a political militant who had been arrested in 1965 as part of a failed guerrilla operation in Três Passos, Rio Grande do Sul, one of the first efforts to overthrow Brazil's dictatorship.[62] The so-called Operation Três Passos became a thing of lore among dissidents, and Aluízio had been excited to learn that this hero figure was also imprisoned at Ahú. When Aluízio finally had the opportunity to meet Alberi inside the prison, the encounter was underwhelming. Shaped, of course, by a retrospective knowledge of the events to come, Aluízio remembered feeling uncomfortable after his initial conversation with Alberi. In Aluízio's retelling, Alberi had just returned to Ahú after a trip to the Army Hospital in Curitiba, and he invited Aluízio to escape from prison: "His plan was completely unhinged. I thought it was weird that this guy—who had just met me—shows up and tells me to join an action that would involve people on both sides of the prison walls.... He kept insisting, but it really put me on guard, and I tried to avoid him."[63] It would be another five years before Aluízio would see Alberi again, on a fateful afternoon in Buenos Aires.

NEW TORTURE IN OLD SETTINGS

Aluízio was routinely taken out of his cell in Ahú and held at the DOPS building, located four kilometers away on Rua João Negrão. Under the command of Ozias Algauer, the head of DOPS in Curitiba, Aluízio was placed in the parrot's perch and questioned about his political activities.[64] João Bonifácio Cabral remembered that Aluízio was among the handful of prisoners escorted away

CHAPTER 4

from Ahú: "They came back broken, tortured. They went out at night and were taken for torture. Then they were brought back."[65] Vitório Seratiuk similarly recalled that Aluízio was often taken out of the cell, and "when he returned, he came back all messed up, with trauma injuries from torture."[66]

Aluízio remembers that the students in Ahú always tried to help him, even when they were not sure how to relate to him. "When they saw me, they were apprehensive," Aluízio said. "[Because] when I came back, I came back a different person. Every time I left, I came back different."[67] Aluízio also witnessed the same changes in other prisoners. Another political prisoner in Ahú was Jane Argolo, a journalism student from Rio Grande do Sul who had been arrested for allegedly being part of the armed struggle.[68] Jane, who decades later still maintained that she had been wrongly imprisoned by the dictatorship, suffered so much abuse and neglect in prison that she weighed under ninety pounds.[69] One morning, Aluízio saw Jane being brought back to Ahú after a night at DOPS. She looked even smaller and weaker than normal. As she later told Aluízio and the other prisoners, along with being placed on the parrot's perch, she was stripped naked and made to stand on top of two jars, the glass rims painfully pressing into the bottom of her feet.[70] Hearing about the torture of other prisoners like Jane must have been deeply disturbing for Aluízio: seeing the effect of violence on others was also a mirror on his own suffering. And learning about new methods of torture was a sign of the trauma that might await him.

One of the cellmates, Políbio Braga, kept a diary while in Ahú, which he published as a book thirty years later. Políbio wrote about Aluízio several times, observing that "[Aluízio] doesn't speak much and his eyes move with apparent surprise and no direction, but they're also determined—like the eye of Antônio Conselheiro or any other type of fanatic. This man has been a main topic of conversation among the prisoners."[71] In another entry, Políbio noted that "Aluízio was taken this evening by the guards. We watched them, hoping to hear an explanation.... The other prisoners have a mixture of respect and fear [for Aluízio]. Everyone is worried that he'll be tortured to death."[72] Although most of Aluízio's interrogations took place in the nearby DOPS building, on this occasion—the incident observed in Políbio's diary—the army flew him to Foz do Iguaçu. There, in the city where he had placed so much of his political and personal hopes, Aluízio suffered arguably the worst psychological abuse of his time in prison.

After a short plane ride from Curitiba to Foz do Iguaçu, Aluízio was driven to the town of Matelândia and then into Iguaçu National Park. He had not been in the park since February, when the group disbanded its guerrilla presence in the region. Accompanied by a handful of officers and a guard dog, Aluízio was forced to walk into the forest. The dense canopy of trees made it difficult to find his way. The officers showed him an interrogation report from Rio de Janeiro—one of his arrested comrades had said that Aluízio knew where the group had hidden a machine gun inside the park. This was correct information, and Aluízio had hidden several guns in the forest; his preferred method had been to stash supplies (weapons, medicine, food) in small tunnels or animal burrows in the ground, which he then covered with branches and dirt. Now he had to locate a long-hidden weapon at night, at gunpoint, in an area where he had not been for over seven months. "I swear to you, I wanted to find the gun," Aluízio recounted in one of our interviews. "I did everything I could to find it, but I couldn't. They started hitting me and tied me to a tree. They put a blindfold over my eyes."[73] It seemed as though the officers were going to execute him. "They were threatening to shoot me. I told them, 'Stop, I'll find the gun, I want to find this fucking gun!'" Even knowing that the military would use it as proof of his guilt, Aluízio still wanted to locate the weapon: "I was so scared that I wanted to find it so that they would leave me in peace and return me to my life in prison [at Ahú]. Because that was hell, being in the forest and them threatening to kill me. Between that and jail, I preferred jail." His guards then released him from the mock execution. But he did not immediately return to Curitiba. From the national park, the guards drove him to the army battalion in Foz do Iguaçu.

Aluízio was kept in a cell for several days and beaten severely. He remembered that the officers seemed angry. When he was last in their battalion, Aluízio had withheld the full extent of his militancy, and it was only after he left Foz do Iguaçu that the dictatorship uncovered the MR-8's wider network.[74] Perhaps this new information made the officers in Foz do Iguaçu look bad, or perhaps they were simply content to abuse a familiar prisoner. The army officer in charge of Aluízio's torture was a lieutenant named Mário Espedito Ostrovski. Along with punching Aluízio in the stomach, Ostrovski also taunted him with information about Eunice's pregnancy. The military had found out that Eunice was pregnant and Ostrovski used that information as a form of torture. "He told me he'd go arrest her, that he'd make her lose the baby," Aluízio said in our very first interview, conducted in the aftermath of Ostrovski's lawsuit in December 2019.[75] In the detention cell, Ostrovski told Aluízio that the baby's death would be his own fault, because Aluízio had made his child a political subversive even before birth: "[Ostrovski said] that ideas and ideology are passed down through blood."

Aluízio was not Ostrovski's only victim, nor was it an idle threat to torture women to the point of miscarriage. Three months earlier, a woman named

CHAPTER 4

Izabel Fávero had been brought into the Foz do Iguaçu Battalion—Izabel was a militant in another armed group, and she had been captured on May 5 in the Paraná town of Nova Aurora. Under Ostrovski's watch, Izabel was tortured every night. "I was two months pregnant," Izabel recalled. "And they knew that. On the fifth day [in prison], after so many shocks, the parrot's perch, electric shocks, threatening to rape me, insulting me, I miscarried."[76] Izabel was then placed in solitary confinement for several days, where she was tended to by a nurse. Once she was deemed sufficiently recovered, Ostrovski started the tortures again. Izabel later testified that long after her torture, she had difficulty sleeping, and when she could calm herself enough to doze off, she would often wake up sweating. Ostrovski also haunted Aluízio. Fifty years after he threatened to terminate Aluízio's unborn child, long after Brazil had transitioned back to democracy—though under a president who sought to return the country to military rule—Mário Espedito Ostrovski would reappear and find new ways to threaten Aluízio.

THE ARMED STRUGGLE AT A CROSSROADS

The torture in Foz do Iguaçu and the mock execution in the national park were a result of the MR-8's downfall. Aluízio had only been taken to Foz do Iguaçu because other members of the MR-8 had, under torture, told the military of the group's guerrilla activities along the border. After the first wave of arrests in late April and early May, the dictatorship used the extracted information to locate and capture more dissidents. A second wave in early June resulted in new arrests and also the group's first death, the twenty-three-year-old Reinaldo Silveira Pimenta.

On June 27, police raided an MR-8 safe house on Rua Bolivar in the Rio de Janeiro neighborhood of Copacabana. According to the military's official report, Reinaldo committed suicide. As reported two weeks later in the *Correio da Manhã* newspaper, the government claimed that Reinaldo "threw himself against a window that was closed, falling down to the building's interior courtyard. He died soon after, at the hospital."[77] Although Brazil's Truth Commission could not prove that the military had thrown Reinaldo to his death, a consensus among militants and journalists was that he had been murdered and then presented as a suicide—the same cover-up used by the dictatorship the following decade when it committed arguably its most infamous murder, that of the journalist Vladimir Herzog.[78] Within a week of Reinaldo's death, further raids led to the capture of more MR-8 militants in Rio de Janeiro and Curitiba, including Iná Meireles de Souza, Milton Gaia Leite, and João Manoel Fernandes, the latter of whom was shot in the throat, suffering permanent damage to his voice box. Five days later, agents also arrested Jorge Medeiros Valle, the "Bom Burguês" who was the group's main financier. As a member named Sebastião Medeiros Filho told me, "It was a disaster. It all happened really fast, so fast. Everything we had tried to build for three years, it was over in a few months."[79] Except for a few members and sympathizers who managed to avoid detection, by mid-July 1969, the MR-8 was entirely in the hands of the military regime.

Other armed groups in Brazil met a similar fate. The Nationalist Revolutionary Movement (MNR, one of the first groups to take up arms against the dictatorship) had already dissolved because of arrests, and by early 1969 many COLINA leaders were captured. In collaboration with members of the VPR—which had also suffered its own recent string of arrests—COLINA then formed a new organization, the Revolutionary Armed Vanguard–Palmares (VAR-Palmares, Vanguarda Armada Revolucionária Palmares), whose name was an homage to the seventeenth-century maroon society of former enslaved people. Of the various armed movements that formed in the aftermath of the 1967 schism within the Brazilian Communist Party, only the ALN, under Carlos Marighella, still maintained much of its structure and leadership. As the dictatorship made these arrests, newspapers—shaped by government censorship—kept the Brazilian public informed of the military regime's war on subversion.

From July onward, Brazil's major papers covered the downfall of the MR-8. A July 17 headline in the *Correio da Manhã* proclaimed that "police believe the MR-8 has been dismantled."[80] Soon afterward, the navy invited journalists to Ilha das Flores to see the imprisoned members of the MR-8. With a headline of "MR-8 Sought to Create Guerrilla Focos," the *Jornal do Brasil* included images of the prisoners (fig. 4.1), separated into groups of men and women, being escorted on the island to be "exhibited to the journalists."[81] As with the *Manchete* photographs reproduced in chapter 3, the image here shows how the military and its media allies gave prominence to women revolutionaries as a means to call attention to the subversion at stake: even middle-class white women—nicely dressed in respectable sweaters and skirts—could fall victim to the allure of revolution. The dictatorship released the full names of all the prisoners, which were then published in newspapers. Two weeks later, the magazine *Veja* featured a lengthy exposé on armed groups in Brazil, even reproducing a section of Aluízio's seized diary that detailed the MR-8's guerrilla training in Iguaçu National Park.[82] The government had turned Aluízio and his fellow imprisoned militants into notorious figures at the national level.

For the armed Left, a silver lining of the cascade of arrests and media coverage was that it provided an opportunity for a new group. In mid-1969,

CHAPTER 4

FIGURE 4.1. Photos of MR-8 prisoners on Ilha das Flores. *Jornal do Brasil*, July 30, 1969, 12.

student activists from Rio de Janeiro, most of whom had belonged to the DI-GB dissidência of the PCB, formed an organization dedicated to urban guerrilla action. They gave themselves the same name as the group that had just been dismantled—they called themselves the MR-8. Because the government had so widely trumpeted the MR-8's collapse, the militants wanted to make the Brazilian public think that the regime had exaggerated its claims about defeating subversion. As a counter to the headlines and images circulating in the press, the MR-8 would continue to stage actions against the dictatorship. Daniel Aarão Reis, a member of the second MR-8—and who would later become a prominent historian of the military period—told me that there were two main goals for adopting the name MR-8: "First, we needed to hide from the dictatorship, and second and most important, we would make a counterpropaganda. [The regime] had said in April or May that it had destroyed the MR-8, but look, now the MR-8 was doing major actions again. That was a great idea we had. ... The name stuck and so we went with it. We thought the name was more heroic, more epic."[83]

On September 4, only a few months after the government had brought journalists to see the militants imprisoned on Ilha das Flores, the second MR-8 helped pull off the most dramatic action to date: in collaboration with Marighella's ALN, the MR-8 kidnapped Charles Burke Elbrick, the US ambassador to Brazil. Elbrick's capture, which lasted for seventy-eight hours, was the first of four diplomatic kidnappings that armed groups in Brazil would stage over the next sixteen months. In exchange for Elbrick's release, the militants demanded the release of fifteen political prisoners and the public distribution of the group's manifesto. The dictatorship agreed to both demands. The imprisoned militants were freed, and the manifesto was read aloud on national television and radio programs, media platforms that were otherwise heavily censored. The high-profile kidnapping showed that even if the repressive policies of AI-5 and a growing national security apparatus had enabled the regime to dismantle several armed organizations, it had not yet extinguished all dissent.

A FATHER BEHIND BARS

While a small number of militants outside of prison continued to mobilize against the dictatorship, Aluízio remained at Ahú in Curitiba. Perhaps to compensate for his inability to take part in the struggles beyond the prison walls, Aluízio's attention seemed to turn inward, focusing largely on Eunice and her pregnancy. During the five months that Aluízio was detained at Ahú, he wrote at least fifteen letters to Eunice.[84] These letters reflected a deeply conflicted emotional state. Some of the letters reflect poorly on Aluízio, but based on the fact that he published them on his website, they do not seem to embarrass him.[85] The files only show a one-sided conversation. Although Eunice had kept the letters from Aluízio for decades afterward, Aluízio could not retain Eunice's messages during the duration of his imprisonment. We can only infer from his letters what Eunice was thinking and feeling.

Aluízio, who had recently turned twenty-six years old, clearly felt guilty that his imprisonment had left Eunice—only twenty-one years old—in such a difficult situation. On July 13, he wrote "I am often tormented by the thought of how you are carrying the burden of our relationship.... So far you have not received what you deserve from me. Our life so far has been really tough.... I was very selfish and I didn't think about us. Better days will come, believe me."[86] Aluízio's letter suggests that Eunice was confronting a lot of gossip and animosity about her imprisoned husband. Trying to reassure her, and perhaps lessen his own guilt, Aluízio wrote that "I know you had a hard time, due to the mentality of these people, who don't understand the purpose of our lives. But it's like I told you, little by little this will pass and people will understand more with time."[87]

However much he expressed his remorse, Aluízio also sought to convince his wife that they were both making sacrifices for a larger goal. On July 8, in his second letter from Ahú, he told Eunice to "think of the wives of so many other patriots, who went through this phase and who still suffer from forced separation. You are not the first or the last, our prisons are full of men who stood up against oppression and social injustice."[88] On another occasion he urged his wife to "never forget, for a single minute, that I am a political prisoner. I am here for having fought, and living out my ideals. For those who want a better and democratic Brazil. I am a patriot. History, and only History, will be able to judge me."[89] This was a consistent theme, and he would later reiterate that "I am satisfied with history's judgment."[90] Much of what Aluízio wrote to Eunice oscillated between these two poles of guilt and conviction. In one particularly revealing letter, Aluízio sought to stay confident in the face of torture, personal hardship, and the collapse of his political group:

> I have my bad moments, my love, but I try to be fully serene and stoic, and I have a deep belief that I have within myself the moral force I need ... and the ability to use it so that I don't fall into despair. And I avoid those vulgar emotional states known as pessimism and optimism. My state of mind combines these two feelings and overcomes them: I am pessimistic in thought but optimistic in will. In all situations, I think of the worst possible outcomes in order to tap into reserves of strength and be capable of overcoming those obstacles. I equipped myself with limitless patience, not passive or inert, but animated by perseverance.[91]

Try as he might to remain steadfast, Aluízio grew shakier as the months wore on. Especially as Eunice's due date inched closer, he got needier and more anxious. His guilt at being separated from his pregnant wife seemed to combine with the disorienting experience of prison, in which he had little contact with the outside world and no control over his own fate. Throughout their correspondence, Aluízio always asked Eunice for more information; although she did write him letters, he felt that they were either too infrequent or not detailed enough. To cite one example, on July 8 he wrote, "My love, I really need news from you."[92] When he reflected on the pending arrival of their child, however, he wrote in a brighter tone. On September 14, he told Eunice that "soon we will welcome a child, to this world of happiness and sorrow, of Tostão and Pele, of hunger and love, of war and peace, of liberty and prison."[93] He wrote another letter the following day, and in a more contrite tone he acknowledged that "I know what you've been going through. The situations you didn't chose. I know that. Better days are approaching, and we can affirm, like in a song I heard the other day, that 'you can close your umbrella, the rain has stopped, the sadness has gone and happiness is here.'"[94]

On September 16, Eunice gave birth to their daughter, Florita, named after Eunice's mother, Flora. The next day, Eunice sent a telegram to Curitiba, which got passed on to Aluízio. In a letter a few days later, Aluízio felt hurt that the telegram had been so short: "It only said, 'Papa Aluízio Daughter arrived all is well Eunice.'"[95] Ten days after Florita's birth, the sorrow he had been feeling over the previous months spilled over: "I'm writing this letter in a very conflicted mood. On the one hand is happiness motivated by the news [of our daughter], on the other is sadness, a reflex of the lack of news from you. . . . At this point I'm thinking of everything, I don't know, my mind goes to a thousand and one things. I'm thinking of your health and our daughter. What's happening?"[96] Imprisoned within Ahú and feeling the full weight of his helplessness, Aluízio pleaded for more news. On October 9, he wrote to Eunice, asking her to "take a bit of your time to write to me, okay? You can't imagine how I need to know these things. I want to follow all the events from a distance, I want to feel the growth of our daughter along with you. . . . The lack of news has increased the sense of impotence that I already suffer from. . . . And about a photograph, send one when possible, in the meantime I wait for the day when I can put the image of our daughter next to yours that I kiss every day."[97] Although he had acknowledged in earlier letters that his imprisonment had put Eunice in a terrible situation, the attrition of life behind bars took its toll. From his letters, it appeared that Aluízio could not fully appreciate that perhaps Eunice was angry with him, whether broadly because his militancy had put their family in its current situation, or more specifically about missing the birth of their child. Nor did Aluízio seem to consider that perhaps Eunice did not write because she was too busy recovering from birth and caring for a newborn.

Regardless of how attuned Aluízio was to Eunice's emotional and physical needs, nothing could change the reality that while his wife and newborn daughter began a new phase together in Foz do Iguaçu, Aluízio remained in a military detention center with no sign of freedom. In his final months at Ahú, Aluízio's anxiety seemed to diminish a bit, and every letter to Eunice included some lines of poetry or expressions of love. In late October, only weeks before he would be transferred back to Rio de Janeiro, Aluízio wrote that "I do everything I can to forget, to not think about [our situation], but today there was a really nice full moon. And the moon, I don't know why, maybe because of how we're raised, it influences how we feel. Despite all the cruelty and injustices, we're always romantic."[98]

In the middle of November, Aluízio was sent back to Rio de Janeiro as part of the navy's IPM tribunal. In his last letter to Eunice from Ahú, Aluízio told her that he would likely be transferred to Rio on November 15 or 16. As he explained

CHAPTER 4

in the letter, although the army investigation in Paraná was still pending, the navy had recently announced a new set of charges against him in Rio de Janeiro. Aluízio was accused of violating Articles 21 and 23 of a new law that had been passed in March 1969, a modification of the 1967 National Security Law that helped accelerate the dictatorship's grip on power. As Aluízio wrote to Eunice, "This is the end of the world! I've never seen anything like this. In addition to being charged twice for the same reason, which is already a legal anomaly, a new law that came out in [March] will be used against me."[99] Aluízio explained that the two articles in the navy case carried sentences of between eight and twenty years, and five and fifteen years, respectively: "That's crazy! Adding up the minimum for the articles in both cases gives me seventeen years and six months; adding up the maximum gives me forty-five years and six months, which would make the longest sentence ever given to a political prisoner in Brazil. This is so wrong, I'm living in a state of permanent persecution." Although Aluízio's trial in Paraná remained open, the new charges in Rio de Janeiro then took priority and he did not return to Curitiba.

In his memoir, Aluízio recalled the Cenimar agents coming to his cell to escort him back to Rio: it "was very emotional. My friends in prison knew that in Rio I would go through new torture sessions. When the prison guards opened my cell door, people started to sing the 'International.' The lyrics of that revolutionary song followed me as I walked down the corridor."[100] Despite the traumas experienced in Paraná, Aluízio had at least become familiar with the routine at Ahú. He could rely on the support and solidarity from the student prisoners to help him weather the abuse. And with a system in place to receive visitors and exchange letters with Eunice, prison in Paraná had provided a certain amount of stability. Going back to Rio de Janeiro, with new charges looming, was an unknown.

CHAPTER 5

PRISON, WAITING

ALUÍZIO'S RETURN to Rio de Janeiro brought him back to a familiar location: the Ilha das Flores detention center in the Guanabara Bay, a stone's throw from Niterói. In the nearly six months since he had first been sent to this naval prison, even more political prisoners had been brought to Ilha das Flores, including several MR-8 militants. As during Aluízio's initial stay on Ilha das Flores, the prisoners were often taken to the small house known as the Ponta dos Oitis.

Fifty years after the Ponta dos Oitis was used as a navy torture center, the building remained largely unchanged. Although other locations on the island were rebuilt—including as a museum of the island's history as an arrival point for immigrants—the Ponta dos Oitis was left untouched, saltwater spray and sun slowly degrading its facade. In October 2014, a delegation from the National Truth Commission went to the island with former political prisoners who had been tortured on Ilha das Flores. This visit took place two months before the commission released its final report, part of the publicity campaign in the lead-up to publishing its findings.[1] Accompanied by several photographers and a videographer, the visitors spent much of their time on the island at the Ponta dos Oitis. Many of the building's red shingle tiles had fallen off the roof and the blue shutters hung precariously from their frames, but overall, the small structure looked much like it did half a century earlier.

Upon arriving at the Ponta dos Oitis, the visitors hesitated before entering. Not only was the house itself in decrepit condition—somebody yelled "watch out, the building is unsafe"—but returning to a site of trauma was a highly

CHAPTER 5

FIGURE 5.1. Screenshot from a video posted on YouTube by the National Truth Commission of its visit to Ilha das Flores, October 21, 2014. *Left to right:* Iná Meirelles, Ziléa Reznik, Marta Alvarez, and Tânia Marins. Comissão Nacional da Verdade, "Ex-presos reconhecem casa na Ilha das Flores onde ocorreu tortura," recorded and posted on October 21, 2014, YouTube, 9 min., www.youtube.com/watch?v=8NSFunW2YH0&t=97s.

emotional experience. The visitors spoke about their torture, and three women in particular, Iná Meirelles, Ziléa Reznik, and Marta Alvarez (fig. 5.1), shared memories of the violence they had suffered. Ziléa, who had spoken to Aluízio through the vent in their adjacent cells when he first arrived on the island in 1969, described the events that took place in the house. With her voice slightly shaking and her eyes hidden behind a pair of large sunglasses, Ziléa recalled that "they took you here, and made you take off your clothes. And then the guys starting using their hands.... I stood right here, and they formed a circle, all of them, just men. And then the beating started. They threw me to one side, they threw me to the other. And I heard Luiz Carlos and Tiago also being tortured [in the other room]."

For Ziléa, Iná, and Marta, this was not the first time they had sought to tell the world about the abuses on Ilha das Flores. On December 8, 1969, only a few weeks after Aluízio was sent from Curitiba back to Ilha das Flores, the three women, along with thirteen other female prisoners, wrote a statement that was then smuggled off the island. The letter was passed to Jether Pereira Ramalho, a lay leader in the Brazilian Congregational Church, and his wife

Lucília, who soon traveled to the United States. In New York City, Jether and Lucília, in coordination with other Brazilian exiles, met with William Wipfler, an Episcopal cleric in the National Council of Churches. Like Jether and Lucília, the other Brazilians had also brought various documents written by political prisoners. As Wipfler would later recall in an interview with historian James Green, "Several were scrawled on scraps of filthy paper, paper bags or wrinkled envelopes, and were difficult to decipher. Another was transcribed in minute lettering on a single square of toilet paper; reading it required a magnifying glass."[2]

The smuggled documents now in Wipfler's possession were the first cache of evidence about torture in Brazil to enter international circuits. Four months later, the materials would get printed in English as an eighteen-page stapled pamphlet called *Terror in Brazil: A Dossier*. Despite its low-budget publication, the dossier had wide influence, helping inform editorials in the *New York Times* and the *Washington Post*.[3] While preparing the pamphlet, one of the first documents to circulate was the statement of the women on Ilha das Flores. In February 1970, the *New York Review of Books* reproduced the document in full, as part of a lengthy letter to the editor submitted by the Brazilian Information Front, an organization of exiles and allies that had chapters across Europe and also in Algeria, whose main task was distributing news about the repression of political prisoners.[4] The Ilha das Flores statement opened with the following declaration:

> We, prisoners held at the Ilha das Flores (Flower's Island), in Rio de Janeiro, wrote this letter, at a moment when the Brazilian public begins to be informed about the atrocities committed against political prisoners in our country and still may doubt that these crimes are really happening. We can assure everyone that torture does exist in Brazil. And more—everything that is said about torture methods is very little, compared with the true facts. We have been victims and witnesses of tortures inflicted here and we consider it our duty toward truth and justice to denounce them.[5]

Many of the prisoners on Ilha das Flores were members of the MR-8, and the group featured centrally in the statement. To both personalize and bear witness to the torture being committed in Brazil, the document summarized the violence against each of the sixteen signatories. The first five all belonged to the MR-8:

CHAPTER 5

1. Ziléa Reznik, 22, arrested on June 5, 1969, accused of belonging to the MR-8 revolutionary organization, was kept incommunicado for forty-five days—thirty-five more than even the military law allows—during which time she was often beaten.

2. Rosane Reznik, 20, Ziléa's sister, was arrested on the same charges on July 27, 1969. Stripped naked by her torturers, she was beaten and suffered electric shocks on various parts of the body, including her nipples.

3. Iná de Souza Medeiros, 20, married to Marco Antonio Faria Medeiros, arrested on the same charges in Curitiba, Paraná, on July 6, 1969. In Curitiba she was made to witness the tortures inflicted upon one of her friends, Milton Gaia Leite, who hung naked from a pole while the radio transmitted, at its loudest, a mass in order to cover up his cries. At the DOPS's (political police) jail, she was informed that her husband, arrested two months before, had died. She panicked, but this information was later proven wrong. Brought to the Ilha das Flores prison, she was beaten, received electric shocks and threats of sexual assaults.

4. Maria Candida de Souza Gouveia, 22, arrested in Curitiba on July 3, 1969, on the same charges, was immediately beaten and kicked. Her wrists and ankles were brutally twisted. She was also stripped.

5. Marta Mota Lima Alvarez, 20, arrested in Rio de Janeiro on July 9, 1969, on the same charges, was stripped and beaten. One of her fingers was broken, as can be seen from photographs taken by the press when invited to meet the members of MR-8.

The statements from the other eleven women told similar stories and the document also said that at least twenty-five male prisoners had been tortured on the island, over half of whom belonged to the MR-8, including Aluízio Palmar, Umberto Trigueiros Lima, César Cabral, and João Manoel Fernandes. The women ended their letter by declaring, "We know that our present attitude, denouncing tortures, can spark reprisals against us. We fear, for it would not be the first case, the simulation of an escape or a suicide, to try to hide the truth we are now stating. We call the attention of all those interested in finding out the truth and in punishing the guilty to the fact that we are at the mercy of all types of violence and need now, more than ever, the decisive help of all."

Through emerging solidarity networks, the Ilha das Flores letter brought new attention to the existence of torture in Brazil. In the years to come, the denunciations of military violence served as a rallying cry for coalitions of Brazilian exiles, human rights activists, and progressive sectors of the Church, both in Brazil and abroad. Eventually, the pressure brought by these movements would help force the dictatorship to enact new policies of democratization. Most notably, the 1974 policy of *distensão* (political decompression) marked the official, if incipient, end of the heaviest phase of repression, paving the way for the 1979 laws of *abertura* (reopening) that accelerated the return of key electoral and political freedoms. This process took place over the course of a decade, and despite its importance, offered little immediate relief for political prisoners at the dawn of the 1970s.

As global pressure campaigns began to call attention to violence in Brazil, Aluízio remained in jail. After less than two months on Ilha das Flores, Aluízio was transferred again. At some point in the early months of 1970, most likely in February, the navy sent Aluízio to another island prison in the Guanabara Bay, called Ilha das Cobras.[6] Connected by a bridge to the Mauá Plaza in downtown Rio de Janeiro, two kilometers north of the Santos Dumont airport, Ilha das Cobras had long been used as a detention center. In the late eighteenth century, the leader of an independence movement, Joaquim José da Silva Xavier (better known as Tiradentes), was imprisoned on the island for three years prior to his public execution by colonial authorities in 1792. And in 1910, after a mutiny known as the Revolt of the Whip—Afro-Brazilian and mixed-race sailors rose up, among other grievances, against the use of whips by white officers—over 600 sailors were detained on Ilha das Cobras, including the leader of the revolt, João Cândido Felisberto, known as the Black Admiral. At the time of Aluízio's imprisonment, he was not aware of the island's history, though in hindsight, he was proud to have been detained in the same spaces as some of Brazil's most celebrated freedom fighters.[7]

Ilha das Cobras is essentially an outcrop of rock, and the navy built prison cells into the island's stone foundation. As many as fifteen people were put into each cell, where prisoners slept on hammocks that hung from hooks bolted into the walls.[8] Because of the prison's proximity to the headquarters of the First Naval District at Mauá Plaza, the military had transferred most of the imprisoned MR-8 members to Ilha das Cobras. It was in a naval courtroom on Mauá Plaza that the militants would finally stand trial for the charges of subversion and conspiring to overthrow the social order.

The prisoners did not know when a trial would begin. When they arrived on Ilha das Cobras, they were placed in almost total isolation, confined to their stone cells, and visited only a few times each day by guards who delivered barely edible food. After nearly a year in prison, and with a trial somewhere on the horizon, Aluízio and his cellmates decided to take action. Soon after arriving at Ilha das Cobras, a dozen MR-8 prisoners staged a hunger strike.

The hunger strike had two main demands: visitation rights for family members and better food. In the memories of prisoners, these two objectives were bolstered by broader goals of calling attention to the plight of dissidents across Brazil. As Aluízio recalled, "There were also a lot of people dying out there [killed by the dictatorship], so we decided to hold a hunger strike."[9] João Manoel Fernandes said the strike was a way "to resist our imprisonment, a way to make our captors have a guilty conscious."[10] In countless examples across the world, hunger strikes have served as a key strategy for political prisoners—by denying food to their bodies, prisoners sought to highlight their mistreatment and cast a wider spotlight on their political cause.[11] The strike on Ilha das Cobras was part of an emerging wave in Brazil, where at least two dozen hunger strikes took place between 1970 and 1979, culminating most famously with the thirty-two-day strike in Rio's Frei Caneca jail demanding an amnesty law that would free them from prison.[12]

The dictatorship had proved its ability to violently squash all manner of dissent, so why might officials be swayed by the actions of political prisoners already under their control? As with the rationale for Aluízio's preventative detention—a veneer of legal legitimacy in which an otherwise macabre situation enabled small privileges like letter-writing—prisoners had contact with the outside world and their ability to call attention to their inhumane treatment could give lie to the regime's claim to moral and legal authority. The women's letter from Ilha das Flores was a telling example. And as we will see, the dictatorship's insistence on following prosecutorial rules also meant that prisoners like Aluízio would be allowed to give testimony in a military court. Whether recounting their experiences of torture or their decision to undertake a hunger strike, prisoners used the regime's own systems to denounce their mistreatment.

For Aluízio and his fellow MR-8 hunger strikers, the task at hand was to improve the conditions of daily life in prison. In terms of food, the prisoners had become fed up with the navy's offerings. "The food was terrible," Aluízio said. "They gave us things of cornmeal, some pasta, all poorly cooked. It seemed rancid."[13] Of the many ills suffered within the walls of Brazil's military prisons, bad food became a low-scale, though incessant, form of abuse. In our interviews, Aluízio often described his experience in a particular prison based on the quality of its food. In contexts of stress, food could trigger further sensorial trauma. "There's a gastronomic memory of the prisons I went through," Aluízio recalled. "That stays in your taste buds, too, it helps you remember things."[14] At the frontier battalion in Foz do Iguaçu: "I didn't eat a damned thing, because they slide the food under the cell bars, and it was this gross pasta, cold, it was all messed up."[15] And on Ilha Grande, where he would be sent later in 1970: "If the food on Ilha das Cobras was bad, then don't get me started on Ilha Grande. That food was totally unhygienic, something horrible... the leftovers you gave to pigs."[16] These experiences left lasting imprints. One of Aluízio's daughters, Andrea, told me that her father's "traumas affected our daily life at home. He doesn't eat reheated food, because in prison... he ate a lot of reheated and rotten food. All his food needs to be made fresh."[17]

During the hunger strike, prison guards tried to tempt the militants by offering steak and chocolate bars, but the strikers held firm. In Aluízio's retelling, after several days on strike, the prisoners were tied up in their cells on stretchers and forcibly given fluids through an IV.[18] After nearly a week, once several of the strikers had fainted from malnutrition, authorities at Ilha das Cobras gave in to the prisoners' demands. Although the food remained underwhelming by normal standards, it began to improve. One small aspect of life in prison became a little more tolerable.

The hunger strike also won the second demand of visitation rights—something that had previously been allowed for most of the prisoners as part of their preventative detention but which authorities had denied on Ilha das Cobras, in advance of the trial proceedings. Family members could now visit the prison. On one of the visits with his parents, Aluízio's mother, Luzia, surprised him by saying that she was glad he was in jail. Aluízio recalled that Luzia told him, "'My son, thank God that you're imprisoned... because if you were out there they would have killed you. At least they don't kill you in jail.'" At the time, Aluízio was taken back by his mother's comments, and that conversation still seemed to unnerve him fifty years later: "Every day [back then] you heard about people dying. She didn't know if I was alive or dead. Think about what that means for a mom, to not know, not knowing about your child. With me in prison, she knew where I was."[19] This was a core predicament for political prisoners during the most repressive years of dictatorship. Being in prison meant the threat of torture and an entirely uncertain future, yet it also represented a degree of security, at least in relation to what might happen to other militants.

For Aluízio, life on Ilha das Cobras after the hunger strike settled into a dull routine. Perhaps because they would soon testify in front of a military court, the prisoners were not tortured on Ilha das Cobras, seemingly the first

CHAPTER 5

respite from physical violence during Aluízio's time in jail. While waiting to be summoned for their trial, the prisoners had little to do but stay in their cells. Visitors brought books, which helped pass the time, and the militants also played card games among themselves. Aluízio was occasionally summoned to make a statement about other political prisoners, such as when navy officers made him answer questions about Liszt Vieira, Aluízio's former classmate in Niterói who had joined the VPR.[20] Aside from these rare trips off the island, life on Ilha das Cobras was largely spent sleeping, eating, and waiting.

As the months dragged on, news from the outside world plunged Aluízio further into a depressive state. In late April, he learned about the death of Juarez Guimarães de Brito, a COLINA militant who later joined the VPR and then the VAR-Palmares. Although the military often framed the murder of a militant as suicide—such as with the MR-8's Reinaldo Silveira Pimenta the previous June—Juarez did take his own life. On April 18, Juarez and his wife, Maria do Carmo Brito (the militant leader who had been Aluízio's university classmate), were discovered by security agents near the Botanical Gardens in Rio de Janeiro. Rather than be captured alive, Juarez shot himself in the right temple. Maria do Carmo was taken prisoner; she was released two months later as part of the exchange for the kidnapped West German ambassador, the third of four diplomatic kidnappings by armed militants in Brazil. The morning after learning about Juarez's death, Aluízio refused to get out of his hammock when the prison guard came by for morning rounds. Normally, every prisoner had to stand at attention and respond "Here!" when the guard called their names.[21] But in that moment, Aluízio felt no motivation to either get up or respond. As recounted in his memoir, "Well, why should I go stand there if I'm already in jail, totally immobilized as is? It was often impossible to stay calm and live in a normal way . . . especially when we were getting constant news about the tortures and deaths of our companions."[22] When Aluízio refused to stand at attention for the guard, a sergeant and several soldiers came into his cell and threw him down from his hammock. As punishment, he spent several days in solitary confinement.

A few weeks later, Aluízio's mood changed dramatically when he was visited by Eunice and Florita—he had not seen his wife for nearly a year, and he had never met his baby daughter, who was now eight months old.[23] When I asked him what it felt like to hold his daughter for the first time, Aluízio said that "it is very difficult to describe that emotion." They sat in a large waiting room, the first time the three of them were together as a family. Despite the harsh surroundings of a naval prison, Aluízio was happy: "I was chatting with [Florita], giving her kisses, it was very emotional." Aluízio was also allowed to introduce

Florita to his cellmates. "I picked her up and brought her to that cave on Ilha das Cobras, our cell," Aluízio remembered. "I held her close and everyone could meet her. It was amazing. It was good, that moment right there." The visit with Eunice and his daughter only lasted an hour, but it helped sustain him.

It did not take long for another event to bring a second burst of cheer to the prisoners on Ilha das Cobras: the 1970 World Cup, held that year in Mexico. As Brazil's dictatorship continued to tighten its grip on power domestically, military leaders saw the World Cup as a global platform to showcase a strong, modernizing nation. The Brazilian national team—known as the *Seleção*—had won two previous World Cups, in 1958 and 1962. Brazil went undefeated in the 1970 tournament, winning its third title by outscoring its opponents 19 to 7; led by its star players Pele and Tostão, the 1970 Seleção was arguably the greatest team, from any country, of all time.[24] The victory further emboldened the military regime, which during this time was also enjoying the so-called Brazilian Miracle, a phase of infrastructure- and industrial-led economic growth marked by a nearly 10 percent rise in gross domestic product. Shortly after the World Cup final, General Emilio Médici, the country's indirectly elected military president, declared, "I identify this victory, achieved in the fraternity of sport, with ascension of faith in our struggle for national development."[25] And in a not-so-subtle swipe at its detractors—those within the country as well as exiles abroad—the Médici government started a public relations campaign that famously included the slogan *Brasil, ame-o ou deixe-o*—Brazil: love it or leave it.

In the run-up to the World Cup, it was unclear how the political prisoners on Ilha das Cobras should feel about the tournament and its context of authoritarian nationalism. Umberto Trigueiros Lima remembered that the prisoners debated whether to support Brazil: was cheering for the Seleção a tacit endorsement of the military regime or could it be a form of resistance? And given the prisoners' current hardship, did they not deserve a fun distraction? This decision became more heightened when the naval guards, in a rare showing of goodwill, offered a television to watch Brazil play. "At first the group didn't want [the television]," Umberto said. "But the soldiers brought it in anyway. Some prisoners were super in favor of watching the games, they were really adamant. And others weren't. I was one of those against it. But the television was there."[26] Aluízio, in a Facebook post during the 2018 World Cup, wrote that for Brazil's first game against Czechoslovakia, he and several others began by rooting against the Seleção and for "our comrades from Eastern Europe."[27] In our interview, he said that when Czechoslovakia scored the opening goal in the eleventh minute, the prisoners chanted, "'Viva Czechoslovakia! Viva!' We were all against the Brazilian team, [it] belonged to the dictatorship, so we were on the side of Czechoslovakia."[28] When Brazil tied the score 1–1 on a Rivelino goal in the twenty-fourth minute, Aluízio stayed quiet, even a bit sad. But when Pele put the Seleção ahead in the second half, Aluízio switched allegiances: "We started going wild, we became Brazilians again."[29] Amused by his patriotic turnaround, Aluízio laughed and said that "when Brazil [scored two more times], we became even more Brazilian!"

During the month-long tournament in June 1970, politics were never entirely out of the picture. Prior to Brazil's quarterfinal game against Peru on June 14, the guards on Ilha das Cobras removed the television. Three days earlier, armed militants from the VPR had kidnapped the West German ambassador, and according to Umberto, the military took away viewing privileges as a form of retribution.[30] But this meant that the guards on duty also could not watch the matches, and they maneuvered to bring a radio into the cell block. This allowed the imprisoned militants to listen to the final three games of Brazil's World Cup victory.

MILITANCY ON TRIAL

The Seleção's march to the title, and the distraction it offered to the prisoners of Ilha das Cobras, coincided with the start of the regime's trial against the MR-8. As the haze of soccer glory spread across Brazil, the trial constantly yanked Aluízio back to the reality of his situation. The proceedings against the group had technically opened in December 1969, though it was not until the following May, once all the militants had been gathered in prisons along the Guanabara Bay, that the trial actually began. In what was officially logged as appeals process no. 38.495 of the Supreme Military Court (STM, Superior Tribunal Militar), thirty-three people were charged with violating an array of articles from the 1967 National Security Law.[31] Over the course of a nearly year-long investigation and trial, the original list of thirty-three accused prisoners would eventually get shortened to twenty-six "confirmed" MR-8 militants.

Reflecting the dictatorship's obsession with maintaining a veneer of orderly bureaucracy, the proceedings were not simply a show trial against subversives. Even if a guilty verdict was likely predetermined from the start, the military followed normal courtroom guidelines: the prosecution had to present evidence and build an argument, each militant was treated as a defendant and given access to legal counsel, and they could also address the charges brought against them. In terms of documentation, the tribunal yielded over 8,400 pages of testimony and supporting evidence.[32]

For most of the month of June, Aluízio and the other accused militants were summoned repeatedly to a courtroom at the First Naval District at Mauá Plaza. The first person to testify was Sebastião Medeiros Filho on June 3, the same day as Brazil's opening World Cup match against Czechoslovakia. Aluízio was summoned four times between June 11 and June 23, twice on his own and twice with others to give collective testimony. During the first month of the trial, most of the questioning related to the same themes from the militants' earlier interrogations in jail, requiring them to again go into great detail about the group's entire history. The prosecution focused much of its attention on the bank heists and procurement of weapons. For Aluízio, who had not participated in any of the armed actions in Rio de Janeiro and Niterói, the prosecution still sought to show how his activities in western Paraná had been central to the group's larger goals. At one point during the June proceedings, Aluízio was asked to provide evidence of his innocence. According to the summary deposition afterward, he "replied [that] despite having socialist ideas, of being organized, his participation in putting these ideas into practice were limited to meetings and studying the reality of Brazil."[33] Asked again whether he had any proof of his innocence, Aluízio "declared that no, he had no proof."

Although Aluízio could not provide evidence to counter the charges, he and the other prisoners did testify about their torture in jail. As Aluízio recalled, when the prisoners were summoned to give their statements, "we decided to denounce our torture in front of the court. Even if it didn't change anything, at least it would get recorded what happened. Each of us went there in front of the tribunal, one by one as we were called up, and said, 'I was tortured like this, like this, and like that.'"[34] Although not registered in the transcripts of the court proceedings, Aluízio told me that their denunciations of torture seemed to enrage the military prosecutor: "He screamed, he yelled, called us terrorists this, gunslinger that, robbers, criminals. He said we should be sentenced to life in prison."[35] As it would for several more years, the dictatorship was still denying its use of torture. Behind the scenes, however, spaces like the MR-8 trial provided a platform for torture victims to be heard. Aluízio's declarations to the STM in June 1970 described the "brutal tortures" he endured, including the parrot's perch, telephone slaps, beatings, simulated drowning, and repeatedly being placed in isolation.[36] As the Paraná State Truth Commission later observed, this represented "one of the rare opportunities" to have the details of torture recounted in military court, and Aluízio "managed to succinctly register what took place in the veritable dungeons of repression."[37] As the trial wore on, and as the prisoners had to return each day to their stone cells on

CHAPTER 5

Ilha das Cobras, the remaining sectors of the armed insurgency continued to battle against the dictatorship.

Similar to how the World Cup had broken up the routine of seemingly constant court appearances during the month of June, something happened on July 1 that jolted Aluízio from the looming question of his trial. That morning, four young Brazilian militants hijacked an airplane, intending to win the release of forty political prisoners. Aluízio's name was on the list of forty prisoners to be freed.[38] The hijackers were members of the ALN: Jessie Jane and her partner Colombo Vieira de Souza—the brother of MR-8 member Iná Meirelles—along with two siblings, Eiraldo and Fernando de Palha Freire. The four boarded a Caravelle PP-PDX plane, operated by Cruzeiro do Sul, that flew from Rio de Janeiro to Buenos Aires. Less than thirty minutes into the flight, the four militants stormed the cockpit. The plan was to force the plane back to Rio de Janeiro and hold hostage those onboard—thirty-four passengers and seven flight attendants—in exchange for the released prisoners. At 10:49 a.m., less than an hour after the plane had taken off, it was back at the Galeão airport in Rio.[39]

During the ensuing standoff, once the militants had announced their demands and presented the list of forty prisoners, a soldier came into Aluízio's cell on Ilha das Cobras and informed him of the hijacking. Aware of the diplomatic kidnappings over the previous year that had already won the release of several dozen political prisoners, Aluízio was hopeful.[40] On the tarmac at Galeão, the plane was surrounded by sixty Air Force soldiers, twenty military policemen, and eight fire engines. Negotiations broke down after four hours and the military charged into the plane. As fire engines sprayed water on the sides of the aircraft—blocking those inside from seeing what was happening—fifteen soldiers entered on a moving staircase. With hoses connected to a pair of specially equipped firetrucks, the soldiers filled the plane with smoke.

Coverage in the following day's *Correio da Manhã* described what happened next: "[The trucks] spray so much foam that the plane seems to disappear. The muffled sound of two gunshots could be heard by journalists. . . . Sometime later a young man leaves the plane, carried on a stretcher."[41] Eiraldo had been shot, though he survived. The militants were taken to a detention center in the Tijuca neighborhood, where security agents tortured them. Three days later, Eiraldo was dead. The military claimed that he had succumbed to his initial gunshot wounds, though according to Jessie, who was held in the same room as Eiraldo, he was tortured to death.[42] For Aluízio, the brief window of hope brought by the hijacking closed almost as quickly as it had formed. His attention turned back to the trial.

Aluízio's lawyer was Augusto Sussekind de Moraes Rego, one of a dedicated group of lawyers—including Heleno Cláudio Fragoso, Jorge Tavares, and Antônio Evaristo de Moraes—who defended various political prisoners. Aluízio was impressed with his lawyer, recalling that even though Moraes Rego was not a leftist, he was a liberal who believed in the rule of law.[43] For his advocacy, the dictatorship even imprisoned Moraes Rego for one night on baseless charges.[44] Once the prisoners had given their statements during the trial's opening month, the defense was allowed to present its case. Aluízio's defense took place on July 14, and Moraes Rego built a three-tiered argument.[45]

First, Moraes Rego sought to pick apart the prosecution's case. Claiming that the accusation against Aluízio was "patently inept," Moraes Rego argued that because of how the National Security Law was phrased, nobody could be tried simultaneously for violating two separate articles—Aluízio was being charged under Articles 21 and 23 of the 1967 law, which related, respectively, to "trying to subvert the current order or sociopolitical structure" and to "carrying out acts intended to provoke revolutionary war or subversion."[46] Second, he depicted Aluízio not as a hardened subversive determined to overthrow the government but rather as a young dissident who did not understand the full implications of his militancy. As argued by Moraes Rego, Aluízio and the MR-8 may have claimed to seek a dictatorship of the proletariat, but in reality "that was a mere illusion of his, an illusion, [nothing but] a mere illusion." Because the prosecution had presented the MR-8 as a sophisticated political organization, Moraes Rego called attention to a "certain disorientation in the methods" used by the group, "noting in particular the absence of any political line to be followed." And finally, Moraes Rego closed his argument by discussing torture. Because the prosecution relied heavily on the defendants' own statements, and because those declarations had originally been obtained through "violent physical and moral torture," Moraes Rego argued that the evidence was inadmissible. Given that the Brazilian state continued to deny the use of torture, it was unlikely that the closing argument would persuade a military judge. But for Aluízio, and likely for other militants as well, he considered it a moral victory to make the regime confront its own abuses.[47] In the meantime, all he could do was wait.

After nearly three months of proceedings, twenty-five MR-8 militants were summoned to the courtroom to hear the verdict. The only charged militant not present that day was Ivens Marchetti do Monte Lima, who had already been released as part of the exchange for the kidnapped American ambassador. On August 29, 1970, the defendants were ushered back to Mauá Plaza. Aware of their likely fate, the group decided that when their verdicts were announced they would stand up and sing Brazil's Independence Anthem—the song from 1822 to mark the end of colonial rule. Reflecting back on the day of the verdict, Aluízio recalled that "they started reading off our sentences; 'It is decreed these many and these years of imprisonment,' they go through all of us, and when they get to the end . . . that's when we stand up and start to sing."[48] In a room filled with armed soldiers, the militants sang the anthem's chorus: "Either keep the Fatherland free, or die for Brazil. Either keep the Fatherland free, or die for Brazil." Aluízio remembered the confused reaction from security agents in the courtroom: "They were pretty taken aback, they didn't know what to do. Were they going to arrest us? We were already prisoners. We weren't singing anything subversive, we were singing the Independence Anthem. Basically, that was our last act of rebellion against the navy."[49] The militants had guessed correctly, and they were all found guilty.

The verdicts brought varying sentences. Aluízio was sentenced to six years of imprisonment, plus an additional three years of suspended political rights. The other MR-8 members received similar sentences, ranging from a high of twelve years (João Manoel Fernandes and Sebastião Medeiros Filho) to a low of one year (Paulo Roberto das Neves Benchimol). The average length of the sentences was five years and ten months, almost exactly what Aluízio received.[50] For the militants, most of whom had already been held in military prisons for nearly a year and a half, these verdicts were a bitter, if unsurprising, development. Still in the throes of the most violent period of Brazil's dictatorship, the MR-8 confronted a feeling of helplessness: while activists continued to mobilize against the regime, the newly sentenced militants prepared to spend most of the next decade behind bars.

A FINAL ISLAND PRISON

After receiving their sentences at the naval tribunal, the militants returned to Ilha das Cobras. The next morning, they were driven to the Hélio Gomes prison, located seventy kilometers away, just north of the Guanabara Bay. Hélio Gomes was a state-run penitentiary, but the military used it as a processing center for political prisoners. When the MR-8 militants arrived at the prison, they were subjected to a cavity search. "We had to stand with our legs open," Aluízio remembered. "They looked inside our anus to see if we were sneaking in drugs, or something like that. I guess that was standard for an inspection system in that type of prison. It was totally humiliating."[51]

Once inside, they were placed in a large cell with other "common"—meaning nonpolitical—prisoners. This was the first time that Aluízio had been housed with common prisoners, and the experience startled him. Shortly after arriving, prisoners in an adjacent cell started yelling, "Hey comrades! Hey comrades! ... Viva Che Guevara!" Thinking at first that there were other militants at Hélio Gomes, Aluízio realized that the prisoners were messing with him: "They told us, 'Hey, in here all of us are also MR-8!' [Our] group was in the headlines all the time. So those street guys [*malandros*] from Rio, they started to talk as if they were in the MR-8 to get in our good books. They wanted cigarettes from us." Aluízio was not worried about being teased, but it saddened him that others could speak so casually about being political prisoners. To Aluízio, it was proof that Brazilian society on the whole still knew nothing about the violence inflicted by the military regime—"They thought that because we were middle-class students, that when we were arrested, they assumed that we weren't made to suffer. That it was easy being in prison. They had no idea about the torture."

After one night in Hélio Gomes, the MR-8 militants were taken out of their cells before dawn on August 31 and placed in three large buses. They were not told where they were being taken. After several hours driving west, when the convoy stopped at the small port town of Mangaratiba, the militants realized that their next destination was another island detention center: the Cândido Mendes prison on Ilha Grande.[52] Unlike their previous jails in the Guanabara Bay, Ilha Grande was a proper island, nearly 200 square kilometers in size, and difficult to access from the mainland. Aluízio and the other prisoners were placed in a flat-bottom fishing boat, and, with the putt-putt of what seemed like a very old motor, they made the hour-long passage from Mangaratiba to Vila de Abraão, the main settlement on Ilha Grande. After being weighed by a doctor, they were taken to the cell block for political prisoners. Each cell contained a bunk bed shared by two people and was enclosed with a heavy iron door.[53] Aluízio shared his cell with another MR-8 militant, Sebastião Medeiros Filho. Although they could talk quietly among themselves in their cell, communicating elsewhere in the prison was more of a challenge. When taken for their twice-daily meals, prisoners were prohibited from talking. Although militants from several armed groups were also detained on Ilha Grande—including the MR-8 and the ALN—common prisoners comprised a majority of the detainees. It was from the nonpolitical prisoners that Aluízio and the other militants learned how to communicate silently in jail, including an elaborate system of hand signals and folding letters into paper airplanes and sending them to other cells.[54]

Interactions with common prisoners also offered lessons on class and racial prejudices. Aluízio told me that most of the prisoners on Ilha Grande were Black and poor, and had been imprisoned for a wide range of convictions including theft and running *jogo do bicho* (an illegal, and widely popular, street lottery). Compared to these prisoners, the MR-8 militants were almost all of privileged backgrounds: "We were these cutesy, white, rich kids or middle class, from well-off families, some of us were even medical and engineering students."[55] Even in the context of the traumatic time in prison, being confronted with his own privilege helped Aluízio realize the shortcomings of the political theories he and the MR-8 had followed.

Although the MR-8 had professed to study the roots of inequality, a larger social critique had rarely formed part of their actual practice. The contradictions of this approach persisted in Aluízio's memories. Similar to his recounting of the conversations with common prisoners at Hélio Gomes, Aluízio spoke about the inmates on Ilha Grande in a somewhat condescending way, saying that they "didn't understand" how the MR-8 militants had ended up in jail: "[They] wanted to know, 'What the hell, why are you in jail, that's not how things go, it's unnatural, it's against the laws of nature.'" While perhaps meaning to signal his awareness of poverty in Brazil—the long-standing economic challenges of being poor materialized in different ways than the political repression of dictatorship—Aluízio's statement that the common prisoners could not "understand" the dynamics of an armed insurgency also revealed a nested set of assumptions about lower-class Brazilians. Despite what the militants had told themselves, they had not represented a so-called vanguard movement that spoke on behalf of all Brazilians. They still had much to learn about Brazilian society.

With their trial now completed and facing the reality of a long stay in prison, the MR-8 militants tried to settle into a new routine. With access to family networks and material resources that the common prisoners on Ilha Grande did not possess, the militants successfully advocated for a few small privileges on the island.[56] This included a daily period outside, where they could sit in the sun, as well as the right to receive gifts from family members—despite having visitation privileges on Ilha Grande, traveling to the island was very complicated and Eunice did not make the trip from Foz do Iguaçu. Unable to see his wife and baby daughter, and with no clear plan for the future, Aluízio's time on Ilha Grande dragged by slowly.

In December 1970, events on and off the island heated up again. As he later wrote in his memoir, toward the two-year mark of his imprisonment, Aluízio mouthed off to the prison warden. Upset because guards had confiscated books that his parents had sent him, Aluízio demanded to meet with the warden—in another sign of his privileged position on Ilha Grande, the meeting was granted. When the warden refused to hand over the books, Aluízio lost his temper and began yelling about conditions in the prison. Before Aluízio could finish his rant, the warden punched him in the stomach and kicked him on the ground. Guards then took him to a "punishment cell."[57] Unlike the solitary confinement at previous detention centers, this was a shared room just barely big enough for two people: a small dark cell with no windows, no toilet, and no sink. The only saving grace of the punishment cell was that he shared it with his MR-8 comrade Sebastião, who had also been sent there for insubordination. Luckily for the two of them, Sebastião had managed to bring a small transistor radio. One day in early December, the radio delivered news that changed Aluízio's life.

TOWARD FREEDOM

On December 7, 1970, Carlos Lamarca led a group of VPR militants in an operation to kidnap Giovanni Enrico Bucher, the Swiss ambassador to Brazil. At 8:40 a.m., while Bucher was being driven to the embassy, a group of VPR militants blocked the ambassador's car in the Laranjeiras neighborhood of Rio de Janeiro. Bucher's Brazilian police guard, a forty-four-year-old named Hélio Carvalho de Araujo, tried to stop the VPR militants but was shot and killed. The Rio police set up a roadblock around the city, and despite locating one of the four cars used in the kidnapping, they could not find Bucher.[58] Thus began the longest standoff of all the diplomatic kidnappings in Brazil.

As previously mentioned, there had been three prior kidnappings.[59] First, on September 4, 1969, the ALN and the (second) MR-8 kidnapped the US ambassador, Charles Burke Elbrick. This led to the release of fifteen prisoners who took up exile in Mexico. It became one of the most symbolic moments in the history of resistance to the dictatorship—one of the kidnappers, Fernando Gabeira, later chronicled the event in a best-selling memoir, adapted into a 1997 movie that received an Oscar nomination for best foreign film. Half a year after the kidnapping of the US ambassador, on March 11, 1970, the VPR staged a second kidnapping, of Nobuo Okushi, the Japanese consul. Okushi was released five days later, in exchange for five political prisoners, as well as the three young children of one of the militants, all of whom went to Mexico. Three months later, on June 11, a joint effort by the ALN and the VPR kidnapped Ehrenfried von Holleben, the West German ambassador. After four days of negotiation, forty political prisoners were released and taken to exile in Algeria. The VPR's abduction of the Swiss ambassador lasted much longer and yielded more released prisoners than the first three combined: after thirty-five days of negotiations, the Brazilian government agreed to the VPR's demand of seventy political prisoners.

CHAPTER 5

Aluízio learned about the kidnapping on the transistor radio that Sebastião had snuck into the punishment cell. When the news first came on, Aluízio was so excited that as he went to turn down the volume—to keep the guards on patrol from hearing—he accidentally pushed the dial in the opposite direction. With the sound blaring, guards came and took away the radio.[60] Hopeful but with no way of knowing what the news meant for him or his fellow prisoners on Ilha Grande, Aluízio waited. Umberto Trigueiros Lima recalled a sense of anxious excitement as news of the kidnapping spread across the island: "We had some information that the kidnapping was happening . . . [but] we didn't know who was going to leave, who wasn't going to leave. Because there were prisoners all over Brazil, so we didn't know."[61] Several days passed with no news, and Aluízio assumed that either his name had not been included on the VPR's list or that something had gone wrong, like it had with the plane hijacking in July.

What Aluízio did not know was that the VPR had demanded the release of seventy prisoners and the dissemination of an antigovernment manifesto on TV and radio stations. The Brazilian government told the VPR that although it had no intention of meeting the group's publicity demands, it was willing to discuss the release of prisoners.[62] But the regime balked at the size of the VPR's request—the three previous kidnappings had won the release of sixty militants in total, and the VPR now wanted seventy people. During these negotiations, the regime dispatched over 2,500 soldiers to search the city for the ambassador. On December 19, once the VPR delivered a handwritten note from Bucher as proof that he was still alive, the authorities agreed to release fifty-one of the seventy requested prisoners. Aluízio's was among the fifty-one names.

Much to his relief, guards eventually came to remove him from the punishment cell. Sebastião was also removed, though he was sent back to a regular cell. Aluízio was ushered to a separate part of the prison where he saw a handful of other political prisoners, including Umberto. "We imagined that, 'Well, we must be on the list because they took us here,'" Umberto recalled. "That's the only explanation, so we waited. But it took a long time."[63] On December 23, after almost two weeks, the prisoners were informed that they were on the list. Taken to a room filled with security agents, Aluízio had to decide whether he consented to being part of the exchange. As Aluízio remembered, "[They said] that if the ambassador died during any type of standoff, because he was being kept hidden somewhere, that I would also be killed as retribution."[64] The agents told Aluízio that if he declined to participate, they would shorten his prison sentence. But nothing could change Aluízio's mind. Following a script that was dictated to him, Aluízio wrote and signed a statement that read,

"I declare that I accept the exchange of my freedom for that of Mr. Giovanni Enrico Bucher, ambassador of Switzerland, kidnapped in Brazil on December 7, 1970, and that I am aware of the banishment imposed on me in accordance with the laws of the country."[65] The power to banish people from the country had come about the previous year as Institutional Act 13. The law was passed on September 5, 1969—one day after the kidnapping of the US ambassador. As legal scholar Ricardo Sontag and his colleagues have noted, the policy of banishment came into being as a means for the regime not only to deport those involved in a prisoner exchange but also to claim a moral victory over the armed insurgents.[66] According to official logic, the prisoners had not "won" their freedom but were instead being banished.

Four other political prisoners on Ilha Grande were also on the VPR's exchange list, including two members of the MR-8, Umberto Trigueiros Lima and Antônio Rogério Garcia Silveira.[67] It is difficult to know why certain prisoners were put on the list while others were not. Perhaps some militants had stronger connections with the VPR kidnappers. Aluízio believed that his name had been included by Zenaide Machado, his former university classmate and fellow MR-8 militant who became a VPR leader and helped organize the kidnapping. When I mentioned this in my interview with Zenaide, she dismissed the notion, saying that Aluízio's name was already on a list that had been circulating among the VPR leadership.[68]

Whatever the reason, it meant that despite the unprecedented number of released prisoners, many were left behind. João Manoel Fernandes, for example, who had received the longest MR-8 prison sentence, was not included. For João Manoel, who was still recovering from the gunshot to his throat, not being part of the prisoner exchange was difficult: "[I heard] that they considered offering my name in exchange for the Swiss ambassador, but in the end, it wasn't necessary. In that process, I guess they had enough people."[69] Sebastião was a similar case. He told me that when guards came to his cell, he thought to himself, "I'm finally getting out of this shithole."[70] But when a guard opened the door and asked if he was Marco Antônio Maranhão da Costa (another militant who was on the list), Sebastião had to say that he was not. The guard then shut the door and went off looking for Marco in another cell. Sebastião and João Manoel, like many other militants—as well as Ilha Grande's entire population of common prisoners—remained behind bars.

After signing their banishment statements, Aluízio and the other prisoners were taken to the medical office, where they were fingerprinted, made to strip naked and photographed from several angles, and given a brief physical exam.[71] As he did when testifying at the trial, Aluízio took advantage of his medical

CHAPTER 5

exam to again denounce his torture; the doctor's summary notes include that "the patient related that he was detained on the April 4, 1970, and was placed in the 'parrot's perch,' for several hours; and he said he did not receive medical help." The doctor, however, observed that Aluízio's body bore no outward traces of torture: "A direct examination reveals an absence of injuries or functional consequences, currently, related to the alleged event." It had been a year since his sustained rounds of torture, and Aluízio's body had likely benefited from the relatively few physically traumas inflicted on him in the lead-up to his trial. So even when he was able to have his testimony recorded, it was still discredited by government officials.

After the medical exams, the prisoners returned to a separate cell on Ilha Grande. The militants waited anxiously in what Aluízio referred to as "total isolation."[72] Umberto recalled the uncertainty of that period: "Christmas came and went, then New Year's came and went, the negotiations dragged on . . . and we had no clue what was happening."[73] Although the government had consented to exchange fifty-one prisoners, the VPR held firm on its demand for all seventy. As more time went on, however, there was an increased risk of the operation backfiring. The police might find Bucher—negating the need for a prisoner exchange—or else something could go wrong within the VPR, leading to the ambassador getting hurt or killed. For Aluízio and the other militants, any setback would have disastrous consequences.

The VPR's gambit paid off. Nearly a month after the kidnapping, the Brazilian government agreed to release all seventy prisoners. On January 7, Aluízio and the four other prisoners on Ilha Grande were placed on a helicopter and flown off the island.[74] Being on the helicopter did not bring any immediate relief. Aluízio thought that because they were handcuffed, if the helicopter crashed, they would all die, and Umberto feared that the military was going to throw them into the sea.[75] Though for others on the flight, the helicopter ride away from Ilha Grande brought immense relief. In my interview with Pedro Alves, a member of the second MR-8 and one of the four other Ilha Grande prisoners released in the exchange, he told me that flying toward Rio was "the most spectacular journey I've ever been on. You can't imagine what it's like coming from Ilha Grande by helicopter, passing by Restinga de Marambaia [a coastal sandbank], and then to Rio de Janeiro by Corcovado and Sugarloaf Mountain. The view is beautiful. It's spectacular."[76] Whether terrified or awestruck, the imprisoned militants were overcome with emotion as they made their way back to Rio.

Aluízio relaxed a bit once they were flying over the mainland and landed at a hangar at the Santos Dumont airport. From there, the helicopter went to pick

FIGURE 5.2. Imprisoned militants prior to their release from Brazil, January 13, 1971. Aluízio is kneeling in the second row, in the center. Collection Serviço Nacional de Informações, National Archive, Brazil.

up others at the Presídio de Bangu, a women's detention center. Eventually, the group of some fifteen prisoners were put on a bus and taken to a military battalion in the São Cristóvão neighborhood, where they remained for nearly a week. Early on January 13, the prisoners were loaded back onto vans and driven to the Galeão airport. On what became their final day in Brazil, the militants were subjected to one last form of abuse. It was an exceptionally hot summer day, and the soldiers left the vans parked in the sun. "They left us there roasting like in an oven," Umberto told me. "It was pure sadism and dirty tricks. They laughed and yelled to themselves, 'Check it out, man, those guys are getting hot, we must have forgotten to turn on the air conditioning.' . . . We could barely breathe through the few vents, our brains felt like they were going to burst. It was horrible!"[77] After spending most of the day inside the vans, the prisoners were taken to another section of the airport, where they were united with the remaining militants (fig. 5.2).

Aluízio had never been together with so many members of armed organizations. In a reflection of how militancy in Brazil tended to concentrate in certain regions, the 70 prisoners came from only five states: São Paulo (29), Guanabara (25), Rio Grande do Sul (8), Minas Gerais (6), and Pernambuco (2).[78] Most of the prisoners were in their twenties, though a few were older, including two in their forties and three in their fifties. Eleven of the militants were women.[79] An archived military dossier shows that prior to being released, all

CHAPTER 5

seventy prisoners were again photographed, twenty-seven of whom were made to stand fully naked, perhaps as a final act of repression and humiliation.[80] The seventy prisoners were eventually given a small amount of food and taken to a runway where a Varig Airlines Boeing 707 waited for them.[81] With over sixty journalists gathered nearby, the militants posed for photographs in front of the plane.[82] Video footage taken by the Associated Press shows the prisoners handcuffed in pairs of two, moving slowly in a line toward a boarding staircase.[83] Aluízio was handcuffed to Pedro França Viegas—who had taken part in a mutiny within the navy—and the two made their way onto the airplane.

It was only in those final moments, once they were loaded onto the Boeing 707, that the militants were informed of their destination: Chile. Throughout the thirty-five days of negotiations, the VPR had proposed three different locations of exile: Chile, Mexico, or Algeria.[84] The Brazilian government eventually consented to the VPR's first choice and chartered a plane to Chile for the seventy prisoners and the three young children of a militant named Geny Cecília Piola. At two minutes past midnight on January 14, 1971, the plane took off from Rio's Galeão airport and flew westward across the Southern Cone.

In our interviews, I asked Aluízio about the mood on the plane. It took him a moment to find an answer: "I guess there wasn't even space to think about anything, because we weren't allowed to talk. It was total silence, there was that fear of what could happen next. I can't remember any thoughts."[85] At 4:22 a.m., the plane landed at the Padahuel airport, fifteen kilometers outside of downtown Santiago. One by one, the militants had their handcuffs removed. Stepping off the plane, many raised their fists in celebration. Aluízio and a few others draped themselves in a large Chilean flag, and they all shared a seemingly endless exchange of hugs. The newly liberated Brazilians celebrated on the runway with a mix of laughter and tears of relief.[86] "It was really emotional," Umberto said. "It was so joyful to be able to escape that situation, because we had all been sentenced to many years in jail. To be honest, we didn't know how long that would last. . . . There was a lot of joy, a lot of emotion."[87]

A large contingent had come to the airport to welcome the Brazilians. This included a group of Brazilian exiles already living in Chile, a few trade union leaders, and several representatives of the Chilean government.[88] Two months earlier, the socialist candidate Salvador Allende had been sworn in as Chile's new president, leading a Popular Unity coalition that sought to bring about socialism through democratic means. For the seventy liberated militants, the conditions on both ends of their recent flight could not have been more different: boarding a plane as a prisoner in an authoritarian Brazil and emerging as a free person in a left-wing Chile.

After introductions and a few statements from Chilean officials, the Brazilians shuffled onto buses organized by the government and, with a police escort, they drove into Santiago. Daylight was starting to illuminate the Andes that rose above the city, and the Brazilians gazed out the windows at their new surroundings. At this time, new metro lines were being built across Santiago, and Umberto remembered watching scores of Chilean workers walking to their worksites in the morning light: "[Our arrival] must have been announced in all of the newspapers and television reports, because the workers cheered for us, they sang, raising their fists and clapping."[89] After the horrors of prison in Brazil, seeing this solidarity on the streets of Santiago felt transformative. And in many ways, the lives of Aluízio and the sixty-nine other liberated militants did change upon arriving in Chile. At first, those changes seemed to be for the better. But as they would soon discover, the repression they had just escaped in Brazil would continue to spread across the continent, shadowing them along their recent path to freedom.

CHAPTER 6

EXILE IN CHILE

ONE WEEK after the Brazilian prisoners arrived in Chile, they were visited by the US film crew of Saul Landau and Haskell Wexler, two documentarians who were already in Santiago to make a film about Salvador Allende. Landau and Wexler had read about the seventy prisoners in a Chilean newspaper, and they wanted to see if the Brazilians would be willing to talk on camera. The resulting fifty-five-minute film was titled *Brazil: A Report on Torture*.[1]

Many of the Brazilians, still too traumatized to discuss their time in prison, refused to speak with Landau and Wexler. But seventeen of the recently released Brazilians agreed to be recorded, providing in-depth descriptions of the violence they experienced as well as the strength and solidarity that allowed them to persevere. And in a somewhat macabre twist, some did more than just give their testimonies—several insisted on reenacting the tortures they had suffered. The filmmakers were surprised that the Brazilians wanted to give such graphic displays. As Landau later recalled to the historian James Green, "We had to restrain them in the recreation of the torture. They wanted to go in a much more realistic way. . . . They wanted to show how truly terrible it was, and we said, 'Take it easy. People can imagine.' [But] they really wanted people to see the incredible brutality of it."[2]

In one scene, a man strips almost naked and allows his comrades to place him in the parrot's perch, with his hands and feet bound around a pole. In another scene, a young woman is hung upside down while her friends play the role of prison guards and pretend to beat her. During these reenactments, various Brazilians—some offscreen, some in picture—narrate the details of each torture method. Interspersed with these demonstrations were lengthy close-up interviews, with the camera often zooming in and out on a subject's face, offering an at-times blurred vision that leaves viewers feeling disoriented and queasy.

No level of cinematographic recreation could give a true sense of what it was like to be tortured. But paired with the testimonies of former political prisoners, the reenactments became a powerful form of bearing witness that reached global audiences. The film aired on New York public television and at venues such as the Whitney Museum and the Los Angeles International Film Exposition.[3] Given that the Brazilian government still officially maintained that there was no torture in Brazil, the documentary became a public relations problem. In one report on the film's screening in Washington, DC, the minister of foreign relations, Mario Gibson Barboza, dismissed it as a "biased" project that romanticized a group of "banished Brazilian terrorists." Intent on stopping further reporting, Minister Barboza announced that should Landau and Wexler ever try to visit Brazil, they would never be issued an entry visa.[4] The film became an early spark in the growing solidarity movement that shined a light on the violence of Brazil's military regime. Much of this work was led by exiles, whether those who had left of their own volition or former political prisoners like the seventy Brazilians who now found themselves living in Chile.

Aluízio appeared only briefly in the documentary. In fact, I did not even notice him the first time I watched the film—after reading an early draft of this chapter, Aluízio told me to rewatch it more closely. About five minutes in, he can be seen standing behind a woman named Maria Auxiliadora Lara Barcelos, better known as Dora, who had been member of the VAR-Palmares armed group. While Dora speaks into the camera, describing the torture and sexual violence she suffered, Aluízio dips in and out of the frame, wearing a white shirt and smoking a cigarette. In total, he is on screen for a little more than thirty seconds, saying nothing but watching intently from the background. His fleeting presence in the film hinted at the type of exile that he would choose to pursue, the isolation that eventually came to define his time outside of Brazil, and his larger pattern of staying just on the margins.

CHAPTER 6

Aluízio's experience in exile is the focus of this and the following chapter (map 6.1), with particular emphasis on his continued role in clandestine politics and its impact on him and his family. These chapters help reveal the lesser-known history of the small number of former prisoners who returned to armed struggle while on foreign soil. Whereas many of his fellow exiles stayed in Chile until a 1973 coup overthrew Allende and established a brutal dictatorship under Augusto Pinochet, Aluízio decided to leave long beforehand. And unlike many of his comrades who emerged more fully into public life—whether appearing on camera for international audiences or enrolling as students in foreign universities—Aluízio went underground again. With his belief in revolutionary tactics not yet extinguished, Aluízio joined a small group of Brazilian exiles, based in Chile, who remained committed to armed struggle. As we will see, Aluízio's continued militancy required a series of difficult decisions that were political as well as personal—he chose to forego a more open life in democratic Chile, and he brought his family along for the uncertain, and highly risky, path of clandestine exile. This chapter chronicles Aluízio's time in Chile from January 1971 to March 1972, exploring why militants like him decided to reenter revolutionary politics so soon after winning their freedom.

Chapter 7 will trace his wayward and increasingly difficult trajectory in Argentina, from March 1972 to May 1979. This path took Aluízio to Argentina's rural borderlands, where, disguised as a farmworker on a tea plantation, he passed messages between various revolutionary groups and helped militants sneak back into Brazil. With the shadow of authoritarianism seeming to stalk him across the Southern Cone—a coup in Chile in 1973 and then Argentina in 1976—Aluízio felt trapped (afraid of getting caught by three different dictatorships) and politically aimless, unsure of how to maintain his activities and sense of self in increasingly difficult circumstances. After bringing his family to live with him in exile, the responsibility—and guilt—of needing to protect his wife and young children eventually led him to abandon all political work. He spent the final years in exile living anonymously in the northeastern Argentine province of Chaco. At Aluízio's insistence, during these years he and his family had no communication with friends and loved ones back home, and they did not return to Brazil until 1979, just before the government passed its Amnesty Law.

In hindsight, knowing that his continued efforts to build an armed insurgency would fail, and that his time in exile would often become lonely and depressing, Aluízio became fairly embittered about this experience. As mentioned in chapter 3, Aluízio belongs to a WhatsApp group called Amigos e Amigas de 68, which he mostly enjoys being a part of. But he gets frustrated when people on the thread discuss exile. To again quote one of Aluízio's most

MAP 6.1. Locations of Aluízio Palmar's exile in Chile and Argentina. Courtesy of Gabe Moss.

telling reflections: "They always talk about their time in exile, in Germany, in Switzerland, Sweden, in Paris, Rome. I think to myself, and I tell them, 'Fucking hell, while you all were living it up in exile, I was God knows where.'"[5]

A NEW LIFE IN CHILE

With no identification documents and wearing the same ragged clothes from the Ilha Grande prison, Aluízio arrived at the temporary housing provided by the Chilean government, a building called the Hogar Modelo Pedro Aguirre Cerda—named after Chile's left-wing president during the Popular Front coalition of the late 1930s.[6] In the context of Latin America's Cold War, Chile under Allende became a refuge for exiles. Some chose to continue onward, whether to Cuba, Mexico, or Europe, but many opted to stay in Chile, seeing Allende as a beacon of hope. A medical doctor by training and a Marxist by political formation, Allende had first made his impact in Chilean politics as the minister of health under Aguirre Cerda's Popular Front government, and he later became a federal senator. After three unsuccessful campaigns for president, Allende finally won in 1970, promising to achieve socialism through the ballot box. What made Allende's presidency so exciting for leftists across the region and globally would soon attract the same authoritarian reactions that had engulfed Brazil. For the moment, however, Chile seemed ripe with possibility.

The seventy Brazilians stayed at the Hogar for nearly a month, while Chilean officials helped arrange paperwork that allowed them to live and work in the new country. Staff at the Hogar also cooked for them and washed their clothes. The Brazilians received an outpouring of donations from Chileans as well as Brazilians who had already relocated to Santiago. Support also came from Brazilians living elsewhere in the world, who had eagerly followed the news of the released prisoners.[7] President Allende himself met with the Brazilians, inviting a group of them to Valparaíso for a celebratory lunch. Aluízio told me that he was among the dozen Brazilians who met with Allende, and that he remembered the president saying that the government would facilitate jobs and places at the university for whoever wanted to stay in Chile, or air travel to other countries for those who preferred to settle elsewhere in Latin America or in Europe.[8] Having so recently escaped the repression of prison in Brazil, and finding themselves now living in country governed by a socialist president, the arrival in Chile felt to Aluízio like "a moment of euphoria."[9]

Despite the hospitality, beginning a new life in Chile was complicated. Aluízio spoke only a little Spanish, which he had picked up by reading translated Marxist texts and by living in the border region of western Paraná. And he felt disoriented being outside of Brazil for the first time in his life.[10] The Hogar had a phone that the Brazilians could use to communicate with their family back home, but because Eunice's house in Foz do Iguaçu did not have a phone, he could not call his wife—having been unable to speak with Eunice over the previous weeks while waiting to be freed, Aluízio could only hope that she had learned about his release in newspapers or from family.[11] Although he remained extremely grateful to the Chilean government and its population for all of the support, the spectacle of their arrival in Santiago also wore on him. The public could not enter the Hogar, but according to Aluízio, many Chileans would stand on the street and try to catch a glimpse of the Brazilians inside: "There were so many people, because it was all over the news. I felt like a little animal in a zoo, everyone out there peeking in. If they had had cell phones in those days everyone would've been taking pictures."[12] After two years of close confinement in jail, Aluízio longed for some privacy.

But the biggest initial challenge in Chile was the same one they had experienced in Brazil: the physical and psychological effects of repression. One of the first services provided at the Hogar was a medical check-up, and Aluízio remembers that even a year removed from his last bout of torture, he still had terrible problems with his hearing—the lingering effects of military officers pounding both of his ears at the same time, the "telephone."[13] For the Brazilians who had been captured later than he had, and thus subjected to torture more recently, the impact of their traumas seemed much more glaring. In a potential blending of Aluízio's memories from the time and his awareness of events afterward, when he talked about the struggles of his fellow Brazilians in Chile, he described scenes from the Landau and Wexler film. He mentioned Dora, who featured centrally in the documentary, telling me that "in the video she talks about torture and she has this wry smile, out the side of her mouth; she wasn't okay."[14] He also talked about Frei Tito, the Dominican friar who had been arrested and tortured by Sérgio Fleury under false allegations of supporting the armed underground. Aluízio told me that "you can see in the video when [Frei Tito] gives an interview, in that film made by the American, he was unhinged. . . . That's the word, right? Unhinged [*desestruturado*]. I can't make any sort of diagnosis, I'm not a psychiatrist, but he was unhinged." The traumas that seemed so evident in the documentary would follow both Dora and Frei Tito like a shadow. Only a few years later, while living in exile in Germany and France, respectively, they each committed suicide.

After Aluízio had been in Chile for nearly a month, Eunice and little Florita arrived in Santiago (fig. 6.1). Aluízio had not been sure whether his family would be able to travel to Santiago, and he was away from the Hogar when they

CHAPTER 6

FIGURE 6.1. Aluízio, Florita, and Eunice in Chile, ca. 1971.
Courtesy of Aluízio Palmar.

arrived, spending a few nights with some members of the Chilean Communist Party. When he returned to the Hogar, his friends said, "Hey Aluízio, there's a surprise for you, can you guess what it is?"[15]

In our interview, I asked Aluízio about how it felt to see his family for the first time as a free man. This was only our seventh interview together, coming barely a month into our sustained exchanges, and we were still figuring each other out. I already had the sense that Aluízio was not an overly sentimental person, though I still imagined he might draw from some of his more effusive moods to describe the reunion with his wife and daughter. Instead, he began stammering his words, saying, "This heaviest thing, most traumatic, most complicated."[16] Soon, he ended the conversation entirely. Granted, we had been talking for nearly two hours—a bit longer than usual—but his memories of Eunice's arrival in exile seemed to trigger something. With his mind perhaps drifting to the years of isolation that would soon follow him and his family, Aluízio seemed overwhelmed by his memories.

Having not yet encountered this side of his storytelling, I sent Aluízio a message after our interview, thanking him for the conversation and wishing him a nice afternoon. He replied almost immediately: "I'm sorry, really I'm so tired. And licking wounds hurts a lot. But we have to lick wounds so they heal. That's what wild animals and oxen do."[17] In the coming months, as we conducted more interviews and as I read deeper into his online archive and collection of writings, I realized how infrequently he discussed his family. Despite speaking constantly about his own experiences as a militant, a prisoner, an exile, and later as a human rights activist, he rarely spoke unprompted about his wife and children. Perhaps some wounds were deeper than others, pushing certain memories to the margins of his accustomed narrative.

Over the course of the nearly two years during which we recorded interviews and exchanged messages, I never again saw Aluízio react in this same way. But when we discussed his family, or when he asked me about interviews that I had done with his children, his normally stoic manner of narration would often shift. If Aluízio's accustomed memory script tended to focus on himself and his own political biography, he seemed on shakier ground when asked to bring his family into the story. This contrast between a fluency in self-narration and a difficulty in accounting for the impact that his political work had on his family suggests an awareness, even if rarely articulated as such, that his choices led to the sufferings of his loved ones. Reading between the lines of Aluízio's memory script reveals the emotional undertones of what it meant to transform his life—and by default, that of his family—into a public story.

TAKING UP ARMS IN EXILE

With his wife and baby daughter now in Chile, Aluízio had to figure out what to do next. During their stay at the Hogar, Aluízio would talk with the other Brazilians about how, or if, they could continue their political work. Of the seventy recently released prisoners, many continued as activists, whether with Chilean student and worker organizations or overseas as part of solidarity networks. Although Aluízio was determined to rejoin the fight against Brazil's dictatorship, he also participated in more localized, less militant campaigns. Figure 6.2 shows Aluízio, Eunice, and another woman at a rally in November 1971 to welcome Fidel Castro during his official state visit to Chile. In the photo, Aluízio dangles a small flower between his teeth, and Eunice wears her hair shortly cropped and framed by stylish sunglasses. The young couple looks relaxed in their new Chilean setting. But any sense of contentment that Aluízio may have felt in these early moments of exile would soon give way to an antsy need to mobilize again. For a handful of the released prisoners in Santiago, the recent experience in Brazil had not yet dissuaded them from their goal of overthrowing the Brazilian military regime. Along with two other MR-8 members—Umberto Trigueiros Lima and Antônio Rogério Garcia Silveira—Aluízio joined the VPR, the People's Revolutionary Vanguard.

FIGURE 6.2. Aluízio (*center*) and Eunice (*right*) at a rally to welcome Fidel Castro, Santiago, Chile, November 1971. Courtesy of Aluízio Palmar.

In her book on the VPR, the historian Carla Luciana Silva notes that by this point in 1971, exiles like Aluízio comprised a large portion of the organization.[18] The group had originally been formed in 1968 by militants who split from the POLOP and MNR armed groups. The following year, in July 1969, the VPR dissolved and formed, with members of the COLINA armed group, a new organization, the VAR-Palmares, which in turn, dissolved two months later. It was at this point, in September 1969, that militants reconstituted the VPR—known sometimes as VPR II. The undisputed leader of the newly reformed VPR was Carlos Lamarca, the dissident army captain, who oversaw a series of bank robberies and, in October 1969, established a guerrilla training camp in the Ribeira Valley in the interior of São Paulo state. In March 1970, the military discovered the VPR's training site, though most of the eighteen would-be guerrillas escaped capture. That same month, Lamarca himself left the VPR to join the second MR-8—a year and a half after splitting from the VPR, Lamarca would be assassinated in the northeastern state of Bahia. As the VPR's numbers and capacity diminished in Brazil, militants abroad sought to revitalize the movement.

In our interviews, Aluízio provided a fairly short explanation for why he joined the VPR. According to him, a few days after arriving in Chile, the three former MR-8 members (Aluízio, Umberto, and Rogério) were visited by Maria do Carmo Brito and Ângelo Pezzutti, who had recently returned from Algeria, where they had started their exile after the prisoner exchange for the West German ambassador. Both Maria do Carmo and Pezzutti were members of the VPR, and they had traveled to Chile to make new contacts and build the organization. Aluízio told me that "because of our friendship, political activism in the student movements, and general political alignment, we immediately joined the VPR."[19] Given the lengthy stories he had shared about his path from student activist to communist militant to armed insurgent, I was a bit surprised at the almost offhand manner in which he recalled giving up his newfound freedom to reenter the armed struggle. There seemed to be no outward consideration of what it meant for Eunice and his young family, or even whether the remaining revolutionary organizations offered a viable route. The dizzying sequence of organizations and acronyms outlined in the paragraph above—dissolving, reforming, dissolving again—shows just how difficult it was to build an armed Left. Yet in Aluízio's retelling, and perhaps even at the time, joining the VPR was a simple product of political conviction (his determination to overthrow the dictatorship) and circumstance (Maria do Carmo's invitation came right as he was figuring out his next move). Whatever the reason, Aluízio now plunged back into revolutionary politics.

After leaving the Hogar, Aluízio and his family lived in a series of apartments connected to the VPR. Eventually they moved into a large house in Puente Alto, a working-class neighborhood on the southern periphery of Santiago. There, Aluízio served as an administrator of sorts, tasked with coordinating the movement of different cadres in Chile and across borders.[20] One of the VPR's main goals at this moment was arranging for exiles to sneak back into Brazil, often by crossing the western Paraná frontier, the exact region where Aluízio had done his MR-8 guerrilla training. Aluízio enjoyed the work in Santiago, and relished being part of a militant organization again, even if being an administrator was a cumbersome and sometimes boring role. With money from bank robberies in Brazil and donations from militants abroad, the VPR maintained a modest budget for members to use on daily expenditures. To earn extra money for himself and his family, Aluízio also picked up odd jobs in Santiago, including as an extra on Chilean television shows. At one point he and Pedro Alves, who had been imprisoned with him on Ilha Grande, played the role of prison guards, dressing in clothes like those of their captors.[21]

To prepare for an eventual guerrilla insurgency back in Brazil, VPR members in Chile organized a series of trainings, including overnight hikes in the Andean foothills while carrying heavy packs and weapons.[22] The VPR also coordinated with foreign insurgent groups like the Chilean Revolutionary Left Movement

(MIR, Movimiento Izquierda Revolucionaria) and the Argentine People's Revolutionary Army (ERP, Ejército Revolucionario del Pueblo). Aluízio served as the VPR's main contact with the Cuban embassy in Santiago, and he helped organize the trips of several Brazilians to Cuba.[23]

Even in the comparatively open climate of Allende's Chile, the VPR operated as a clandestine organization, relying on a system of security measures to shield their actions and protect their members. A Brazilian exile named José Carlos Mendes remembered feeling that militants in the VPR were never safe: "There were probably spies from the Brazilian surveillance branches, or even the CIA, or other groups to monitor us. So everything was really discreet."[24] Although this was several years before the official formation of Operation Condor—which facilitated the surveillance and repression of militants across the Southern Cone—agents of authoritarian regimes were nonetheless able to track the movements of exiles. And more pressingly for Aluízio and his fellow VPR members, though they were not yet aware of the danger, Brazil's dictatorship had already infiltrated their group: after being captured by the dictatorship, a radical navy officer named José Anselmo dos Santos—known as Cabo Anselmo—became a double-agent and lured six VPR militants into a fatal ambush in January 1973. VPR militants in Chile did not learn about Cabo Anselmo's deception until after the murder of their comrades in 1973, but in the Cold War climate of the early 1970s, they operated on the assumption that security forces could be lurking around any corner. Aluízio described some of their safety precautions: "I would wait in a dark place for a car to pass by, and I would get in. When I got in the car, I had to get in with my eyes closed, and then they'd put a hood on me, something over my eyes so I wouldn't see."[25] Aluízio's fear of government surveillance was not unwarranted. The archives of Brazil's dictatorship show that while he was living in Santiago, security forces were keeping tabs on him. The intel was not always correct, such as when agents reported that Aluízio was spotted in Asunción, Paraguay, or that he and Eunice had won scholarships to study in Denmark. But the regime seemed intent on tracking his movements on foreign soil.[26]

Given Aluízio's return to revolutionary organizing, the presence of his wife and young daughter in Chile made for difficult decisions. At first, the couple was determined to keep their family intact. This was, after all, the first time that the three of them had ever lived together, and they all stayed in Santiago for nearly half a year.[27] In Aluízio's memories, what seemed to stand out most about this period was the shock of a radically new climate: early in the morning of July 8, he and his family woke to something they had never experienced in Brazil, an earthquake that was large even by Chilean standards—a magnitude of 7.8 that killed nearly 100 people. A series of winter blizzards added further novelty, and homesickness, for the Brazilians.

As the months drew on, Aluízio's work with the VPR became a steady source of tension with his wife. Aluízio told me that Eunice did not share his political commitments: "I knew perfectly well what I wanted. [But] Eunice was torn. It was complicated, because [as militants] we couldn't project our situation, our lives, on other people."[28] By September, they decided that Florita should return to Brazil, and they arranged for Eunice's mother, Flora, to come to Chile and bring her granddaughter back to Foz do Iguaçu. Eunice, who had never been away from her daughter, stayed with Aluízio for three months. In late December 1971, Florita returned to Santiago, again accompanied by her grandmother. After a few weeks together for Christmas and New Year's, the three women (toddler Florita, Eunice, and grandma Flora) went back to Brazil. Throughout these various trips, Brazil's surveillance system kept tabs on the family. An army intelligence report from late December 1971 noted the anticipated travels of Eunice and Florita.[29] And two months later, a memo from the Federal Highway System stated that while Aluízio was conducting guerrilla training in Chile, Eunice had already settled back in Foz do Iguaçu.[30] In this case, both surveillance reports were accurate: Aluízio had indeed recommitted himself to the armed struggle, and Eunice and Florita were living in Brazil. Upon returning to Foz do Iguaçu, Eunice began a new job as a teacher, and she and Florita would remain in Brazil until rejoining Aluízio eighteen months later.

Aluízio, meanwhile, never felt entirely comfortable in Santiago. Initially, he had been relieved to escape prison and to be reunited with Eunice and Florita. But even after his family returned to Brazil, with nothing but political work to occupy his mind, Aluízio could not settle into the type of routines that many of the other exiles seemed happy with. "Those of us in the VPR, we lived in a parallel universe." Aluízio said. "It was a parallel reality. We didn't participate in Chilean politics. We had our own Brazilian reality, and we were organizing to return to Brazil. . . . Sure, we would go to speeches, and marches, all of that, but without any real engagement, because we were getting ready to go back."[31]

Yet Aluízio did not return, at least not for another eight years, and only after abandoning the armed struggle. Despite his commitment at the time to helping rebuild bases of operations in Brazil, his tasks in the VPR remained logistical, not tactical or military. I never asked him why he did not go back when others did. Perhaps I should have. With Brazil's dictatorship still at the height of its most repressive period, choosing to sneak back so soon after being released, however lofty the motivation, may have felt too risky, even for him.

CHAPTER 6

In early 1972, the VPR decided that Aluízio could better coordinate the movement of militants if he were closer to the Brazilian border. So in March he prepared to leave Chile and settle in northeastern Argentina. This was a dangerous move. Since 1966, Argentina had been ruled by a series of military generals, and conflicts between the government and civil society had steadily escalated: the so-called Cordobazo of 1969—the bloody repression of student and labor protestors in the city of Córdoba—sparked new cycles of violence that persisted into the early 1970s. Being a clandestine militant in Argentina came with a constant threat of danger. Having arrived in Chile to great fanfare and international attention the previous year, Aluízio now had to find a way to leave the country and secretly enter Argentina.

CLANDESTINE AGAIN

One of Aluízio's most trusted contacts in Chile was an actress named Sara Astica, who had helped arrange him some paid work as a television extra. (Sara herself would later become an exile, forced out of the country after Pinochet's coup.) For Aluízio's clandestine exit from Chile, the VPR produced a fake passport, with the identity of a made-up businessman from the Portuguese island of Madeira. To look like a more convincing *madeirense*, Aluízio went to Sara's studio, where she glued on an oversized fake mustache, died his blond hair black, gave him contact lenses to turn his blue eyes brown, and used stage makeup to puff out his cheeks.[32] To finish the look, Aluízio wore a nice suit, an imported Italian tie, and dress shoes that were so polished "you could use them as a mirror to comb your hair."[33] With his fake document and changed appearance, Aluízio boarded a flight in Santiago, heading to the northwestern Argentine town of Mendoza. Going to Buenos Aires would have been more convenient for his final destination on the Brazil-Argentina border, but the VPR wanted to avoid the capital city, as it was believed to have a heavy presence of Brazilian spies.

Aluízio's problems started while still on the runway in Santiago. As he waited in his seat, the flight attendant kept asking for a passenger named José Augusto to please come to the front. Aluízio did not think much of it, but after several repetitions, he realized that *he* was José Augusto—the name of his Portuguese identity. In his nervous effort to keep a low profile, he had forgotten his own fake name. Assuming that his cover had been blown, Aluízio thought to himself, "Shit! I'm getting caught before even leaving Chile. I guess that's the end of the road."[34] Luckily for him, he had simply forgotten to hand in a travel document during the boarding process, and once he did, he returned to his seat. José Augusto could now travel onward to Argentina.

But soon after landing in Mendoza around ten at night, Aluízio again found himself in hot water. After getting off the plane and waiting in the customs line, Aluízio was told to stand to the side while Argentine officials took away his passport. Apparently the VPR had not included a travel visa as part of his documents. Although Brazilians did not need a visa to enter Argentina, citizens of Portugal did, meaning that José Augusto did not have permission to leave the Mendoza airport.[35] Long after the rest of the passengers had cleared customs, the immigration officers came back and told Aluízio that he would have to spend the night there, in the airport waiting room, until a supervisor could come in the morning. Terrified at the thought of being discovered, Aluízio began shouting at the immigration workers, and speaking in the condescending tone of a self-important businessman, he said that he refused to sleep in the airport and could only stay at a luxury hotel: "A hotel of 5 stars, 10 stars, 500 stars, the best hotel in Mendoza!"[36] Eventually the officers allowed him to leave, but they kept the passport to make sure that he would come back the next morning.

Aluízio walked out of the airport, where he was met by the VPR's pre-arranged contact, a Bolivian militant named David Acebey Delgadillo. This was the first time that Aluízio met David, who was known by his codename of Pepe, and who would serve as Aluízio's bodyguard and travel companion over the next few years. Rather than head to a hotel as he had told the immigration officers, Aluízio and Pepe took a taxi to the Mendoza bus station and began a 2,000-kilometer series of bus rides. After an overnight bus to Cordoba, they transferred to Rosario, and then to Entre Rios, before heading due north on smaller buses for nearly a thousand kilometers until arriving at their destination of Campo Grande, in the northeastern province of Misiones, a pinky finger of a border region surrounded by Paraguay to the north and Brazil to the south.

Only a few hundred kilometers to the closest Brazilian border point—and roughly the same distance, as the crow flies, from his family in Foz do Iguaçu—Aluízio had a difficult task. He had to block out any potential desire to return home while staying focused on the VPR work of coordinating the travel of other militants. In the coming years, when the VPR dissolved and with the repression of military regimes seeming to encroach from all directions, his time in exile would devolve into a period of political and personal seclusion.

CHAPTER 7

EXILE IN ARGENTINA

For a biography of Aluízio Palmar, his period in Argentina presents several challenges. Given that he spent nearly eight years living under a pseudonym and trying to avoid detection, most of the sources for this chapter come from his own recollections, primarily from our interviews and his memoir. Of all the sections in this book, the present chapter is the one that relies most heavily on Aluízio's own memories. But to deepen and corroborate his stories, I also include the perspective of other militants who overlapped with him in exile, two of his neighbors from Argentina, and his two oldest daughters, who shared with me some of their earliest memories. And to provide a fuller picture of what these years meant to other people in Aluízio's orbit, I also offer two examples of what I call "memory vignettes"—not quite a memory script, which requires a larger corpus of a person's recollections, these vignettes offer step-back summaries and analysis of my interviews with other people in Aluízio's life. The first is of David Acebey Delgadillo, aka Pepe, the Bolivian militant who was Aluízio's bodyguard, and the second is of Aluízio's daughter, Florita. Especially because the present chapter otherwise draws largely on Aluízio's memories, I use these vignette discussions of Pepe and Florita to show the types of lives that overlapped with, and were affected by, Aluízio's path as an exile. The two vignettes explore the methodological and emotional dimensions of my interviews with people other than Aluízio.

MEMORY VIGNETTE: PEPE

Before continuing with Aluízio's experience in the Argentine borderlands, it is useful to introduce readers to his bodyguard. Pepe had been a militant in various Bolivian insurgent groups, seeking to overthrow the series of military juntas that had ruled Bolivia since 1964. Although the Southern Cone dictatorships are the most notorious of the authoritarian regimes during Latin America's Cold War, dictatorships first emerged in the landlocked countries of Paraguay (1959) and Bolivia (1964), helping establish a precedent of violent counterinsurgency that would proliferate across the region. Pepe eventually fled the repression in Bolivia and made his way to Santiago, where he met the Brazilian exile Onofre Pinto, a founder of the VPR.[1] Onofre gave Pepe a place to stay at a VPR safe house in Santiago, and because Pepe still had a valid passport, he was able to contribute to the VPR's cross-border operations. With press credentials and a set of camera equipment, Pepe posed as a photographer and made several trips to the Argentina-Brazil border, running messages and helping transfer militants. Prior to joining the armed underground in Bolivia, Pepe had served in the army, and with a basic level of military training—something that most other militants lacked—he became one of the VPR's bodyguards.

Of all my interview contacts, Pepe was among the most difficult to track down. He lives on his own in Santa Cruz, Bolivia, and his eyesight has worsened to the point that he can barely read. In terms of the logistics of making contact and planning an interview, Pepe was also an outlier; on the whole, technology was never a barrier for most of my interviewees, even for those in their seventies and eighties. But Pepe does not have an internet connection in his home and relies solely on a cellphone, with which he posts poetry on Facebook—after his younger decades as a political militant, Pepe spent much of his adulthood as a writer, including as the author of books on Indigenous groups in Bolivia.[2]

Given the nature of Aluízio's clandestine time in Argentina—having few contacts, moving secretly between various small towns—Pepe was one of the only consistent figures in Aluízio's life. As such, I hoped that an interview with him could help fill in my understanding of this period of Aluízio's biography. In some ways our conversations did provide context and a few new anecdotes, but my interviews with Pepe were most insightful not for their details about Aluízio but rather for his process of remembering these stories. If my biography project focuses primarily on the memory script of one person, it was always useful to be reminded that a person's life story is also comprised of a wide range of other people's parallel and overlapping memories. Compared to Aluízio, who has made the narration of his life a central practice of his political work, many people struggle to recall their past. Pepe helps illustrate this process.

When I first contacted Pepe, he received my messages warmly but warned me that he rarely does interviews anymore, in large part because he no longer trusts his memory. He agreed to speak with me on the condition that I send him a transcript of our conversations, so that he could see whether what he said was, in fact, what he meant to say. In one of our initial exchanges—a series of back-and-forth audio messages on WhatsApp—Pepe told me that "you are free to think whatever you want about me, I won't object to anything there, but I want to know if the words that you publish, if you do end up publishing them . . . actually represent what I told you. Sometimes I say things thinking they mean one thing, but they actually mean something else." Throughout my conversations with Pepe, this sense of uncertainty with his own stories became a steady theme, and he often spoke about his *desmemoria*, meaning bad memory or forgetfulness. He also seemed determined to give me the "correct" memory, telling me at one point that "in fiction it doesn't matter that every character sees the story in a different way, but in a testimony, maybe that is really important, and maybe that's what worries me so much."

Pepe shared with me, almost as real-time commentary, his own process of locating his memories. At times he used the language of a former revolutionary ("I must arm my memories") and at others like a poet, mentioning his desire to "find the thread" of his memories. In the end, two external items proved useful for reacquainting himself with his own stories: my questions, which I sent to him in advance, and his copy of Aluízio's memoir. With my questions, he said that the details they alluded to helped situate him in the particular moments and places of Aluízio's exile in the 1970s. And with Aluízio's book, it was not that he reread the memoir—his poor eyesight is a major obstacle—but that he skimmed his own highlights and margin notes from when he had read it fifteen years earlier. These nudges became a path back to his memories.

To make sure that I received the exact words and memories that he selected for me, most of my "interviews" with Pepe were epistolary. I would send him a question via WhatsApp, and he would write out his answer in longhand, in the style of a personal essay, and then he would record an audio message with him reading his answer out loud. As we had agreed, I would then transcribe his recording and send it back to him, hoping that my typed words were the same ones he had originally written himself. Having spent much of my research communicating with people whose memories were closer to the surface, my exchanges with Pepe were productive, if circuitous. Over the course of our messages and conversations, particularly after Pepe sent me his short essays, he seemed content to know that, when called to do so, he could find the path back to his memories.

CAMPO GRANDE

Pepe was the only person who knew Aluízio's exact location. By design, the VPR used a security system that decentralized information about its members. Aluízio was now more on his own than ever. With little more than the clothes in his day bag and a list of VPR contacts in the region, Aluízio set off to begin his work.

He spent the first few weeks in the Argentine borderlands acquainting himself with an area roughly 100 kilometers wide, between Campo Grande and Posadas. He visited the towns of Santo Encantado and Candelaria, meeting with the small handful of VPR contacts. Eventually he returned to Campo Grande, where he lived in the clinic of a Paraguayan doctor named Alderete, an exile fleeing the Stroessner dictatorship. Aluízio had come to the border region with some money from the VPR, which he spent renting a house in Posadas and helping Doctor Alderete buy a small tea farm on the outskirts of town.[3] Aluízio traveled the border region in an old jeep (also purchased with VPR money), coordinating furtive meetings with VPR members and visiting the rented house in Posadas.

In Aluízio's estimation, during his year conducting VPR work in Misiones (June 1972–July 1973), he helped six militants cross into Brazil, as well as several people who were already based in Brazil but came to Misiones to debrief with Aluízio, including Lauro Consentino and Vera Lucia Tezza, a married couple who worked as dentists in the western Paraná town of Medianeira—Lauro, like Aluízio and many other militants, would later write a memoir about his experience during the dictatorship.[4] Moving between the Alderete farm in Campo Grande and the rented house in Posadas, and with the help of intermediaries like Pepe, Aluízio used a careful system to communicate with militants on both sides of the border. This included placing fake classifieds in local newspapers that would announce the sale of poodle puppies. Interested buyers were told to meet at a certain time and place, whether in Foz do Iguaçu in Brazil or in Posadas in Argentina.[5] According to Pepe, the VPR also set up a small photography and printing laboratory in Posadas, which they used to make falsified immigration documents.[6]

The six militants Aluízio helped cross into Brazil were José Carlos Mendes, Vânia Alves da Silva (the sister of Jessie Jane Vieira de Souza, who had taken part in the failed 1970 hijacking of a Cruzeiro do Sul flight), João Roberto Castro

CHAPTER 7

de Pinho, an Argentine communist named Américo Árias, a young militant known as Mercado (to this day Aluízio does not know his real name), and Ubajara Silveira Roriz.[7] The efforts of the six militants did not bear fruit: the VPR never established guerrilla training bases in western Paraná, and while most militants were able to move clandestinely across borders with no consequences, Ubajara was eventually captured after returning to Brazil. In custody, the police tortured him severely.

The military's interrogation logs of Ubajara show a mixed result of the VPR's security measures.[8] He only knew of Aluízio by the codename "Lucho"—one of the few times that Aluízio appears to have used a codename other than André. As such, when police captured Ubajara they did not know the identity of his main contact. But Aluízio had apparently given Ubajara the details of his mother-in-law's house in Foz do Iguaçu, which, under torture, he divulged to the police. From this information, security agents eventually pieced together who "Lucho" likely was, and when they showed him a photo of Aluízio, Ubajara confirmed the identity of his contact across the border.

Ubajara's arrest and torture, and the relatively small number of militants that Aluízio helped cross the border, represented one of many obstacles confronting the VPR. My interview with José Carlos Mendes offers a window into what this moment felt like, both politically and emotionally. José Carlos had been a student leader in Curitiba, Paraná, and was drawn to the VPR's goal of using militants from Argentina, Paraguay, and Brazil to, in his words, "create massive agitation in the triple frontier era, [a big] armed struggle.... That was the seed of something much bigger that we dreamed might happen."[9] Like many former militants, with the benefit of hindsight José Carlos recalls this period with a tinge of embarrassment at the naivete of their efforts, and also a sense of being lucky to have survived: "Today, looking back, it's good that nothing happened. It would've been a disaster.... We all could have died. A lot of innocent people could have died."[10]

José Carlos credits Aluízio with keeping him alive during such a dangerous period. At the time, José Carlos was only twenty-one years old, making the thirty-year-old Aluízio seem like a seasoned veteran. What struck José Carlos about Aluízio was his ability to perceive potential threats and act quickly, all while projecting a calm demeanor. "We're not dead because of him," José Carlos said. "Because he had this awareness of danger, a feeling, if something was off. He keeps this peaceful face, a really calm face.... A face that's almost absentminded.... Aluízio only looks like a fool, but he's not a fool. He's really smart." The two men became very close in their short overlap as VPR militants; they gave each other playful nicknames from cartoons, with José Carlos calling

FIGURE 7.1. Aluízio on a tea plantation, ca. 1972. Courtesy of Aluízio Palmar.

Aluízio Peninha (the Portuguese translation of Fethry Duck, the very eccentric cousin of Donald Duck) and Aluízio calling his younger, more energetic comrade Pica-Pau (Woody Woodpecker). José Carlos told me that whenever the two of them were together, they "trusted each other like trapeze artists. You jump and you know for sure that his hand will be there to catch you. . . . He never made a mistake, if he set a meeting for this hour, on this day, in this place, he'll be there waiting, no matter what."[11] Years later, when they had both returned to Brazil and sought to rebuild their lives in a new political context, Aluízio became the godfather of José Carlos's daughter.

Although Aluízio's coordination with militants like José Carlos remained his priority in Misiones, he spent the bulk of his time on the tea farm purchased by Doctor Alderete. The plot of land was far from a main road and surrounded by a canopy of Atlantic rainforest, making it well-suited for the VPR's purposes. Under the guise of being the caretaker for Alderete's property, Aluízio moved to the farm, where he lived in a one-room wooden house (fig. 7.1). For most of the second half of 1972 he lived the life of a rural worker.

While maintaining his VPR duties in the region, Aluízio also undertook the backbreaking work of a rural peasant. On the Alderete farm, he kept the rows

CHAPTER 7

of bushes cleared of weeds and picked the tea leaves when they were ready to harvest. To give cover for his assumed identity as a peasant, he also worked on neighboring tea plantations. Often, this work entailed carrying heavy bags full of tea leaves—known as *ponchadas*—from the sorting machines in the fields to the pickup trucks parked several hundred meters away. Prior to leaving Chile, Aluízio had done some training on a farm owned by the VPR, but nothing could prepare him for the life of a peasant. "It was a really radical change," Aluízio told me. "Most of it was a lot of suffering, I was sad. I mean, I was the worker, I wasn't the boss. So the other planters, the farmers, they considered me a peon and I had to obey the boss's orders."[12] He described this manual work as some of the hardest of his life, with particularly dark memories of the heavy ponchadas: "Those immense bags on my back . . . I felt like wanting to die. But I had to do that work and when it was harvest time on the other farms, they would call on me to work. What else would I say? That I wasn't going to, because I had a headache? That I was lazy, wanting to sleep? No, I had to go. Here's the thing, Jake, I couldn't call attention to myself, I had to behave like any other peasant."

The toll of the physical labor made Aluízio feel even lonelier. Having gotten used to being surrounded by other militants in the various VPR houses in Santiago, life in Misiones was difficult. His main company was a neighboring farmer named Maúcho Duarte and his family. Several evenings a week, Aluízio would go to Maúcho's house to drink *chimarrão* tea on the porch: "I'd go over there, stay there for a bit, chatting. I didn't want to be all on my own."[13] In our interviews, Aluízio said that most nights, Maúcho would insist on having one of his three daughters—Alicia, Blanca, and Polaca—walk with him back to his farm, carrying a flashlight to guide them in the dark. Aluízio told me that he had to constantly decline invitations from the three women: "The girls invited me to dances, and I always said that I didn't want to go, that I had a headache, or that I had this that or the other. I was running out of excuses." As with his Facebook post about declining a young woman's advances on the eve of his departure for clandestine militancy, Aluízio again lets his audience know that, should he have wanted to, there were sexual adventures to be had. In his memoir, Aluízio frames this story in an even more evocative manner. While discussing the VPR's security measures, which precluded him from socializing with, let alone dating, locals, he wrote that "our concern for security reached such a point that the women near the farm began to doubt my masculinity."[14]

Normally, this type of memory—a retrospective anecdote tinged by heteronormative bluster—is difficult to corroborate. Yet there is video evidence of this story. In 2008, Aluízio and two other former VPR militants (Roberto de

Fortini and Ladislau Dowbor) returned to Campo Grande for the first time in over thirty years, and they arranged to meet with Alicia Duarte, who still lived near the Alderete farm. This was a few years after the publication of Aluízio's book, and he wanted to give a copy to his old neighbors in Argentina. One of the Brazilians in the group brought a camcorder, and Aluízio posted the resulting eighteen-minute video on YouTube.[15] The recording follows Aluízio as he is driven to Alicia's home, where he gets out of the car, wearing a black leather coat and a black paperboy cap, and receives a big hug from Alicia, who exclaims: "¡Brasileño de mierda, vino!" (You damned Brazilian, you came!). After several minutes of chatter about each other's families, Aluízio mentions the anecdote he had included in his book, about needing to turn down the Duarte women. "When I lived here, you all invited me to dances, but I didn't go." Aluízio says to Alicia. "You didn't think something was going on?" At first, Alicia replies that she knew he had a wife, because her sister Blanca had told her. Later, Aluízio brings the topic up again, and in a far more direct way: "You didn't think I was gay?" (As throughout much of the conversation, Aluízio is speaking in Spanish; his exact question was "¿Te desconfiabas que yo era marica?") Alicia's face grows stern, then with a wry smile she says, "Sí." Everyone laughs.

In addition to the sexualized banter about why Aluízio kept to himself in Campo Grande, the recording also sheds light on just how stressful it was for Aluízio to live on his own as a clandestine militant in exile. Using Aluízio's codename, which is how he was known in the Argentine borderlands, Alicia remarks that "my dad said that André slept on top of the jug, the water tower, out of fear. He slept up there because he was afraid. And he wouldn't go anywhere else [except to our house]. And we had to go and get him." Aluízio does not deny the story, and even adds that he often brought a gun with him to sleep on the tower. And using a Guarani word meaning "single" or "alone," Alicia jokes that at the time they were all "caraya," implying that nobody had much of a social life. Aluízio, too, says that he was caraya, sharing in the memories of an isolated experience.

Although not included in the video recording, the Brazilians also toured the old farm that had served as the VPR's base. As documented in photographs that Aluízio posted to his Facebook page, the three former militants walked around the old Alderete farm, which had changed very little over the years: the one-room house still remained, and they even found the VPR's abandoned jeep on the property, rusted from decades of exposure to the elements.[16] A photo shows Roberto and Ladislau sitting in the front seats, with Aluízio on the back of the open-bed car, smiling and holding an old rifle—a far cry from his days, almost

CHAPTER 7

forty years earlier, of gripping a weapon through the night while perched on top of a water tower, nervously keeping guard in the middle of a forest.

THE DISSOLUTION OF THE VPR

Aluízio's tense experience in Misiones reflected the broader state of the VPR. Based primarily outside of Brazil, the VPR made only halting progress toward its goal of rebuilding an armed insurgency in Brazil. What the militants did not know was that beginning in 1972, key decisions within the VPR were being made by the double agent known as Cabo Anselmo, who had infiltrated the group and assumed a leadership role. Similar to the type of trap that soon killed the militants in the Paraná borderlands—whose bodies Aluízio would devote much of his adult life to finding—Cabo Anselmo led a separate group of VPR militants to their deaths in January 1973. In a macabre twist, both fateful traps involved the exact same number of militants (six) and both lured their victims with the same pretext of creating a secret guerrilla base of operations. The deception by Cabo Anselmo took place in the northeastern state of Pernambuco and came to be known as the São Bento massacre, after the nearby farm where the young revolutionaries were captured and tortured to death by Brazilian security forces. Among the six was Soledad Barrett Viedma, who was five months pregnant at the time.[17]

As news of the São Bento massacre and Cabo Anselmo's deception spread among militants in Brazil and abroad, members of the VPR realized that the group might have reached its end. A meeting was called for July 1973, to be held in a small Chilean town of Talagante, just south of Santiago. Having spent more than a year in the Argentine frontier, Aluízio prepared for a lengthy bus trip to Chile. Despite the stressful circumstances—uncertainty about the VPR and the dangers of traveling with falsified documents—Aluízio was happy to leave Misiones, even if just briefly. Aluízio recalled that after the final of several police control stations along the route, none of which raised any flags on the clandestine Brazilian, "for the first time, in many months, I felt so light, so relaxed."[18] It felt so good, in fact, that as the bus crossed the border into Chile, he found himself singing the chorus to the famous Chilean song, "Si vas para Chile":

If you go to Chile	Si vas para Chile
I beg you to pass	Te ruego que pases
Where my beloved lives.	Por donde vive mi amada.

It's a little house	Es una casita
Very cute and small	Muy linda y chiquita
That is on the side	Que está en la falda
Of a nestled hill.	De un cerro enclavada.

Aluízio's joy upon leaving Argentina was short-lived. Even if he had assumed that the VPR would likely vote to disband at the meeting, it was not a pleasant experience dissolving the group that he had spent several years helping build—and for which he had chosen to be away from his family. In his memoir, Aluízio wrote in a cursory and almost detached manner about the meeting, noting that "it was short. There was no overview and no political positions were discussed, there were only administrative issues on the agenda."[19] When I pressed him for more details on the meeting, he opened up, telling me about how they discussed the infiltration of Cabo Anselmo and the deaths of their comrades in Pernambuco: "There wasn't anything left. Those who died, were dead, and who wasn't dead was in exile. So, what was left?"[20] Aluízio told me that after collectively voting to end the VPR, the general takeaway was "cada um cuidava de si" (everyone for themselves), meaning that each member could decide whether or not to continue clandestine political work. The group divided the remaining money in the VPR coffers—in Aluízio's estimation, the group at that point had US$200,000, of which he received about US$25,000, the equivalent of nearly US$160,000 today.[21] With more money on hand than most militants had ever possessed, but facing an uncertain future, everyone went their separate ways.

With the VPR now defunct, Aluízio was not sure what to do or where to go. The first step was to leave Chile, and he took a bus to Buenos Aires. As he later told the journalist Juliana Machado, he scanned the headlines at a newsstand in Buenos Aires and became frightened by what seemed to be escalating political repression in Argentina and across the Southern Cone—1973 was also the year when Argentina's minister of social welfare, José López Rega, established a right-wing death squad called the Argentine Anticommunist Alliance (AAA, Alianza Anticomunista Argentina), ushering in a three-year period under the Peronist governments that brought 1,500 political murders, nearly 1,000 disappearances, and over 5,000 political prisoners.[22] So even though Argentina's military would not officially seize power until 1976, the scale of repression under Argentina's democratically elected governments was beginning to surpass that of Brazil's dictatorship. Aluízio felt the specter of authoritarian

CHAPTER 7

violence closing in on him. "Looking at those newspapers, I kept thinking, 'My God, I was stuck!'" Aluízio recalled. "I can't go back to Santiago, I can't go to Europe because I don't have any documents, I can't go back to Brazil. What am I going to do with my life?"[23]

Ultimately, Aluízio chose to go back to northeastern Argentina, where Eunice and Florita were just across the border in Foz do Iguaçu. After returning to Posadas, Aluízio got in touch with Américo Árias, the Argentine communist in Posadas, whom he asked to help retrieve his family in Foz do Iguaçu.[24] Aluízio gave instructions about how to contact Eunice: Américo should book a room in the Hotel Normandie, where Eunice's mother worked, and pass on the message that Aluízio was still alive, and that he would like his wife and daughter to reunite with him in Argentina. Américo agreed to help and followed Aluízio's plan. Once contact and details were arranged, Américo crossed the border to Foz do Iguaçu and traveled with Eunice and Florita back to Posadas. Aluízio's family arrived in Argentina in August 1973, and they would stay for six years.

One month after Aluízio's family settled in Argentina, his attention was abruptly thrust back to Chile. On September 11, 1973, General Augusto Pinochet led a coup that overthrew Salvador Allende and established a dictatorship that would oversee a sixteen-year reign of repression that killed at least 3,000 people and forced over 200,000 into exile. Although Aluízio had left Chile a year and a half before the military seized power, scores of Brazilian exiles had remained in Santiago. In the early days after the coup, foreigners became a key target of the military's massive detention sweeps. Because many Latin Americans living in Chile were political exiles, like the seventy Brazilians who had arrived in early 1971, the Pinochet regime considered them particularly subversive, as known dissidents and as symbolic benefactors of the Allende government. The military encouraged Chileans to turn in their neighbors, placing ads in newspapers that called on people to report Allende sympathizers—especially foreigners.[25] By one estimate, eighty-nine Brazilians were among the several thousand people imprisoned by the military in the Estadio Nacional, Chile's main soccer stadium that was turned into a detention and torture encampment, and several dozen more Brazilians were detained in other facilities in Santiago and elsewhere in the country.[26] Five Brazilians died at the hands of Chilean security forces: Jane Vanini (a militant in the ALN), Luiz Carlos de Almeida and Nelson de Souza Kohl (both in the POC), Túlio Roberto Cardoso Quintiliano (of the PCBR), and Wânio José de Matos (a comrade of Aluízio's in the VPR).[27]

Even for the Brazilian militants lucky enough to escape Pinochet's web, the period after September 1973 brought new challenges. All the exiles had to quickly leave Chile. As José Carlos Mendes told me, "There was a mass exodus, nobody knew about anybody else. Pretty soon everyone was getting in touch with their contacts in Europe, in Mexico."[28] José Carlos, for his part, secured travel to the Netherlands, where he stayed for several years. But he had no idea what happened to his good friend in the VPR—"Nobody knew where Aluízio was. Probably dead."[29]

Paired with the recent dissolution of the VPR and the growing violence in Argentina, the coup in Chile shook Aluízio's sense of self and security. With the shadow of dictatorship steadily moving across the Southern Cone—Paraguay, Bolivia, Brazil, Uruguay, and now Chile—and with Aluízio living just across the border from the Brazilian authorities who had initially captured and tortured him, he spent the final months of 1973 taking stock of his situation. The end of the VPR meant that for the first time since he joined the Brazilian Communist Party a decade earlier, Aluízio did not belong to a political organization. And in a regional climate of unrest and persecution, he was unsure whether it was wise to pursue political work of any kind. Having arranged for Eunice and Florita to join him in exile, his most immediate concern was how to support his newly arrived family.

With some of the distributed VPR money, Aluízio rented a house in Posadas on Avenida Santa Catalina. Still in possession of the VPR's camera equipment and printing press, he tried to find work as a commercial photographer and then as a printer. Neither effort proved successful. Eventually, he teamed up with Américo Arias to buy a truck and work as grain wholesalers, buying large sacks of wheat and beans, which they bought in bulk and then sold in smaller parcels to local merchants. Aluízio did not particularly enjoy the work, but it made a bit of money and, importantly for a militant with nothing to do, it kept him busy: "I couldn't just stay snoozing all day, I had to have some kind of activity."[30] As a clandestine exile, working openly in business was risky, and to the extent possible, Aluízio tried to keep a low profile, adopting the name of André Ferreira—his militant codename plus his actual middle name. Because neither Aluízio, Eunice, nor Florita had legal paperwork to live in Argentina, he used the printing equipment to make forged travel stamps every three months, to give the impression that the family transited back and forth routinely and were not permanent residents abroad.

A CLOSE CALL IN BUENOS AIRES

Although Aluízio had paused most of his political work, he occasionally met with contacts. Some of these meetings took place in the border region, and

CHAPTER 7

others much farther away, an effort to keep security forces unaware of his presence along the frontier. One of these trips proved to be among the most consequential of Aluízio's life—not only for what nearly happened at the time but even more so for what it came to represent afterward, becoming the crux of his memory script and his human rights activism in the twenty-first century.

In January 1974, Aluízio went to Buenos Aires to meet with João Roberto Castro de Pinho, one of the six VPRs militants Aluízio had helped sneak across the border. The two were meant to discuss what, if anything, João Roberto should be doing in western Paraná now that the VPR had ended. Aluízio was only in town for a few days, and except for a planned meeting that evening with João Roberto, he had no intention of seeing anyone. But while walking on the sidewalk of Avenida Corrientes, Aluízio spotted Alberi Vieira dos Santos, a fellow Brazilian he had last seen in 1969, when they were both detained in the Ahú prison in Paraná.

The encounter with Alberi stands as one of the most important stories in Aluízio's memory script. It places him at an almost fated crossroads of revolutionary militancy and violent repression, and it serves as an origin story for his eventual human rights work. With no other sources to shed light on why Aluízio reacted as he did upon seeing Alberi, it is not possible to determine how much of his memory was shaped by his retrospective knowledge of what Alberi had become. And as with other parts of Aluízio's memory script, especially those relating to high-stress and potentially dangerous moments, certain details remain fuzzy. All the same, his account of what took place is central to how he narrates his life trajectory.

As described in his memoir and in multiple interviews, Aluízio was unnerved to see Alberi in Buenos Aires. And Alberi was not alone—he was chatting with Onofre Pinto, one of the founders of the VPR, whom Aluízio had not had contact with since the VPR's dissolution. Rather than feeling relief or excitement at spotting the two militants together, Aluízio felt worried; as he recalled to me, "My alarm bells went off and I stopped dead in my tracks."[31] Living in exile had left Aluízio permanently on edge, and he ducked into a café to avoid being seen. But Alberi had apparently spotted Aluízio from across the street and followed him into the café. Onofre went elsewhere. While Aluízio stood at the counter, Alberi came up beside him, grabbed his arm, and told him about a plan for sneaking back into Brazil to stage an uprising.[32] Alberi said that he knew Aluízio was organizing secret groups along the border, and that they should combine forces. Aluízio grew increasingly suspicious. How did Alberi know about his activities, and why was he discussing them so openly in the middle of a café? Trying to maintain his composure, Aluízio said that he was interested and suggested they meet later that night to discuss further. Alberi agreed.

Aluízio then left the café, walked to the bus station, and fled Buenos Aires on a series of late-night buses. His instincts in that moment likely saved his life. A few months later, Alberi led a group of six militants across the border: five Brazilian exiles, including Onofre Pinto, and a nineteen-year-old Argentine student. All six disappeared and Aluízio would spend several decades searching for their bodies.

The chance encounter with Alberi made Aluízio increasingly afraid of being captured. In one of the few moments from our interviews when he used the word "trauma" to describe his emotions, he told me that in the aftermath of seeing Alberi in Buenos Aires, he entered a period of "extreme isolation, total isolation. The type of isolation that left lots of traumas, so much trauma."[33] Unable to connect with his political comrades, and unsure of how to navigate exile with a wife and young daughter, Aluízio felt lost: "I didn't have contact with anyone, I didn't know who was alive. I didn't know if my dad was still alive, or my mother. I didn't know anything and they also didn't know about me. Because there were two problems. One was my militancy, with my friends and comrades, and the other was the question of family. Eunice didn't have any news from her family, her mother, her sisters, she didn't know anything. My daughter didn't know who her grandmother was, or her grandfather. We were in the most severe clandestinity. I don't think anyone had a clandestinity like mine."

MEMORY VIGNETTE: FLORITA

But Aluízio was not the only person living with his choices. Eunice and their daughter Florita remained with him almost every step of the way. Because Eunice does not discuss these matters with people outside of her circle of family and friends, my understanding of her experience, and of the family more broadly, came largely from her children.

Florita's memories, as the eldest daughter, are especially insightful. While living in Posadas at the age of four, Florita was with her father on a permanent basis for the first time. This new life in Argentina was complicated. In many ways, she recalls this period fondly, cherishing the period when it was just the three of them, before her siblings were born in the coming years. "It was a playful time," Florita told me. "There were a lot of games. With Dad at home with his photography. I remember it being a one-room house, a photographer's studio really, very small. It was humble, but we played a lot."[34] Her memories of Posadas are also tinged by the impact that moving to Argentina had on her mother. Florita recalls her mother crying a lot: "My first memory was just me and my mom in a house.... The memory I have is of my mom crying, always out of fear. I have this very strong memory, even in therapy I always remember the feeling of her sadness."[35]

As with almost all my interviews, I sent Florita a set of questions in advance. After several back-and-forth messages on WhatsApp, during which she asked about my interest in her father's story, how old I was, and why I had decided to study Brazil, she agreed to the interview. Though she warned me that "my memories are about my childhood and adolescence and they are not romanticized."[36] I then sent her a list of thirteen questions, covering a range of topics related to her upbringing in Brazil and abroad, her memories of her parents, and her feelings about growing up as a Brazilian in a foreign country. Rather than hearing back from Florita, I received a WhatsApp message from Aluízio: "I'd like to know what questions you asked Florita. She has really strong traumas. She says that she was abandoned as a child, that my militancy deprived her of a lot of things. Your questions triggered her and yesterday she came here crying about all these problems of her childhood."[37]

I was not sure how to proceed. This was not the first challenge of the collaborative biography, but previous issues had related to my interactions with Aluízio. Now, it felt as though the third wall of research had been breached, with Aluízio, my primary subject, wanting to know about my interviews with other people whose memories would feature in the book. Given that Aluízio was the one who had given me Florita's phone number—which he did for all his children—I assumed that he had no major qualms with my talking to her. To my mind, none of my questions to Florita were problematic, and I reasoned that this was a good moment for Aluízio to continue seeing the type of analysis that I would bring to the project: not simply curating his stories and corroborating them with archival evidence, but bringing in other people's memories to make larger observations about his life and his process of self-narration. I decided to send Aluízio the questions. He never replied to them or mentioned them in any form, at least not to me.

My worries then shifted to Florita. After sending her the questions, I received no reply. After six weeks of silence, I sent her a brief message, asking if she was still willing to schedule a time to talk. Three days later, she left me a string of recorded voice messages, apologizing for the delayed response and recounting what had happened after initially getting my list of questions: "That day, I went really angry to my mom's house, it was a terrible family argument. I didn't even want to see my dad's face. I didn't want to. I wanted to talk to my mom, I wanted to know why... I just wanted to talk. You need to understand, Jake, today I can talk to you calmly, but it took me a long time, because it was a lot.... I said, 'Mom, do you have any idea what was going on in my head?'"[38]

Over the coming days, we exchanged more voice messages and eventually scheduled an interview. At several points in our conversation, she brought up the argument with her parents from six weeks earlier, especially as it related to the period when she lived in Brazil with her grandparents, while her mother was in Chile with Aluízio: "I yelled so much at her, it was like I threw up in her face. I was so rude to her, saying, 'You abandoned your daughter to be with a man, and you weren't even a militant.'... But I understand, it was just anger that I had, of imagining myself, a hurt child waiting for her mom to come back.... She wasn't a militant, my mom was in love in my dad, that's it. She did everything out of love for my dad."[39]

Florita, fifty-two years old at the time of our interview, was proud of her ability to process her emotions and her memories, a skill that had only come later in life, and, in her view, thanks to her time in therapy. Our conversation flowed freely and without tension, as she shared stories from what seemed like a difficult childhood. These memories ranged from her sense of identity (she never felt Brazilian nor Argentinian) to her confusion about why she never saw her extended family—she received occasional letters from her "aunts" and "grandma" in Brazil, only to find out later that her mother had written them. Many of her stories circled back to her mother, whom Florita described as always nervous and on edge: "I have memories of my mom at a sewing machine, one of those machines that make noise. And I slept with my siblings in another room... and [through the wall] I heard the noise of that machine and I felt, I don't know if this makes sense, that when it was very fast, I imagined that my mom was nervous. And when it was a little slower, she was sad. I stayed up until dawn, because my mom would be on the machine all night."

FURTHER ISOLATED IN EXILE

Aluízio lived with his family in Posadas for over a year, from July 1973 to August 1974. Throughout this time, he never felt comfortable, always fearful that Brazilian security forces would find him so close to the border. Seeking to put more distance between him and Brazil, Aluízio decided to leave Posadas and move to Resistencia, a small city in the Chaco province, 300 kilometers to the west. Aluízio had previously visited Resistencia, and the city left a decent enough impression on him.[40] With no obvious alternative, he, Eunice, and Florita moved to Resistencia. In his memoir, Aluízio describes his arrival in the Chaco as a form of existential crisis. "I cried on the night that we moved to Resistencia," Aluízio wrote. "I felt trapped in a situation that was completely different from what I had imagined for myself. . . . I was no longer a militant revolutionary at the center of major events, in the middle of intense political agitation. That new phase of my exile was a rupture, the uprooting of an entire universe that had given meaning to my life."[41]

With the remaining money that had been distributed to him by the VPR, Aluízio bought a small soda factory in a neighborhood called Villa Libertad. At this stage in his clandestine exile, Aluízio was using a fake identification card that allowed him to maintain a bank account, paying for large purchases like the soda business.[42] The factory included several gasification tanks, a bottling machine, two Ford-29 trucks, a cart, a buggy, and two mules. Aluízio bought the factory from an older man called Don Blanco.[43] The soda factory was adjacent to a house, also owned by Don Blanco, which Aluízio purchased. Aluízio kept the business's existing client base, and with three employees, he oversaw the production of various flavored sodas, which would get bottled and loaded onto the trucks and the mule-drawn buggy and delivered across town. In addition to soda, which was made in-house, they also sold beer and wine, purchased at a distributor and sold to clients in Resistencia. Although Aluízio had previously worked as a grain wholesaler in Posadas, running a small factory felt like an entirely new experience, especially for somebody whose identity had always been wrapped up in political work: "The failure of my political and personal project forced me to play a new role. Now, I was a merchant."[44] The pretense of that idea—playing a role—weighed on Aluízio in the coming years, as he often felt pressure to ignore what felt like his true self in order to put on a performance in exile.

Life in Resistencia was not all bad. It was where he and Eunice had two more children: Andréa, born in February 1975, and Alexandre, born in January 1976. And despite being entirely cut off from family back in Brazil, they became friends with some of their neighbors, above all with Don Blanco. Together with their families—Don Blanco and his wife María also had three children—the neighbors would have churrasco barbecues, drink wine, and play soccer in the open field that conjoined their two properties.[45] Aluízio has fond memories of joining the Blancos for meals of a *chaqueño* dish called *locro*, a meat and corn stew. As Aluízio wrote in his memoir, "Aside from the isolation, we were able to have some nice moments during our time in the Chaco."[46]

I interviewed one of Don Blanco's daughters, María Mercedes, known by her nickname Chona. Twenty-five years old at the time of Aluízio's arrival in Resistencia, Chona recalls being struck by the humility of these strange new

Brazilian neighbors. "Here comes this man, blond, tall, handsome . . . and my father says, 'Will you stay and join us for dinner?' [And Aluízio says,] 'Yes, yes, yes, of course.' And that was the key to winning the affection of my parents. . . . He won over their hearts with his humility, his simplicity, he was good. . . . Aluízio and his wife, too, they lived here a long time, and they never changed. He was always good."[47] Chona laughed a lot when sharing her memories of Aluízio, whom she often called Don Ferreira, including when I asked about his appearance at the time. Rather than answer my question about what kind of clothes he wore, she again brought up his good looks: "His eyes were so blue that they looked like headlights. A handsome man, let's call it what it is. A handsome man, and he still is, even at his age now." The two families became very close. "We shared many experiences, many meals, many lunches, many dinners, many nice things," Chona told me. "Many difficult things too. We shared life. Afterward we missed them so much. . . . When they went back, we missed them so much."

Despite the close bonds with the Blancos, Aluízio and his family had to maintain their false identities and keep secret the true nature of their stay in Resistencia. Perhaps because he became good friends with the Blancos, Aluízio spoke with bitterness when telling me about having to lie to them to maintain his family's cover in exile: "We were totally isolated from everything and had to make up stories, inventing and living a lie. Living a lie, lying to people you know. People would ask where you're from, who's your father, his name. And you'd have to lie, with a straight face. That was tough, that was really tough."[48]

Especially in his initial years in the Chaco, Aluízio struggled to stay wholly committed to his role as a merchant. Even though the VPR had dissolved, and even in the aftermath of the coup in Chile, Aluízio proved unable to abandon politics entirely. While living a supposedly isolated and clandestine life, Aluízio conducted political work on behalf of the ERP, the Argentine guerrilla group. The ERP had been formed in 1969 to fight against the military regime of Juan Carlos Onganía, kidnapping government and business leaders, robbing banks, and killing policemen and soldiers.[49] The ERP remained active even after the 1973 return to civilian rule. Under the presidency of Juan Domingo Perón, the ERP shifted its focus from urban operations to a rural campaign. Perón died on July 1, 1974—the same month that Aluízio moved to Resistencia—and his wife, Isabel, assumed office and oversaw an even more violent crackdown, often through the AAA death squad. In response, militant groups like the ERP accelerated their own actions.

Aluízio had met a few ERP militants during his days in the VPR, and now that he was settled in the Chaco province, his contacts in the ERP asked him to gather intelligence in the region. Under the cover of his soda distribution company, Aluízio traveled the region to take photographs of government sites like police and army barracks, and prisons where militants were reportedly being detained. Aluízio would develop the photographs and prepare a written report that he delivered periodically to Buenos Aires.[50] When I asked if Eunice knew about his political work, Aluízio told me that she probably had a sense that he was doing something, but he never told her.

A sequence of events in 1976 finally pushed Aluízio to abandon his political work—a move that helped protect him and his family but which left him depressed, drinking heavily, and feeling more isolated than ever. First, on March 24, the Argentine military staged a coup that overthrew Isabel Perón, and the resulting junta killed as many as 30,000 people during a six-year period. Even in the perverse exercise of comparing which Southern Cone dictatorship was "worst," the staggering scale of violence in Argentina makes it stand out. At one point during our interviews, Aluízio sent me a WhatsApp message recalling his terror at the news emanating outward from Buenos Aires: "There were announcements on the radio for foreigners to come forward. Neighbors and businessmen friends of mine asked if I had already presented myself to the police. It was suffocating. I had a feeling that at any moment Eunice and I would be arrested. I was really afraid. I knew that the government was killing and disappearing people, even children."[51] Yet this fear did not seem to dissuade Aluízio from his political work, at least not yet. For much of 1976, against a backdrop of an increasingly violent dictatorship, he maintained his collaborations with the ERP.

But toward the end of 1976, a second event pushed Aluízio to give up his politics.[52] At some point between October and December—Aluízio could not remember the exact date—he was set to travel from Resistencia to Buenos Aires, to deliver some of his surveillance reports to the ERP. At the airport in Resistencia, Aluízio was waiting near the departure gate with his ERP contact, Marcos Antonio Álvarez, when a wave of police began asking to see the ID cards of all passengers. Aluízio grabbed the bag of documents from Marcos and ducked into a nearby bathroom, where he went into a stall and tried to flush the papers down the toilet. But the documents kept coming back up. After several attempts, Aluízio abandoned the material and went back to the gate. He told Marcos to get on the flight without him and without the materials for the ERP. In his telling, Aluízio was able to leave the airport without being stopped by the police, and he went straight home.

In his memoir, Aluízio describes his shock the following day, when he saw articles in the local press announcing the discovery at the airport of subversive material from Brazilian militants.⁵³ Aluízio was simultaneously scared and angry at himself: "I made a mea culpa and I stopped all contact with the Argentine guerrillas. Because of an irresponsible attitude, I almost put my family's life at risk." Seeking to destroy the evidence of his political activity, Aluízio threw his typewriter into a nearby river—he had been using a Brazilian typewriter with the Portuguese cedilla (ç), which he assumed was how the police knew that the documents from the airport had been written by a Portuguese speaker. As he told me with an increasingly fevered sound in his voice, after getting rid of the typewriter he burned his books, he burned his music records, he burned the remaining surveillance documents he had compiled, he smashed his camera equipment, and he gathered all the ashes and broken pieces of plastic and metal and buried everything in the back of his garden.⁵⁴

Thus began the most difficult period of Aluízio's time in exile, from late 1976 through the middle of 1979. Aluízio's description of feeling trapped in Resistencia merits a lengthy quotation. It reflects not only his circumstances at the time but also how he would come to frame his own history in relation to the exile of other militants:

> We stayed there, we stayed there in Resistencia. Trying to go back to Chile, that wouldn't work. . . . So we were stuck, we couldn't go back to Brazil. . . . Me with a precarious document, I didn't have a passport, Eunice without any document. I couldn't leave Argentina, I was stuck in Argentina, right? . . . I couldn't travel to Europe, or the United States, or Central America, anywhere. I was stuck in Argentina. . . . Because my friends and companions who were in Chile, they left. Some went to Panama, others went to Cuba, others went to Mexico, others to France, others to Sweden, Germany. Everyone left and I was there alone, isolated. You understand? I was completely isolated, from the family, from my father, from my mother, from my brothers, they didn't know where I was. Nobody knew where I was. Eunice was also isolated, we were all isolated, it was like we were inside a bubble. Trapped, isolated, completely isolated, isolated from everything. We cut all ties, everything that connected me to the movement, to the Brazilian resistance, everything that connected me to family, friends, everything was gone. . . . Nobody knew who I really was. Sometimes, if I drank a little wine, I would start talking about politics, but Eunice wouldn't let me talk politics. She would kick me, hit me under the table like that so I would stop. . . . I should've gone [overseas] because somebody would've helped me, some kind of help would come from Europe. I don't know if it was

from Italy or France, help would come for me. But [at the time], I thought that I shouldn't go."⁵⁵

From 1977 through 1979, as the military junta took violent root across Argentina, Aluízio tried his best to lay low. He stopped buying newspapers, and reading books, and listening to music, and devoted himself to the soda business and to keeping up appearances with neighbors. He had to force himself to tune out rumors of the ongoing repression in Argentina, Brazil, and Chile. Aluízio admitted to me that he drank a lot during this period: "Sometimes I would get home very late at night and I would stay up drinking, this type of fermented drink, really strong, that they have in Argentina. Almost like vodka. . . . It was really difficult to completely change myself and to not have any access to news, or anything political at all. A radical change."⁵⁶ His desire to return to politics was constantly outweighed by his worries about his wife and children:

> My situation was really difficult. If I was captured, I would be killed in Argentina or in Brazil. I wouldn't survive. But the problem was even more serious, because I was getting my family involved, three kids and a wife. . . . So much responsibility. At any moment a tragedy could happen. It would be one tragedy among the 30,000 tragedies from Argentina. . . . What happened in Argentina was a genocide, and I barely escaped. I only escaped because I decided to blend in, me and my family, into the population. Like I was a chameleon. . . . So for two years it was just survive. Survive.⁵⁷

Aluízio's daughters told me several stories that indicated the stress of these final years in exile. Similar to her father's sense of being stuck in Argentina, Florita felt trapped in her neighborhood: "We weren't allowed to leave the neighborhood. We were all blonde, in an area where everyone else was *moreno*, I didn't know how to speak Portuguese—my parents didn't teach me—and school was just on the other side of our house, so I had no freedom at all."⁵⁸ Once, Florita ran away, taking a local bus to the center of town, where a neighbor happened to recognize her and bring her home. Florita told me that when she returned, her mom wanted to hit her as punishment, but her dad intervened. In hindsight, she understands how terrifying it must have been for her parents: "Nowadays my mom will tell me, 'Imagine having a daughter in that situation, you disappeared and what if I had to go to the police?'" The dual fear of a missing daughter, and an inability to report it to the police, caused what Aluízio described as a "major merda" (shit fest)—"We felt like throwing up, pissing ourselves, shitting ourselves, we were so panicked."[59] Aluízio also told me a detail about Florita running away that showed just how starved she was for family: she had left her parents a note, written in Spanish, saying that she was leaving to go live instead with her *abuelita*, her grandmother.[60]

Andrea was six years younger than Florita but still old enough to retain memories from the final years in Resistencia. She remembers the confusion of being torn between two identities, living her life as an Argentinian but also knowing that somehow, she was Brazilian, too: "I felt entirely Argentinian. . . . And I guess because we were clandestine, we couldn't exactly take pride in our Brazilian roots."[61] Andrea also shared one of her earliest memories, about her parents' reaction to seeing on the news that the authorities were searching for her father. It is difficult to know if such a report had indeed aired on television, or whether the memory blends the details of her stressed home life with knowledge that she would gain later. Either way, the memory reflects a young child's frightened state: "What really stuck with me the most was the day my dad broke the television at home. . . . [On TV] they were announcing the search for my dad, and I remember him and my mom being really nervous. We were all in the living room, and broken glass and the pieces of the TV were everywhere. There was a silence that echoed, until my dad said, 'I already said that we should stop watching TV at home.'"

For Aluízio, these years were defined by a constant fear of being discovered. One event stands out in his memories, even more frightening perhaps than when he had almost been caught with the ERP materials at the airport. As detailed in his memoir and in our conversations, one day the Argentine police came to his house, in what seemed like a sweep of the entire neighborhood. "Holy shit," he told me. "They entered through the courtyard, with a truck, jeeps, and those German dogs, those big dogs."[62] In his memoir, he recalled that a helicopter circled above.[63] Aluízio snuck out the back, hoping to stay out of sight. The police knocked on the door and told Eunice to show them the family's identification papers. They also asked where her husband was, the one who ran the soda business. In nearly perfect Spanish, Eunice said that her husband André had gone to the bank, and that he had taken all their documents with him. Stalling for time, Eunice invited the police inside and offered them some sodas to drink. While in the kitchen, Eunice pinched her children really hard, which had the intended effect of making them cry. With a chorus of three wailing kids echoing in the house, the police seemed to lose patience. Along with causing a commotion with her children, Eunice had also prayed to Nuestra Señora de Itatí, a Catholic figure venerated in northern Argentina, asking for divine intervention to make the police go away.[64] The crying and the prayers worked, and the police soon left. When the coast was clear, Aluízio returned. In his memoir, he wrote that he found his Eunice "shaking like a leaf in the wind."[65]

The memories of that near-miss never left him. Similar to how he broke down emotionally when telling me about Eunice's initial arrival in exile—his WhatsApp message about feeling like an animal licking its wounds—he sent me the following text about Eunice's encounter with the Argentine police: "To this day, I cringe when I remember these things. I have unresolved trauma."[66] With no end in sight to Argentina's violent dictatorship, the longer that Aluízio stayed in Resistencia, the more he feared for him and his family. Despite the military's continued rule in Brazil, Aluízio could not help but think that perhaps returning to his home country, even if risky, might be the lesser of two evils.

HOME AGAIN

By early 1979, changes seemed to be taking place in Brazil. Human rights activists had made huge strides in calling global attention to the violence of military rule, and toward the end of the decade a wave of student and labor strikes helped build opposition to the dictatorship. In late 1978, at end of the presidency of Ernesto Geisel, the government allowed Institutional Act No. 5 to expire, ending the regime's most authoritarian policy. For much of the decade, momentum grew for an amnesty law that would allow exiles to return and for persecuted politicians to regain their rights. An amnesty law would not be passed until August 1979, but the movement for an amnesty bill helped change the calculus for people like Aluízio, who asked themselves whether it was finally time to return to Brazil.

The logistics of going home were not simple. Because he and his family were living in Argentina with false documents, crossing the border would be complicated—to say nothing of the fact that Aluízio was still banned from returning to Brazil. In early 1979, Aluízio enlisted the help of a trusted neighbor who traveled to Foz do Iguaçu to meet Eunice's mother, Flora, and travel with her back to Resistencia.[67] Eunice had not seen her mother in nearly five years, and it was the first time that Andrea and Alexandre had met their grandmother. Over the course of a few more visits to Resistencia, Flora helped coordinate a plan for Aluízio and his family to sneak back: one of Eunice's sisters, Arlete, worked for the Receita Federal (Brazil's customs agency), and she would wait for them at a border checkpoint and allow them to cross into Brazil.

In the early months of 1979, while planning their return, Aluízio received several bits of promising news. At one point, Eunice's brother-in-law Eloy

(Arlete's husband) visited Resistencia and brought a message from a lawyer in Rio de Janeiro, explaining that Aluízio's banishment from Brazil had been revoked several months earlier. In December 1978, President Geisel signed a law rescinding the banishment of over 120 political exiles. The one condition, however, was that the exiles would have to present themselves to the police upon arrival.[68] Perversely, and perhaps in a sign of the regime's disorganization, nearly a dozen names on the list of people allowed to return were ones whom the military had already disappeared, including five of the six militants who had fallen into Alberi's trap in 1974. The requirement of presenting himself to the authorities scared Aluízio too much—he did not trust the government—but the official revocation of his banishment felt like an important step.

A court decision in late March drew Aluízio's attention even more back to Brazil. In a case relating to several former MR-8 militants, a judge in the First District Naval Court annulled both of Aluízio's standing judgements. In Aluízio's case, a public defender argued the illegality of Aluízio's having been tried in two different military courts for essentially the same set of accusations—the reason that he had "ping-ponged" back and forth between the army prisons in Curitiba and those of the navy in Rio de Janeiro. Judges on the court's permanent council found this argument convincing and decreed unanimously that Aluízio's prior sentencing should be overturned. Several of Brazil's largest newspapers reported on the verdict.[69]

Media coverage also focused on a somewhat morbid plot twist—Aluízio was not dead. Previously, his name had appeared on a list of "dead and disappeared" compiled by the Committee for Amnesty in Brazil (Comitê Brasileiro pela Anistia), and a general presumption had grown that the military had killed Aluízio. Even his lawyer noted the various stories about Aluízio being dead. An article in *Folha de São Paulo* ran under the title of "Dead Former Banished [Prisoner] Absolved in Rio."[70] Rumors of Aluízio's death had also spread among his friends—two of whom, Umberto Trigueiros Lima and Lauro Consentino, named their sons André in homage to their supposedly fallen comrade.[71]

When the news of the court verdict eventually made its way to Aluízio—via his family's visits to Resistencia—he was relieved in many ways but also anxious about what it might imply. As he wrote on Facebook decades later, Aluízio worried that the widespread news coverage of the verdict could nudge him or his family members to let down their guard, "thus opening cracks, leaving clues for the regime to find me."[72] In this climate, the family had to maintain their clandestinity while also organizing a secret return to Brazil.

Aluízio tried to sell his soda business, but he could not find a buyer in the short time before needing to leave Resistencia. So he gave it back to the Blanco family. Chona confirmed this story, telling me that one day Aluízio said that they were returning to Brazil, and that he wanted to leave them the business and the house: "He left us ev-er-y-thing! He left us the deed to the house, the documents for the trucks, he just gave it all."[73] Chona and her husband, Julio, moved into the house, where she lives to this day.

On a prearranged day in May, Eunice's brother-in-law Eloy arrived early in the morning, and Aluízio told his kids to pack only a few belongings. In Florita's memory, they could only bring what they could carry in their arms—they also had to leave their dog behind.[74] Andrea, four years old at the time, told me that her parents only announced that they were leaving on the day of the departure: "In less than an hour, we left all our things behind. I cried because I couldn't say goodbye to my friend Pili."[75]

The whole family drove together, crammed into Eloy's Ford Falcon, with Aluízio, Eunice, and the three kids in the passenger seats.[76] The drive took nearly an entire day. It was already night when they arrived in Puerto Iguazú, on the Argentina side of the Iguaçu River that forms the border with Brazil. Rather than use the bridge to cross the water, Eloy drove onto a ferry boat that took them to the Brazilian side. As planned, they went to a specific customs post, where Eunice's sister was waiting. Florita told me that her mother made a game out of the secret border crossing: "Mom said, 'Okay, now you and your siblings need to put your head down. Aunt Arlete will be there, but it's a game, we're going to pretend that it's a game where we're all hiding. Put your head down and don't say anything.'"[77] To the family's relief, the plan went smoothly and Arlete waved them through. Eloy drove straight to Eunice's family house in Foz do Iguaçu, where Flora had arranged a welcome-home party.

I asked both Florita and Andrea how it felt arriving in Brazil. Florita said that what most struck her was the color of her new surroundings: "I remember that fantastic green in Brazil, I opened my eyes and it was a different type of green. That green flooded my eyes, it almost startled me. Here in Foz do Iguaçu we have a lot of this bright green. I looked around and said, 'I guess this is Brazil!' I wondered why it took us so long to live in such a beautiful place."[78] Andrea shared with me a poem that she wrote decades later, to mark her family's return to Brazil. The poem opened with the following lines:

> My father was banished from Brazil for political reasons and my mother accompanied him.
>
> From one coup to the next, until Argentina "asylumed" them.
>
> Land where my mother gave birth to me and where I learned to speak.

Until, they started chasing him again.

My father and mother sought refuge in the arms of their Brazilian motherland.

Clandestine

Innocent

Patient.[79]

Florita remembers a joyous and festive scene upon their arrival, with her mother jumping out of the car and hugging everyone, looking relaxed for the first time. But that moment was fleeting. Soon after the party started, her mother took Florita aside and told her the bad news: her father had left.[80]

Aluízio had wanted to join in the festivities. "I wanted to get out of the car and hug everyone," he told me. "I wanted to eat Brazilian food, eat some feijoada, drink cachaça, hang out in the street. But I couldn't."[81] While preparing to bring his family back to Foz do Iguaçu, Aluízio had also arranged for his own onward travel. Fearing that he was a risk to his family, he decided to travel all the way back to Rio de Janeiro, where he would stay in hiding until an amnesty law was passed. As the family celebration began, Aluízio barely had time to get into another car, which Eloy then drove east to Curitiba, before changing cars again and continuing to Rio. Even if no longer an exile on foreign soil, Aluízio left his family behind and entered another form of exile—alone and in a country still governed by the same military that had tortured him a decade earlier. It was not clear how long this new form of exile would last.

CHAPTER 8

TRANSITIONS

How long Aluízio would have to remain clandestine in Brazil depended not only on when Congress would pass an amnesty law but also on whether it would cover former political prisoners like him, those who had been labeled as "terrorists" and banished from the country. As with debates about democratization and transitional justice across Latin America and globally, the question of amnesty in Brazil had a complex history.

Although calls for amnesty had begun within a year of the military's 1964 coup, an organized movement did not take shape until 1974, when General Geisel's distensão policy envisioned a "slow, gradual, and secure" return to democracy. In the less repressive environment of distensão, opposition politicians from the Brazilian Democratic Movement party (MDB, Movimento Democrático Brasileiro) started to draft policies that would allow persecuted figures to resume a role in government and the military. Civic groups also began to campaign for the return of Brazilian exiles and the reinstatement of those who had lost their jobs and their political rights. The most influential coalition was the Women's Amnesty Movement (MFPA, Movimento Feminino pela Anistia), founded in São Paulo in 1975 by Therezinha Zerbini, a lawyer and the wife of a persecuted military officer.[1] Other amnesty organizations formed throughout the mid-1970s and drew support from politicians in the MDB as well as civic bodies like the Catholic Church, the Brazilian Bar Association, and various student associations.[2] In February 1978, the Brazilian Amnesty Committee (CBA, Comitê Brasileiro pela Anistia) was founded in Rio de Janeiro with the aim of consolidating a national social movement. Throughout 1978 and 1979 CBA branches were founded across Brazil and it soon became the largest sector of the amnesty movement.

The amnesty movement debated whether impunity should be given to the perpetrators of state repression. In July 1978, the CBA leadership drafted a list of demands, including that amnesty *not* be extended to torturers.[3] But the CBA's stance against amnesty for perpetrators never gained traction as a core goal of the broader movement. Especially after General João Baptista Figueiredo assumed the presidency in March 1979 and announced his interest in passing an amnesty law, a focus on exiles and the return of political freedoms took precedence over the question of perpetrators. Among the most famous events in the lead-up to Brazil's Amnesty Law was a thirty-two-day hunger strike by political prisoners from July to August. Crucially, the strikers did not emphasize criminal trials for state agents, instead using the strike to demand an "anistia ampla, geral e irrestrita" (broad, general, and unconditional amnesty) that would cover everyone who had been persecuted by the military, including those, like them, who were still in prison. It would only be in the years and decades to come, long after the 1979 passage of the Amnesty Law and the 1985 return to democratic rule, that leftists would mobilize more forcefully to overturn amnesty and enable criminal trials for perpetrators. Even then, as we will see, not everyone on the left agreed, with some fearing that former militants could also be liable for their armed actions, and others content to turn the page and focus on contemporary political struggles.

Despite ongoing debates about what an amnesty could look like and who it would benefit, the movement had become a primary vehicle for a large range of opposition groups. As noted by Rebecca Atencio in her cultural study of memory in Brazil, the "pro-amnesty banners, bumper stickers, and leaflets became ubiquitous in streets, soccer stadiums, and other public places. The pressure on the government to enact an amnesty law became impossible to ignore."[4] And for exiles, amnesty was a ticket home that promised either the possibility of renewed political engagement (they could openly participate in the campaign to end military rule) or a quieter life after years of activism, militancy, prison, and exile. For those still abroad, there was little to do but watch and advocate from afar. This was also the case for people like Aluízio, who had sneaked back into Brazil in the hope of a forthcoming amnesty. Waiting, and having to do so clandestinely, became an exercise in attrition, frustration, and loneliness.

AMNESTY IN WAITING

After changing cars in Curitiba, Aluízio drove with Eloy all the way to São Gonçalo, on the periphery of Niterói where he had spent his adolescence. In

CHAPTER 8

São Gonçalo, they met Aluízio's oldest brother, Evaldo, a lawyer who agreed to let Aluízio stay at his house in São Pedro da Aldeia, a small beach town further up the coast. The house was not yet ready, so Aluízio first had to spend several days in a hotel in Cabo Frio, a resort area known for its colonial-era buildings and pristine beaches.[5] He was not sure where Eloy had received the money that covered his travel and accommodation, though in hindsight, he thinks that his expenses were paid for by César Cabral, his former MR-8 comrade who had married one of Eunice's sisters.[6] In the decade since Aluízio had last seen him, César had embarked on various business ventures along the border that would make him a wealthy and highly influential figure in the region—attributes that would feature centrally in Aluízio's search, two decades later, for the bodies of the six disappeared militants.

At the hotel in Cabo Frio, it finally hit Aluízio that he was back in Brazil, but he could not fully relax while needing to stay clandestine, so he rarely left his hotel room. After several days, Eloy returned and drove Aluízio to the safe house in São Pedro da Aldeia. The house was directly on a beach called Praia do Sudoeste, with a volleyball court and large patio. Especially on the heels of a decade living on the run, staying on his own in the house felt decadent. It also felt disorienting, and Aluízio struggled to balance his fears of being discovered with his desire to enjoy himself for the first time in years. He had to prepare mentally for potentially coming "above ground" and rejoining society—what he described to me as "trying to adapt to a new reality."[7] To keep busy, and to catch up on the political news, he listened to the radio, paying special attention to the developments on the Amnesty Law. Aluízio's anxiety lessened after several days in the big house, and he began to enjoy life on the beach. From mid-May to early July, Aluízio's days followed a fairly set routine: spend all morning at the beach, come home to prepare some food, go back to the beach all afternoon, then return home for dinner and an evening of listening to the news. "I didn't have contact with anybody, but that's okay. I didn't want to have contact with anyone," Aluízio said. "It was the life of a tourist. I was basically just a tourist. Somebody who's just on holiday at a resort."[8]

After five or six weeks of the same daily schedule, rarely seeing or talking to anybody, Aluízio decided to go further into town—until then, he kept to a small radius that included the beach directly in front of the house and some small food shops nearby. On June 29, he joined the large crowds that had gathered for the Festa de São Pedro, the yearly saint's day festival, in which locals adorn fishing boats with bright colors and host a maritime procession for a statue of Saint Peter. In two different interviews that we conducted, spaced over a year apart, Aluízio shared a version of the same story: Standing on the beach, happy to blend in with a large gathering of people, Aluízio watched as the boats brought the large statue of Saint Peter to shore. But when he saw that the statue was beginning to teeter while being passed down from the boats, he instinctively stepped in and helped keep it aloft. He then noticed a large flash of light. A photographer had taken a picture of the statue, with Aluízio squarely in the frame. Aluízio's self-narration of this story reflected the repetitive nature of his memory script, and a tendency to retell the same anecdotes. The first time he spoke about this story in one of our interviews, he said, "I was really worried. Son of a bitch. I survived so many different things, and now to get caught because of Saint Peter!"[9] Sixteen months later, he brought it up again, seemingly unaware that he had already told me this story. As he recounted a second time, when he saw the photographer's flash, he thought to himself, "Son of a bitch, I'm going to get caught because of Saint Peter!"[10] Almost by its nature, storytelling depends on repetition, reflecting just how much a person can internalize, and then perform repeatedly, certain narratives and memories.

The photographer on the beach snapped Aluízio back to the reality of his situation, and the happiness he had felt at being surrounded by people quickly dissipated. He returned straight away to the house, aiming to keep a low profile as he wound his way through the crowds. Aluízio stayed in São Pedro da Aldeia for another week, during which time he did not deviate from his standard, lonely, routine. In early July, Eloy returned and drove him to São Gonçalo, where he stayed for a few days with his sister Maria Célia. He enjoyed the time with his sister, especially because it enabled him to see his parents. But staying with family felt risky, as he was still clandestine in Brazil. It came as a relief, then, when a former MR-8 comrade named Iná Meirelles showed up at his sister's apartment and told Aluízio that he would come stay with her.[11]

Aluízio ended up spending nearly two months living with Iná, who was very active in the amnesty movement. Iná brought Aluízio to several demonstrations, and moving once again in the spaces of political activism seemed to boost his morale. Despite the risks involved, Aluízio felt safe with Iná: "I went everywhere with her. She took care of me, she was like my bodyguard. She wouldn't let me be alone. . . . She never told anybody who I was. I went to all these meetings, but without exposing myself. . . . I was having a political life again."[12] For as much as he enjoyed the activism, he also knew that his general state of nervousness could make him unpleasant to be around. When I asked him if he had been happy to see old friends and comrades, he described the tense months of July and August, when he and many other former exiles waited anxiously for news of the Amnesty Law. "In that climate of fear, I wasn't very good company," Aluízio said. "I was somebody who at any moment could be captured and made to finish out my prison sentence.... I was moving about freely but without actually being amnestied, and even worse, I didn't have any documents."[13]

Such statements call to mind the lyrics of Caetano Veloso's hit 1967 song "Alegria, Alegria," an anthem of sorts for Brazilians of Aluízio's generation who were in the throes of the global counterculture yet also on the cusp of a descent into violent authoritarianism:

Walking against the wind	Caminhando contra o vento
Without handkerchief, without documents	Sem lenço e sem documento
In the almost December sun	No sol de quase dezembro
I go!	Eu vou!
...	...
Between photographs and names	Por entre fotos e nomes
Without books and without guns	Sem livros e sem fuzil
Without hunger, without a phone	Sem fome, sem telefone
In the heart of Brazil	No coração do Brasil

Like Caetano's song, Aluízio also inhabited a deeply conflicted state: he was happy to be back in Brazil, but he was still afraid of capture. And although he felt rejuvenated again as a militant, he remained restless and uncertain of his next move.

With Iná's encouragement, Aluízio went to the office of a lawyer named Ana Maria Müller, one of the leaders of the national amnesty movement, and a cofounder of the Brazilian Amnesty Committee (CBA) in Rio de Janeiro. Ana's husband, Samuel, had also been on the plane with Aluízio in 1971, one of the seventy exchanged prisoners flown to Chile. As Ana explained to me, in the late 1970s her office in downtown Rio was a busy hub for political dissidents and their families, especially in July and August 1979 when the Amnesty Law was being debated in Congress. Even amid the normal bustle of her work, the arrival of Aluízio shocked her: "I almost fell over, because I said to myself, 'My God, I must be seeing a ghost.' Because that man was banished from Brazil. What's he doing in Rio de Janeiro, in the center of Rio de Janeiro, in a lawyer's office, busy and open to anyone?"[14] Ana asked Aluízio why he was there, and he said that he hoped to make an official statement of having returned to Brazil. In case the authorities captured and disappeared him, Aluízio wanted a record of his being alive in Brazil. "I almost died, it was so moving," Ana told me. "So I said to him, 'For the love of God take care of yourself.' . . . It was a real act of courage, to show up and say, 'I'm alive, I came back, and I want to leave a document so that if they do something, if I disappear, it's because I'm dead, they killed me.'"

Aluízio's fate largely depended on that of the Amnesty Law. On June 27, Brazil's recently appointed president, General Figueiredo, submitted his amnesty proposal, which stipulated that impunity would be granted to military authorities, and he allotted forty days for Congress to deliberate. Figueiredo's bill reflected how the military considered amnesty for state crimes a nonnegotiable part of its agreement to gradually transition to democratic rule, and only rarely did opposition groups take a concerted stand against it.[15] Here, it is important to remember that the military government had stacked Congress in its favor—an advantage that held strong until the passage of the Party Reform Act that reestablished a multiparty system at the very end of 1979.[16] A lengthy debate did take place around an amendment proposed by the MDB senator Djalma Marinho that, if passed, would have instituted the broader type of amnesty championed by certain sectors of the opposition, including the political prisoners on hunger strike. But the Marinho amendment was narrowly rejected on August 21, clearing the way for a final vote one week later.

Congress passed the Amnesty Law on August 28, 1979. Along with allowing exiles to return to Brazil and all persecuted leaders to regain their political rights, the law returned professors, public employees, members of the judiciary, and diplomatic personnel to their jobs. As a central part of the military's negotiation to eventually hand over power, the law also included a blanket pardon for those involved with state torture.[17] Brazil's pacted transition thus folded two amnesties into one (referred to as a reciprocal amnesty, or a bilateral amnesty), making it an outlier compared to other Latin American countries where amnesties for dissidents and perpetrators were dealt with in separate stages. Despite the longer-term worries about what impunity would mean for those seeking truth and justice, the passage of the Amnesty Law was a cause for celebration for most exiles, their families, and supporters across Brazil. But for people like Aluízio, who were technically "banished" and not "exiled," it was not immediately clear if the law would apply to them.

As Aluízio and his friends in Rio discussed his situation, Iná suggested that he go public and bring attention to his cause. On August 29, the day after Congress passed the Amnesty Law, Aluízio returned to Ana Maria Müller's office and sat down with a journalist from *Veja*, Brazil's most popular weekly magazine. Aluízio was extremely nervous. He told me that when a photographer took his picture, the camera's rapid shutter triggered him, reminding him of the sounds of a machine gun: "He showed up already taking photos, clicking off a million pictures. That made me nervous and the interview turned to shit."[18] Aluízio's frayed nerves were also evident to the *Veja* reporter, who, in the resulting article, described Aluízio several times as "inseguro" (anxious). The article profiled Aluízio and one other person, a former student leader named Carlos Alberto Muniz. Under the title of "Back in the Open," *Veja* explored what it meant for formerly clandestine militants to reemerge into public life.[19] Wary of giving too much insight into his past, Aluízio gave a false version of his time in exile, saying that after leaving Brazil in 1971, he had remained in Chile all the way through the Pinochet coup in September 1973. He made no mention of his extensive period in Argentina, claiming instead to have spent the rest of the decade in Peru. His emotional description of exile, however, rang true: "Those were really hard times, I took any odd jobs I could find and the isolation really stressed me out." The article commented on the uncertainty that surrounded Aluízio: "Still a bit anxious and scared, Palmar has no set plans. He does not know what he will do for work." Looking back on how he felt at the time of the interview, Aluízio agreed with the article's description of him. "Of course I was anxious," he told me. "I was anxious about Brazil, anxious about my own future, anxious about what I would do."

During the two months that Aluízio lived clandestinely in Brazil, he had no contact with Eunice or his children, waiting until after the passage of amnesty to get in touch. When Aluízio learned about the Amnesty Law's passage on August 28, he called Eunice. But rather than expressing any excitement to reunite with her in Foz do Iguaçu, he tried to convince Eunice to come to Rio, saying that the city was buzzing with political energy and opportunity. He recalled telling his wife that "we were going to bring about democracy and build a new society."[20] Aluízio felt emboldened by the new political climate, and he wanted to remain in Rio de Janeiro to take part in the next—and hopefully final—campaign to end military rule. Eunice did not share her husband's desire to be on the front lines of the fight for democracy. Having so recently moved back to her hometown, and on the heels of an extremely difficult decade in exile, Eunice's patience seemed to have run out.

Aluízio's memories of what Eunice then said to him reveal the refracted ways that certain stories get repeated. Like the earlier memory about the photographer on the beach in São Pedro da Aldeia, which he repeated in multiple interviews with me, Aluízio has retold this story about Eunice's ultimatum, though in subtly distinct ways. In a 2018 Facebook post on the August 28 anniversary of the Amnesty Law, Aluízio wrote that "my wife put me up against a wall: 'You have to choose, either you continue your politics here with your family or you stay there on your own.'"[21] Compared to this softer phrasing, in which Eunice seemed to offer him a chance to combine family and politics, in our interview—inflected perhaps by the male banter that ran as a steady undercurrent in many of our exchanges—he recalled the conversation in a more direct way. While still using the same idiomatic phrase at the beginning of the anecdote, he told me that, "She put me up against a wall. 'You decide, your revolution or your family.'"[22]

Aluízio did not argue with Eunice, and he began preparing himself, logistically and emotionally, to leave Rio and travel back to Foz do Iguaçu. Perhaps he thought that he would find a way to remain active in the democratization movement, even from the western Paraná borderlands. Or maybe he felt that Eunice was not bluffing, and that he could lose his family if he stayed in Rio. Either way, he had to make peace with leaving Rio de Janeiro at precisely the moment when the passage of amnesty and the return flow of exiles would make the city a center of popular mobilization. Aluízio prepared to head back to the border.

With the help of his brother Evaldo, Aluízio secured a statement of amnesty, which was signed on September 10 by a judge in the First Naval District in Rio de Janeiro—the same circuit in which his imprisonment and trial had taken place. The amnesty declaration was the first official documentation he had held in Brazil for over a decade, and it allowed him to travel relatively worry-free. But in terms of his personal feelings, the move to Foz do Iguaçu was complicated. Aside from his family, Aluízio did not know many people in Foz, and compared to major cities like Rio de Janeiro, it felt like a small and isolated town. Aluízio told me that he was sad to move to a place that he considered to have no politics, or culture, or sports: "Here, it was like the end of the world. The backlands! There was nothing here. Here it was just a frontier."[23] Aluízio's situated choice of the word "here" reflected the fact that after moving to Foz do Iguaçu in September 1979, he never left. It has remained his home for over four decades.

At the time, however, Foz do Iguaçu felt like a rupture. He told me that he cried on the drive from Rio to Foz. "I knew that I was leaving behind a dream," he said. "But I would have to build a new dream, starting from scratch, completely from scratch. I didn't have the Chaco anymore, I didn't have Rio anymore, my reality was Foz."[24] Forever seeking a way to balance the two priorities

CHAPTER 8

in his life—his revolution and his family, in Eunice's words—Aluízio moved to the western Paraná border to be with his wife and children, and he also soon found his way back into political activism.

FOZ DO IGUAÇU AND DEMOCRATIZATION IN A BORDERLAND

Upon settling back in Foz do Iguaçu, Aluízio confronted several challenges, ranging from the pressing need to find a job—which he had not had in Brazil since the mid-1960s—to the broader process of adapting to normal life as a regular citizen. It did not take him much time to resolve the first task, and he soon got hired as a journalist for local newspapers. The second task proved a far more enduring problem. He was now living freely, but he was not at peace with himself, unable to shed the psychological weight of his experiences over the previous decade. As he recalled to the journalist Juliana Machado, "That year in prison, and all the torture, my years of clandestinity, all my friends who had died, other friends that I still hadn't heard news about.... It took me a long time to adapt. We carry all of that, it doesn't go away, we carry it. Even after all those years, it will never go away."[25]

While struggling to find his emotional balance, Aluízio explored his options for work. Doing so required him to obtain an identification card, which in Brazil at the time was handled by the police. This meant that Aluízio had to go to the police precinct in Foz do Iguaçu, the same building where he had been detained and tortured twelve years earlier. He was scared to enter the precinct, though his fear soon gave way to frustration, when the officer in charge of processing identification cards seemed unfamiliar with the recently passed Amnesty Law. The officer looked up Aluízio's record and saw that there were several years outstanding of his prison sentence. In Aluízio's memories, he had to repeatedly explain to the officer that he had been amnestied and that his prison sentence had been annulled.[26] After an afternoon filling out paperwork, Aluízio received an ID card, a critical step toward rejoining society.

Despite the relief of finally having documentation, Aluízio struggled to adapt to his new circumstances. When I asked him about these difficulties, he again compared himself to exiles who had gone to Europe. "Everything was a new reality, because I had been living in a type of bubble outside of reality," Aluízio told me. "Those of us who were clandestine lived in a parallel universe that we had to construct with our own imaginations. Those who were in Europe were so much more in touch with reality.... Exiles in Portugal or Sweden or Germany or France, they had contact with other exiles, they could read newspapers, they were in constant contact with the reality of [what was happening in] Brazil."²⁷ In this framing, Aluízio felt that he not only had to adapt to the daily minutia of having a nonclandestine life, but he also had to give himself a crash course in Brazilian politics—a rather shocking realization for somebody who had considered himself a dedicated observer of politics and society. To get a feel for his new surroundings, Aluízio spent much of his initial weeks in Foz do Iguaçu walking around the city talking to people. This routine helped calm his anxieties, reminding him that he was still a social person who could communicate normally and lead a regular life.

But Aluízio had never lived a "normal" existence. He had been a full-time activist and militant since the age of sixteen, and now, almost twenty years later, he needed to figure out a new profession. He considered returning to university to finish his undergraduate degree. The Amnesty Law gave him the right to continue where he had left off in 1967, but that would require returning to Niterói, which Eunice was not willing to do. Aluízio thought a lot about what skills he had. "I didn't really know how to do anything," he told me. "I only knew how to make a revolution. I am a professional militant, that's my job. I don't know things beyond that."²⁸

Aluízio sought advice from a lawyer named Adolfo Mariano da Costa, whom he had known in the late 1960s, while organizing with the MR-8. Adolfo lived in Medianeira, some fifty kilometers from Foz do Iguaçu, and he had a lot of contacts throughout the region. In their meeting, Adolfo asked Aluízio what jobs he might want to pursue. Remembering how much he had enjoyed writing the student pamphlets in Niterói, and eager to immerse himself in political news, Aluízio said that he wanted to work as a journalist. Luckily for Aluízio, Adolfo knew the owner of a newspaper in Cascavel, who then put in a call to another newspaper in Foz do Iguaçu called *Hoje Foz*, which offered Aluízio a job as a reporter. The newspaper's editor at the time was João Adelino de Souza, who shared with me his initial memories of Aluízio: "When he arrived, he seemed really dejected. He was tired, sad. But at the same time, he seemed like somebody who wanted to rebuild his life. I think he was someone who suffered a lot in exile, far from his home. And he really threw himself into his work. He lifted his head and marched forward."²⁹ Something that also stuck out to João Adelino was that Aluízio almost never spoke about his past, choosing instead to stay focused on the political challenges of the moment.

Hoje Foz was not an alternative or opposition newspaper, but it maintained a relatively open editorial line and João Adelino encouraged his writers to cover political topics. The main story in the region at this time was the construction of the Itaipu hydroelectric dam, which was slated to become the largest dam on the planet. Itaipu was the crown jewel of the dictatorship's development policies, yet the local impact of the dam served as a counternarrative to the triumphalist image that the military regime hoped to install in the twilight of its rule. Over 40,000 Brazilians would be displaced by the dam, including smallholder farmers, peasants, and the Avá-Guarani Indigenous community. The dam's construction itself was proving very dangerous, with scores of workers getting injured and dying. Aluízio was one of several reporters at *Hoje Foz* who wrote about the ongoing drama at Itaipu.

Aluízio was fired after two months at the newspaper. *Hoje Foz*, as it turned out, had recently been sold, and the new owner wanted to get rid of Aluízio and another reporter named Juvêncio Mazzarollo, who was writing a book about the communities displaced by Itaipu. In Aluízio's telling, the paper had been purchased by someone directly connected to the Itaipu dam, and the change in ownership was a way to stop their news coverage. Aluízio and Juvêncio's departure was soon followed by that of their editor, João Adelino, who resigned from the paper. Newly unemployed, Aluízio found short-term work with another Paraná newspaper, *Correio de Notícias*, and he also wrote a few stories for national publications like *O Globo* and *Veja*—with the growing spotlight on the Itaipu dam, Aluízio became a well-placed stringer to provide local reports on Foz do Iguaçu and the western Paraná borderlands.[30]

Meanwhile, Aluízio stayed in close touch with Juvêncio and João Adelino, his former colleagues at *Hoje Foz*, and they had a sequence of increasingly serious conversations about starting their own newspaper. Sensing a need in the region for an explicitly political newspaper, the three men began to map out the necessary steps. The first hurdle was financing. As Aluízio jokingly told me, "Putting all our money together was barely enough to buy a Coca-Cola."[31]

NOSSO TEMPO

To raise funds to start their newspaper, Aluízio, Juvêncio, and João Adelino established an investment cooperative (*sociedade*) of local business owners. According to Aluízio, he and his colleagues sought to capitalize on Foz do Iguaçu's political situation: although the military regime had allowed local elections in most of the country—unlike its cancellation of direct elections for president and senators—Foz do Iguaçu had been designated as one of Brazil's sixty-eight "national security zones," for which the national government appointed mayors from outside the region. These appointed leaders, as well as a key number of presidentially appointed federal senators, became known informally as "biônicos" (bionics)—a cultural reference to the popular US television show *The Six Million Dollar Man* and its spinoff, *The Bionic Woman*, whose protagonists possessed extraordinary power and influence. At the time, Foz's mayor was an army colonel named Clóvis Cunha Vianna, who had been appointed in 1974. As a result of the city's lack of mayoral elections, elites in Foz do Iguaçu harbored a grudge against their limited ability to influence local politics. "There was a contradiction between the politicians and businessmen from the city and the military officers who came from elsewhere," Aluízio said. "So we looked for people who were against the mayor and who wanted elections to come back. We aligned ourselves with them. We pitched them on the idea of starting a newspaper to stand against the appointed mayor."[32] João Adelino still remembers the exact number of investors they recruited: eleven people agreed to join the paper's sociedade, with each contributing money and agreeing to have the paper registered collectively in all of their names.[33] The funds went primarily to the purchase of a printing press and a rented office in the Vila Yolanda neighborhood. In the lead-up to their first issue, Aluízio and his colleagues posted fliers around the city announcing the creation of an alternative newspaper.

The fundraising and leafleting caught the attention of authorities. In a sign of how power and surveillance existed in Foz do Iguaçu, much of the monitoring of Aluízio and his collaborators was conducted by the security branch of the Itaipu dam—what was known as Special Committee for Security and Information (AESI, Assessoria Especial de Segurança e Informação). In November 1980, a month before the newspaper's first publication, a report from AESI warned that "subversive materials" would soon circulate throughout the region.[34] AESI was one of many such committees (*assessorias*) that Brazil's dictatorship used to gather information on entities such as universities and businesses, and it coordinated closely with the dictatorship's National Information Service. In the coming years, AESI would play a leading role in surveilling the unfolding drama at the Itaipu dam—and in the eventual standoff between the dictatorship and Aluízio's newspaper.

As for what to call the newspaper, the three coeditors eventually settled on a title that they hoped would serve as a symbol of political change: *Nosso Tempo* (Our time). The first issue of *Nosso Tempo* came out on December 3, 1980, barely half a year after Aluízio, Juvêncio, and João Adelino began their efforts to start a newspaper. The opening editorial introduced readers to the paper's ideological pillars: "We at *Nosso Tempo* seek to chart our own path. We choose freedom. As such we strive for independence. We will resist until the end. . . . Nobody can push us from this path. Our ideals cannot be bought. We will never make this organ of communication an executioner of our beliefs."[35] Taking bold aim at the repression that still shadowed Brazilian society—locally in Foz do Iguaçu as well as nationally—the paper's front cover was a graphic illustration of torture. Depicting the parrot's perch torture method that Aluízio and countless other prisoners had suffered, the cover image showed a naked man hanging upside down, his hands and ankles tied together, while menacing security agents squeezed his head and burned his face with a cigarette. The main story of this first issue focused on allegations of torture in Foz do Iguaçu's military prisons. The tortured prisoners were no longer political prisoners like Aluízio and his MR-8 comrades a decade earlier but rather common prisoners who told *Nosso Tempo* about the ongoing use of the telephone torture method (the simultaneous pounding of both ears) as well as severe beatings that resulted in broken ribs.[36] Although the abertura's gradual return of political freedoms had made it less provocative to speak openly about such allegations of torture, *Nosso Tempo* caused a stir in Foz do Iguaçu. João Adelino recalled that the content and cover illustration of the first issue "shocked the city. Because most people didn't know that torture was going on. So that had a really strong impact."[37]

If Aluízio had initially been hesitant to move to Foz do Iguaçu, considering it a boring political backland, ensuing events showed that under a dictatorship, any region of the country could become a hub of political agitation. *Nosso Tempo*'s office in Vila Yolanda provided a welcoming space for militants, activists, and various social movements in the region, including progressive religious organizations such as the Indigenist Missionary Council (Conselho Indigenista Missionário) and the Justice and Peace Commission (Comissão de Justiça e Paz). One of the key organizers in western Paraná was a Lutheran pastor named Werner Fuchs, who had recently moved to Foz do Iguaçu to help lead the Justice and Peace Commission campaigns for Indigenous rights and land rights for smallholder farmers. Pastor Fuchs remembers being very impressed with *Nosso Tempo*'s political orientation, describing the newspaper as "one of the main avenues we had to get out a different message. Other papers at the time, like *Folha de Londrina* or the one in Cascavel, they were commercial media, they didn't have a political vision to fight the dictatorship."[38] Pastor Fuchs also credits Aluízio with helping him connect the local struggles in western Paraná to the larger problems facing Brazil: "I remember him opening my horizon to see these crises, these questions about the military regime. His trajectory had given him this structural perspective, which was new to me. Aluízio was a good communicator. It's not that he was a big talker or anything, but more than most people, he could express what he was thinking."[39]

Starting an alternative newspaper in the climate of dictatorship was a risk. Aluízio told me that in the early days of the paper, it received menacing phone calls and even a few bomb threats. "The threats always came at night,

anonymous calls, threatening to bomb the newspaper, terrorist attacks really," Aluízio said. "The paper was a battleground of struggle, because more than just a newspaper it also became a center for the dissemination of political ideas."[40] According to João Adelino, the military also pressured the sociedade investors to withdraw their funding: "People at the army battalion went about threatening each of the members, saying, 'How can you get mixed up with these communists?'"[41] The pressure worked and several investors pulled out, deepening an already difficult financial situation. It did not take long for the authorities to directly target *Nosso Tempo*. At the time, the government's policy was that to work as a journalist, one needed to have official authorization from the Ministry of Work. None of *Nosso Tempo*'s staff had such credentials, and the three coeditors were tentatively charged under Article 47 of the Misdemeanors Law—surveillance logs kept by the Federal Police noted that Aluízio was charged for "not being credentialed as a journalist while practicing the profession."[42] Fortunately, upon returning to Foz do Iguaçu the previous year, Aluízio had reinitiated contact with Fábio Campana, his friend and comrade from the late 1960s, who worked as a journalist in Curitiba. Aluízio told Fábio about *Nosso Tempo*'s predicament, and Fábio agreed to come on board as an editor. In our interview, Fábio explained to me that his position was in name only, but it allowed his accreditation to cover the newspaper.[43] As a result, the misdemeanor charges were dropped.

THE LAST POLITICAL PRISONER

But a separate effort to silence the newspaper proved far more successful: the dictatorship charged Juvêncio Mazzarollo—one of *Nosso Tempo*'s coeditors—with having violated the National Security Act (LSN, Lei da Segurança Nacional), eventually imprisoning him for nearly two years. Juvêncio was jailed from 1982 to 1984, only winning his freedom when an international solidarity campaign—and his two hunger strikes—pressured the military regime to release him. After two decades of dictatorship, with democracy supposedly on the horizon, Juvêncio became known throughout Brazil as "the last political prisoner."

Juvêncio's story is complex and fascinating, shedding light on the contradictions of the abertura period, the dynamics of politics in a border region like western Paraná, and the grassroots movements that helped bring about the end of military rule in Brazil. I have written about Juvêncio Mazzarollo elsewhere, chronicling the saga of his imprisonment in the detail that it deserves.[44] In fact, my research on Juvêncio and *Nosso Tempo* was part of the project that initially put me in touch with Aluízio. Rather than dive into Juvêncio's story, which would offer a digression, however important, from our primary narrative of Aluízio's life and memories, it is more useful here to summarize the main reasons for Juvêncio's imprisonment. And because Aluízio knew how familiar I was with Juvêncio's saga—and motivated perhaps by a desire to keep our interviews focused mostly on himself—Aluízio volunteered relatively few anecdotes about these tense years at *Nosso Tempo*.

How was it that a largely unknown journalist at a small alternative newspaper ended up becoming the last political prisoner of Brazil's dictatorship? Put simply, military authorities threw Juvêncio in jail for a combination of two escalating factors. First, *Nosso Tempo*'s exposés about the unelected leaders of Foz do Iguaçu spurred local elites to try and silence the newspaper. Second, the paper's coverage of the farmers' protest against the Itaipu dam caught the attention of national leaders who wanted to protect the government's highly curated image of the dam as a patriotic triumph. The cascade of these two factors embodied the tensions of Brazil's abertura. For local elites who felt removed from the democratization process, Juvêncio's repression was an attempt to exercise their quickly fading power. For the national government, the coverage given to the farmers drew attention away from the triumphant narrative of Itaipu that they hoped to leave as a legacy before the full return of democratic rule. And for opposition groups throughout Brazil, Juvêncio transcended his role as a dissident journalist to become a rallying point for democratization.

Juvêncio's trial started in November 1981 and almost seven months later he was found guilty of violating Article 33 of the LSN—relating to offenses against government authorities. For Aluízio and the other staff at *Nosso Tempo*, Juvêncio's imprisonment became a challenge on many levels. Most immediately, they did everything possible to publicize the flagrant abuse of their friend and colleague—*Nosso Tempo* devoted extensive coverage to Juvêncio's situation, printing a running tally of the length of Juvêncio's time in jail on the front page of almost every issue. In terms of the logistics of running a newspaper, the imprisonment of an editor and key writer meant even more work for everyone. In one of the few memories that Aluízio shared with me about these events, he said that either he or another writer named Jessé Vidigal would drive almost every week to Curitiba to visit Juvêncio in prison and take back the articles that he wrote in his cell, which would then get published in *Nosso Tempo*.[45] And according to João Adelino, the situation put added strain on the paper's finances—several staff members took on part-time work as freelance writers or photographers in order to channel some extra money back into the newspaper and keep it from going deeper into debt.[46] For a small opposition paper like *Nosso Tempo*, Juvêncio's saga showed that despite the official narrative of a changing society, military rule remained embedded in daily life.

After nearly two years in prison, at a time when no other political prisoners remained behind bars in Brazil, Juvêncio staged what became a sixteen-day hunger strike, casting an even greater spotlight on his imprisonment, both in Brazil and globally, with Amnesty International organizing a letter-writing campaign on his behalf.[47] Nearly six months later, Juvêncio staged a second hunger strike, and after ten days, Brazil's Supreme Court ordered his release on April 6, 1984. The complete return of civilian rule would not occur until the following March 1985, but Juvêncio's freedom reflected Brazil's democratic opening. Sentenced in 1982 by a military tribunal, Juvêncio Mazzarollo was freed two years later by a civilian court when a solidarity movement made him into a rallying cry for democracy in Brazil. Upon his release, Juvêncio wrote an article in *Nosso Tempo* that praised the efforts of opposition forces in Foz do Iguaçu, across Brazil, and throughout the world, saying that it was only through grassroots mobilization that "the last political prisoner in the country could leave from where, in justice, he should never have entered."[48]

WORK AND POLITICS

Although Juvêncio's imprisonment occupied much of Aluízio's attention and his work at *Nosso Tempo*, he also took advantage of being "above ground" for the first time in fifteen years. In the context of accelerating political change, Aluízio spent much of the early 1980s involved in a wide range of activities. The final report of Paraná's State Truth Commission contains a list of Aluízio's political activities during this time, compiled from years-long surveillance reports.[49] The list, of which I summarize key entries below, reflected the progression of local politics in Foz do Iguaçu and the rebuilding of a broader political culture:

- February 22, 1980. Was part of the personal security detail for Leonel Brizola upon his return to exile via Foz do Iguaçu and participated in the refounding of the Brazilian Democratic Labor Party (PDT, Partido Democrático Trabalhista).

- July 14, 1980. Represented the Justice and Peace Commission at deliberations in Santa Helena between Itaipu Binational and local farmers.

- March 1981. Participated in a meeting of the Paraguayan Communist Party.

- 1982. Registered as the PDT's candidate for federal deputy in the elections of November 15.

- October 1983. Wrote an article in *Nosso Tempo* in defense of the Chilean president Salvador Allende.

- August 1984. Chaired a meeting for "Solidarity with the People of Paraguay," with the goal of denouncing the dictatorship of that country.

- 1985. Served as president of the PDT's Municipal Leadership in Foz do Iguaçu.

- March 17, 1985. Helped organize the first meeting of the Landless Rural Workers of Santa Terezinha do Itaipu, whose goal is to advance agrarian reform and the rights of landless workers.

The final entry above, for Aluízio's presence in the landless workers movement—which would become one of the leading social movements in the Western Hemisphere—took place three days after Brazil's dictatorship officially ended. Many elements of military rule continued for years afterward, including amnesty for human rights abusers and the lack of direct election for president, which did not happen until 1988. But when General João Figueiredo stepped down on March 14, 1985, it marked the end of Brazil's twenty-one-year dictatorship.

As noted in the list, prior to the official return of democracy in 1985, Aluízio spent the final years of military rule as an active organizer with the local branch of the PDT, the Democratic Labor Party. The opposition leader Leonel Brizola had founded it in 1979 as a means to revive the previous Brazilian Labor Party (PTB) of Getúlio Vargas in the 1950s and João Goulart in the 1960s. While maintaining his full-time job at *Nosso Tempo*, Aluízio also dedicated himself to building the PDT (fig. 8.1). As a former member of the Brazilian Communist Party, Aluízio sought to bring radicals like him into the PDT, seeking to transpose some of the far-left views from his earlier militancy into the democratizing climate of the 1980s. Aluízio told me that even though he was "more to the left" of the PDT's official platforms, and disagreed at times with the party, he found it refreshing to work within large political networks.[50] With the PDT he experienced something that had never occurred during his younger days as a far-left militant: winning. "We started gaining power, getting mayors elected, and governors. Those were some major wins, getting progressive governors elected in several states." In addition to the victories of the PDT, Aluízio also

FIGURE 8.1.
Aluízio at a May Day event with the PDT, either 1982 or 1983. Courtesy of Aluízio Palmar.

noted an increase in his own influence. As an example of his new stature in Paraná politics, Aluízio told me that during Juvêncio Mazzarollo's imprisonment, he met several times with Paraná's governor, José Richa, to lobby for Juvêncio's freedom. "We gained a lot of clout," Aluízio recalled. "I could show up at the governor's office without needing to ask permission.... No appointment, I didn't need to ask anyone, and I'd speak with the governor. That was a big change."

FAMILY

Aluízio's newfound status reflected a long-standing issue: his dedication to politics often came at the expense of his family. My interviews with Aluízio's three oldest children help paint a picture of the Palmar household after the family's return to Brazil. For Florita (who had been born in Brazil in 1969 and raised in Chile and Argentina) as well as Andrea and Alexandre (born in Argentina in 1975 and 1976, respectively), their lives in Foz do Iguaçu in the 1980s were complicated. To be sure, they enjoyed being surrounded by family after so many years on their own. Aluízio, Eunice, and the three kids moved into a house on a large plot of land owned by Eunice's family—nicknamed Villa Almeida, her maiden name—on which Eunice's parents and several siblings also lived. As Andrea told me, her mother's "dream was to be close to her family in Foz," and living immediately adjacent to so many siblings and cousins provided a welcome torrent of activity after such a long time on their own.[51] But even among their family, Aluízio's children felt like outsiders. Their Brazilian cousins often made fun of them for speaking with an accent and dressing like Argentinians, which also extended to their experience at school, where classmates mocked their "Portunhol" (Spanish-inflected Portuguese).

In addition to the challenges of adapting to a new life in Brazil, the children also had to navigate Aluízio's past experiences and his present activism. At the time, they knew almost nothing about their father's past—Aluízio and Eunice shared few details with their children about why the family had fled Brazil. But even to the young children, it was clear that something had happened to their father. In what she now assumes to be the traumatic effects of Aluízio's torture, Andrea told me that her father "would get jumpy when he heard the sound of keys. We couldn't make any noise with keys. I think this must remind him of the jailers walking down prison corridors, on their way to torture someone."[52] She also said that Aluízio could not stand bright lights, perhaps a legacy of his time in jail. This awareness would only come with time. Aluízio's children would not learn about the full extent of his past until he published his memoir in 2005.

All three of his oldest children told me that Aluízio worked more than they would have wanted, though Florita was the most unflinching in her response. Along with telling me stories about the family's financial struggles (not having enough food in the house, or having to wear hand-me-downs from her cousins), Florita gave a frank assessment of people like her father: "I came to the conclusion, Jake, that a political militant, man or woman, they shouldn't have a family. There's no way [to do both]. I think they should choose not to have children, because the family suffers a lot."[53] Although not as direct as their sister, both Alexandre and Andrea shared similar sentiments of dealing with a father who often seemed to care more for politics than family. To see Aluízio more, Alexandre and Andrea spent as much time as they could in the offices of *Nosso Tempo*—Alexandre even had several of his birthday parties at the newspaper, and his interest in emulating his father set him on the path to eventually becoming a journalist.[54]

A frequent theme in their memories was the contrast between Aluízio's impassioned activities outside of the house and his detached presence inside it. While telling me that he now understands how difficult it must have been for his father to balance his work and his family, Alexandre also shared his frustrations from childhood: "How could there be so much love, so much desire to fight for the world outside, but nothing like that in the home?"[55] Florita recalled a similar dynamic. "My dad outside of the house was always one thing, a different person, and inside the house he was someone else," Florita said. "He was more closed-off . . . always tucked away in his study, with his head in a book, reading, writing. My mom, trying to get him involved in our lives, she would have to yell at him. I think she must have yelled at him all day long."[56]

Because the family never discussed Aluízio's past, the children knew very little about how their parents met. Similar to how Aluízio's kids eventually learned about his militant days by reading his memoir, their parents' early life together was also revealed by reading. Eunice had kept years' worth of letters, which she kept in a large trunk and allowed her kids to read. Alexandre told me that when he and his sisters were young, they would spend hours going through the letters: "My mom was always a romantic, very dreamy, really in love with my dad, and my dad with her, too. . . . There were hundreds of letters in the trunk. I'm not talking about dozens of letters, I'm saying there were hundreds of letters."[57] But those letters seem to have vanished. In Alexandre's opinion, his mother probably destroyed them in reaction to one of his father's transgressions—perhaps the affair that led to the birth Aluízio's youngest daughter, Amanda, perhaps a different affair that I was not told about, or perhaps something else entirely. "Those letters ended up disappearing into thin air," Alexandre told me. "Something that my dad must have done made my mom get rid of them. I don't know if she burned them or threw them out. Such an important record of things. A shame that they're lost to history now."[58] For Aluízio's children, these letters symbolize what went unsaid for years in the home, and serve as a reminder of the trade-offs of how he chose to live his life.

By the mid-1980s, Aluízio was at a crossroads. The return of civilian rule in 1985 was undoubtedly a great step for Brazilian society, but it also meant that for the first time in over two decades, Aluízio did not have an obvious target against which to mobilize. Although he remained active in various social movements that sought to overturn the policies of military rule, ranging from agrarian rights to education and housing reform, he also had to figure out his political identity beyond the official context of dictatorship.

Nosso Tempo also underwent changes. João Adelino left the newspaper in 1985, having been invited to work in City Hall on the heels of Foz do Iguaçu's first mayoral elections in several decades. And although Juvêncio Mazzarollo returned to the newspaper after being released from prison in 1984, he also began to get more involved with the Justice and Peace Commission—a social justice body linked to progressive branches of the Catholic Church.[59] This left Aluízio as the only original coeditor still working full time, and as the years went on, he came to dislike what the paper became. As with any organization or business, *Nosso Tempo* changed as it grew, and Aluízio felt like his role as an administrator was overtaking his role as a journalist. "The character of the [newspaper] was totally lost," Aluízio recalled. "It was like selling out, dealing with invoices, and accounts, having to organize everything, [it was a] bureaucracy."[60] And with the military no longer in power, Aluízio sensed that *Nosso Tempo*, a newspaper founded to fight against the dictatorship, did not quite fit the moment at hand: "That's the bad thing about outdated ideas, isn't it? You create something and it has an end. If you adapt, it's not always possible to maintain that life as it was before. That main quality is lost and then everything is lost."

Despite his misgivings about *Nosso Tempo*'s direction, he stayed at the paper until 1992. That year, Foz do Iguaçu's mayor, Dobrandino Gustavo da Silva, won reelection as part of the center-left Brazilian Democratic Movement Party (PMDB, Partido do Movimento Democrático Brasileiro), and he invited Aluízio to work as the city's head of communications. According to Aluízio, when conservative forces in local government found out that he had been nominated, they pressured the mayor to not appoint a former communist to an important public relations position. As a compromise, Dobrandino withdrew the communications position and instead tapped Aluízio to work as the city's secretary of the environment. Aluízio accepted the job, and after more than a decade running *Nosso Tempo*, he resigned from the newspaper.

From 1993 to 1997, Aluízio worked in city government, helping lead a series of environmental campaigns that included the creation of new parks and reforestation of city streets, cleanup projects for local rivers, and efforts to curb the use of pesticides within city limits. When telling me about his work in city government, Aluízio said that they accomplished "a revolution in terms of the environment, it was a revolution."[61] I told Aluízio that I found his use of the word "revolution" very interesting, given its connotations of armed struggle that had defined much of his earlier life. I wondered if he would have used that phrase at the time, or whether his ability to equate environmentalism with revolution reflected more contemporary ideas. "Yeah, it's really different," he acknowledged. "But it was also continuing the same fight to improve people's quality of life. So it was making people's lives better through environmental education, an environmental revolution, planting trees, protecting, protecting, protecting. . . . It was a different type of revolution."

Aluízio's new position in civil society mirrored broader changes in Brazil during the 1990s. Although amnesty remained the law of the land—meaning that no perpetrators could be held liable for human rights abuses—Brazilians found new ways to reckon with the country's recent history of authoritarian rule. In 1992, for example, Brazil's most popular television station, Globo, ran a telenovela called *Anos Rebeldes* (Rebel years), about a fictional group of high school students in the 1960s; some of the characters, like Aluízio in real life, joined the armed underground only to eventually get imprisoned and tortured by the military regime. The show's depictions of censorship and torture suggested that Brazil was starting to more directly confront its recent past. And in the realm of national politics, the mass demonstrations in 1992 demanding the impeachment of President Fernando Collor de Mello, coupled with the 1994 election of Fernando Henrique Cardoso (a former sociology professor who lived in exile during the dictatorship) reflected a population eager for more accountability from its leaders. It remained to be seen what might result from these changing cultural and political winds.

While Aluízio worked in city government, the shadows of his former life as an armed revolutionary reemerged. In the years after his return from exile, as democracy gradually returned to Brazil and as former militants and human rights activists grappled with the extent of violence committed by the dictatorship, Aluízio found himself thinking about his comrades who never came back—those who had been disappeared by the military, their bodies discarded, leaving their families without answers or closure. His mind kept returning to Onofre Pinto and the group of militants who disappeared in 1974. That Aluízio had nearly fallen into the same trap added a dark undertone to his concern about their disappearance, injecting him with what he described as a "restlessness that for many years tormented my soul."[62] As the transition years of the 1980s gave way to a new, if still wayward, period in the 1990s, Aluízio's interest in the 1974 disappearances would grow into an obsessive crusade to uncover the truth.

CHAPTER 9

THE SEARCH

THE MAJORITY of Aluízio's memoir is a chronicle of his search for the six disappeared militants. Across much of his 300-page book, Aluízio goes into extreme detail on the various twists and turns of his investigations that spanned the early 1990s through 2010. In this chapter, I provide only a summary of the search, highlighting the main phases of his investigation and complementing his narrative with additional interviews and documents. I also describe various people involved with the search, providing a glimpse into the biographies of different activists and politicians working to find the bodies of the disappeared. And given that Aluízio's search during these years proved to be the spark of his memory script, my overview of his investigations also highlights key moments—and tensions—in the stories that he would begin to tell as part of his human rights activism.

Ever since his return from exile, Aluízio had always kept an ear out for rumors about what happened to Onofre Pinto in 1974. Within radical circles it was widely assumed that Pinto, the former VPR leader, and a few other militants had been killed after being lured back to Brazil.[1] It was unknown exactly how many people died or where the murders took place. It was believed that the plan had been orchestrated by a double agent named Alberi Vieira dos Santos, whom Aluízio had encountered, and fled, on that fateful afternoon in Buenos Aires in January 1974. Especially as details had come to light about the São Bento massacre in 1973, which had been orchestrated by another double agent known as Cabo Anselmo, a similar trap of Onofre Pinto seemed possible.

In his memoir, Aluízio wrote that he first started to think that Alberi might have been involved in the 1974 disappearances when a journalist named Marco Aurélio Borba came to Foz do Iguaçu in 1980. Borba was writing a story about Cabo Anselmo, and he asked Aluízio about the exiled militants in Chile.[2] Still on edge after a decade of being clandestine, Aluízio spoke cautiously with Borba, sharing only a few stories about the VPR.[3] From an initial discussion about the São Bento massacre organized by Cabo Anselmo in 1973, Aluízio's conversation with Borba eventually turned to another VPR mystery: the 1974 disappearance of Onofre Pinto. Borba had no concrete details about the case, but he mentioned the same stories that Aluízio had heard elsewhere, namely that Onofre was part of a group that had sneaked back into Brazil, where they were presumed to have been killed.

Aluízio sat with these thoughts for several years. When he finally wrote about Onofre Pinto, for *Nosso Tempo* in 1984, he did not mention his own militancy in the VPR, nor did he indicate that Alberi had invited him to join the group. *Nosso Tempo* ran a front-page exposé on the life and death of Alberi, who had died under suspect circumstances.[4] As described in *Nosso Tempo*, Alberi was killed in the town of Medianeira in February 1979, with an autopsy indicating that he had been shot four times by a 9-millimeter pistol—the standard-issue weapon for army soldiers at the time. Why might the authorities have killed Alberi? According to family members interviewed by *Nosso Tempo*, Alberi was planning to publish a book that would reveal details of his criminal activities along the border—a story that would have implicated army officers with whom he was collaborating. The newspaper story teased what Aluízio had long presumed: "Was [Alberi] also a traitor like Cabo Anselmo?"[5] It would take nearly a decade for more information to come to light. When it did, the new details came from a former military agent.

In November 1992, around the same time that Aluízio left the newspaper to work in the mayor's office, an officer came forward. Marival Dias Chaves had been a sergeant with the Army Intelligence Center, and he now seemed ready to clear his conscience. There was no legal obligation for Marival to give his testimony, but, driven by a desire to move forward with his life—and perhaps to help Brazil start its own process of accountability—the former intelligence agent gave a lengthy interview to *Veja*, the nation's largest magazine. Under the title of "Autopsy of a Shadow," a twelve-page story provided details on numerous cases of murder and espionage staged by the dictatorship.[6] The *Veja* material did not include anything related to the disappearance of Onofre Pinto's group, but its publication led several human rights organizations to get in touch with Marival in hopes that he could shed light on other cases.

One such group was Tortura Nunca Mais (Torture never again), a coalition based in Rio de Janeiro that formed in 1985, becoming a leading advocate in the movement for truth and justice. The group had been trying to gather information on the 1974 disappearances, and it wrote to Marival soon after the testimony in *Veja*. Within a month, Marival sent his reply and provided the first confirmation from within the military apparatus of what had happened. In a letter dated January 7, 1993, Marival confirmed that Alberi had indeed been a double agent who lured the militants back to Brazil by claiming that he was organizing a resistance base along the Paraná border.[7] Marival also gave the names of five militants whom he knew to have been part of the group: Onofre Pinto, José Lavéchia, the brothers Daniel and Joel José de Carvalho, and Enrique Ruggia, a seventeen-year-old Argentine student. These were five of the six militants who disappeared in 1974. The sixth, whom Marival seemed unaware of, was a man named Victor Carlos Ramos.

Family members of the disappeared saw this as revelatory, if still insufficient, news. For many years, Liliane Ruggia had lobbied both the Argentine and the Brazilian governments to comment on the disappearance of her brother, a student activist who had become friends with several Brazilian exiles living in Argentina. A psychologist from Buenos Aires, Liliane had tried to find information about her brother, but given that he had likely died in Brazil, authorities in her home country had been unhelpful. Marival's revelation offered the first semblance of an answer to her brother's death, and she contacted Cecília Coimbra, one of the founders of Tortura Nunca Mais, who suggested that Liliane visit the border region where her brother likely disappeared.[8] Cecília also put Liliane in touch with Aluízio, and the two had a series of long conversations in Foz do Iguaçu. For Liliane, who had felt alone in her search for answers, Aluízio seemed like a kindred spirit. In our interview, Liliane told me that meeting Aluízio "was fantastic. A kind person, friendly, and who was really interested in the case. . . . That for me was tremendous, tremendously emotional, really incredible. To meet someone who knew what I was talking about, who knew the people that were with my brother."[9] Aluízio also arranged for Liliane to give an interview to *Nosso Tempo*, resulting in an article about the disappearances titled "Betrayal at the Border."[10]

The burst of interviews and revelations in 1992 confirmed Aluízio's hunches. He had been correct to not trust Alberi when they had their chance encounter in Buenos Aires, and he was correct in guessing certain details about the subsequent disappearances. But he would have to wait several years for more clues to emerge.

A FALSE LEAD

In the decade that the search for Onofre Pinto's group largely went dormant, the campaign for truth and justice in Brazil saw the passage of an important, if limited, law. In December 1995, the government of President Fernando Henrique Cardoso passed Law No. 9.140, known as the Law of the Disappeared (Lei dos Desaparecidos). The law determined that the Brazilian state was responsible for the murder of 136 people who had been disappeared for political reasons, and it also created the Special Commission on Political Deaths and Disappearances (CEMDP, Comissão Especial sobre Mortos e Desaparecidos Políticos).

Through the CEMDP, families could present evidence about the disappearance of their loved ones, with the aim of having the person added to the official list of disappeared.[11] The commission could also distribute financial compensation to families. The Law of the Disappeared represented the government's largest effort to-date at truth and reconciliation, but as noted by the legal sociologist Cecília Santos, many families and human rights groups remained critical of the law, believing "that the government, by refusing to revise the Amnesty Law and to declassify documents on [key events of military violence], was promoting a politics of forgetfulness and impunity."[12] Similarly, Cecília Coimbra, who had put Liliane Ruggia in touch with Aluízio, told me that the 1995 law was "extremely perverse. It forced the burden of proof into the hands of family members. We were the ones who had to prove that someone died under the watch of the state."[13] The law required an immense amount of grassroots mobilization, presenting a logistical nightmare for families already dealing with tragedy. While telling me more the Law of the Disappeared and her work with families, Cecília reflected on the impact of this trauma. "This is terrible, my friend, it is a constant and daily torture," she said. "Because the family will never know if their loved one is actually alive or not. There were mothers here in Rio de Janeiro who didn't change their phone number or address because they thought that one day their child could appear. A lot of mothers died with that hope. So many of them. It is a terrible thing."

Scholars have devoted great energy to the study of disappearance—as a historical process, as a perversion of language, and as an ontological form of violence. Across Latin America, tens of thousands of people were disappeared by authoritarian regimes.[14] Although the disappearance of one's enemies predated Latin America's Cold War, with roots in the Nazis' doctrine of Night and Fog, the region became a perverse laboratory for refining the process. The

CHAPTER 9

logic of disappearance functioned in a self-fulling cycle of denial and impunity: because there was no body, no proof of military violence, a dictatorship could deflect blame by claiming that a missing person was a subversive who had chosen to go underground, and was likely still at large, still plotting an attack. In this view, if a family member could not find their loved ones, it must be because the person in question chose to abandon them. Layers of emotional manipulation thus permeate an ambiguous loss. As the Argentine scholar and essayist Marguerite Feitlowitz has written, "A *desaparecido* was neither living nor dead, neither here nor there. The explanation was at once totally vague and resoundingly final. Night and fog drawn like a curtain in the collective mind."[15]

For families and activists in search of the bodies of the disappeared, memory serves as a key mechanism for navigating the meanings and legacies of past violence. In his ontological analysis of disappearance, Marco Antonio Ramos observes that "the question of when an act of violence stops, for instance— when it moves from the present into the past—does not have an answer that is already given. As any memory activist in Latin America will tell you, violence does not come ready made as memory. Rather, it *becomes* memory through labor. An anthropologist records an interview with a survivor; a forensic technician digs up the bones of a victim; a genetic test spits out results that indicate parentage."[16] Even if the search for disappeared people is not successful, the long, often harrowing process of searching helps make authoritarian violence visible. The labor of that search—emotional, logistical, physical—gives shape and purpose to memory.

By the turn of the century, Aluízio had retired from his work in the mayor's office and was preparing for a more relaxing next stage of life. But in June 2000, a newspaper article changed his plans. He did not write the article. Rather, he was interviewed by a journalist from the *Folha do Paraná* for a series about the dictatorship's surveillance and repression in the border region, including Operation Condor—the secret intelligence and security system shared by military dictatorships across the Southern Cone.[17] The journalist, Valmir Denardin, told me that he was struck by how emotional Aluízio became when talking about the 1974 disappearances: "He was really distressed about it, he wanted to find a way to clarify what had happened.... I remember that he cried a lot during the interview. He cried because he remembered, 'I want to know what happened to my companions, I need to know.'"[18]

As part of the report, Valmir quoted Aluízio about the disappearance of Onofre Pinto, Enrique Ruggia, and the others. The information he discussed in the article seemed fairly innocuous, offering a summary of what had been revealed in the testimony of Marival seven years earlier. There was no indication that

Aluízio was actively investigating the case, but someone who read the article evidently wanted to nudge him onto the chase.

As chronicled in his memoir, and as Aluízio told me in our interviews, a few days after the article was published, somebody called his house.[19] Aluízio was out at the moment, but the caller told Eunice that he had information to share about Operation Condor. The caller did not leave his name or a return number. The same thing happened for several more days, until Aluízio happened to be home when the mystery call came in. Without saying his name, the man identified himself as a former army officer who knew where the bodies were buried. He said that he was currently passing through Curitiba, the state capital of Paraná, and that Aluízio should come meet him. Foz do Iguaçu is a nine-hour drive away, but Aluízio arranged for a friend and former militant named José Carlos Mendes, who lived in Curitiba, to go in his place. José Carlos met the man, who claimed that he "was having a crisis of conscience" and wanted the truth to be known. Before leaving quickly, he gave José Carlos a hand-drawn map of where Onofre Pinto and the militants were allegedly buried. The map, which José Carlos sent to Aluízio by fax, pointed to an old airstrip outside the town of Nova Aurora in western Paraná, less than 200 kilometers from Foz do Iguaçu. Aluízio felt cautious but hopeful at the possibility of finally bringing closure to the families.

The next morning, Aluízio contacted Nilmário Miranda, the head of the Special Secretariat of Human Rights, a body within the Ministry of Justice that helped coordinate forensic searches. Nilmário and Aluízio had much in common. Nilmário had been a political prisoner in the early 1970s, and, once out of prison, he established an opposition newspaper in Belo Horizonte, the state capital of his native Minas Gerais. After the return to civilian rule, Nilmário became an elected official, serving first as a state deputy and, beginning in 1991, as a federal deputy, a position in which he eventually oversaw the creation of Brazil's first-ever human rights commission. Throughout the 1990s and early 2000s, Nilmário was among the most influential figures in Brazil's search for disappeared persons. Even for someone as experienced as Nilmário, Aluízio's tenacity—and stubbornness—stood out. Nilmário told me that Aluízio was "someone who never took a break . . . he was always present. Very tough, he would just go after it. He wouldn't wait for people to come find him, he went and found everyone he thought was important [for the case]."[20]

With Nilmário's help, the logistics of a search in Nova Aurora began taking shape. The following year, in May 2001, a team of geologists from the Federal University of Minas Gerais and forensic scientists from Argentina spent two days using ground-penetrating radar to identify subsoil anomalies.[21] The binational effort was thanks in part to Liliane Ruggia, who lobbied her government to help with the possible exhumation of her brother, Enrique, an Argentine citizen. Due largely to the particularly brutal nature of Argentina's dictatorship from 1976 to 1983, the country's forensic scientists in subsequent years had become experts in locating human remains. Liliane closely followed news of the potential excavation, staying in telephone and email contact with Aluízio. In July, she sent an email—which Aluízio reproduced in his memoir—that opened with the following lines: "I THANK YOU WITH ALL MY HEART for your interest in the case of my brother and his companions, as well as the detailed information on these updates, which has you as the protagonist. Your information is of great emotional importance for me because it allows me to continue filling in this story, whose end continues to be the discovery of my brother's body."[22]

The initial survey of the Nova Aurora site was promising. In tandem with the map drawn by the mystery army officer, the scientists noted two potential areas where human remains might be buried. The next step was coordinating an excavation, which took place on August 3 and 4. Nilmário Miranda came to Nova Aurora to oversee the dig. Liliane Ruggia traveled to attend, as did the daughter of Onofre Pinto.[23] Also present was Suzana Lisboa, a representative of the CEMDP. During the dictatorship, Suzana had been an armed militant with the ALN, and she later became a leader in Brazil's amnesty movement. She was also intimately aware of the challenges and turmoil of searching for the disappeared. In 1990, the bones of her husband, Luiz Eurico Tejera, were discovered in the Dom Bosco cemetery in São Paulo, part of the first official excavation to identify disappeared victims of the dictatorship. Suzanna had not crossed paths with Aluízio prior to the 2001 dig at Nova Aurora, but she felt an immediate connection with him. "Finding a person like Aluízio, with total dedication to this subject, it was a huge thing for me," Suzana recalled in our interview. "Because the seriousness with which he treated this subject, his search, all his efforts and commitment, it really won me over from the very first moment."[24] With so many like-minded people gathering at Nova Aurora, hopes were high for a major breakthrough.

On the first day of excavation, the forensic team worked from daybreak until well past nightfall. Aluízio told me that the site turned into a festival: "It was like a circus, with two or three television stations, national stations, Rede News, Band News ... and vendors selling popcorn, cotton candy, sandwiches, everything.... The whole town came out to watch."[25] Photos published in a local newspaper show dozens of people standing around a roped-off area while several men wield shovels in a waist-deep trench.[26] But the spectacle was for nothing.

The forensic team found no human remains or clues of any kind. The search continued early the following day, but when nothing was found by midday, Nilmário Miranda called it off.[27] As the official government representative at the excavation, Nilmário took no pleasure in ending the dig. The majority of similar searches, often relying on fragments of information, ended in the same fashion, and Nilmário told me that he had long since learned to "live with that kind of frustration."[28] To Nilmário, failed searches like Nova Aurora were products of the 1979 Amnesty Law, and however badly he wanted to compel former military officers to testify, as a government official he had to follow the rule of law—even when it meant conducting his work within the stifling confines of impunity.

To Aluízio, who did not have the same perspective of someone like Nilmário Miranda, the failed search was devastating. Aluízio admitted to me that he cried from frustration. This despair was evident to those around him. Liliane Ruggia told me that the failure at Nova Aurora, and the similar results that unfolded in the coming years, "really knocked him about. Each of those frustrations was really tough. Because he would fight and fight and fight until the end. Always wanting to go further, always thinking there was more to do. But there wasn't anything more."[29] Suzana Lisboa saw how despondent Aluízio became, and she tried to council him based on her own history of accompanying similar excavations: "It's a sad job visiting burial sites, taking part in all of this, it's really difficult. [And most often] it creates enormous frustration."[30] And Nilmário Miranda likewise felt Aluízio's anger at having to follow government protocols: "Aluízio was unhappy with us because we couldn't take things past a certain point. We had to explain to him that there was a limit [to what we could do]."[31]

Despite Aluízio's wide range of personal and political setbacks as a clandestine militant, he had never experienced this particular type of disappointment. But in the years to come, as he entered more fully into the spaces of memory activism, he learned to identify the false lead at Nova Aurora as a form of personal reawakening. In the opening section of his memoir, which he wrote only a few years after the failed excavation, Aluízio observed that "the frustrations at Nova Aurora gave me more courage to continue the search. Sometimes, I think that this fixation was driven by a curiosity to know what my own death would have been like if I had accepted Sergeant Alberi's invitation to join the group. On top of that was my guilt for not having warned those comrades that they were being led into a trap. But who would I have told? And how? Would anyone, in that moment, even have believed my suspicion?"[32] In a swirl of survivor's guilt and political conviction, Aluízio remained determined to discover the truth.

At this moment in 2001, Aluízio had just been led on a wild goose chase by someone who seemed eager not only to keep the truth buried but to embarrass Aluízio and other activists. Yet as part of what would soon grow into his memory script, Aluízio sought to find purpose in a moment of great frustration. This resolve drove his activism in the decades to come.

A PERPETRATOR COMES FORWARD

For much of the next two years, Aluízio traveled across the western Paraná border chasing down leads in small towns the militants might have passed through back in 1974. Most often, Aluízio felt lost and overwhelmed by the search. As he wrote in his memoir, the six militants "could have been buried anywhere in the immense area flooded by the Itaipu dam's reservoir, or even somewhere in Argentina. Without a doubt, that work was like trying to find a needle in a haystack."[33] Most often, the snippets of potentially useful information that Aluízio gathered ended in a dead-end, leading to even more questions. Compounded by the lack of progress in his search, part of what made the work so tiring was the hostile reception that Aluízio sometimes received: "People didn't want to talk to me. Some tried to fight, or shout at me, saying really nasty things."[34] As a former torture victim himself, Aluízio tried to empathize, knowing that he would likely react in a similar way if a stranger were to show up and start asking about their personal histories of hardship. "They didn't want to touch these subjects anymore," Aluízio told me. "They had already suffered a lot. It was clear that people were traumatized and still very afraid." Aluízio invited his son to join him on several of these visits—Alexandre had recently begun working as a professional journalist, including having written several articles on the Nova Aurora excavation for the *Folha do Paraná*.[35] The father-son bonding was a silver lining in an otherwise daunting process.

It was also during this period that Aluízio's solo investigation gained some official authority. In November 2002, the CEMDP issued him research credentials, allowing him to spend several months in the archives of the Federal Police Station in Foz do Iguaçu.[36] Paired with his visits along the border, his archival searches helped him gather more information about Alberi and the operations of the military's security systems in the 1970s. Aluízio told me that his time in the archives felt like "a marvelous journey, because I learned so many things! I came across all kinds of documents about Japan, about the Arabs, about the Soviet Union, I found things about Chile, Uruguay, Itaipu, so much about Itaipu. I was diving into that world of surveillance information and all the documents sent by the army, the navy, the air force, federal police, civil police, highway police!"[37] This material, while useful for understanding the mechanisms of surveillance and repression at the time, contained no concrete evidence about what happened to Onofre Pinto's group.

The year 2003 seemed to promise several fresh starts, for Brazil and for Aluízio. In January, Luiz Inácio "Lula" da Silva was inaugurated as president, marking a sea change in national politics. A former factory worker with a second-grade education, Lula had become a prominent opposition figure against the dictatorship, helping lead a wave of strikes from 1978 to 1980. During the abertura process, he was a founding member of the Workers' Party (Partido dos Trabalhadores), for which he ran as a presidential candidate in 1989, 1994, and 1998—the latter two losing to Fernando Henrique Cardoso. On his fourth presidential campaign, in 2002, he finally won. Thus began a string of four-straight PT administrations that, bolstered by a strong export economy, oversaw a wave of social policies aimed at lifting millions out of extreme poverty.

During the first year of Lula's presidency, Aluízio also discovered the biggest clue yet in his search for the VPR militants. In July 2003, Aluízio helped run a mayoral campaign in the border town of Capanema, just south of Iguaçu National Park. Aluízio took advantage of the several months he spent on the campaign to continue his search.[38] In September, as he was preparing to return to Foz do Iguaçu, Aluízio met the nephew of the double agent Alberi, a man named Valdir who still lived in the area. In Aluízio's telling, his conversations with Valdir offered what appeared to be the key to solving the mystery: the identity of the driver who had accompanied Alberi on the ambush that killed the six militants. The driver's name was Otávio Rainolfo, and he would soon testify to having been present at the murder of five of the six militants.

Before describing how Aluízio discovered Rainolfo, it is useful to summarize how the deaths most likely happened. Key details of Rainolfo's story would be corroborated a decade later by Paulo Malhães, a former army officer who became one of the few perpetrators to voluntarily testify to Brazil's Truth Commission. In addition to Malhães's most headline-grabbing admission of having tortured prisoners at the notorious Casa da Morte (House of Death) detention center in Petrópolis, he also discussed the 1974 deaths of the VPR militants, stating that the murders had taken place near Medianeira and that they had been organized at the upper levels of the military regime.[39] Prior to Malhães's testimony to the Truth Commission, the more detailed sequence of events was uncovered by Aluízio's search. The story is as follows.

CHAPTER 9

MAP 9.1. Paraná borderlands and likely location of 1974 massacre. Courtesy of Gabe Moss.

On July 11, 1974, the double agent Alberi traveled with the six militants from Buenos Aires to the Brazilian border. By the next day, they had crossed into Brazil near the town of Santo Antônio do Sudoeste. The militants spent a day and night on a small farm, which they were led to believe was a base for the armed movement that sought to topple Brazil's dictatorship. At dusk the next day, July 13, Onofre stayed at the farm while the other five militants were driven into Iguaçu National Park for a planned meeting with other would-be rebels (map 9.1). After driving for about ten kilometers on an old road through the park—what was known as the Estrada do Colono (Settler's Road)—the car stopped, and the militants were told they now had to walk to the meeting point. The five militants walked alongside Alberi and Rainolfo, the driver. After walking for fifty meters, the group reached a clearing. Suddenly, bright lights flashed and gunfire erupted. Alberi and Rainolfo, seemingly aware of the planned ambush, threw themselves to the ground and took cover behind a fallen tree trunk. The five militants were shot to death. Onofre Pinto would later be killed back at the farm.

While there is no doubt that Aluízio's investigation uncovered this story, what is debatable is precisely *how* he discovered it. In his book, Aluízio writes that during his investigations along the border, he eventually tracked down Alberi's nephew, who claimed to have seen his uncle and the militants being taken to the family's farm, presumably before being driven to their deaths. Aluízio wanted to find out if Alberi was accompanied by anyone else, and the nephew replied that there was also a driver, whose name was Otávio Rainolfo.[40] This became a pivotal moment of Aluízio's search. In his telling, Aluízio remembered having seen Rainolfo's name mentioned in the police archive—he even told me that in several documents, Rainolfo's name often appeared alongside that of the double agent Alberi.[41] With what seemed to be biggest break in the case yet, Aluízio was eager to locate this person who might have participated in the murder of the six militants. As luck would have it, Rainolfo happened to still live in Foz do Iguaçu, only a short drive from Aluízio's home. As detailed in his memoir, Aluízio was able to find Rainolfo's address "with the help of some friends." The book goes on to say that although Rainolfo refused to speak with Aluízio, he did meet with Aluízio's two friends—a police officer and a wealthy businessman—and that Rainolfo then confessed to the full sequence of events described above.

Aluízio's recounting of this story raises several questions. First, how did Alberi's nephew know the full name of the driver whom he claimed to have seen only briefly during a secret military operation thirty years earlier? Second, who were the two friends who found Rainolfo, and why was the alleged perpetrator willing to share the details with them? The first question is perhaps unknowable, and the second leads us to informed conjectures.

The blurriness of how Aluízio found Rainolfo revolves around the pair of friends that helped secure the testimony. The first was a police officer named Adão Almeida. In the 1980s, Adão was fired from the police force following an internal investigation into still-undisclosed transgressions, after which he worked for several years at *Nosso Tempo*. Adão's dismissal was later reversed and from the 1990s onward he again served as a federal police officer in the border region. Adão also became close with the second person connected to Rainolfo: César Cabral, one of Aluízio's oldest friends. César had been a militant in the MR-8, joining Aluízio in the national park for guerrilla training sessions in 1968, before he, too, was arrested by the dictatorship. César was also Aluízio's brother-in-law, each having married a sister from the same family. César eventually settled in Foz do Iguaçu and set up a lucrative import-export company based in Paraguay. As mentioned in chapter 8, Aluízio believed that the money for his return to Brazil and his hideout in the Cabo Frio hotel came from César's budding enterprises along the border. Most of César's wealth came from cigarettes, and some of his business dealings over the years caught the attention of authorities for potential smuggling. No charges were ever brought against César, though he worked closely with a Paraguayan firm called Tabesa that was the subject of several investigations, including the code-named Operation Heart of Stone run by the US Drug Enforcement Administration.[42] César died of cancer in 2014, so I could not interview him about his role in the search for the disappeared militants. Aluízio spoke candidly with me about his old friend, and we even spent the bulk of one interview discussing César and their complicated relationship over the years.[43]

I was curious how exactly Rainolfo ended up divulging his memories about the 1974 disappearances. Compared to the relatively short version in Aluízio's book, which made only a passing gesture to Aluízio's "two friends," he gave me a lengthier story in our interviews. Aluízio told me that one night, at some point after having discovered Rainolfo's name, he was out having a beer with César, and they got to chatting about his ongoing search: "I didn't know if they were buried in Nova Aurora, or if they were thrown in the lake . . . but I said that I had a lead, of the only person who witnessed it . . . but that I didn't know who he was. César asks for the name, and César laughs and says, 'Don't worry my friend, [that guy] works for me.'"[44] In a twist that reflects the plausible overlap between contraband and policing in a border region, the story then goes that Rainolfo was a lackey of sorts for César—Aluízio used the word "capanga," meaning henchman.[45] As such, César had no trouble getting Rainolfo to admit what happened in 1974. Aluízio explained that Rainolfo refused to speak with him directly, only sharing details with César and Adão Almeida, the police officer. It was thus to Aluízio's two powerful friends, and never to Aluízio himself, that Rainolfo told his version of the story.

DIFFERENT TRUTHS

The truth that Rainolfo supposedly revealed was never verified—not in the early 2000s or at any point since. None of the bodies, or clues of any kind, have ever been found. Rainolfo's revelation to César Cabral set in motion another excavation. Because the new site was within Iguaçu National Park—a nearly 700-square-kilometer stretch of dense Atlantic rainforest—it required far more bureaucracy and logistical coordination than the dig at Nova Aurora. Approval had to first be granted by Brazil's Ministry of the Environment, and several preliminary aerial visits had to be made by helicopter prior to an excavation. Rainolfo himself participated in one of the helicopter survey trips. The team's primary detail for identifying the murder site was Rainolfo's memory of having traveled for a few kilometers through the park before seeing a small river at a turn in the road, after which they continued for what felt like another five kilometers. This approximation was vague enough to begin with, and was now even more difficult because park officials had closed the road back in 1986. The search thus had to follow instructions from a forty-year-old memory along a now-defunct dirt road in the middle of a massive rainforest.

Despite these obstacles, between March and May 2005, the search team identified a clearing within the park that seemed to match Rainolfo's testimony of where the ambush had taken place. Nearly a year after Rainolfo had first told his version of facts to César Cabral and Adão Almeida, an official excavation took place from May 5 to 10.[46] A collaborative team of Argentine and Brazilian forensic scientists lead the search, and Aluízio participated in a nontechnical supervisory role. The dig began much as it had at Nova Aurora: nothing was found. After a few days with no results, the decision was made to bring Rainolfo back and to allow him to survey the area from the ground. Aluízio was not present on the day of Rainolfo's visit to the excavation site—in a sign of the tension that festered in the years to come, Rainolfo refused to meet with Aluízio, insisting on being accompanied by Adão Almeida. Rainolfo's visit to the park made little difference. After a few more days of searching, the forensic team declared that the details of Rainolfo's testimony were inconsistent with the site, and the dig was cancelled.

For Aluízio, not finding the bodies was even more deflating the second time. "It was so frustrating. Such tremendous frustration," Aluízio said. "One day I finished a whole thing of whiskey, I drank a liter of whiskey. It was so frustrating not finding anything there."[47] After securing the testimony of somebody who claimed to have taken part in the disappearances, Aluízio struggled to understand how they could not find a single tangible clue.

Here is where we must venture into the world of informed hypotheses. Although Rainolfo's testimony yielded the same amount of evidence—zero—as in Nova Aurora, Rainolfo did work for the military in Foz do Iguaçu in 1974 and he maintained connections with Alberi in subsequent years. These facts, and his willingness to publicly attach his name to the murder of six people, suggest that his memories were likely more accurate than the "information" of the mystery caller who sparked the wild goose chase to Nova Aurora. Perhaps Rainolfo could not remember the precise location, within an immense national park, where the ambush happened? Or maybe the bodies had been scattered by animals and the elements in this dense stretch of Atlantic rainforest? To this day, a definitive answer remains elusive.

CHAPTER 9

Regardless of whether Rainolfo was telling the truth, what is clear is that his ability to make his statement, to declare that he had been an accomplice to the disappearances, was the result of a prevailing culture of impunity, through which the dictatorship's 1979 Amnesty Law shielded state agents from prosecution. Like with Marival Chaves in the early 1990s, Rainolfo could come forward because he knew that there were no legal consequences for doing so. In a context of impunity, where perpetrators could freely share details of past crimes, people like Rainolfo felt untouchable. A paradox of testimony in postdictatorship societies is that the search for truth often required perpetrators to willingly reveal their memories of human rights abuses. Because of a lack of evidence that has hindered most cases, perpetrators serve as gatekeepers to some semblance of truth. For any sense of justice to be achieved for the six disappeared militants, Rainolfo needed to come forward. Yet the reliance on his testimony was part of the exact problem that Aluízio and other activists were trying to confront.

An unintended legacy of Rainolfo's testimony was that it led Aluízio to write his memoir. The excavation in Iguaçu National Park took place in May 2005. After the failed dig, Aluízio wrote a short report about the search for the CEMDP. Aluízio shared the report with Fábio Campana, his friend and former comrade in the MR-8, who had lent his journalist credentials to *Nosso Tempo* in the early 1980s. After the end of the dictatorship, Fábio continued to work in media and eventually became the head of a small publisher in Curitiba called Travessa dos Editores. Fábio encouraged Aluízio to expand the report into a book-length text and offered to serve as its editor.[48] Aluízio accepted Fábio's proposal. As part of his writing process, Aluízio spoke with old comrades to confirm his memories about certain episodes, and he went on his own into Iguaçu National Park to seek inspiration from the forest landscapes where he believed the murders to have taken place.[49]

The more Aluízio wrote about the six disappeared militants, the more he found himself writing his own story. Aluízio told me that he was surprised by the process: "It was like breaking a silence that had been there for decades. . . . Writing broke that silence, about [all the things] I never spoke about in my house, that I never wrote about in the newspaper, that I never mentioned in all my years living in Foz do Iguaçu, more than thirty years, no? I broke all that silence by writing. I say that I went in search of the disappeared and I ended up finding myself."[50]

In hindsight, Aluízio wishes that he had not taken so long to write about himself. "I guess it's because [early on] my mission was the return of democracy, I wasn't interested in chewing on the past," Aluízio told me. "That was a mistake, of course it was a mistake. I'm not sure why, I don't know if it was a question of silence, I don't know if it was trauma, having some type of post-traumatic syndrome. Whatever it was, I'm not sure why I stayed silent [for so long]."[51] In telling me about his book, Aluízio again brought up the narrative of how his exile was harder than that of the Brazilians who went to Europe—and his comments also betrayed a hint of jealousy at the fame received by exiles like Fernando Gabeira and Alfredo Sirkis, whose books were, and remain, the most influential works in the large genre of militant memoirs. Aluízio noted that a lot of former prisoners shared his initial tendency to remain silent about the past. The lone exception, in his mind, were the exiles who went abroad. "Only those who went to Europe, who stayed in contact with Brazil, with what was going on in Brazil, those were the guys who came back already talking, having a party," Aluízio said. "Those guys, Alfredo Sirkis . . . and Gabeira . . . they were in touch with reality, they were ready to talk about the past. But not me. I didn't live that reality. I was here in the interior adapting to a different reality, suffocating."

For Aluízio, writing his book seemed like the only way to reconnect with his past. But it retained silences. On only a few occasions in his memoir does he discuss his family, offering little acknowledgment of the impact that his militancy and his exile had on Eunice and their children. Another silence relates to Otávio Rainolfo, the army officer who drove the VPR militants to their death. Although throughout this book I have referred to the driver in 1974 by his real name—Otávio Rainolfo—for most of Aluízio's search, the person in question was publicly known as Otávio Camargo. According to Aluízio, César Cabral had demanded that he not include Rainolfo's name, even threatening to kill Aluízio if he did.[52] Aluízio opted for a middle path and used the real first name but a fake last name—a solution that did not satisfy César, leading to a falling out between the one-time close friends. As such, the initial version of the memoir referred to the driver as Otávio Camargo, which persisted through the fifth edition in 2018, two years after Rainolfo died at the age of sixty-nine. In Aluízio's telling, even though he used a fake last name in the memoir, Rainolfo still hated him.

Regardless of the interpersonal drama behind the pages of Aluízio's memoir, its publication in 2005 launched him, at the age of sixty-two, as a full-time memory activist. At the suggestion of Fábio Campana, Aluízio had chosen a title that he hoped would reflect the unfinished status of the search and also the broader demand for truth and justice: *Onde foi que vocês enterraram os nossos mortos?* (Where did you bury our dead?).

The book brought Aluízio new levels of prominence among human rights circles and also the general public (fig. 9.1). A book launch was held at the

CHAPTER 9

FIGURE 9.1. Aluízio (*seated*) at a book signing, Porto Alegre, 2005. Courtesy of Aluízio Palmar.

National Archive in Rio de Janeiro, he was interviewed in several media outlets, and the memoir was discussed in the *Folha de São Paulo*.[53] Reflecting the cyclical power of a person's memory script, the more attention that Aluízio's memoir brought to the case of the six disappearances, the more attention he gained as an activist, which, in turn, allowed him to continue talking about his search for the disappeared. If his memoir was the most tangible part of his memory script, it also served as an open-ended platform for the script itself: many of Aluízio's speaking engagements and presentations in the coming years revolved around the memoir, providing him with an accessible tool for sharing his memories and his life history.

ANOTHER SEARCH IN THE NATIONAL PARK

Even though two major excavations had failed to unearth any clues about the deaths of Onofre Pinto and the five other militants, the publication of Aluízio's memoir and his growing profile as a human rights activist helped keep interest in the case alive. Five years later, in November 2010, he convinced the Brazilian government to stage a second excavation within the national park. A new minister of human rights had recently been appointed, Paulo Vannuchi, who prioritized the discovery of disappeared bodies. As we will see in the next chapter, this was part of a larger move toward historical

FIGURE 9.2. Aluízio at the excavation site in Iguaçu National Park, November 2010. Courtesy of Aluízio Palmar.

clarification that soon culminated with the creation of a National Truth Commission.

Within this context of a growing human rights culture, Aluízio could also point to a new piece of evidence in the Paraná case. Since his original testimony earlier in the decade, Rainolfo had changed his statement, telling César Cabral that the bodies were several kilometers away from his original indication.[54] Rainolfo had initially said that their drive into the park had started near Porto Lupion (the southern entrance of the Estrada do Colono [Settler's Road]), but he now said that they had actually entered the park near Capoeirinha, at the park's northern entrance. The change in direction implied an entirely different location along the seventeen-kilometer road through the park. With this new information, Minister Vannuchi authorized another excavation.

Even with a new set of geologists and geophysicists, the forensic team again found nothing (fig. 9.2). After a few days of fruitless searching, the excavation was suspended and Rainolfo was again brought by helicopter into the national park to visit the dig site. Accompanied by representatives from the Ministry of Justice, Rainolfo walked around the site and the surrounding forest, repeating his testimony, and describing how he remembered the events taking place. Although Aluízio was not present during the visit—Rainolfo, as ever, refused to meet with him—the conversation was recorded and later transcribed. Aluízio eventually posted it on his website and included it as an appendix in subsequent editions of his memoir.[55] (This was one of the instances I discovered of Aluízio publishing documents without authorization.) Aluízio was frustrated by Rainolfo's refusal to meet with him, but he endeavored all the same to publicize the testimony that might one day lead to the discovery of the disappeared bodies.

Aluízio's inability to speak directly to Rainolfo served as a small sideshow to the larger issue at hand: the complete lack of clues. After Rainolfo's visit to the dig site, the excavation continued for several more days. As with all previous searching, the additional time in the national park yielded no breakthroughs.

By this point, Aluízio had been actively searching for nearly a decade, and that amount of experience—and exposure to failure—had given him new perspective. The abject frustration he had felt after the 2001 dig in Nova Aurora no longer resurfaced in the same way, and he instead resigned himself to a different form of closure. He had not located any clues about the six militants who disappeared in 1974: Onofre Pinto, José Lavéchia, Daniel and Joel José de Carvalho, Victor Carlos Ramos, and Enrique Ruggia. None of their bodies, or any concrete evidence about them, were ever discovered. Yet Aluízio took solace in the fact that his search had brought new attention to their disappearances and to the broader history of violence unleashed by Brazil's dictatorship.

Even in his most optimistic moments, Aluízio never knew whether he would unearth the full story of what took place. But especially as he grew older, and as he witnessed a growth in human rights activism across Latin America and globally, his initially hardened pursuit of "truth" (tangible proof of crimes) and "justice" (trials for perpetrators) gave way to a broader sensibility that ideas like truth and justice were also important as a process, and not just as a goal. Asking questions could hold just as much power as finding answers. In the closing lines of his memoir, Aluízio offers a summary of these feelings: "The executioners are out there, I believe almost all of them are alive, perhaps reading this book comfortably in their homes. I don't know if they have nightmares at night, or if their children know what they've done or if they regret it. But I am sure of one thing: it is necessary to clarify the crimes committed by state agents. Society has the right to truth and memory."[56]

CHAPTER 10

MEMORY IN THE TIME OF IMPUNITY

BRAZIL WAS AMONG the last countries in Latin America to have a truth commission investigating its military dictatorship. While most countries established a state-sponsored truth commission within a few years of their transition from military to civilian rule, it took Brazil nearly three decades. The dictatorship ended in 1985, and it was not until 2011 that the Brazilian government created a commission "for the purpose of examining and clarifying the serious violations of human rights practiced during the period [in question], in order to solidify the right to memory and historical truth and to promote national reconciliation."[1] The commission was signed into law by President Dilma Rousseff of the Workers' Party, herself a former political prisoner and torture victim, who had assumed office at the beginning of 2011. During the first two Workers' Party administrations under Lula (2003–10), little progress had been made toward a truth commission, but enough momentum built under Dilma that a commission finally became possible.

As we saw in previous chapters, the National Truth Commission (CNV, Comissão Nacional da Verdade) was both a reflection and a product of Brazil's disjointed path of transitional justice. Because the 1979 Amnesty Law continued to provide legal protection for perpetrators of human rights abuses, government initiatives were sporadic and constrained, most notably the 1995 Law of the Disappeared that created the CEMDP to coordinate excavations and pay economic reparations.[2] As legal scholar Marcelo Torelly has written, in the context of ongoing impunity, government bodies like the CEMDP relied largely on the investigations of social movements and victims groups, most notably the 1985 *Brasil: Nunca mais* report and the 1996 *Dossiê dos mortos e desaparecidos políticos*.[3] During the 1990s and early 2000s, although certain government initiatives—catalyzed and substantiated by grassroots pressure from below— made important inroads, such as establishing a baseline number of 363 victims of military violence, amnesty remained untouched and no perpetrators were made to stand trial.[4] In 2010, the Brazilian Supreme Court reinforced the legal status quo, with judges voting 7-2 to uphold the 1979 law, declaring that the reciprocal amnesty (applying to state perpetrators as well as armed dissidents) constituted a political agreement that served as the foundation for the democratic constitution of 1988.

The Supreme Court ruling was a blow to activists' hope for legal accountability, but government and civil society actors continued to organize toward a truth commission.[5] Throughout 2010, a congressional working group was formed to draft a bill for establishing a national truth commission—toward the end of the year, the bill was approved with minor modifications by both the Chamber of Deputies and the Senate. Even then, it took another thirteen months for the bill to become law: on November 18, 2011, President Dilma Rousseff signed the bill and authorized the CNV to conduct its investigations between 2012 and 2014. The commission's purview was investigative and not prosecutorial, meaning that it could only document instances of human rights abuse and political persecution. The commission could not file any legal charges.

Especially in the CNV's first year, a series of internal debates and political crises threatened to derail the investigation. These issues included whether hearings should be public or held behind closed doors and to what extent the CNV's final report should include recommendations for further action, especially in regard to overturning the 1979 Amnesty Law. Part of what made the CNV's work difficult was a lack of consensus on the left about amnesty. Although a vocal contingent of activists, victims' groups, and politicians called for the end of amnesty, others did not want it to be a priority. In part, this related to what Paulo Abrão and Marcelo Torelly call the "time factor," meaning that because the worst violence of military rule was now an entire generation in the past, various civil society actors had begun to pursue a "practical desire to move forward."[6] Especially with a leftist government in power, certain sectors preferred to spend their political capital enacting progressive policies. This reluctance to overturn amnesty features across Latin America, perhaps most notably in Uruguay, where President José Mujica, himself a former armed militant and political prisoner, was for many years a vocal opponent of reversing his country's amnesty law.[7] And finally, some people in Brazil did not want to touch amnesty as a matter of self-preservation in the face of legal uncertainty. Because the 1979 law applied to state agents and dissidents alike, would the law's overturning also open the door for trials against militants? There was no definitive answer. And if this prospect was nerve-wracking in the early 2010s under a Workers' Party government, any potential rightward shift in national politics would only exacerbate worries about the weaponization of amnesty. The election of Jair Bolsonaro in 2018 was not preordained, but the intractable shadow of prodictatorship forces meant that potential backlash always loomed on the horizon.

During the deliberations over Brazil's truth commission, the Inter-American Court of Human Rights (IACtHR) declared that the 1979 law was illegal, using a case relating to the 1972 disappearance of dozens of militants from the Araguaia guerrilla movement to declare that Brazil's Amnesty Law is incompatible with the American Convention on Human Rights.[8] Although Brazil is a member of the Organization of American States (the parent body of the IACtHR) and formally recognizes the court's jurisdiction, the nonbinding ruling did not override the earlier decision by Brazil's Supreme Court. Nonetheless, the IACtHR decision emboldened antiamnesty activists and highlighted the various challenges facing the CNV. The tensions within the CNV also frustrated those watching from the sidelines. In July 2013, a little more than halfway into the commission's work, a coalition of human rights activists and victims' groups issued an open letter criticizing the CNV for its lack of transparency and slow pace.[9] Aluízio Palmar was one of the letter's signatories.

Aluízio's involvement in Brazil's truth commission took many forms. As a victim of dictatorship, he delivered a testimony about his personal experience; as the leading figure in the search for the disappeared VPR militants, he contributed his extensive research; and as a representative for the Center for Human Rights and Popular Memory in Foz do Iguaçu, he participated in the planning of several local events meant to boost public awareness of the commission. Although he worked closely with people involved in the national truth commission—even attending the CNV's official inauguration in Brasília— most of his efforts related to the Paraná state truth commission.[10] The parallel existence of a state and a national truth commission may seem odd, if not inefficient, but the slow progress of the CNV had spurred civil groups and local governments to create their own commissions. By 2012, over fifty local commissions existed across the country. Not wanting to be outflanked, the CNV eventually issued official notes of cooperation with twenty-seven local commissions; as Torelly observes, "This decision helped to reduce the tension between the [CNV] and the human rights movement. [And] a substantial amount of what became the [CNV's] final report pays tribute to the local commissions' work."[11] The Paraná State Truth Commission signed its cooperation agreement with the national CNV in November 2012, thereby linking Aluízio's life story to Brazil's largest effort to-date to reckon with its violent past.[12]

The official name of the Paraná commission was the Comissão Estadual da Verdade do Paraná–Teresa Urban, in honor of a former militant who had been imprisoned by the dictatorship and who later became a leading journalist in the state. (Teresa Urban had been one of Aluízio's earliest contacts in Paraná; her boyfriend at the time, Fábio Campana, hosted Aluízio on his initial scouting trips for the MR-8 in Foz do Iguaçu.) Beginning in June 2013, the state commission held fifty-one weekly hearings, all of which were open to the public, in addition to collecting the testimony of almost eighty people. Many of the events took place in the Palácio Iguaçu, the state's capitol building in Curitiba, with others in various cities across Paraná. In fact, the inaugural hearing on June 28 did not occur in Curitiba but in Foz do Iguaçu—the opening presentation, at 9 a.m., featured Aluízio talking about what was now being called the "Medianeira Massacre" of the six VPR militants in 1974.[13] Aluízio described to me the buoyant atmosphere on that first day: "It was a marvelous gathering, when we had the public hearing of the [State] Truth Commission in Foz do Iguaçu. The council chamber was full, the plenary was packed."[14] On a later occasion, Aluízio would again testify to the state truth commission, offering personal testimony about his experience as a militant, a political prisoner, and a torture victim, mentioning several times the name of Mário Espedito Ostrovski, the army lieutenant who would file a defamation lawsuit six years later.[15]

In addition to delivering these two testimonies, Aluízio stayed active in various activities for both the state and national commissions.[16] One of the leaders of the Paraná commission was a human rights lawyer named Ivete Caribe, who told me about the key role that Aluízio played: "[He] was a tremendous collaborator, sharing so many of the things he knew and putting us in touch with people for the commission [to interview]."[17] Aluízio's gained national attention as well. Marcelo Rubens Paiva, a well-known writer whose father had been disappeared by the dictatorship, wrote about Aluízio in *O Estado de São Paulo*. The article described Aluízio's militant past and his recent memory work, a one-man sweep of history reflected in the profile's title: "Comissão Pessoal da Verdade" (Personal Truth Commission).[18]

But the truth commission was not always a positive experience for Aluízio. As part of the investigation into the 1974 disappearances, Otávio Rainolfo was called to testify. The inclusion of perpetrator testimony reflects what the sociologist Leigh Payne calls a "contentious coexistence," in which the unsettling accounts from human rights abusers must be weighed as part of a "democratic debate over past state violence."[19] Across postconflict societies but especially in places like Brazil where there have been no trials or forms of legal accountability, the ability to know what happened in a country's violent past often relies on perpetrator memory. Sometimes there are other forms of proof—archival documents, bystander testimony, forensic evidence—but discovering the truth about human rights violations often depends on those who had been involved in the crimes. Their memories, however contentious and potentially misleading, are a key part of the process. And as the example of Rainolfo will show, they can also be understood as a type of memory script, with their own elements of being practiced, repetitive, and performative.

This story about Rainolfo is not a part of Aluízio's standard narrative. If I had not brought it up, Aluízio likely never would have mentioned it. And as far as I could tell, it received zero news coverage. Outside of those immediately involved with the truth commission, this particular testimony seems to have barely registered. Especially compared to the more headline-grabbing statements of perpetrators like Paulo Malhães, Rainolfo's testimony remained on the margins. Rainolfo was called to testify in June 2013, but he did not show up on his scheduled day. As told to me by the retired police officer Adão Almeida—one of Rainolfo's two unofficial handlers—Rainolfo did not want to be in City Hall, but he agreed to meet with representatives of the CNV in a supposedly "neutral" location: the house of César Cabral.[20] Most of Rainolfo's testimony covers the details he had shared in previous years about how the six militants were lured back to Brazil and then killed in the national park.

But three-quarters of the way into his two-hour testimony, Rainolfo made what seemed to be an absurd and vindictive statement. While discussing the double agent Alberi who had orchestrated the ambush, Rainolfo obliquely suggested that perhaps Aluízio was also a double agent who had collaborated with the dictatorship. "I'm not saying this because I'm mad at him," Rainolfo stated. "It's just that you shouldn't trust him, he's not what he says he is."[21] When given an audience with Brazil's truth commission, Rainolfo tried to turn the tables by accusing Aluízio. And later in his testimony, having already made the provocative insinuation against Aluízio, Rainolfo also made an overt threat. As a sign of the risks involved with turning one's memories into a public narrative, Rainolfo's threat was couched in a reference to Aluízio's memoir. "Just seeing that book gets me angry," Rainolfo said. "If he doesn't like me, well then I won't like him. And I'll find a way to tell him . . . you've made an enemy."[22]

Rainolfo's official testimony reflects a paradox at the core of what it means to search for truth within a culture of impunity. On the one hand, his memories of 1974 are the foundation of what is known about how the six militants were most likely killed. Although key elements of his story were corroborated by the testimony of Paulo Malhães, Rainolfo's memories have been the main source base for these events. On the other hand, while detailing what allegedly happened in the national park, he also accused Aluízio of being a double agent. These assertions were widely seen as malicious. I asked Ivete Caribe about Rainolfo's accusation, and she told me that it was not uncommon among the small number of former military officers who testified. "Look, we didn't take his statement too seriously," Ivete said. "Because the majority of those who gave testimonies, there weren't many ex-military who did so, they always tried to belittle and smear the people who fought against the dictatorship. . . . They try to discredit the human rights activists."[23] Without Aluízio's investigations, Rainolfo's participation in the 1974 massacre would have likely stayed a secret. The accusations leveled at Aluízio reflect a global trend. Human rights activists around the world have been the target of such widespread abuse—physical violence like torture and execution, as well as harassment, defamation, and arbitrary imprisonment—that the UN Office of the High Commissioner for Human Rights (OHCHR) spent fourteen years negotiating for the UN General Assembly to adopt a Declaration on Human Rights Defenders.[24] Although Aluízio did not suffer the type of overt attacks experienced by some human rights activists, the slander that he had to navigate nonetheless showed the dangers of telling one's life story. Rainolfo could attack Aluízio because Aluízio was a public figure, and because Aluízio had turned his life story into a matter of public record. Rainolfo could also attack Aluízio because there were essentially no consequences for doing so.

It is useful here to analyze Rainolfo's testimony as a form of memory script, with its three main characteristics. First, Rainolfo's testimony was practiced. He learned how to frame his memories of the murders in a similar way to how other perpetrators had done when they went public with their admissions over the previous decades. Because there were no legal requirements for former officers to come forward, when they did, they often drew on a similar set of phrases and justifications—of only being an accomplice, of just following orders, and of now seeking praise for voluntarily coming forward. This narrative circulated not only in Brazil but across Latin America and internationally, in the aftermath of the political violence of the global Cold War. Second, Rainolfo's memories were repetitive. At every excavation, between 2004 and 2010, he was brought into the national park to repeat his testimony and to guide the forensic team through the supposed murder site. Even if certain details shifted—like when Rainolfo changed the massacre's location in 2010—the broader narrative of events and the roles played by perpetrators had to remain consistent. The repetition of his story was a crucial part of his self-depiction as a relatively innocent soldier who was just following orders. For the sake of self-defense, his memories had to follow the same script.

Finally, Rainolfo's memory script was performative. He was performing innocence and a form of patriotic duty. As evident in his accusations against Aluízio, he was aware of the spotlight cast by the truth commission, and he could turn his testimony into a public spectacle. In this sense, his performance of memory was not so different than the actions six years later of Lieutenant Ostrovski, Aluízio's torturer, whose lawsuit was also an incendiary performance of countermemory. The changing context between the two perpetrator memories meant that Rainolfo's provocations under a democratic government could be cast aside as vengeful bluster, while Ostrovski's lawsuit, in the reactionary climate of Jair Bolsonaro, would pose a much greater threat.

Both at the time and in the decade since, Rainolfo's testimony reveals a troubling reality at the core of these platforms for truth-telling. In the long-standing absence of legal accountability, where any approximation of the truth must rely on the testimony of perpetrators, people like Rainolfo retained a lot of power to withhold or manipulate memory. When it suited them, they could change their script. Why, for example, do we trust Rainolfo's testimony concerning the details of the massacre but not his accusations against Aluízio? Context and common sense help distinguish probable truths from probable slander. But in a search for memory there exists a suspension of disbelief through which society is eager to find answers, even when they are delivered by people we are naturally inclined to distrust.

My analysis of Rainolfo's testimony is a final example of revisions that I made after Aluízio commented on a chapter draft. In previous sections, I drew readers' attention to instances when, after showing Aluízio my initial draft, he brought up an anecdote or detail from our interviews that I had not included. Often, these stories were inflection points in how Aluízio understood his youth and his commitment to political militancy—his political discipline in not accepting a "bribe" from older comrades to study in Europe, and his personal discipline in turning down a one-night stand with a beautiful woman before he began his guerrilla training. But here, rather than *adding* material in light of Aluízio's comments, I opted to *remove* some of my previous writing.

Aluízio took great exception to parts of this chapter. It was the only time during our collaboration that he seemed genuinely upset. Several weeks after I had emailed him the chapter, he replied tersely: "Hi Jake. Attached are my comments on the draft. This was hard, an inglorious task, looking over these fake news statements. Hugs, and I'm sorry. I do support your work and I try to collaborate."[25] In light of Aluízio's comments, and as part of my constant effort to balance my duties as a biographer with my relationship to the subject of the biography, I made a few key revisions. I removed a few additional quotations from Rainolfo's testimony, and I framed the accusations in a more obviously negative way—the words "absurd" and "vindictive" had not appeared in the original version. In our conversation a few weeks later, once Aluízio had read the new chapter, he was happier with the text, though he still worried that readers might take Rainolfo's accusations seriously. Especially because the anecdote comes in the last chapter of the book, he wanted to leave a good final impression, telling me, with a slight chuckle, "You always remember your last kiss."[26]

Over the course of its two-year investigation, the CNV heard the testimonies of 1,116 people, mostly victims, family members, and witnesses, but also perpetrators like Rainolfo. The CNV produced its findings in a final report that ran to almost 4,500 pages, which it issued on December 10, 2014, at the end of a year that had included a long series of commemorations relating to the fiftieth anniversary of the military coup in 1964.

Given the context of the CNV report and the commission's lack of subpoena power to compel the testimony of perpetrators, the report offered little in the way of new information. The CNV did update the total of known victims from 363 to 431, and it identified 377 military and police officers as culpable of gross human-rights violations. It also made the symbolically important decision to include types of repression that went beyond torture, death, and disappearances, with chapters and appendices on violence against Indigenous communities and the targeting of trade unionists, student activists, and LGBT people. Returning to Torelly's analysis of Brazil's truth commission, the CNV's main accomplishment "was not to report new facts but to assemble everything that was already known in a systematic way, thickening the narrative with testimonial evidence and legitimizing an account of violence that the regime had mostly tried to cover up."[27] If a primary goal of truth commissions is to establish a historical narrative that explains the patterns and causes of past violence, then the CNV was a success.[28] As the transitional justice scholar Rebecca Atencio has written, the CNV "appeared to have settled the debate over the meaning of the 1964 coup and the ensuing brutal regime—and discredited the military's celebratory narrative once and for all."[29] To that end, activists and contributors like Aluízio Palmar had to content themselves with the knowledge that even if their efforts had not led to trials or any significant new information, the process had forced Brazil to systematically confront its collective past.

History, of course, is not linear. Nor is the advance of human rights norms. Although observers at the time might have felt like the CNV had helped change the narrative about what had happened during military rule, the shadow of dictatorship did not dissipate. Two years later, in 2016, right-wing forces would stage a legislative coup against President Dilma Rousseff, exploiting a relatively benign political scandal to stir up backlash sentiment against the social reforms and antipoverty measures overseen by the Workers' Party over the previous four administrations. In many ways, the CNV represented the exact type of initiative that conservative forces sought to reverse. During the impeachment proceedings against Dilma, a previously marginal congressmen named Jair Bolsonaro cast his vote in honor of Colonel Carlos Alberto Brilhante Ustra, among the dictatorship's most notorious human rights violators—Ustra was also one of the army officers who had tortured Dilma. The impeachment effort succeeded. Dilma's removal from office brought to the surface right-wing sympathies that helped pave the way, two years later, for Bolsonaro to run for president on a campaign to reclaim the memory and legitimacy of military rule. Bolsonaro's victory in 2018, on the heels of the 2016 impeachment of Dilma, represented Brazil's most serious political and social crisis in many years.

But in 2014, when the CNV issued its report, this descent back toward authoritarianism was not yet obvious. In the meantime, Aluízio was satisfied by the progress, both symbolic and tangible, embodied in the truth commission. He was motivated as well by the CNV's limitations. As always, there was more work to do.

ARCHIVING MEMORY

Aluízio had started visiting archives in the early 2000s as part of his search for the six militants. To find traces of information about the double agent Alberi or the militants themselves, Aluízio spent much of his free time looking through the police archives in Foz do Iguaçu—his ability to do so resulted largely from a law passed in 1991, which regulated public access to classified material.[30] In the archives, his interests expanded beyond the case of the VPR militants to include all manner of documents relating to the military regime. In the years

CHAPTER 10

between the failed national park excavations in 2005 and 2010, much of his archival work was in the service of a human rights network called Memória, Verdade e Justiça (Memory, truth, and justice).[31] As a member of the group, Aluízio visited archives across the country, most notably the DOPS secret police holdings in Rio de Janeiro and those of the Air Force in Brasília. He also started researching his own archival record, finding various documents relating to his arrest, imprisonment, and torture. As part of his searches, Aluízio began to make digital copies of any document that he thought might be useful, using a hand scanner to create jpg files.

At the time, he had no long-term goals for his budding collection of digital files. When I asked Aluízio what motivated his archival efforts, he said that it was mostly out of "curiosity. Just to find out more. I had no plans or anything to become a guardian of memory. I never thought of being a memory keeper. I did it to learn things, and with time I just kept compiling more."[32] Eventually, Aluízio had the idea to post his archives on the internet, and in February 2009 he launched a website called Documentos Revelados.

The site would grow to become one of the largest private archives of its kind in Latin America. As of September 2024, it has over 75,000 documents. And according to the Google Analytics data that Aluízio shared with me, it averages 11,000 views per month. The documents are all tagged by keyword and theme, and Aluízio has curated them across 3,250 posts, each with a short essay describing the documents and their historical context. Aluízio has written every single one of the essays, and he alone maintains the website, storing all the material on a series of external hard drives at his home in Foz do Iguaçu. Although Aluízio occasionally secured partnerships to cover some of the site's operating costs, most often he financed it himself. When I asked him if he pays for the site out of his own pocket, he said, "Of course, who else would pay? Jesus Christ? He doesn't pay my bills, only I do."[33]

Given the ad hoc nature of the website, and the fact that Aluízio runs it almost entirely on his own, I asked whether he ever worried about the legal implications of posting so much material. Aluízio seemed a little annoyed by my question: "I never asked for anyone's permission, I never asked for authorization. They are [from] public archives, that makes them public documents."[34] Although the vast majority of documents are from Aluízio's own research, some come from other sources. As mentioned previously, two people that I interviewed (one a historian, the other a human rights practitioner) told me that Aluízio published material on his website without their permission.[35] Aluízio did not tell me about these examples of unauthorized posts. But he did say that when documents related to torture, he would try to contact the person named in the document. "With police reports I would always be cautious, because the information in those reports is rarely true, they have so much false information . . . extracted by torture." Occasionally, Aluízio was able to contact the person named in the report, and he would tell them about the website. Nobody ever told him not to post the archival material, but most people did not share his eagerness to publicize the past: "A lot of people, after the return to democracy, they wanted to stay hidden." Aluízio told me that the only time when somebody asked him to take a document off the website was in the aftermath of Bolsonaro's election in 2018, when the daughter of a former VPR militant got in touch with him, saying that she was afraid that her father would now get targeted by the Far Right.

The tumultuous four years of Bolsonaro's presidency gave a renewed sense of the website's importance. According to a post on Aluízio's Facebook page, Documentos Revelados had its highest-ever month of traffic in November 2022, the month after Bolsonaro lost reelection to President Lula.[36] With nearly 1 million views during the month, the site's three most popular types of post related to torture during the dictatorship, urban guerrilla warfare, and the music of the popular left-wing singer and composer Chico Buarque. As an archive of historical memory, an outlet for an anxious society, and a source of inspiration, Aluízio's website embodied the ongoing effort in Brazil to make sense of the country's past and find its purpose in the present.

As a public memory space, the website could also be targeted by online trolls. Aluízio told me that from the early days of the site, he received a steady stream of vitriol, to the point that he changed the settings to require him to approve or reject any comments. I asked him to share some examples with me, but that was not always simple, given that he normally deletes the most blatantly offensive comments. But in early February 2023, barely a month after supporters of the recently defeated Bolsonaro stormed government buildings in Brasília, Aluízio forwarded me a server notification. The message indicated that there were 169 pending comments to approve or reject.

Aluízio called my attention to one post in particular. Someone identifying themselves as André Matiads Miguel wrote the following: "I think that torture under the military dictatorship wasn't very much, it should have continued and been stronger, going all the way to death and even dismembering bodies, death to dilma rousseff."[37] Aluízio often removes such comments, though perhaps knowing that he had shared it with me, he approved this post and, later that same night, replied directly: "André, this is horrible. You should be ashamed of the nonsense you write. So, are you in favor of torture, rape, and the disappearance of bodies? How can a person defend the murder of those who fight against a dictatorship that led Brazil into poverty and caused immense suffering to Brazilian families?"[38] The troll in question remained silent for over a month, before resurfacing and shifting his threats from the former president to Aluízio himself: "I dare you to say all this in person, I guarantee that you'll wish for death and regret your cowardly comment." The post must have alarmed Aluízio enough to share its existence with colleagues, because the Paraná Federation of Journalists soon issued a denouncement of precisely that threat.[39] Even with Bolsonaro out of power, journalists and human rights activists continued to face right-wing backlash. According to one study, although overall harassment of journalists decreased after Bolsonaro left office, 181 journalists were targeted in 2023, including forty cases of physical violence.[40] The threats against Aluízio and others showed that *bolsonarismo*, and the memory wars that gave it power, would not go away any time soon.

MEMORY IN ACTION

While overseeing the Documentos Revelados site, Aluízio's was also building a nonprofit in Foz do Iguaçu, the Center for Human Rights and Popular Memory. The CDHMP was officially established in 2012, but its origins stretched back a decade earlier. In the late 1990s and early 2000s, Aluízio had felt somewhat lost politically, no longer a member of any party and without an organization to anchor his activism. Especially after retiring from his job at City Hall, he needed a space and a community. There had previously been an organization in Foz do Iguaçu called the Center for Human Rights, and Aluízio wanted to use that same name, but with the addition of *popular memory*. "From the beginning that was the idea, because I had been working for many years on questions of memory," Aluízio told me. "Without memory you can't build a new society. So I thought it was important that beyond a center to defend human rights, it also needed to be a center for the construction of memory, to rescue memory. The memory of popular struggles in Foz do Iguaçu and in the region."[41]

It took several years for Aluízio to start an actual center. Initially, he and his collaborators would meet at community spaces in Foz do Iguaçu, most often at a church run by a progressive priest. Aluízio eventually had the idea to seek a partnership with Itaipu Binational, the entity in charge of the hydroelectric dam—Itaipu was, and remains, the largest nongovernmental funder of civil initiatives in the region. (The irony was not lost on Aluízio that he would collaborate with Itaipu administrators, whose predecessors in the 1980s had tried to silence his newspaper). During the time of the dam's construction, Itaipu built several neighborhoods of worker housing on the outskirts of the city, much of which had fallen into disrepair. With the help of a few friends who worked in Itaipu's administration, Aluízio was told that he could choose among a series of abandoned houses. "The buildings were horrible," Aluízio recalled. "Really broken down, in ruins. I was getting tired looking at so many of them, but when I saw one that was more or less okay, it seemed like the best [option] and I ended up choosing that one."[42] The building had no electricity or gas connections, and it needed new floors and a new roof. The remodeling, curiously enough, was financed almost entirely by the VPR, his former armed group of exiles. In the 1970s, the VPR had purchased land along the Brazil-Argentina border for use as a training site. In the three decades since, the plot stayed in the hands of a few former VPR militants, and as the comrades began to get older, they had the idea to sell part of it. The group had originally wanted to use the funds to build a monument to Carlos Lamarca in Bahia, but that project never got off the ground. Aluízio proposed instead that the money help establish the CDHMP in Foz do Iguaçu. The VPR money funded a complete remodel, which included hiring a local artist to paint the building's exterior in the style of Chilean political murals from the 1970s.

With time, other organizations and families moved into the neighborhood, making the surrounding area more pleasant. The center has since become a hub of social activism in Foz do Iguaçu. An entirely volunteer-run organization, the CDHMP works on campaigns related to land rights and the rights of Indigenous people, women, and workers, most often in the western Paraná border region but also in solidarity with movements elsewhere in Brazil. Aluízio was not the sole person in charge of organizing events at the CDHMP, but the types of activities to which he contributed also reflect his efforts later in life to grapple with questions of machismo and patriarchy. Of the hundreds of events hosted at the center, examples include a two-day symposium in 2013 against sex tourism along the border, a 2016 roundtable discussion of trans rights, and a 2020 exhibition of local female artists—in addition to the bevy of protests and solidarity actions during the Bolsonaro years.[43] And in terms of the popular memory side of the CDHMP, Aluízio has organized a long series of presentations on the history of dictatorship in the Triple Border region, and he collaborated with local university students to record life-history interviews with elderly residents in the region.

LEGACIES, PUBLIC AND PRIVATE

Aluízio's work with the center and his website made him into a highly respected figure in Foz do Iguaçu. In July 2016, the City Council voted to confer on him

CHAPTER 10

the title of "citizen of honor." A television news segment about the ceremony shows an auditorium packed with friends and family members, some of whom held a large banner that read "Fora Temer" (Out with Temer) in reference to then president Michel Temer, hinting at Brazil's larger political climate after the ousting of President Dilma.[44] Wearing a suede brown jacket and thin-rimmed glasses, Aluízio sat on the council bench and listened to a series of speeches and poems in his honor. The ceremony ended with a sing-along of Geraldo Vandré's 1968 protest song "Pra não dizer que não falei das flores" (So they don't say I never spoke of flowers)—an unofficial anthem of the antidictatorship movement, which tells the story of activists who had no choice but to take up arms against the military. The song surely resonated with Aluízio as he reflected on the arc of his life, especially while being celebrated by a city that he had initially derided as a political and cultural desert.

On the heels of a tumultuous youth spent as an armed militant and clandestine exile, Aluízio's move to Foz do Iguaçu defined his life's work. There is no way of knowing whether he would have followed a similar path if he had stayed in Rio de Janeiro—no way to know what might have happened if he had rejected Eunice's ultimatum of choosing family over politics. But living in Foz do Iguaçu from 1979 onward provided a unique space to build his legacy. Compared to Rio de Janeiro, Foz do Iguaçu might have indeed felt like a boring frontier, but with time, and due in no small part to Aluízio himself, it became a vibrant space of political activism.

I interviewed several dozen colleagues and friends of Aluízio, and, along with my questions about their interactions with him over the years, I asked them to describe Aluízio. Everyone spoke about his tireless energy and his commitment to political activism. It is useful here to provide a sampling of what people said.

- Beth Fortes, who was imprisoned with Aluízio in the Ahú detention center: "Even if I use all the adjectives praising him, it's not enough. The research, the tireless collection of material, searching in the most difficult recesses of the dictatorship, it's all magnificent!"[45]

- Cecília Coimbra, of Tortura Nunca Mais, a group that awarded Aluízio its 2021 Chico Mendes Medal of Resistance: "His work is so important. It should be done by the State, but the State never did it and won't do it. So those dangerous memories will always be cast to the margins. Aluízio's research is of the highest importance. He's not doing it for himself, it's for the future, for the next generations."[46]

- Fábio Campana, former MR-8 member and eventual publisher of Aluízio's book: "Aluízio is an example of tenacity, Aluízio does not give up.... He seeks clarity, he has an almost Franciscan patience for listening, talking, and discussing."[47]

- Vitório Seratiuk, a student activist who shared a prison cell with Aluízio: "What was fantastic is that he came from a region different from ours, culturally very different from the region here in Paraná. He came from the state of Rio de Janeiro, and generally the Carioca is more open and boastful. But not Aluízio. He was a calm, sweet person. You can think of a revolutionary like Emiliano Zapata, a vigorous man with strength. [Not Aluízio,] no, he was a person with soft gestures, a very sweet, affable manner."[48]

- Ana Maria Müller, lawyer and leader of amnesty movement: "Aluízio is a very steady person, very courageous. He is a person who always stays active, denouncing [injustices], bringing memory, honoring his companions, in a firm way, but very delicate, very smooth.... He's really tireless, he's a tireless person. We have to applaud his fight, his memory, and all this legacy he leaves us, because it's not just talking, it's something he's working on for future generations."[49]

- Suzana Lisboa, member of the Special Commission on Political Deaths and Disappearances: "Aluízio is, above all, a man of character. I'd say that's the first definition [of him], because there are lots of people who don't have character. But he has character. He's a militant committed to his past, to his present, committed to the future as he fights so that we don't forget, so that it doesn't happen again. He does everything with a lightness, with joy, with an enormous energy. He has much more energy than me, I'm going to be seventy years old, he's already eighty—I always tell him that he has a thousand times more energy, more health than I do."[50]

Not everyone in Aluízio's life has such uncomplicated views of him. Above all, Aluízio's children have a far more tangled opinion. Previous chapters of this book have provided a glimpse of what it was like to grow up with Aluízio Palmar as a father—someone who worked tirelessly, but whose dedication to political causes could make him absent or distant at home. I interviewed five of his six children, and every one of them painted a complex picture. On the one hand, they praised his contributions to politics and human rights, but just as often, if not more so, they expressed a variety of frustrations.

Janaína, Aluízio's fifth child, told me that while she is proud of the fact that late in life he began working on questions of gender and sexism, she also draws a direct line between her own feminist politics and her frustrations with him. "I'm a feminist because I always saw an inconsistent man at home," Janaína said. "A man who fought for social rights but rarely looked at his own actions."[51] And when I asked about having a father who worked so much, she gave a two-word response: "horrible, absent."

For Aluízio's youngest daughter, Amanda, the feeling of having an absent father was even more tangible. Amanda is half-siblings with Aluízio's other children, the result of Aluízio's affair with her mother in the mid-1990s, when he was over fifty years old. Aluízio's affair was one of the few topics that I decided to not discuss directly with him, an approach that I deemed useful for our collaborative biography, though which perhaps foreclosed a larger reflection on how he balances his self-perception of having been a faithful militant but not always a faithful husband.

Amanda told me that when she was young, she did not have much contact with her father, seeing him perhaps once a month. It made her sad that he rarely sent presents on her birthday, and that he did not always remember how old she was. "He always said that it's more important that he send a present when he felt it was important and not just on a [specific] date. Those are his values." Amanda told me. "Those are things that can be frustrating, but sometimes they can be good, too." As Amanda got older, their visits became more frequent, and she enjoyed spending time with him and hearing him share his memories: "He's a real storyteller. So when he'd come here to the house, he'd sit down and just start telling me his stories."[52] Amanda was proud to be the daughter of a well-known figure in Foz do Iguaçu, but it also bothered her that their time together would often get interrupted by people wanting to talk to him: "Sometimes if we'd go out to a movie or a café, and other people would come up and shake his hand, really talk him up. Wow, a lot of people really love my father. And so that was very frustrating, having Aluízio Palmar as a father has been a source of great pride but also a lot of frustration because whether he likes it or not, he's a public figure."

Alexandre is Aluízio's only son, and in many ways, he has the closest relationship with their father. Alexandre also became a journalist, even working alongside Aluízio at several stages of the investigations into the disappeared militants. He also helped edit Aluízio's 2005 memoir, an experience gave Alexandre an entirely new window into Aluízio's life and personality. While growing up, however, Alexandre yearned for his father's attention: "I remember one day, I must have been twelve or thirteen years old, I came home and talked with my mom, asking her why it was so hard to get a hug from my dad or any words of affection. . . . To have so much maternal love, but I felt a lack of paternal love. I wanted my dad to say that he loved us."[53] Speaking with me in 2020, at the age of forty-four, Alexandre said that over the years he has come to see his father differently. "Today, looking back on earlier moments, reviewing all his efforts, over time I understood how difficult it was to balance [his politics] with his life as a husband, his life as a father," Alexandre said. "At the time, I wondered why he had so much love, so much willingness to fight for the outside world, and why this didn't happen at home. But today this is resolved for me, it's not an issue because I understand better what happened. I know that there were failures on his part, but today I can look back and find examples of his love and fatherly presence in other ways. If in the past I had some resentment, today it's not something that I hold against him."

Aluízio's oldest child, Florita, shared a similar sentiment. For a long time, Florita harbored deep resentment against her father. As mentioned earlier, she credits therapy with her ability to process her feelings of abandonment from being raised in relative isolation across multiple countries during Aluízio's exile. In recent years, Florita has found something closer to a peaceful relationship with Aluízio. After one of our interviews, she sent me a photo of a card she had made for her father. The card included two pictures, a recent photo of Aluízio smiling and one of Florita with her parents as a toddler. On top of the images, Florita included an inscription that reflected her desire for reconciliation: "I had a very playful childhood thanks to him. These memories make me forgive all the issues we have today! Aluízio Palmar, a difficult but brilliant genius [*gênio difícil, mas genial*]!"[54]

A FINAL SEARCH

In May 2018, a Brazilian academic named Matias Spektor discovered a shocking US government document. In 1974, the director of the CIA, William Colby, sent a memo to Secretary of State Henry Kissinger about a recent meeting between Brazil's military president, Ernesto Geisel, and several of his most important generals. According to Colby's memo, the generals discussed the ongoing threat of "dangerous subversives" and said that "104 persons in this category had been summarily executed by the [Army Intelligence Center] during the past year."[55] One of the generals proposed that "extra-legal methods should continue to be employed," and the memo also states that João Baptista

Figueiredo—who would soon oversee the abertura process of democratization as the final military president of the dictatorship—"supported this policy and urged its continuance." Spektor's archival discovery offered the most tangible proof to-date of the military's extrajudicial killings.

A minor scandal ensued, with activists on the left demanding further action from the government of Michel Temer, and detractors on the right seeking to downplay the document. The discovery coincided with the 2018 presidential campaign, and Jair Bolsonaro, at the time a leading candidate, dismissed the memo in the abrasive manner that would become his trademark. As quoted in *O Estado de São Paulo*, Bolsonaro shrugged off the military's sanctioning of summary executions, saying, "Who's never given their kid a spank on the butt and then regretted it? These things happen."[56]

In addition to fanning the flames of an already heated presidential race, the revelation of the 1974 CIA memo sparked new efforts to discover the remains of disappeared militants. This included Onofre Pinto and the five other VPR militants, who disappeared three months after Geisel's meeting with his generals. When the CIA memo came to light, eight years had passed since the last excavation in Iguaçu National Park. During that period, Aluízio's involvement with the case had shifted from an active investigation to a more narrative approach: rather than devote himself to searching for the bodies, he honored the six militants by telling their story as much as possible. He had mixed feelings about the new search, which felt to him like a propaganda effort from the Temer government to bolster its human rights record. Aluízio had great respect for Eugênia Augusta Gonzaga, the head of the CEMDP who oversaw the dig, but he remained skeptical. "It was a really important action from [Eugênia], in the middle of the Temer government," Aluízio recalled. "But on the other hand, it was also for show, for the TV cameras."[57] Eugênia invited Aluízio to join the excavation, which took place over two days in May. Aluízio declined, citing a recent flareup up of his diabetes.

Rede Globo, one of Brazil's main television stations, produced an eight-minute story about the search, complete with sweeping aerial views of the Iguaçu waterfalls and national park, ominous music that followed the forensic team, and a computer-generated reenactment of what the ambush might have looked like.[58] Several minutes into the segment, the program cuts to Aluízio in his backyard, a set of garden shears in hand as he trims the hedges outside his home. The program then uses Aluízio's life history as an anchor to tell the story of the disappearances: Aluízio is interviewed about his time in prison and in exile as a VPR militant, and Rede Globo outlines Aluízio's investigation, his memoir, and the multiple excavations that he helped lead in the early 2000s.

Several of the images used in the television program even came from Aluízio's Documentos Revelados website. The segment builds up suspense when the forensic team discovers two anomalies, a piece of metal and a subterranean hole. Both were false alarms. The metal did not come from a weapon and the hole was most likely an armadillo burrow.

As with every previous search, the 2018 dig found no evidence of any kind. Aluízio was disappointed, if unsurprised. Although he still believed that the bodies were most likely somewhere in Iguaçu National Park, the multiple failures across nearly two decades also nurtured the thought that maybe they were looking in the wrong place. Perhaps the bodies were in Nova Aurora, where the mystery caller had first directed his attention. Maybe the murders had happened somewhere else entirely. Or maybe, as was the case across Latin America, the dictatorship had burned the bodies, or thrown them into a river or the ocean. As much as Aluízio wanted to stop thinking about the case, the persistent lack of evidence made it hard to find closure: "How can I give up if the bodies have never been found? I was searching so much, and he who searches can't rule anything out. Anything is possible, anything is possible."[59]

CONCLUSION

OUT OF THE SHADOWS

IN OCTOBER 2018, five months after the failed search in Iguaçu National Park, Jair Bolsonaro was elected president. After his inauguration on January 1, 2019, Bolsonaro installed a sixteen-person cabinet that included eight active-duty or military reserve officers—the largest number of noncivilian ministers since the return of democracy in 1985—and he sought to reverse much of the social policies from the previous two decades. He withdrew key public resources and legal protections for women and Indigenous groups, he championed deforestation in the Amazon, and he constantly attacked freedom of the press.[1] As an unabashed apologist for Brazil's dictatorship, Bolsonaro repeatedly used the specter of military rule to threaten his enemies.

One of Bolsonaro's early acts as president was to reinstate the March 31 commemorations of the 1964 coup, and in response to criticism from Michelle Bachelet (the UN Human Rights commissioner and former president of Chile), he praised the Pinochet dictatorship that had tortured her father. As an example of how he fused his nostalgia for dictatorship with his current attacks on the rule of law, Bolsonaro taunted the president of the Brazilian Order of Lawyers (OAB, Ordem dos Advogados do Brasil), Felipe Santa Cruz, whose father was among the nearly 500 people disappeared by the dictatorship. At a press conference, Bolsonaro said that "one day, if the president of the OAB wants to know how his father disappeared during the military period, I'll tell him."[2]

The same afternoon of Bolsonaro's attack on Felipe Santa Cruz, Aluízio helped write a note condemning the president's statement. As he shared on his Facebook page, he joined a collection of ten human rights groups from across the country to denounce Bolsonaro's attack on Santa Cruz and the OAB. The letter stated,

> The Brazilian Network of Memory, Truth, and Justice . . . vehemently repudiates the attack perpetrated by the President of the Republic. . . . The despicable declaration took place today, when, in a press conference, the President of the Republic, in order to intimidate the president of the OAB, Felipe Santa Cruz, was once again vile and repulsive. . . . Like other Brazilians, [Felipe's father] Fernando Santa Cruz was captured and tortured to death; his body, like that of so many others, men and women alike, was never found again. Bolsonaro's statement is repugnant, gloating about a painful situation in the life of a son who lost his father during the dictatorship.[3]

For Aluízio, it seemed like he was constantly producing such letters of condemnation, or helping organize protest marches, or gathering with other activists to coordinate their efforts. Mobilizing under Bolsonaro became an endless task. Aluízio remained committed to his political work, but he was also seventy-six years old and diabetic. He was tired. And he worried that Bolsonaro would dismantle the hard-fought victories of Brazil's wayward, and still incomplete, historical reckoning. It was toward the end of Bolsonaro's first year in office, four decades after the violence he had suffered as a political prisoner, that Aluízio was visited again by the shadow of dictatorship.

One morning in early December 2019, somebody knocked on the door of Aluízio's home. He answered, and a person identifying themself as a court employee handed him an envelope. Aluízio read the enclosed documents to discover that he was being sued in the Second Civil Court of Foz do Iguaçu by Mário Espedito Ostrovski—his former torturer. Toward the second half of our interviews, several months after the lawsuit had been dismissed, I asked Aluízio about his initial reaction. Speaking with the benefit of hindsight, Aluízio said that rather than feeling dejected by the lawsuit, the news was invigorating: "I said, 'Thank you God,' because I was finally going to face a torturer in court. Finally, this was the thing I wanted most. My whole life I wanted the chance to be face-to-face in court with this guy, to denounce all of his atrocities."[4] Aluízio might well have relished the chance to confront his torturer in a court of law. But the fact remains that in the aftermath of being sued by Ostrovski, Aluízio did everything that he could to mobilize *against* the lawsuit. Any potential political and moral victories seem to have taken a backseat to the legal jeopardy at hand, to say nothing of the financial risk to Aluízio's livelihood: Ostrovski's lawsuit was seeking a staggering BR$39.9 million (US$10 million) in damages. In the context of Bolsonaro's Brazil, this was serious.

Ostrovski's human rights abuses had already been well documented, including in the 1985 report on torture, *Brasil: nunca mais*, and also in the 2013 proceedings of the National Truth Commission.[5] During the commission's testimony, Aluízio discussed his torture at the hands of Ostrovski, as did Isabel Fávero, another political prisoner whom Ostrovski had victimized so brutally that she suffered a miscarriage.[6] Ostrovski had been invited to speak to the truth commission, but he declined. On the afternoon of Ostrovski's scheduled testimony, protestors engaged in a political action common in Latin America known as an *escrache* (*escracho* in Portuguese). To expose Ostrovski, who had been living a quiet life as a lawyer, the crowd marched to his law office and held a noisy rally to "out" him as a torturer. Aluízio did not take part in the protest, but he did publicize the event on Facebook.[7] And it was precisely Aluízio's act of sharing the protest on Facebook that Ostrovski cited in his claim for legal and financial restitution.

But if the event in question took place in 2013, why did Ostrovski wait six years to pursue a lawsuit? Simply put, Bolsonaro's election in 2018 year made the long-standing culture of impunity even more brazen, calling to mind what the legal scholar Cass Sunstein calls the unleashing effect, through which an erosion of social norms—of the type that bubbled to the surface during Bolsonaro's campaign and subsequent presidency—"unleashes people, in the sense that it allows people to reveal what they believe and prefer, and to act as they wish."[8] The unleashing under Bolsonaro emboldened former officers like Ostrovski to push back against Brazil's gradually expanding culture of human rights. The lawsuit against Aluízio was symptomatic of a double injustice at play. Not only was a survivor of torture being preyed on once again by his former abuser, but the lack of accountability over the previous forty years was being compounded to such a degree that a torturer could claim that *his rights* were being abused. Under Bolsonaro, torturers like Ostrovski could seek to pervert the legal system to not only silence victims and critics but also to attempt to redefine whose rights actually matter.

If Aluízio's memory activism had been a cause of the lawsuit, it also helped protect him. Having built a large network of allies during his two decades of grassroots campaigning, Aluízio was able to mobilize a solidarity campaign, with dozens of organizations in Brazil and abroad denouncing the lawsuit. I saw his posts on Facebook and I decided to get involved. My article, the only one written for Anglophone audiences, played a very small role in the larger effort to bring attention to the perversion of human rights under Bolsonaro.[9] The campaign seemed to work: seven months later, a judge dismissed the lawsuit. Bigger challenges remained, including Bolsonaro's attacks on the rule of law, Brazil's ongoing culture of impunity for crimes of the dictatorship, and the unfolding COVID crisis. But at least for a moment, Aluízio and his allies celebrated.

The saga of Aluízio being sued by his former torturer reflects the numerous levels at which a memory script functions. As a human rights activist, Aluízio became adept at using social media to publicize his search for the disappeared militants as well as the wider range of his political activities, many of which drew from stories of his own life. And it was his presence on Facebook that made him a target of his former torturer. But it was also the wide reach of social media, cultivating a network of contacts and allies, that eventually got the lawsuit dropped. Moreover, if not for the practiced, repetitive, and public nature of Aluízio's memory activism, I may not have gotten involved and our collaborative biography might never have happened. One platform of memory begets another.

INTO THE SPOTLIGHT

The title of this conclusion—"Out of the Shadows"—has many meanings. As an allusion to the presidency of Jair Bolsonaro, it suggests that after three decades of democratic rule, the proauthoritarian forces in Brazil, which had been out of power but never entirely out of sight, had reemerged. The shadow of military rule had always lurked ominously, and now it ruled from the presidential palace. As a reference to Lieutenant Ostrovski's lawsuit against Aluízio Palmar, it exemplifies the type of attacks that Bolsonaro's election had unleashed. Ostrovski and scores like him could now come out of the shadows, emboldened and feeling unaccountable. And as a nod to Aluízio himself, and to this book about him, it brings our analysis back to the process—and to the impact—of writing his biography.

The publication of this book will amplify the spotlight on Aluízio's life, both in Brazil and in the English-speaking world, where he was almost entirely unknown, and where college students, academics, and perhaps even some members of the general public will now have an extremely intimate familiarity with him. Aluízio may never entirely escape the traumas of dictatorship, but he is capable of carving his own path out of the shadows. By virtue of this book, Aluízio will be better-known than scores of other Brazilians and Latin

Americans exactly like him: former militants and political prisoners from the era of military rule who became active in human rights campaigns after their countries' return to democracy. Many of these as-yet-unexamined figures also made the narration of their backgrounds a key part of their transition from militant politics to grassroots activism. As it was for Aluízio, talking about their lives constituted a form of legitimacy in the present and also a search for memory about their past. Their life stories surely include the same type of personal, political, and emotional tales as Aluízio's, and biographies of them would be equally fascinating and yield many of the same insights.

If not for the circumstances of how I came to know Aluízio, this book would not exist. I did not set out to write a collaborative biography, nor did I initially seek to understand the off-the-beaten-path experiences of repression and resistance during Brazil's dictatorship. Originally, I did not even have a clear idea of how I would engage the theoretical and methodological questions about memory. My goal was to write about Aluízio's life.

It was only over the course of my two years of interviews and research, and through the process of writing this book, that my main interventions came into focus. First, a memory script framework for analyzing how people narrate their own life in a way that is practiced, repetitive, and performative. Second, the methodology and the challenges—both ethical and authorial—of a collaborative biography. And third, the question of history from the margins, and the insight that can be gained from the experience of people like Aluízio who chose a series of peripheral paths. In his case, this included joining an armed resistance that sought to build a rural insurgency, choosing a clandestine exile with his family in tow, and charting an activist career in a border city. This sequence of events, which fundamentally shaped Aluízio's political and personal trajectory, rarely features in more established narratives. There is much to be learned from studying the lives that are both in the middle of history and on its margins.

So far, most of this biography has been an analysis from me about Aluízio. To reverse some of this asymmetry between author and subject, and to shift the balance more evenly back to Aluízio, I now conclude the book with a long reflection from Aluízio on his life and his memories. We thus end with a sustained example from Aluízio's memory script.

REFLECTIONS ON A LIFE REMEMBERED

In many ways, all my interviews with Aluízio were reflections on his life. By its nature, his memory script was self-reflective: every story, every detail, every moment of frustration or humor was the product of his efforts to make sense of, and bring attention to, his life trajectory. As a learned, repetitive, and performative process, his memory script required not only a high level of introspection but also an ability to translate his internal assessments in a way the public could relate to. Although this occurred throughout our interviews, one session in particular became an extended conversation about how Aluízio sees his own life. This was the sixteenth of what ended up being a total of twenty-five interviews. Having already covered an initial chronology of his life during our previous conversations, our interview that day became contemplative in a new way.[10] It took place on September 11, 2020, and perhaps the anniversary of Pinochet's coup in Chile made him especially reflective. Or maybe the ongoing context of Bolsonaro and the COVID pandemic nudged him to take stock of a lifetime's worth of accomplishments and frustrations.

    The interview was the same length as most of our conversations, lasting one hour and sixteen minutes. But its content was unique. Rather than cover specific stories or anecdotes from Aluízio's life, we mostly talked about how he felt about his life. A summary of the interview serves as a fitting end to this book. Unlike most of the chapters so far, in which I weave together direct quotations as part of a larger chronological narrative, the interview excerpts here are longer, with fewer of my own authorial interventions. The transcribed text of the whole interview runs nearly seventeen pages, so I have edited mainly for length, to provide readers with a feel for Aluízio's narrative style. Otherwise, his narration stays largely in its original form.

    Our conversation started much as it always did. We chatted for a few minutes, about the weather in our respective parts of the world and about the state of politics. Normally, our discussions about politics would soon transition to the life-history interview. But on this day, Aluízio's brief update on his current political work set in motion a much broader reflection. He told me about trying to build a "united front" against Bolsonaro—an effort to collaborate across the political aisle toward a common goal of defending democracy. His biggest frustration, he explained, came from people not on the right but on the left, who criticized him for working with centrist and conservative leaders. "Many comrades tell me that I'm wrong, that the revolution is this and that, and all about the proletariat. The Trotskyists are giving me a lot of shit," Aluízio said. "But I don't care. I defend a broad political front, so broad that it hurts, because we have to sit next to our opponents, even those who staged a coup against President Dilma. We are calling for a political front, to sit down together, because the priority at the moment is to defeat fascism, no matter who joins us."

CONCLUSION

I asked Aluízio whether he would have had this same perspective if he had been a student activist under Bolsonaro. He laughed slightly and admitted that he was now doing precisely what he had criticized fifty years earlier: "In the 1960s, we denounced the Partidão [Brazilian Communist Party] for its stance on a united democratic front, elections, all of that, to defeat the dictatorship. We were critical of that and we left the party. Today I'm defending that same stance. Nowadays I'm that old guy in the party. But it's not a question of youth, or even a question of being older, it's not about age. It's about context." Aluízio continued riffing on the idea of context, drawing out its implications across his own life course. "Life changes according to the situation, it is the situation that changes. I don't change because I want to change, it's not a matter of wanting," Aluízio told me.

> In the 1960s I was a developmentalist because at the time Brazil was substituting its imports, and independent development was necessary. So I was a national developmentalist, with the goal of reaching socialism, but at that moment I was together with the national developmentalists in the government of Juscelino Kubitschek. [And then] in the Jango government [João Goulart's leftist presidency in the early 1960s], we defended basic reforms, structural reforms, but always with our minds tuned to social justice, right? The indignation before the injustice, that is, the social question was stronger than the institutional question. Democracy would be a means of achieving social justice, it was not a goal in itself. The goal was social justice within the republican democratic system. When the dictatorship came, we couldn't fight for social justice or have a democratic regime for that fight, so to return to democracy and keep fighting for social justice in a country as unequal as Brazil, it was necessary to overthrow the dictatorship. As there was no form of legal struggle, we went to armed struggle. We didn't take up arms because we wanted to, we were forced to because there was no other way.

Especially in the context of Bolsonaro's Brazil, Aluízio felt that violence was no longer a viable route: "The fight against fascism will take place through institutions. Bolsonaro wants violence because if we practice violence, the State's violence is much more powerful than ours and we'll get wiped out. Today our struggle is through institutional means: the Supreme Court, national courts, state courts, municipal courts, political parties, elections. Today, there's no other way. Tomorrow could be different and we have to change according to the moment."

Aluízio's reflections on Bolsonaro and the return of authoritarianism led to a lengthy discussion about memory—or rather, the lack of memory, and the tendency in Brazil to collectively forget uncomfortable truths. He spoke in a way that blended the contemporary (using the lexicon of modern human rights activism) and the historical, tracing the question of memory back to the age of slavery:

> The crimes committed under slavery were never made public, they were always hidden. And the vision we have of abolition [was] of Princess Isabel, a good-hearted princess, who cried, who felt the pain of the Blacks and so she freed them. So the fight for freedom was hidden. So the memory that we have of slavery is not a memory of violence but a type of romanticized memory. And why is that? Because there was never any transitional justice. The same thing happened during the dictatorship. There was no transitional justice and that memory fell into oblivion. The victims, too, a lot of victims didn't want to remember.

Aluízio went on to tell me about several of his former comrades who had been traumatized by the dictatorship and who no longer had any interest in revisiting the past. These were examples of the type of leftists who were not interested in overturning the 1979 Amnesty Law. Some of them, in his telling, worked in the Workers' Party administrations, and from their position of political power they preferred to look forward and not backward: "Many of our comrades who even held positions in the Lula government, important positions as ministers, for example, when we talked about transitional justice and memory, do you know what they said to us? They said the following, '*Companheiro*, now we have to move forward and we're not going to look in the rearview mirror.'"

And in one of the few instances when he discussed the impact that his politics had on his wife, Aluízio then told me that whenever he plays Chilean protest music like Víctor Jara or Inti-Illimani, he has to keep the volume down so that Eunice does not hear—"I have to listen really low, I can't put it on high because Eunice, my wife, she doesn't want to listen to it. It makes her nervous to listen, because she suffered a lot during that period, she has trauma. I told you about that, right? She doesn't want to talk, she doesn't want to remember." In contrast to people like Eunice and countless others, Aluízio treats memory almost like a personal crusade: "I want to remember, I seek paths of memory. I want to remember, I want to write, I want to talk. Other people don't want to remember, they don't want to talk. They want to forget. You're a historian, you must always think about these questions, no? Forgetting and remembering."

CONCLUSION

Aluízio often expressed frustration that Brazilians want to forget more than they want to remember. He spoke with envy about the memory initiatives in other countries. Mostly he talked about Argentina, the country where he spent most of his decade in exile. He mentioned several times the number of memory spaces in Argentina that commemorate sites of torture and spaces of resistance: "In Argentina, no matter the city, even all these small cities, they have a memory space." He also cited the memory work in Chile and South Africa. As he had done in an earlier interview, he again talked about a German film from 1990, *Das schreckliche Mädchen* (released in English as *The Nasty Girl* and in Portuguese as *Uma cidade sem passado*), about a young girl, who for a class project, starts researching her town's history during the Holocaust. His discussion of the film flowed uninterrupted into a transnational reflection on the importance of archives, before rounding back to the errors committed by his generation in the 1960s. The throughline was the question of memory:

> I told you about the film that had a great impact on me, about a girl from a small town in Germany, who did some research for her homework. She talked to the residents and only discovered the true behavior of the city during the Third Reich when she went to the public archive of the municipality, in City Hall. So the archive is really important, without it history will always remain on the story of the winners and never with the true story. Even today the Soviet Union doesn't know its history, with each side saying something different. The Stalinists tell one story, the anti-Stalinists tell another story. There are governments that say that Stalin was a great leader and I don't know what, others say he was a demon—after all, he either was a demon or he wasn't a demon, right? So the history, the memory is very important, and archives are for people to know the history of their country, the mistakes, the successes. I work a lot with this, not biased memory, you know? I don't want to be biased. You have to tell the reality the way it was and how it happened, admit the mistakes. We made many mistakes, too many mistakes. Lots of delusion, my generation was the generation of delusion. The popular struggle took away students who were almost graduating in the last year of medicine, engineering, and sent them to the countryside to work with a hoe, to become a peasant, to be able to join the people. It was a mistake. We made mistakes, our MR-8 guerrilla foco was a mistake. So we admit these mistakes and correct them, but we have to admit it, we have to tell it, we can't hide it, right? I can't hide it, say it didn't happen. It happened.

Aluízio is happy that Brazil has at least one major memory center: the Memorial de Resistência de São Paulo, a museum established in 2009 in a former detention center of the DOPS secret police. But he wants many more like it, especially where he lives. "It would be such a great thing for Foz do Iguaçu," Aluízio told me. "People would come visit the waterfalls, do some shopping in Paraguay, go see Itaipu and then make a small trip to a memory space. But there's just not enough interest." Over the years, Aluízio made several efforts to raise money and government support for a memory museum in Foz do Iguaçu, but nothing ever materialized. He spoke sadly about this process, and I shifted the conversation to his website, telling him that he had already created a space for memory. He did not disagree, but he told me that his website is mostly for researchers like me. What he really wants is something for the general public.

Hearing his tone of frustration, I asked Aluízio what he is most proud about from his life and what are his disappointments. Rather than mention anything related to politics, he talked about his family. Regardless of whether he would have given that answer at an earlier stage of life, he seemed genuine, telling me that he sometimes thinks about what would have happened if he had not moved to Foz do Iguaçu: "I wouldn't have the family that I have today. I could have died [if I had stayed a militant in Rio de Janeiro]. I have six children, eight grandchildren, and I think that's a really big accomplishment. And they're all well-educated, engaged people, with a social consciousness." Aluízio also told me about a second source of pride, of having helped people learn and think more deeply about society: "A lot of people came under my wing. All of that makes me proud. I'm proud of not having gone through life like a vegetable, of having left roots, and [having] showed what it is to dream, to try and build something. From my time in City Hall, I'm proud of my work as secretary of the environment, of protecting water sources and forests. And I'm proud of the Documentos Revelados website, and of building the Center for Human Rights. Those are what I built over my lifetime."

When we talked about his disappointments, Aluízio's answer was not quite what I expected. Elsewhere in our conversation, he had spoken a lot about the mistakes he had made as a young revolutionary and the naive approach of university students who "thought that a group of a dozen people could create a peasant rebellion." And I already knew about his deep frustrations at having never found the bodies of the six VPR militants. I imagined that he would talk about some version of these political disappointments. Or maybe he would even talk about his shortcomings as a father and a husband.

Instead, Aluízio told me that his great regret is not having been able to travel: "It's frustrating to live in a democratic world where people have freedom

CONCLUSION

to go wherever they want to, and I didn't have the means to do that. I never really had the money." He regrets having never properly visited Europe. His only experience came in 1984, when he spent a few days in Rome and Frankfurt while transiting to and from Iran, where he was one of several journalists from the Global South invited by the government to tour the country. Aside from those brief layovers, Aluízio has not known Europe. This was a refraction of the frequent narrative in our earlier conversations that his clandestine exile in Argentina was much harder than the experience of others who spent their exile in Europe. Given that he was now approaching eighty years old, and knowing that his health was far from perfect, he was no longer certain of one day traveling to Europe. But he was inspired by the groups of elderly Japanese tourists that he often saw pass through Foz do Iguaçu. "I would be like those Japanese people who move in an entourage of old folks. The elderly travel around the world together. It would be good for my mental health to join a group of older people and travel around, taking pictures, chatting, having a good time."

Even if overseas travel is no longer possible, I asked Aluízio if he might start to relax more, to work a little bit less, especially given the stressful climate of Bolsonaro and the pandemic. As with his earlier answers, Aluízio surprised me. He talked about gardening, saying that it was one of the few activities that allowed him to turn off his mind: "Sometimes I like to get my hands dirty. I go [to my garden] and work with my plants, taking care of my rose bushes. I'm starting to learn how to make seedlings, deal with the roots. I've been studying botany." I was struck by the similarity to *Candide*, Voltaire's eighteenth-century novella, in which the protagonist has a series of harrowing, if satirical, adventures around the world, famously realizing in the end that the secret to happiness is to "cultivate one's garden." I asked Aluízio if he was familiar with the book and its conclusion. He said nothing about the book and kept talking about gardening. He also sprinkled in the lyrics from a 1977 song, "O cio da terra," by Milton Nascimento and Chico Buarque. "I see that the earth is asking to be sown," Aluízio rhapsodized. "The earth is in heat [*o cio da terra*], the earth wants to be fertilized."

Even though we were speaking over WhatsApp audio, it was like I could see a calmness in his face. Aluízio spoke with a tone I had rarely heard in our two years of interviews. Given the traumas of his life, and his deep conviction for bringing about a more peaceful future, perhaps he may never feel entirely at peace. But in these moments, Aluízio seemed happy enough to sit back and appreciate his contributions: "Something will happen. You see the plant, you watch the seeds sprout. It's beautiful, you know, sprouting is a very beautiful process, very beautiful in nature. It's life being born, exploding up from the ground. I like to watch it unfold."

Five days after this lengthy, reflective conversation, we had another interview. Mainly, we talked through a few clarification points and pending questions from the previous month of interviews. At one point we turned to the topic of our interviews themselves. I asked Aluízio why he had accepted my invitation for the biography project. As I quoted in the introduction to this book, he said that he had known me for a while, that he trusted me, and that he was very comfortable sharing his life story: "I was already used to talking, it's not like you got me when my mouth was shut. I had been making this speech for a long time."[11] But he admitted that he was surprised by the focus on memory that had gradually developed over the course of our conversations. "I didn't expect the work to be so deep. The research is really digging down into those themes. I think that's good, because if you're going to write a biography about a political militant, about a victim of state terrorism, you have to talk about memory, in a context bigger than them."

I then told Aluízio that I had come up with a working title for the book. I was thinking of calling it *Searching for Memory*. He said, "That's okay," and then went silent for several seconds. Perhaps thinking back on the excavations for the bodies of his former comrades, and his frustrated efforts to unearth the truth of Brazil's violent past, Aluízio offered an alternative: *O garimpeiro da memória* (*The Memory Miner*). I liked his suggestion, telling him that even if it did not end up in the title, I would find a way to include it in the book.

NOTES

ABBREVIATIONS

AN-RJ	Arquivo Nacional, Rio de Janeiro, Brazil
APERJ	Arquivo Público do Estado do Rio de Janeiro, Brazil
CEPEDAL	Centro de Pesquisa e Documentação sobre o Oeste do Paraná, Brazil
CEV-PR	*Relatório da Comissão Estadual da Verdade do Paraná*
CGIPM	Comissão Geral de Inquérito Policial-Militar
DOPS	Departamento de Ordem Política e Social
IPM	Inquérito policial militar
SNI	Serviço Nacional de Informações
STM	Superior Tribunal Militar

INTRODUCTION

1. Colombia issued its final Truth Commission report in 2022, though it related to a period of armed civil war rather than a military dictatorship. And in 2020, Mexico president Andrés Manuel López Obrador signed an executive order to form the country's first-ever truth commission, related to state-sponsored violence in the 1970s. The Mexican commission remains pending.

2. Jelín, *Los trabajos de la memoria*; Stern, *Memory Box of Pinochet's Chile*.

3. Palmar, *Onde foi*. Unless otherwise noted, all citations to this book come from its fourth edition, printed in 2012. For an analysis of the genre of militant memoir, see Atencio, *Memory's Turn*, 28–58.

4. The website is called Documentos Revelados: https://documentosrevelados.com.br.

5. In the late twentieth and early twenty-first centuries, Latin America has been a center of new legal norms and social movements relating to global human rights. For more, see Sikkink, *Justice Cascade*.

6. Gaffey, "Imagining the Words of Others," 4.

7. Ernst Van Alphen discusses the ritualized repetitions of narrative of suffering in his study of art, memory, and the Holocaust, in *Caught by History*. Freud discusses "acting out" in relation to "working through" past traumas in "Remembering, Repeating, and Working-Through."

8. Taylor, "Performing Gender," 302.

9. Puga and Espinosa, *Performances of Suffering in Latin American Migration*.

10. Schippert, Grov, and Bjørnnes, "Uncovering Re-traumatization Experiences."

11. A useful guide is "Interviewing," in Office of the High Commissioner for Human Rights, *Manual on Human Rights Monitoring*.

NOTES TO CHAPTER 1

12. Pioneering examples include Felman and Laub, *Testimony*; and Caruth, *Unclaimed Experience*. It should also be noted that "trauma theory" has come under criticism for the heritage of *trauma* as a Western medical and psychoanalytical term. For more, see Visser, "Trauma Theory and Postcolonial Literary Studies."

13. Fivush and Graci, "Autobiographical Memory."

14. Ehlers and Clark, "Cognitive Model of Posttraumatic Stress Disorder."

15. The estimated number of armed militants in Brazil as given in Green, *Exile within Exiles*, 88.

16. Other armed groups that would also seek to build a rural insurgency included the second formation of the People's Revolutionary Vanguard and the Revolutionary Armed Vanguard–Palmares.

17. Personal collection of author.

18. Blanc, "Inversion of Human Rights."

19. Aluízio Palmar, Facebook, October 22, 2018. All citations in this book of Aluízio's Facebook page refer to www.facebook.com/aluiziopalmar.

20. For example, Aluízio Palmar, Facebook, November 15, 2016, and November 15, 2018.

21. In Latin America, the genre of testimonial biographies, known as *testimonio*, has a long and at times contentious history, most notably as it relates to the testimonio of Rigoberta Menchú, an Indigenous Guatemalan woman, whose recounting of her life story to the French anthropologist Elizabeth Burgos-Debray was later the object of academic and political scrutiny. In part to avoid the questions of authorial voice raised by Menchú's published testimonio, other scholars have collaborated with activists—most often of Indigenous backgrounds—through an adapted approach of "testimonial biography," in which the scholar serves primarily as a coauthor; for example, Reuque Paillalef and Mallon, *When a Flower Is Reborn*; and Llamojha Mitma and Heilman, *Now Peru Is Mine*.

22. Aluízio Palmar, interview, September 16, 2020.

23. Aluízio Palmar, WhatsApp message to author, June 13, 2024.

24. Aluízio Palmar, interview, September 16, 2020.

CHAPTER 1

1. Information from Aluízio Palmar, Facebook, May 1 and 12, 2019.
2. Aluízio Palmar, interview, May 19, 2020.
3. Aluízio Palmar, interview, May 19, 2020.
4. Aluízio Palmar, Facebook, May 12, 2019.
5. Machado, *O mel e o sangue*, 61.
6. Aluízio Palmar, Facebook, April 19, 2019.
7. Aluízio Palmar, interview, May 26, 2020.
8. Coppe Caldeira, "Bispos conservadores brasileiros no Concílio Vaticano II."
9. Palmar, *Onde foi*, 172.
10. Aluízio Palmar, personal essay, n.d., shared with author.
11. Aluízio Palmar, Facebook, May 12, 2019.
12. Aluízio Palmar, Facebook, August 24, 2018.

NOTES TO CHAPTER 1

13. Aluízio Palmar, interview, May 19, 2020.
14. Aluízio Palmar, interview, May 19, 2020.
15. Palmar, *Onde foi*, 172.
16. Friendly, "Changing Landscape of Civil Society," 223.
17. Instituto Brasileiro de Geografia e Estatística, Censo demográfico, 1940–2010, https://seriesestatisticas.ibge.gov.br/series.aspx?vcodigo=POP122.
18. Palmar, *Onde foi*, 173.
19. For more, see Nunes, *A revolta das barcas*.
20. Palmar, *Onde foi*, 174.
21. Aluízio Palmar, interview, May 19, 2020.
22. Aluízio Palmar, interview, May 19, 2020.
23. Green, *Exile within Exiles*, 29–30.
24. For an analysis of revolutionary masculinity in Brazil, see Green, "Who Is the Macho Who Wants to Kill Me?" Normative ideas about masculinity also shaped political trajectories on the right; see Cowan, *Securing Sex*.
25. Palmar, "As marquises de Niterói."
26. As quoted in Machado, *O mel e o sangue*, 65.
27. Reis, *A revolução faltou ao encontro*, 45.
28. Aluízio Palmar, interview, May 19, 2020.
29. Palmar, *Onde foi*, 176.
30. Aluízio Palmar, interview, May 19, 2020.
31. Umberto Trigueiros Lima, interview, August 24, 2020.
32. Carvalho, *Niterói na época da ditadura*, 19.
33. Minutes of the Congresso Continental de Solidariedade a Cuba, March 28–30, 1963, www.marxists.org/portugues/tematica/1963/03/cuba.htm.
34. Aluízio Palmar, interview, May 19, 2020.
35. Carvalho's memoir traces his life through some of twentieth-century Brazil's most impactful eras, Carvalho, *Vale a pena sonhar*.
36. Lima, interview.
37. Lima, "Encontro com Apolônio," 292.
38. Aluízio Palmar, interview, May 19, 2020.
39. For more on the PNA and education programs under Goulart, see Favero, *Cultura popular e educação popular*.
40. Unless otherwise noted, details in this paragraph from Aluízio Palmar, interview, May 19, 2020.
41. File on Aluízio Palmar, no. 354, IPM. Personal collection of Aluízio Palmar.
42. In the decade after her imprisonment, Iná helped found the Workers' Party (Partido dos Trabalhadores) and over the course of a career as a medical doctor also became one of the most influential leftist women in Brazil.
43. Iná Meirelles, interview with Claudia Santiago, April 30, 2014, part of the Quintas Resistentes history series, posted April 30, 2014, by Núcleo Piratininga de Comunicação, YouTube, 1:24:51, www.youtube.com/watch?v=YNw8nP9ktPU.
44. Aluízio Palmar, interview, September 16, 2020.
45. As reproduced in Goulart, *Discursos selecionados*, 84–85.
46. Aluízio Palmar, interview, September 16, 2020.

CHAPTER 2

1. Aluízio Palmar, interview, May 26, 2020.
2. Aluízio Palmar, interview, May 19, 2020.
3. Palmar, *Onde foi*, 171.
4. Knauss and Maia, "Niterói, 1964," 106–7.
5. Palmar, *Onde foi*, 170.
6. Palmar, *Onde foi*, 171.
7. Aluízio Palmar, Facebook, August 14, 2018.
8. Aluízio Palmar, interview, May 26, 2020.
9. Aluízio Palmar, interview, May 26, 2020.
10. As quoted in Machado, *O mel e o sangue*, 66.
11. Aluízio Palmar, interview, May 26, 2020.
12. Aluízio Palmar, interview, May 26, 2020.
13. Aluízio Palmar, interview, May 26, 2020.
14. Article 14, Law no. 4.464, November 9, 1964.
15. Aluízio Palmar, interview, June 2, 2020.
16. Aluízio Palmar, "Os esbirros da ditadura controlavam estudantes e professores da Universidade Federal Fluminense," essay posted March 22, 2012, https://documentosrevelados.com.br/os-esbirros-da-ditadura-controlavam-estudantes-e-professores-da-universidade-federal-fluminense.
17. The military arrested Liszt in 1970. After several months of torture, he was released as part of an exchange for another kidnapped diplomat. He spent most of the 1970s in exile in Algeria, Cuba, Chile, and Europe, then returned to Brazil after the Amnesty Law in 1979. Three years later, he was elected as a state legislator on the Workers Party (PT) ticket.
18. Vieira, *A busca*.
19. Liszt Vieira, interview, August 6, 2021.
20. Online blog post by Aluízio Palmar, March 22, 2012, www.plural.jor.br/documentosrevelados/repressao/forcas-armadas/os-esbirros-da-ditadura-controlavam-estudantes-e-professores-da-universidade-federal-fluminense.
21. Vieira, interview; Maria do Carmo Brito, interview, September 7, 2020.
22. Brito, interview.
23. Umberto Trigueiros Lima, interview, August 24, 2020.
24. Aluízio Palmar, Facebook, July 19, 2020.
25. Aluízio Palmar, interview, May 26, 2020.
26. Lima, interview.
27. Lima, interview.
28. Palmar, *Onde foi*, 182.
29. Lima, interview.
30. Aluízio Palmar, interview, May 26, 2020.
31. Langland, *Speaking of Flowers*, 100.
32. For more on Prestes's cadernetas, see Reis, *Luís Carlos Prestes*, 332.
33. A recent biography offers a useful overview of the historian's political trajectory and influence: Pericás, *Caio Prado Júnior*.
34. Huberman and Sweezy, "Régis Debray and the Latin American Revolution."

NOTES TO CHAPTER 3

35. Aluízio Palmar, interview, June 2, 2020.
36. Lima, interview.
37. For more on the armed struggle, see Reis and Ferreira de Sá, *Imagens da revolução*; and Ridenti, *O fantasma da revolução brasileira*.
38. Ridenti, *O fantasma da revolução brasileira*, 30.
39. Aluízio initially told me the story in interview on June 2, 2020, and he retold it to me, after having read the chapter draft, in a subsequent interview on November 10, 2021.
40. Justiça Militar, 1ª Auditoria da Marinha, file 2364, July 10, 1970. Sentencing report on "Jorge Medeiros Valle e outros," Brasil Nunca Mais Digital.
41. The military records only provide the names of men, though from interviews with multiple former MR-8, we know that the two women, Ziléa and Iná, were also founding members.
42. Aluízio Palmar, interview, June 2, 2020.
43. Ministry of War, November 6, 1969, report no. 2828/S-102/CIE, folder F-151, file 60.985, AN-RJ.
44. Aluízio Palmar, interview, June 2, 2020.
45. Aluízio Palmar, interview, June 2, 2020.
46. Zenaide Machado, interview, October 26, 2021.
47. Sebastião Velasco Cruz, interview, July 28, 2021.
48. Aluízio Palmar, interview, June 2, 2020.
49. Surveillance report from May 15, 1967, DOPS, Rio de Janeiro, Legal Department, section "Prontuário," folder RJ, file 34160, APERJ.
50. Aluízio Palmar, interview, June 2, 2020.
51. Aluízio Palmar, interview, June 2, 2020.
52. Palmar, *Onde foi*, 187.
53. Aluízio Palmar, interview, June 2, 2020.
54. Another example of younger militants taking up arms include those involved with the "O" in Minas Gerais in 1967, which would lead to the establishment of a guerrilla organization two years later, the Revolutionary Armed Vanguard–Palmares.
55. Partido Comunista Brasileiro, "Resolução política," December 1967, www.marxists.org/portugues/tematica/1967/12/informe.htm.
56. Langland, *Speaking of Flowers*, 101.
57. Ridenti, *O fantasma da revolução brasileira*, 32.
58. Aluízio Palmar, interview, June 2, 2020.
59. Two rural uprisings in the region were the so-called Porecatú War in 1949 and the 1957 Squatters Rebellion; for more, see Blanc, *Before the Flood*, 203.
60. Aluízio Palmar, interview, June 9, 2020.
61. Aluízio Palmar, interview, June 2, 2020.

CHAPTER 3

1. Fábio Campana, interview, March 15, 2021.
2. Aluízio Palmar, interview, June 2, 2020.
3. Palmar, *Onde foi*, 190.
4. Comments on draft sent to author, by email, on March 7, 2022.

NOTES TO CHAPTER 3

5. Aluízio Palmar, Facebook, April 4, 2021.
6. Colling, *A resistência da mulher à ditadura militar no Brasil*.
7. Aluízio Palmar, interview, June 2, 2020.
8. Palmar, *Onde foi*, 188.
9. Aluízio Palmar, interview, June 9, 2020, and IPM report, May 9, 1969, signed by Colonel Ajudante Jayme de Paiva Bello, Palmar collection, CEPEDAL.
10. Aluízio Palmar, interview, June 9, 2020.
11. Aluízio Palmar, interview, June 9, 2020.
12. Palmar, *Onde foi*, 191.
13. Palmar, *Onde foi*, 189.
14. Langland, *Speaking of Flowers*, 107.
15. Aluízio Palmar, Facebook, June 27, 2018.
16. Aluízio Palmar, interview, June 28, 2021.
17. Portelli, *Death of Luigi Trastulli*, 73.
18. Aluízio Palmar, WhatsApp message to author, October 27, 2021.
19. Aluízio Palmar, interview, July 15, 2020.
20. LaCapra, "Trauma, History, Memory, Identity," 391.
21. Aluízio Palmar, interview, June 9, 2020.
22. IPM report, May 9, 1969, Palmar collection, CEPEDAL. The conversion rate in March 1968, for example was NCr$3.2 to US$1.
23. DOPS, Paraná, "Informações referentes às detenções de alguns integrantes, no Paraná, do MR-8," November 18, 1970. Posted on Acervo Digital Universidade Federal do Paraná, https://acervodigital.ufpr.br/handle/1884/66928.
24. IPM report, May 9, 1969, Palmar collection, CEPEDAL.
25. Digitized archival evidence about the Ramírez Villalba brothers can be found at the National Security Archive: https://nsarchive2.gwu.edu/NSAEBB/NSAEBB262/index.htm.
26. SNI sentencing report no. 61-CGIPM, December 3, 1969, Palmar collection, CEPEDAL.
27. Campana, interview.
28. Aluízio Palmar, interview, June 9, 2020.
29. Aluízio Palmar, interview, June 9, 2020.
30. João Manoel Fernandes, interview, August 20, 2020.
31. Aluízio Palmar, interview, June 9, 2020.
32. Memo no. 147-E2/69, April 18, 1969. Included in Arquivo Público, Paraná, DOPS, folder "Aluízio F. Palmar."
33. Fernandes, interview.
34. DOPS, Paraná, "Informações referentes às detenções de alguns integrantes, no Paraná, do MR-8," November 18, 1970. Palmar collection, CEPEDAL.
35. Unless otherwise noted, details on the MR-8 in this section come from two documents. The first is Encaminhamento no. 61-CGIPM, December 3, 1969, DOPS collection, "Prontuário" series, folder RJ, file 34160, APERJ. The second is DOPS, Paraná, "Informações referentes às detenções de alguns integrantes, no Paraná, do MR-8," November 18, 1970, Palmar collection, CEPEDAL.
36. Ridenti, *O fantasma da revolução brasileira*, 197.
37. Zenaide Machado, interview, October 26, 2021.

NOTES TO CHAPTER 3

38. Iná Meirelles interview, as recorded in the documentary *Torre das Donzelas*, dir. Susanna Lira, 2018.
39. Jessie Jane Vieira de Souza, interview, July 30, 2021.
40. Machado, interview.
41. Iná Meirelles interview, as recorded in *Torre das Donzelas*.
42. Sebastião Medeiros Filho, interview, May 11, 2021.
43. Fernandes, interview.
44. Umberto Trigueiros Lima, interview, August 24, 2020.
45. "Banco de Ipanema assaltado em NCr$10 mil," *Jornal do Brasil* (Rio de Janeiro), January 7, 1969, 1, 14.
46. Police sketch of alleged robber. In dossier of Ação Penal no. 70/69, Apelação STM no. 38.495, page 376, Brasil Nunca Mais Digital.
47. Umberto Trigueiros Lima, WhatsApp message to author, April 12, 2021.
48. Details on the second robbery from "Ladrões agem à tarde e roubam outro banco," *O Jornal* (Rio de Janeiro), May 8, 1969, 1.
49. SNI report on Iná de Souza Medeiros, no. 03/70-SS.16, January 30, 1970, file 14654, AN-RJ.
50. Sebastião Medeiros Filho, interview. For a short biography of Valle, see Almeida, "O 'Bom Burguês.'"
51. "MR-8 racha e rompe com a esquerda radical," *Jornal do Brasil* (Rio de Janeiro), July 24, 1983, 4.
52. "MR-8: as armas da subversão," *Manchete* (Rio de Janeiro), August 16, 1969, 24–29.
53. A reference to the date of their first meeting, August 6, 1968, is found in a letter from Aluízio Palmar to Eunice Palmar, July 6, 1969, written from Ahú prison. Personal files of Aluízio Palmar.
54. Aluízio Palmar, interview, June 28, 2021.
55. Aluízio Palmar, interview, June 9, 2020.
56. Aluízio Palmar, interview, June 9, 2020.
57. Aluízio Palmar, WhatsApp message to author, April 9, 2021.
58. Fernandes, interview.
59. Medeiros Filho, interview.
60. Lima, interview.
61. Aluízio Palmar, email exchange with author, April 2, 2024.
62. IPM report, May 9, 1969, Palmar collection, CEPEDAL.
63. IPM report, May 9, 1969, Palmar collection, CEPEDAL; and Police File on Aluízio Palmar, DOPS, Rio de Janeiro, Serviço de Cadastro e Documentação, May 8, 1969, DOPS collection, "Prontuario" series, folder RJ, file 34160, APERJ.
64. Ivan Palmar, personal essay shared with author.
65. Machado, interview.
66. Encaminhamento no. 61-CGIPM, December 3, 1969, DOPS collection, "Prontuário" series, folder RJ, file 34160, APERJ.
67. Benedito Mariano Leite, interview, July 18, 2021.
68. Lima, interview.
69. Aluízio Palmar, interview, June 9, 2020.
70. Aluízio Palmar, interview, June 9, 2020.

NOTES TO CHAPTER 4

71. SNI sentencing report no. 61-CGIPM, December 3, 1969, Palmar collection, CEPEDAL.
72. Aluízio Palmar, interview, June 9, 2020.
73. As quoted in Machado, *O mel e o sangue*, 72.
74. Aluízio Palmar, interview, June 9, 2020.
75. Conselho de Segurança Nacional, "Processo de Aluízio Ferreira Palmar," file 00144, May 29, 1969, DOPS collection, "Prontuario" series, folder RJ, file 34160, APERJ.
76. Secretaria de Segurança Pública, 7ª Subdivisão Policial, Cascavel, report no. 271/69, April 5, 1969, Palmar collection, CEPEDAL.
77. As quoted in Machado, *O mel e o sangue*, 73.
78. Aluízio Palmar, interview, June 9, 2020.

CHAPTER 4

1. Details on Aluízio's arrest and abuse from CEV-PR, 2:131–51.
2. Weschler, *A Miracle, a Universe*, 54.
3. Aluízio Palmar, interview, June 23, 2020.
4. Aluízio Palmar, interviews, June 9 and 23, 2020.
5. Prisoner report, May 9, 1969, Quartel General da 5ª Região, DOPS collection, "Prontuário" series, folder RJ, file 34160, APERJ.
6. Secretaria de Segurança Pública, 7ª Subdivisão Policial, Cascavel, report no. 271/69, April 5, 1969, Palmar collection, CEPEDAL.
7. Aluízio Palmar, interview, June 23, 2020.
8. As cited in the English translation of the book: Dassin, *Torture in Brazil*, 16.
9. Aluízio Palmar, interview, June 9, 2020.
10. Aluízio Palmar, testimony to the CEV-PR, Cascavel, March 20, 2014, https://acervodigital.ufpr.br/handle/1884/65571.
11. Aluízio Palmar, interview, June 9, 2020.
12. Palmar, *Onde foi*, 31.
13. Aluízio Palmar to Eunice Palmar, July 13, 1969, Ahú prison, Curitiba. All prison letters come from the personal collection of Aluízio Palmar.
14. Secretaria de Segurança Pública, "Relatório," April 7, 1969, Palmar collection, CEPEDAL.
15. Aluízio Palmar to Eunice Palmar, July 13, 1969, Ahú prison, Curitiba.
16. Aluízio Palmar, interview, June 28, 2021.
17. Aluízio Palmar, interview, June 9, 2020.
18. The various testimonial and documentary evidence that implicates Fleury as a leading figure in extrajudicial violence includes a June 8, 1971, report from the US State Department titled *The Esquadrão da Morte (Death Squad)*. A digital copy of the report is housed on the website of the National Security Archive: https://nsarchive2.gwu.edu/NSAEBB/NSAEBB478/docs/doc4.pdf.
19. Aluízio Palmar, interview, June 9, 2020.
20. Palmar, *Onde foi*, 32.
21. Secretaria de Segurança Pública, "Relatório," April 7, 1969, Palmar collection, CEPEDAL.

NOTES TO CHAPTER 4

22. Ministério do Exército, 5ª RM, Curitiba, April 9, 1969, note no. 137-B2/69, Palmar collection, CEPEDAL.
23. Aluízio Palmar, interview, June 9, 2020.
24. Aluízio Palmar to Eunice Palmar, July 13, 1969, Ahú prison, Curitiba.
25. CEV-PR, 2:150.
26. Aluízio Palmar, interview, June 9, 2020.
27. Details on Aluízio's legal processing from CEV-PR, 2:135–38.
28. Transcript of Aluízio Palmar interrogation, Foz do Iguaçu, n.d., Palmar collection, CEPEDAL.
29. "Promotor denuncia plano subversivo," *Tribuna do Paraná* (Curitiba), June 10, 1969.
30. Aluízio Palmar to Eunice Palmar, July 13, 1969, Ahú prison, Curitiba.
31. Aluízio Palmar to Eunice Palmar, July 13, 1969, Ahú prison, Curitiba.
32. Unless otherwise indicated, information on arrests come from Secretaria de Segurança Pública, DOPS, "Informações referentes às detenções de alguns integrantes, no Paraná, do MR-8," November 18, 1970, https://acervodigital.ufpr.br/handle/1884/66928; and Comissão Geral de Inquérito Policial-Militar, Encaminhamento no. 61, Office of the President, December 3, 1969, DOPS collection, "Prontuário" series, folder RJ, file 34160, APERJ.
33. Sebastião Medeiros Filho, interview, May 11, 2021.
34. Aluízio Palmar to Eunice Palmar, July 13, 1969, Ahú prison, Curitiba.
35. Aluízio Palmar to Eunice Palmar, July 13, 1969, Ahú prison, Curitiba.
36. Comissão Nacional da Verdade, "Ex-presos e ex-militar reconhecem locais de prisão e tortura na Ilha das Flores, RJ," October 22, 2014, http://cnv.memoriasreveladas.gov.br/outros-destaques/560-ex-presos-e-ex-militar-reconhecem-locais-de-prisao-e-tortura-na-ilha-das-flores-rj.html.
37. João Manoel Fernandes, interview, August 20, 2020.
38. Anonymized interview with "JM," as quoted in Scelza, "Companheiros, camaradas e amigos," 3.
39. Aluízio Palmar, interview, June 16, 2020.
40. CEV-PR, 2:146.
41. Aluízio Palmar, interview, June 16, 2020.
42. Aluízio Palmar, interview, June 16, 2020.
43. Comissão Nacional da Verdade, photo gallery on "Ex-presos reconhecem casa na Base Naval Ilha das Flores," caption from image 6, http://cnv.memoriasreveladas.gov.br/fotos.html.
44. Aluízio Palmar, interview, June 16, 2020.
45. Aluízio Palmar to Eunice Palmar, July 13, 1969, Ahú prison, Curitiba.
46. Aluízio Palmar to Eunice Palmar, July 13, 1969, Ahú prison, Curitiba.
47. Palmar, *Onde foi*, 199.
48. João Bonifácio Cabral, interview, August 8, 2020.
49. Beth Fortes, interview, September 14, 2020.
50. Palmar, *Onde foi*, 200.
51. Aluízio Palmar to Eunice Palmar, July 13, 1969, Ahú prison, Curitiba.
52. Vitório Seratiuk, interview, March 26, 2021.
53. Aluízio Palmar to Anízio Palmar, October 2, 1969, Ahú prison, Curitiba.

NOTES TO CHAPTER 4

54. Aluízio Palmar to Eunice Palmar, October 25, 1969, Ahú prison, Curitiba.
55. Seratiuk, interview.
56. Aluízio Palmar to Eunice Palmar, July 13, 1969, Ahú prison, Curitiba.
57. Fortes, interview.
58. Laércio Souto Maior, "Irmã Araújo: santa ou revolucionária?," blog post, December 13, 2017, https://medium.com/@laerciosoutomaior/irmã-araújo-santa-ou-revolucionária-a6d890716517.
59. Palmar, *Onde foi*, 200.
60. Aluízio Palmar to Eunice Palmar, July 6, 1969, Ahú prison, Curitiba.
61. Aluízio Palmar to Eunice Palmar, July 13, 1969, Ahú prison, Curitiba.
62. Although the uprising in Três Passos has been traditionally understood to have been organized under the command of Leonel Brizola—the exiled former governor of Rio Grande do Sul—recent scholarship suggests that Brizola played no direct role in the operation. Rippel, "Operação Três Passos."
63. Palmar, *Onde foi*, 201.
64. A list of police and military agents in charge of torture at various locations is included in CEV-PR, 2:150.
65. João Bonifácio Cabral, video testimony for "Depoimentos para a história: A resistência à ditadura militar no Paraná," November 30, 2013, posted December 1, 2013, by Dh Paz, YouTube, 2:10:27, www.youtube.com/watch?v=RcWkDHKlH60.
66. Seratiuk, interview.
67. As quoted in Machado, *O mel e o sangue*, 74.
68. Case summary of Jane Argolo, CEV-PR, 2:202–19.
69. "Susepe e Comitê Carlos da Ré reúnem ex-presas políticas na Capital," October 24, 2012, www.susepe.rs.gov.br/conteudo.php?cod_conteudo=1054&cod_menu=4.
70. Palmar, *Onde foi*, 200.
71. Braga, *Ahú*, 156. Antônio Conselheiro was a millenarian leader of the Canudos settlement in the interior of Bahia; in the 1890s, Canudos was the site of a violent war between the government and the rural settlers.
72. Braga, *Ahú*, 155.
73. Aluízio Palmar, interview, June 23, 2020.
74. Aluízio Palmar, interview, June 9, 2020.
75. Aluízio Palmar, interview, December 18, 2019.
76. As reproduced in Secretaria Especial dos Direitos Humanos da Presidência da República, *Luta, substantivo feminino*, 51.
77. "Denunciados 33 como implicados no MR-8," *Correio da Manhã* (Rio de Janeiro), November 1, 1969, 12.
78. "As duas mortes do estudante Reinaldo em Copacabana," *Jornal do Brasil* (Rio de Janeiro), July 3, 2020.
79. Sebastião Medeiros Filho, interview.
80. "Polícia acredita que MR-8 foi desmontado," *Correio da Manhã* (Rio de Janeiro), July 17, 1969, 8.
81. "MR-8 pretendia criar focos de guerrilhas," *Jornal do Brasil* (Rio de Janeiro), July 30, 1969, 12.

NOTES TO CHAPTER 5

82. "Diário de um jovem terrorista," *Veja* (São Paulo), August 13, 1969, 17.
83. Daniel Aarão Reis, interview, May 14, 2021.
84. It is possible that Aluízio wrote more than fifteen letters, though that was the number that survived in the family's personal belongings.
85. "Cartas do presídio político do Ahú, em Curitiba, 1969," March 23, 2018, https://documentosrevelados.com.br/cartas-do-presidio-politico-do-ahu-em-curitiba-1969.
86. Aluízio Palmar to Eunice Palmar, July 13, 1969, Ahú prison, Curitiba.
87. Aluízio Palmar to Eunice Palmar, September 15, 1969, Ahú prison, Curitiba.
88. Aluízio Palmar to Eunice Palmar, July 8, 1969, Ahú prison, Curitiba.
89. Aluízio Palmar to Eunice Palmar, July 6, 1969, Ahú prison, Curitiba.
90. Aluízio Palmar to Eunice Palmar, July 9, 1969, Ahú prison, Curitiba.
91. Aluízio Palmar to Eunice Palmar, July 13, 1969, Ahú prison, Curitiba.
92. Aluízio Palmar to Eunice Palmar, July 13, 1969, Ahú prison, Curitiba.
93. Aluízio Palmar to Eunice Palmar, September 15, 1969, Ahú prison, Curitiba.
94. Aluízio Palmar to Eunice Palmar, September 16, 1969, Ahú prison, Curitiba.
95. Aluízio Palmar to Eunice Palmar, September 20, 1969, Ahú prison, Curitiba.
96. Aluízio Palmar to Eunice Palmar, September 25, 1969, Ahú prison, Curitiba.
97. Aluízio Palmar to Eunice Palmar, October 9, 1969, Ahú prison, Curitiba.
98. Aluízio Palmar to Eunice Palmar, October 25, 1969, Ahú prison, Curitiba.
99. Aluízio Palmar to Eunice Palmar, November 7, 1969, Ahú prison, Curitiba.
100. Palmar, *Onde foi*, 201.

CHAPTER 5

1. Comissão Nacional da Verdade, video recording of visit to Ilha das Flores, October 21, 2014, "Ex-presos reconhecem casa na Ilha das Flores onde ocorreu tortura," posted on October 21, 2014, YouTube, 9 min., www.youtube.com/watch?v=8NSFunW2YH0.
2. As cited in Green, *We Cannot Remain Silent*, 150.
3. "Terror in Brazil: A Dossier," The American Committee for Information on Brazil, April 1970, 15; "Brazil: Terror and Torture," *New York Times*, April 29, 1970, 39; "Brazil and Torture," *Washington Post*, September 26, 1970, E6.
4. Kelly, *Sovereign Emergencies*, 39.
5. "Statement by Women Prisoners Held at Ilha das Flores (Rio)," *New York Review of Books*, February 26, 1970.
6. The archival record does not indicate the date of Aluízio's transfer from Ilha das Flores, though one document does note his presence on the island as late as January 30, 1970. SNI, file on Aluízio Palmar, no. 01/70-SS.16, January 30, 1970, Palmar collection, CEPEDAL. In interviews, he recalled spending a month or so on Ilha das Flores.
7. Aluízio Palmar, interview, June 16, 2020.
8. Aluízio Palmar, interview, June 16, 2020.
9. Aluízio Palmar, interview, June 16, 2020.
10. João Manoel Fernandes, interview, August 20, 2020.
11. For an overview of hunger strikes as a form of protest, see, for example, Machin, "Hunger Power."

NOTES TO CHAPTER 5

12. Fundação Perseu Abramo, "Relação das principais greves de fome," summary research, April 23, 2006, https://fpabramo.org.br/2006/04/23/relacao-das-principais-greves-de-fome.
13. Aluízio Palmar, interview, June 16, 2020.
14. Aluízio Palmar, interview, June 16, 2020.
15. Aluízio Palmar, interview, June 16, 2020.
16. Aluízio Palmar, interview, June 16, 2020.
17. Andrea Palmar, interview, November 1, 2021.
18. Aluízio Palmar, interview, June 16, 2020.
19. Aluízio Palmar, interview, June 23, 2020.
20. CEV-PR, 2:136.
21. Aluízio Palmar, interview, June 16, 2020.
22. Palmar, *Onde foi*, 194.
23. Aluízio Palmar, interview, June 28, 2021. Aluízio estimates that the visit took place sometime in mid-May.
24. For more on Brazilian soccer in the 1970s, with a particular focus on the politics of its players, see Couto, "Football, Control and Resistance in the Brazilian Military Dictatorship in the 1970s."
25. As reproduced in Shirts, "Playing Soccer in Brazil," 122.
26. Umberto Trigueiros Lima, interview, August 24, 2020.
27. Aluízio Palmar, Facebook, July 6, 2018.
28. Aluízio Palmar, interview, June 16, 2020.
29. Aluízio Palmar, interview, June 16, 2020.
30. Lima, interview.
31. Decreto-Lei no. 314, March 13, 1967; the charges against the MR-8 militants invoked portions of the law that had been updated as part of the 1969 Decreto-Lei no. 510.
32. Ação Penal no. 70/69, Apelação STM no. 38.495. The full dossier compendium of the trial is housed digitally with Brasil Nunca Mais Digital, http://bnmdigital.mpf.mp.br/DocReader/docreader.aspx?bib=BIB_01&PagFis=152557.
33. Ação Penal no. 70/69, Apelação STM no. 38.495, 2374.
34. Aluízio Palmar, interview, June 16, 2020.
35. Aluízio Palmar, interview, June 16, 2020.
36. "Auto de interrogatório: auditoria," statement from Aluízio Ferreira Palmar, Ação Penal no. 70/69, Apelação STM no. 38.495, 1935–36. This particular document is also part of the appendix for the CEV-PR, included as "Anexo Condor 070" in the digital archive of the Federal University of Paraná.
37. CEV-PR, 2:145.
38. DOPS file on Aluízio Palmar, Prontuário no. 1299. Posted on Documentos Revelados website, July 23, 2013, www.plural.jor.br/documentosrevelados/repressao/prontuario-de-aluizio-palmar-no-dops-de-sao-paulo.
39. "Operação militar derrota seqüestradores," *Correio da Manhã* (Rio de Janeiro), July 2, 1970, 2.
40. Aluízio Palmar, interview, June 23, 2020.
41. "Operação militar derrota seqüestradores."

NOTES TO CHAPTER 5

42. Report on Eiraldo de Palha Freire, compiled by the Comissão Nacional da Verdade, accessed June 17, 2021, https://memoriasdaditadura.org.br/personagens/eiraldo-de-palha-freire.
43. Aluízio Palmar, interview, June 16, 2020.
44. For more on lawyers during the dictatorship, see Rollemberg, "Memória, opinião e cultura política."
45. Augusto Sussekind de Moraes Rego, defense statement for Aluízio Palmar, July 14, 1970, Palmar collection, CEPEDAL.
46. Decreto-Lei no. 314, Article 21, March 13, 1967.
47. Aluízio Palmar, interview, June 16, 2020.
48. Aluízio Palmar, interview, June 16, 2020.
49. Aluízio Palmar, interview, June 16, 2020.
50. Summary of Apelação no. 38.495, Brasil Nunca Mais Digital, http://bnmdigital.mpf.mp.br/sumarios/100/093.html.
51. Aluízio Palmar, interview, June 16, 2020.
52. Aluízio Palmar, interview, June 16, 2020.
53. Palmar, *Onde foi*, 196.
54. Aluízio Palmar, interview, June 16, 2020.
55. Aluízio Palmar, interview, June 16, 2020.
56. Aluízio Palmar, interview, June 16, 2020.
57. Palmar, *Onde foi*, 196.
58. "Leftists in Brazil Seize Swiss Envoy," *New York Times*, December 8, 1970, 1, 10.
59. For a history of the diplomatic kidnappings, see Silva, "Sequestros e terrorismo de Estado no Brasil."
60. Aluízio Palmar, interview, June 16, 2020.
61. Lima, interview.
62. Details of the negotiations from Baumann, *Diplomatic Kidnappings*, 82.
63. Lima, interview.
64. Aluízio Palmar, interview, June 16, 2020.
65. Declaration signed by Aluízio Palmar, December 23, 1970, section "Terrorismo," folder 11, 242, APERJ.
66. Sontag, Ferreira, and Jacob, "Banimento 'em sua forma extra-constitucional.'"
67. DOPS memo no. 142/1970, December 24, 1970, section "Terrorismo," folder 01, 44, APERJ.
68. Zenaide Machado, interview, October 26, 2021.
69. Fernandes, interview.
70. Sebastião Medeiros Filho, interview, May 11, 2021.
71. Estado da Guanabara, Secretaria de Segurança Pública, Instituto Médico Legal, "Auto de exame de corpo de delito," December 23, 1970, Palmar collection, CEPEDAL.
72. Aluízio Palmar, interview, June 16, 2020.
73. Lima, interview.
74. Palmar, *Onde foi*, 197.
75. Aluízio Palmar, interview, June 16, 2020; Lima, interview.
76. Pedro Alves, interview, August 20, 2020.

NOTES TO CHAPTER 6

77. Umberto Trigueiros Lima, "40 anos do voo da liberdade," essay written January 14, 2011, reposted on Documentos Revelados site, www.plural.jor.br/documentosrevelados/repressao/forcas-armadas/embarque-dos-setenta-presos-politicos-trocados-pelo-embaixador-da-suica-video-da-france-press.

78. "Subversivos banidos sairão de cinco Estados," *Jornal do Brasil* (Rio de Janeiro), January 11, 1971, 1.

79. The digital platform of the Arquivo Nacional in Rio de Janeiro houses a nineteen-part dossier with full biographical details of the released prisoners as well as documentation of the negotiations between the People's Revolutionary Vanguard and Brazilian government. In series DFANBSB, section V8, subsection GNC.AAA, dossier 71025662, AN-RJ.

80. Dossier on seventy liberated political prisoners, in series DFANBSB, section V8, subsection GNC.AAA, dossier 71025662, AN-RJ.

81. "Brazil Frees 70, Who Fly to Chile," *New York Times*, January 14, 1971, 9.

82. "Terroristas já estão no Chile," *O Globo* (Rio de Janeiro), January 14, 1971, 9.

83. Associated Press footage of the seventy released political prisoners, January 14, 1970, "Embarque dos setenta prisioneiros políticos trocados pelo Embaixador suíço," posted January 14, 2018, by Aluizio Palmar, YouTube, 1 min., 34 sec., www.youtube.com/watch?v=iHpnuFdIZKE.

84. Baumann, *Diplomatic Kidnappings*, 82.

85. Aluízio Palmar, interview, June 16, 2020.

86. Details from interviews with Aluízio Palmar (June 16, 2020) and Umberto Trigueiros Lima (August 24, 2020).

87. Lima, interview.

88. The government's main representative was Minister of the Interior José Tohá. Aluízio Palmar, interview, June 16, 2020.

89. Lima, interview.

CHAPTER 6

1. Saul Landau and Haskell Wexler, dirs., *Brazil: A Report on Torture*, 1971.

2. Green, *We Cannot Remain Silent*, 260.

3. Examples of screenings from, respectively, Green, *We Cannot Remain Silent*, 262; Telegram 052337, received at Brazilian Consulate in New York, September 30, 1971; "'Documentaries' or Propaganda?," *Herald Examiner* (Los Angeles), November 10, 1971. The latter two documents posted at https://library.brown.edu/create/wecannotremainsilent/chapters/chapter-9-denouncing-the-dictator-2/brazil-report-on-torture/, accessed October 30, 2022.

4. Report from Mario Gibson Barboza to the Ministry of Justice, August 11, 1971, https://library.brown.edu/create/wecannotremainsilent/chapters/chapter-9-denouncing-the-dictator-2/brazil-report-on-torture.

5. Aluízio Palmar, interview, July 15, 2020.

6. Aluízio Palmar, interview, June 16, 2020.

7. Pedro Alves, interview, August 20, 2020.

8. Aluízio Palmar, interview, July 9, 2020.

9. Aluízio Palmar, interview, June 23, 2020.

NOTES TO CHAPTER 7

10. Aluízio Palmar, interview, June 23, 2020.
11. Aluízio Palmar, interview, June 23, 2020.
12. Aluízio Palmar, interview, June 23, 2020.
13. Aluízio Palmar, interview, June 23, 2020.
14. Aluízio Palmar, interview, June 23, 2020.
15. Aluízio Palmar, interview, June 23, 2020.
16. Aluízio Palmar, interview, June 23, 2020.
17. Aluízio Palmar, WhatsApp message to author, June 23, 2020.
18. For a recent history of the People's Revolutionary Vanguard, see Silva, *A revolução da VPR*.
19. Aluízio Palmar, email to author, April 2, 2024.
20. Details from Aluízio Palmar, interview, July 9, 2020; and Machado, *O mel e o sangue*, 76–77.
21. Details confirmed by both Palmar, *Onde foi*, 202, and Alves, interview.
22. Aluízio Palmar, interview, July 9, 2020.
23. Aluízio Palmar, interviews, July 9 and 23, 2020.
24. José Carlos Mendes, interview, August 10, 2020.
25. Aluízio Palmar, interview, July 9, 2020.
26. Rede Rodoviária Federal, Departamento de Segurança, report no. 03/72-IDN, Subject "Aluizio Ferreira Palmar," February 23, 1972. Personal collection of Aluízio Palmar; Ministério do Exercito, Gabinete do Ministro, Centro de Informacões do Exército, report no. 329/71/S-102-M3-CIE. December 28, 1971, BR AN.BSB Z4.SNA.TRR.12, part section 269, folder "Sequestro do Embaixador da Suíça—Banidos," AN-RJ.
27. Timeline of the family's movements provided in email exchange with Aluízio Palmar, November 2, 2022.
28. Aluízio Palmar, WhatsApp message to author, November 6, 2022.
29. Ministério do Exército, Gabinete do Ministro, Centro de Informacões do Exército, report no. 329/71/S-102-M3-CIE. December 28, 1971, BR AN.BSB Z4.SNA.TRR.12, part section 269, folder "Sequestro do Embaixador da Suíça—Banidos," AN-RJ.
30. Rede Rodoviária Federal, Departamento de Segurança, Febraury 23, 1972, report no. 03/72-IDN, subject "Aluizio Ferreira Palmar." Personal collection of Aluízio Palmar.
31. Aluízio Palmar, interview, July 9, 2020.
32. Aluízio Palmar, interview, July 9, 2020.
33. As quoted in Machado, *O mel e o sangue*, 77.
34. Aluízio Palmar, interview, July 9, 2020.
35. Aluízio Palmar, interview, July 9, 2020.
36. As quoted in Machado, *O mel e o sangue*, 77.

CHAPTER 7

1. Details in this paragraph from David Acebey Delgadillo, interview, September 9, 2020.
2. For example, Acebey, *Quereimba*.
3. Aluízio Palmar, interview, July 9, 2020.
4. Consentino Filho, *Ocoy*.
5. José Carlos Mendes, interview, August 10, 2020.

6. Acebey Delgadillo, interview.
7. Aluízio Palmar, WhatsApp message to author, November 11, 2022. Ubajara was also known by his codename of Salomão.
8. Army interrogation report no. 0674, July 16, 1974, section "Comunismo," folder 128, file 319, APERJ.
9. Mendes, interview.
10. Mendes, interview.
11. Mendes, interview.
12. Aluízio Palmar, interview, July 9, 2020.
13. Aluízio Palmar, interview, July 9, 2020.
14. Palmar, *Onde foi*, 204.
15. "Retorno ás bases da vpr na fronteiraii," posted November 4, 2015, by Aluizio Palmar, YouTube, 18 min., 9 sec., www.youtube.com/watch?v=PzQSYOVywYA.
16. Aluízio Palmar, Facebook, October 23, 2015.
17. For more on the 1973 deaths in São Bento, see Silva, *A revolução da VPR*, 305–13.
18. Palmar, *Onde foi*, 33.
19. Palmar, *Onde foi*, 39.
20. Aluízio Palmar, interview, July 15, 2020.
21. Aluízio Palmar, email to author, April 2, 2024.
22. Crenzel, "Narrative of the Disappearances," 176.
23. Machado, *O mel e o sangue*, 78.
24. Aluízio Palmar, WhatsApp message to author, March 9, 2021.
25. Schneider Marques, "Frágeis e perigosos," 184.
26. "Lista dos cidadãos brasileiros vitimados no Chile," *Rsurgente*, October 4, 2015, https://rsurgente.wordpress.com/2015/10/04/lista-dos-cidadaos-brasileiros-vitimados-no-chile.
27. "Acusação pode incluir mortos brasileiros," *Folha de São Paulo*, October 23, 1998, 2.
28. Mendes, interview.
29. Mendes, interview.
30. Aluízio Palmar, interview, July 15, 2020.
31. Aluízio Palmar, email to author, April 2, 2024.
32. Palmar, *Onde foi*, 216; Aluízio Palmar, interview, July 15, 2020.
33. Aluízio Palmar, interview, July 15, 2020.
34. Florita Palmar, interview, November 3, 2021.
35. Florita Palmar, interview.
36. Janaína, WhatsApp message to author, September 14, 2021.
37. Aluízio Palmar, WhatsApp message to author, September 15, 2021.
38. Florita Palmar, WhatsApp message to author, November 2, 2021.
39. Florita Palmar, interview.
40. Aluízio Palmar, interview, July 15, 2020.
41. Palmar, *Onde foi*, 210.
42. Palmar, *Onde foi*, 212.
43. Aluízio Palmar, interview, July 15, 2020.
44. Palmar, *Onde foi*, 211–12.
45. Aluízio Palmar, interview, July 23, 2020.
46. Palmar, *Onde foi*, 211.

NOTES TO CHAPTER 8

47. Maria Mercedes Blanco, interview, August 14, 2020.
48. Aluízio Palmar, interview, July 15, 2020.
49. For a history of the ERP, see Pozzi, "Guerrilla argentina y las masas."
50. Aluízio Palmar, interview, July 15, 2020.
51. Aluízio Palmar, WhatsApp message to author, May 9, 2021.
52. Aluízio Palmar, interview, July 15, 2020.
53. Palmar, *Onde foi*, 212.
54. Aluízio Palmar, interview, July 15, 2020.
55. Aluízio Palmar, interview, July 15, 2020.
56. Aluízio Palmar, interview, July 23, 2020.
57. Aluízio Palmar, interview, July 23, 2020.
58. Florita Palmar, interview.
59. Aluízio Palmar, interview, November 25, 2021.
60. Aluízio Palmar, interview, July 15, 2020.
61. Andrea Palmar, interview, November 1, 2021.
62. Aluízio Palmar, interview, July 15, 2020.
63. Palmar, *Onde foi*, 212.
64. Aluízio Palmar, "No fio da navalha. Minha vida na clandestinidade e o retorno ao Brasil," April 8, 2022, https://documentosrevelados.com.br/no-fio-da-navalha-meu-retorno-a-vida-legal.
65. Palmar, *Onde foi*, 213.
66. Aluízio Palmar, WhatsApp message to author, May 9, 2021.
67. Aluízio Palmar, interview, July 23, 2020.
68. Decreto no. 82960, December 29, 1978.
69. For example, "Justiça militar absolve outro ex-banido no Rio," *O Globo* (Rio de Janeiro), March 30, 1979; "Ex-banido processado duas vezes por crimes idênticos é absolvido," *O Dia*, March 30, 1979.
70. "Ex-banido morto é absolvido no Rio," *Folha de São Paulo*, March 30, 1979.
71. Aluízio Palmar, interview, August 5, 2020.
72. Aluízio Palmar, Facebook, September 12, 2014.
73. Blanco, interview.
74. Florita Palmar, interview.
75. Andrea Palmar, interview.
76. Aluízio Palmar, WhatsApp message to author, November 16, 2021.
77. Florita Palmar, interview.
78. Florita Palmar, interview.
79. Poem shared by Andrea Palmar.
80. Florita Palmar, interview.
81. Aluízio Palmar, interview, July 23, 2020.

CHAPTER 8

1. Rodeghero, Dienstmann, and Trindade, *Anistia ampla, geral e irrestrita*, 28.
2. Martins, *Liberdade para os brasileiros*, 131; Mezarobba, *Um acerto de contas com o futuro*, 28.
3. Information on the CBA comes from Atencio, *Memory's Turn*, 16.

4. Atencio, *Memory's Turn*, 11.
5. Aluízio Palmar, WhatsApp message to author, November 16, 2021.
6. Aluízio Palmar, interview, November 25, 2021.
7. Aluízio Palmar, interview, July 23, 2020.
8. Aluízio Palmar, interview, July 23, 2020.
9. Aluízio Palmar, interview, July 23, 2020.
10. Aluízio Palmar, interview, November 25, 2021.
11. Aluízio Palmar, interview, November 25, 2021.
12. Aluízio Palmar, interview, July 23, 2020.
13. Aluízio Palmar, interview, July 23, 2020.
14. Ana Maria Müller, interview, April 27, 2021.
15. Gonçalves, *O preço do passado*, 50.
16. Passed on December 20, 1979, the Party Reform Act abolished the two state-created political parties: the Alliance for National Renewal (Aliança Renovadora Nacional, ARENA), the government party, and the MDB, the "loyal" opposition party. This act was conditioned by changing political realities: by the late 1970s, the MDB had begun to function much more like a real opposition party, while many ARENA politicians foresaw the end of the dictatorship and distanced themselves from the party.
17. Moreira Alves, *State and Opposition*, 211–12.
18. Aluízio Palmar, interview, July 23, 2020.
19. "Volta à superfície," *Veja* (São Paulo), September 5, 1979, 23–34.
20. Aluízio Palmar, Facebook, August 28, 2018.
21. Aluízio Palmar, Facebook, August 28, 2018.
22. Aluízio Palmar, interview, July 23, 2020.
23. Aluízio Palmar, interview, July 23, 2020.
24. Aluízio Palmar, interview, July 23, 2020.
25. Machado, *O mel e o sangue*, 80–81.
26. Aluízio Palmar, interview, August 5, 2020.
27. Aluízio Palmar, interview, August 5, 2020.
28. Aluízio Palmar, interview, August 5, 2020.
29. João Adelino de Souza, interview, September 20, 2020.
30. For example, "Morte na barca," *Veja* (São Paulo), August 13, 1980, 28.
31. Aluízio Palmar, interview, August 5, 2020.
32. Aluízio Palmar, interview, August 5, 2020.
33. João Adelino de Souza, interview.
34. Confidential memo, Itaipu Binacional, November 19, 1980, report no. E/AESI.G/1B/BR/0061/80, Itaipu Binacional Centro de Documentação, Foz do Iguaçu, Brazil.
35. Untitled editorial, *Nosso Tempo* (Foz do Iguaçu), December 3, 1980, 2.
36. "Tortura," *Nosso Tempo* (Foz do Iguaçu), December 3, 1980, 5.
37. João Adelino de Souza, interview.
38. Werner Fuchs, interview, September 15, 2020.
39. Fuchs, interview.
40. Aluízio Palmar, interview, August 5, 2020.
41. João Adelino de Souza, interview.

42. Serviço Público Federal, DPF/FI 011.217, file on Aluízio Palmar, with surveillance logs from April 1969 to September 1981. Personal collection of Aluízio Palmar.

43. Fábio Campana, interview, March 15, 2021.

44. Blanc, "Last Political Prisoner"; also Blanc, *Before the Flood*, 154–69.

45. Aluízio Palmar, interview, August 5, 2020.

46. João Adelino de Souza, interview.

47. The personal files of Juvêncio Mazzarollo contain copies of over 1,500 letters that were sent to the Brazilian authorities as part of the Amnesty International campaign, representing fifteen countries. Files in possession of the Mazzarollo family.

48. "Vencemos," *Nosso Tempo* (Foz do Iguaçu), April 13, 1984, 15.

49. CEV-PR, 135–42.

50. All quotes in this paragraph from Aluízio Palmar, interview, August 5, 2020.

51. Andrea Palmar, interview, November 1, 2021.

52. Andrea Palmar, interview.

53. Florita Palmar, interview, November 3, 2021.

54. Alexandre Palmar, interview, October 7, 2020.

55. Alexandre Palmar, interview.

56. Florita Palmar, interview.

57. Alexandre Palmar, interview.

58. Alexandre Palmar, interview.

59. João Adelino de Souza, interview.

60. Quoted in Machado, *O mel e o sangue*, 80–81.

61. Aluízio Palmar, interview, August 5, 2020.

62. Palmar, *Onde foi*, 17.

CHAPTER 9

1. Onofre Pinto, along with José Lavecchia and the Carvalho brothers, appeared on the unofficial list of disappeared Brazilians, a document that had been compiled beginning in 1979 and was eventually distributed under the title "O dossiê ditadura: mortos e desaparecidos políticos (1964–1985)."

2. Borba eventually published a book on the topic; Borba, *Cabo Anselmo*.

3. Palmar, *Onde foi*, 15.

4. "Vida e morte do Sargento Albery," *Nosso Tempo* (Foz do Iguaçu), May 18, 1984, 1.

5. "Vida e morte do Sargento Albery."

6. "Autópsia da sombra," *Veja* (São Paulo), November 18, 1992, 20–32.

7. Marival Dias Chaves to Cecília Coimbra, president of the Grupo Tortura Nunca Mais, January 7, 1993, as reproduced in Palmar, *Onde foi*, 57–60.

8. Liliane Ruggia, interview, August 18, 2020.

9. Ruggia, interview.

10. "Traição na fronteira," *Nosso Tempo* (Foz do Iguaçu), February 5, 1993, 30–31.

11. A recent ethnography of the family members working through the CEMDP, as well as the civil society group Tortura Nunca Mais, is Azevedo, *Ausências incorporadas*.

12. Santos, "Transnational Legal Activism and the State," 37.

13. Cecília Coimbra, interview, August 31, 2020.
14. Although statistics are, by nature, difficult, one recent attempt to quantify the violence of disappearance is Bernasconi, Jaramillo, and López, "Number of Disappearance." It should also be noted that disappearances continue through the current day; for a recent study of missing people in Brazil, see Willis, *Keep the Bones Alive*.
15. Feitlowitz, *Lexicon of Terror*, 57.
16. Ramos, "Making Disappearance Visible," 669.
17. "Como Operação agiu no PR," *Folha do Paraná* (Curitiba), June 3, 2000.
18. Valmir Denardin, interview, April 17, 2021.
19. Details of the call from Palmar, *Onde foi*, 66–69, and Aluízio Palmar, interview, August 12, 2020.
20. Nilmário Miranda, interview, August 2, 2021.
21. Palmar, *Onde foi*, 74.
22. As reproduced in Palmar, *Onde foi*, 74. Capitalization consistent with original.
23. "Parentes esperam encerrar capítulo aberto pela ditadura," *Folha do Paraná* (Curitiba), August 3, 2001.
24. Suzana Lisboa, interview, September 21, 2020.
25. Aluízio Palmar, interview, August 12, 2020.
26. "Expedição retoma hoje busca de ossadas," *Folha do Paraná* (Curitiba), August 4, 2001, 7.
27. Palmar, *Onde foi*, 76.
28. Miranda, interview.
29. Ruggia, interview.
30. Lisboa, interview.
31. Miranda, interview.
32. Palmar, *Onde foi*, 16.
33. Palmar, *Onde foi*, 77.
34. Aluízio Palmar, interview, August 12, 2020.
35. For example, "Ministério procura no Paraná corpos de vítimas da ditadura," *Folha do Paraná* (Curitiba), August 2, 2001.
36. Palmar, *Onde foi*, 82.
37. Aluízio Palmar, interview, August 12, 2020.
38. Palmar, *Onde foi*, 122–26.
39. Paulo Malhães, testimony to the Rio de Janeiro State Truth Commission, February 18, 2014, http://comissaodaverdade.al.sp.gov.br/upload/010-depoimento_paulo_malhaes.pdf.
40. Palmar, *Onde foi*, 145.
41. Aluízio Palmar, interview, August 12, 2020.
42. In 2010, Wikileaks released documents showing that Operation Heart of Stone was a planned in cooperation with the Drug Enforcement Administration and the Bureau of Alcohol, Tobacco, and Firearms, https://wikileaks.org/plusd/cables/10BUENOSAIRES5_a.html#.
43. Aluízio Palmar, interview, September 2, 2020.
44. Aluízio Palmar, interview, August 12, 2020.
45. Aluízio Palmar, interview, August 12, 2020.

46. Details in this paragraph from Palmar, *Onde foi*, 235–38.
47. Aluízio Palmar, interview, August 12, 2020.
48. Fábio Campana, interview, March 15, 2021.
49. Aluízio Palmar, interview, August 19, 2020.
50. Aluízio Palmar, interview, August 19, 2020.
51. Aluízio Palmar, interview, August 5, 2020.
52. Aluízio Palmar, interview, August 12, 2020.
53. The book launch is reported on in "Palmar narra a morte de seis militantes da VPR," *Jornal da ABI* (Rio de Janeiro), July–August, 2005, 30. Examples of media coverage include "Onde enterraram nossos mortos," *H2FOZ*, September 3, 2005, www.h2foz.com.br/noticia/onde-enterraram-nossos-mortos-10253; and the memoir's inclusion in a review article is "Ditadura militar returna às prateleiras," *Folha de São Paulo*, November 12, 2005.
54. Palmar, *Onde foi*, 240.
55. The online posting is "Revelações da testemunha da chacina do Parque Nacional do Iguaçu," *Documentos Revelados*, July 2, 2012, https://documentosrevelados.com.br/inedito-testemunha-revela-detalhes-da-chacina-do-parque-nacional-do-iguacu-quando-seis-militantes-da-vpr-foram-assassinados. And the document in his memoir is Palmar, *Onde foi*, 245–68.
56. Palmar, *Onde foi*, 243.

CHAPTER 10

1. Law no. 12.528, November 18, 2011.
2. Unless otherwise noted, all details about the CNV come from Torelly, "Assessing a Late Truth Commission."
3. Arquidiocese de São Paulo, *Brasil: nunca mais*; Comissão de Familiares de Mortos e Desaparecidos Políticos, *Dossiê dos mortos e desaparecidos políticos a partir de 1964*.
4. Comissão de Familiares de Mortos e Desaparecidos Políticos, *Direito à memória e à verdade*.
5. One instance of the military's informal veto power constituted what historian Nina Schneider refers to as "blackmail" of then president Lula. Schneider, "'Too Little Too Late' or 'Premature?,'" 153.
6. Abrão and Torelly, "Resistance to Change," 175.
7. For more on Uruguay, see Burt, Amilivia, and Lessa, "Civil Society and the Resurgent Struggle against Impunity in Uruguay."
8. The IACtHR ruling was issued on November 24, 2010, in the case of Julia Gomes Lund vs. Brazil.
9. Open letter to the Comissão Nacional da Verdade, July 15, 2013, www.forumverdade.ufpr.br/blog/2013/07/16/familiares-criticam-comissao-da-verdade.
10. Aluízio Palmar, interviews, August 19 and September 2, 2020.
11. Torelly, "Assessing a Late Truth Commission," 14.
12. Press release from Comissão Nacional da Verdade, November 12, 2012, BR_RJANRIO_CNV_0_PLA_00092000098201516_v_05_d0007de0022, AN-RJ.
13. CEV-PR, "Relatório parcial das atividades," July 2014, BR_RJANRIO_CNV_0_PCV_00092_001400_2014_64, AN-RJ.

NOTES TO CHAPTER 10

14. Aluízio Palmar, interview, August 19, 2020.

15. Aluízio Palmar testimony to CEV-PR, Cascavel, March 20, 2014. Transcript and audio recording at https://acervodigital.ufpr.br/handle/1884/65571.

16. For example, he was a key contributor to the CNV's report on Operation Condor and the transnational system of repression. Comissão Nacional da Verdade, "Relatório," vol. 1, chap. 6, "Conexões internacionais: a aliança repressiva no Cone Sul e a Operação Condor," https://cnv.memoriasreveladas.gov.br/textos-do-colegiado/586-epub.html.

17. Ivete Caribe, interview, September 16, 2020.

18. Marcelo Rubens Paiva, "Comissão Pessoal da Verdade," Opinião, *O Estado de São Paulo*, May 29, 2013, www.estadao.com.br/cultura/marcelo-rubens-paiva/comissao-pessoal-da-verdade.

19. Payne, *Unsettling Accounts*, 3.

20. Adão Almeida, interview, September 15, 2020.

21. Otávio Rainolfo, testimony to National Truth Commission, June 28, 2013, National Archive, digital document number CNV.0.DPO.00092000706201312, 44.

22. Otávio Rainolfo, testimony to National Truth Commission, June 28, 2013.

23. Caribe, interview.

24. The Declaration on Human Rights Defenders was adopted by consensus by the UN General Assembly in 1998, on the fiftieth anniversary of the Universal Declaration of Human Rights, following fourteen years of negotiations led by the OHCHR. The resolution was officially made under General Assembly Resolution A/RES/53/144.

25. Aluízio Palmar, email to author, February 7, 2023.

26. Aluízio Palmar, interview, February 7, 2023.

27. Torelly, "Assessing a Late Truth Commission," 18.

28. An important book on the comparative study of truth commissions is Bakiner, *Truth Commissions*.

29. Atencio, "From Truth Commission to Post-truth Politics in Brazil," 70.

30. Law no. 8.159, January 8, 1991.

31. Aluízio Palmar, interview, August 19, 2020.

32. Aluízio Palmar, interview, August 26, 2020.

33. Aluízio Palmar, interview, August 26, 2020.

34. Aluízio Palmar, interview, August 26, 2020.

35. Valdir Sessi, interview, August 23, 2020; Ivan Seixas, interview, August 18, 2020.

36. Aluízio Palmar, Facebook, December 6, 2022.

37. Aluízio Palmar, email to author, February 10, 2023.

38. All comments on this post from "Tipos de torturas usadas durante a ditadura military," *Documentos Revelados*, November 30, 2019, https://documentosrevelados.com.br/tpos-de-tortura-usados-durante-a-ditadura-civil-militar.

39. "Sindicatos de jornalistas repudiam ameaças a Aluízio Palmar," March 16, 2023, https://fenaj.org.br/sindicatos-de-jornalistas-repudiam-ameacas-a-aluizio-palmar.

40. Federação Nacional dos Jornalistas, *Violência contra jornalistas*.

41. Aluízio Palmar, interview, September 2, 2020.

42. Unless otherwise noted, all details about the center come from Aluízio Palmar, interview, September 2, 2020.

43. Details of these various events are archived on the center's Facebook page, www.facebook.com/cdhmpfoz.

NOTES TO CONCLUSION

44. TV Câmara, news segment on Aluízio Palmar, July 19, 2016, "Título Cidadão à Aluízio Palmar," posted July 19, 2016, by Aluizio Palmar, YouTube, 5 min., 23 sec., www.youtube.com/watch?v=7-9R4ZcUnBU.
45. Beth Fortes, interview, September 14, 2020.
46. Cecília Coimbra, interview, August 31, 2020.
47. Fábio Campana, interview, March 15, 2021.
48. Vitório Seratiuk, interview, March 26, 2021.
49. Ana Maria Müller, interview, April 27, 2021.
50. Suzana Lisboa, interview, September 21, 2020.
51. Janaína Palmar, interview, September 14, 2020.
52. Amanda Palmar, interview, September 16, 2021.
53. Alexandre Palmar, interview, October 7, 2020.
54. Florita Palmar, WhatsApp message to author, November 3, 2021.
55. "Memorandum from Director of Central Intelligence Colby to Secretary of State Kissinger," April 11, 1974, Foreign Relations of the United States, 1969–1976, vol. E-11, part 2, Documents on South America, 1973–1976, doc. 99, US Department of State Archive, Washington, DC, https://history.state.gov/historicaldocuments/frus1969-76ve11p2/d99.
56. "'Quem nunca deu um tapa no bumbum do filho?,' diz Bolsonaro sobre Geisel," *O Estado de São Paulo*, May 11, 2018.
57. Aluízio Palmar, interview, August 19, 2020.
58. "Expedição em Foz do Iguaçu busca vestígios de emboscada na ditadura," television program, Rede Globo, June 4, 2018.
59. Aluízio Palmar, interview, August 19, 2020.

CONCLUSION

1. For example, "Bolsonaro foi autor de 58% dos ataques contra jornalistas em 2019, diz entidade," *Folha de São Paulo*, January 16, 2020, www1.folha.uol.com.br/poder/2020/01/bolsonaro-foi-autor-de-58-dos-ataques-contra-jornalistas-em-2019-diz-entidade.shtml.
2. "Bolsonaro: 'Se o presidente da OAB quiser saber como o pai desapareceu no período militar, eu conto para ele,'" *O Globo* (Rio de Janeiro), July 29, 2019, https://g1.globo.com/politica/noticia/2019/07/29/se-o-presidente-da-oab-quiser-saber-como-o-pai-desapareceu-no-periodo-militar-eu-conto-para-ele-diz-bolsonaro.ghtml.
3. Aluízio Palmar, Facebook, July 29, 2019.
4. Aluízio Palmar, interview, September 11, 2020.
5. Dossier by Mário Espedito Ostrovski, tome 2, vol. 1, *A Pesquisa BNM*, 136–37.
6. Paraná State Truth Commission, April 27, 2013, transcript included in Brazil's National Archive, file BR_RJANRIO_CNV_0_DPO_00092_000088_2014_91.
7. Aluízio Palmar, Facebook, June 28, 2013.
8. Sunstein, "Unleashed," 73.
9. Blanc, "Inversion of Human Rights."
10. Unless otherwise noted, all material in this section comes from Aluízio Palmar, interview, September 11, 2020.
11. Aluízio Palmar, interview, September 16, 2020.

BIBLIOGRAPHY

PRIMARY SOURCES

Interviews

All interviews conducted digitally by the author, via either WhatsApp (audio and video), Zoom, Google Meets, Blackboard Collaborate, or FaceTime video.

ALUÍZIO PALMAR INTERVIEWS

December 18, 2019.
May 19, 26, 2020.
June 2, 9, 16, 23, 2020.
July 9, 15, 23, 2020.
August 5, 12, 19, 26, 2020.
September 2, 11, 16, 2020.
June 28, 2021.
August 5, 2021.
September 2, 2021.
October 26, 2021.
November 10, 25, 2021.
December 15, 2021.
March 17, 2022.
June 7, 2022.
January 20, 2023.
February 7, 2023.

OTHER INTERVIEWS

Acebey Delgadillo, David. September 9, 2020.
Almeida, Adão. September 15, 2020.
Alves, Pedro. August 20, 2020.
Blanco, Maria Mercedes. August 14, 2020.
Brito, Maria do Carmo. September 7, 2020.
Cabral, João Bonifácio. August 8, 2020.
Campana, Fábio. March 15, 2021.
Caribe, Ivete. September 16, 2020.
Coimbra, Cecília. August 31, 2020.
Denardin, Valmir. April 17, 2021.
Fernandes, João Manoel. August 20, 2020.
Filho, Sebastião Medeiros. May 11, 2021.
Fortes, Beth. September 14, 2020.
Fuchs, Werner. September 15, 2020.
Leite, Benedito Mariano. July 18, 2021.
Lima, Umberto Trigueiros. August 24, 2020.
Lisboa, Suzana. September 21, 2020.
Machado, Zenaide. October 26, 2021.
Mendes, José Carlos. August 10, 2020.
Miranda, Nilmário. August 2, 2021.
Müller, Ana Maria. April 27, 2021.
Palmar, Alexandre. October 7, 2020.
Palmar, Amanda. September 16, 2021.
Palmar, Andrea. November 1, 2021.
Palmar, Florita. November 3, 2021.
Palmar, Janaína. September 14, 2020.
Reis, Daniel Aarão. May 14, 2021.
Ruggia, Liliane. August 18, 2020.
Seixas, Ivan. August 18, 2020.
Seratiuk, Vitório. March 26, 2021.
Sessi, Valdir. August 23, 2020.
Souza, João Adelino de. September 20, 2020.
Velasco Cruz, Sebastião. July 28, 2021.
Vieira, Liszt. August 6, 2021.
Vieira de Souza, Jessie Jane. July 30, 2021.

BIBLIOGRAPHY

Archives

Arquivo Nacional, Rio de Janeiro, Brazil.
Arquivo Público do Estado do Rio de Janeiro, Rio de Janeiro, Brazil.
Arquivo Público do Paraná, Curitiba, Paraná, Brazil.
Brasil Nunca Mais Digital, https://bnmdigital.mpf.mp.br.
Centro de Pesquisa e Documentação sobre o Oeste do Paraná, Universidade Estadual do Oeste do Paraná, Marechal Cândido Rondon, Brazil.
Itaipu Binacional Centro de Documentação, Foz do Iguaçu, Brazil.

Newspapers and Periodicals

Correio da Manhã (Rio de Janeiro)
Folha de São Paulo
Folha do Paraná (Curitiba)
Herald Examiner (Los Angeles)
Jornal da ABI (Rio de Janeiro)
Jornal do Brasil (Rio de Janeiro)
Manchete (Rio de Janeiro)
New York Review of Books
New York Times
Nosso Tempo (Foz do Iguaçu)
O Dia (Rio de Janeiro)
O Estado de São Paulo
O Globo (Rio de Janeiro)
O Jornal (Rio de Janeiro)
Tribuna do Paraná (Curitiba)
Veja (São Paulo)

SECONDARY SOURCES

Abrão, Paulo, and Marcelo D. Torelly. "Resistance to Change: Brazil's Persistent Amnesty and Its Alternatives for Truth and Justice." In *Amnesty in the Age of Human Rights Accountability: Comparative and International Perspectives*, edited by Francesca Lessa and Leigh A. Payne, 152–81. Cambridge: Cambridge University Press, 2012.

Acebey, David. *Quereimba: Apuntes sobre los ava-guaraní en Bolivia*. La Paz: Gráficas E. G., 1991.

Almeida, Valesca de Souza. "O 'Bom Burguês': a trajetória de Jorge Medeiros Valle." Master's thesis, Universidade Federal Fluminense, 2015.

Araujo, Ana Lucia. *Slavery in the Age of Memory: Engaging the Past*. London: Bloomsbury, 2020.

Arquidiocese de São Paulo. *Brasil: nunca mais*. Petrópolis: Vozes, 1985.

Atencio, Rebecca J. "From Truth Commission to Post-truth Politics in Brazil." *Current History* 118, no. 805 (February 2019): 68–74.

———. *Memory's Turn: Reckoning with Dictatorship in Brazil*. Madison: University of Wisconsin Press, 2014.

Azevedo, Desirée de Lemos. *Ausências incorporadas: etnografia entre familiares de mortos e desaparecidos políticos no Brasil*. São Paulo: Editora Unifesp, 2021.

Bakiner, Onur. *Truth Commissions: Memory, Power, and Legitimacy*. Philadelphia: University of Pennsylvania Press, 2015.

Baumann, Carol Edler. *The Diplomatic Kidnappings: A Revolutionary Tactic of Urban Terrorism*. The Hague: Martinus Nijhoff, 1973.

Blanc, Jacob. *Before the Flood: The Itaipu Dam and the Visibility of Rural Brazil*. Durham, NC: Duke University Press, 2019.

———. "The Inversion of Human Rights in Brazil." *NACLA*, January 20, 2020. https://nacla.org/news/2020/01/20/inversion-human-rights-brazil.

———. "The Last Political Prisoner Juvêncio Mazzarollo and the Twilight of Brazil's Dictatorship." *Luso-Brazilian Review* 53, no. 1 (2016): 153–78.

Borba, Marco Aurélio. *Cabo Anselmo: a luta armada ferida por dentro*. São Paulo: Global, 1981.

Bozzoli, Belinda. "Public Ritual and Private Transition: The Truth Commission in Alexandra Township, South Africa, 1996." *African Studies* 57, no. 2 (1998): 167–95.

Braga, Políbio. *Ahú: diário de uma prisão política*. Porto Alegre: Movimento XXI, 2004.

Burt, Jo-Marie, Gabriela Fried Amilivia, and Francesca Lessa. "Civil Society and the Resurgent Struggle against Impunity in Uruguay (1986–2012)." *International Journal of Transitional Justice* 7, no. 2 (2013): 306–27.

Caruth, Cathy. *Unclaimed Experience: Trauma, Narrative, and History*. Baltimore: Johns Hopkins University Press, 1996.

Carvalho, Anderson Carlos Madeira de. *Niterói na época da ditadura*. Rio de Janeiro: Gramma, 2019.

Carvalho, Apolônio de. *Vale a pena sonhar*. Rio de Janeiro: Rocco, 1997.

Colling, Ana Maria. *A resistência da mulher à ditadura militar no Brasil*. Rio de Janeiro: Rosa dos Tempos, 1997.

Comissão de Familiares de Mortos e Desaparecidos. *Direito à memória e à verdade*. Brasília: Secretaria Especial de Direitos Humanos, 2007.

———. *Dossiê dos mortos e desaparecidos políticos a partir de 1964*. São Paulo: Imprensa Oficial, 1996.

Comissão Estadual da Verdade do Paraná–Teresa Urban. *Relatório da Comissão Estadual da Verdade do Paraná*. São Paulo: TikiBooks, 2017.

Consentino Filho, Lauro. *Ocoy: o rio que levou boiando capacetes militares . . . e os sonhos*. Self-published, n.d. Accessed June 5, 2020. www.documentosrevelados.com.br/wp-content/uploads/2015/03/dr-lauro-consentino-filho-2.pdf.

Coppe Caldeira, Rodrigo. "Bispos conservadores brasileiros no Concílio Vaticano II (1962–1965): D. Geraldo de Proença Sigaud e D. Antônio de Castro Mayer." *HORIZONTE: Revista de Estudos de Teologia e Ciências da Religião* 9, no. 23 (2011): 1010–29.

Couto, Euclides de Freitas. "Football, Control and Resistance in the Brazilian Military Dictatorship in the 1970s." *International Journal of the History of Sport* 31, no. 10 (2014): 1267–77.

Cowan, Benjamin A. *Securing Sex: Morality and Repression in the Making of Cold War Brazil*. Chapel Hill: University of North Carolina Press, 2016.

Crenzel, Emilio. "The Narrative of the Disappearances in Argentina: The Nunca Más Report." *Bulletin of Latin American Research* 32, no. s1 (2013): 174–92.

Dassin, Joan. *Torture in Brazil: A Shocking Report on the Pervasive Use of Torture by Brazilian Military Governments, 1964–1979*. Austin: University of Texas Press, 1998.

Ehlers, Anke, and David M. Clark. "A Cognitive Model of Posttraumatic Stress Disorder." *Behavioral Research and Therapy* 38 (2000): 319–45.

Farrell, Thomas B. *Norms of Rhetorical Culture*. New Haven, CT: Yale University Press, 1993.

Favero, Osmar, ed. *Cultura popular e educação popular: memória dos anos 60*. Rio de Janeiro: Edições Gerais, 1983.

Federação Nacional dos Jornalistas. *Violência contra jornalistas e liberdade de imprensa no Brasil*. Brasília: FENAJ, 2023.

Feitlowitz, Marguerite. *A Lexicon of Terror: Argentina and the Legacies of Torture*. New York: Oxford University Press, 2011.

Felman, Shoshana, and Dori Laub. *Testimony: Crises of Witnessing in Literature, Psychoanalysis, and History*. New York: Routledge, 1992.

Ferreira de Souza, Rogério. "Memória, justiça e poder: desafios contemporâneos. Uma introdução." *Revista Crítica de Ciências Sociais* 121 (2020): 95–102.

Fivush, Robyn, and Matthew E. Graci, "Autobiographical Memory." In *Learning and Memory: a Comprehensive Reference*, edited by John H. Byrne, 119. 2nd ed. Cambridge, MA: Elsevier Open Access Academic, 2017.

Freud, Sigmund. "Remembering, Repeating, and Working-Through." In *The Standard Edition of the Complete Psychological Works of Sigmund Freud*, 12: 145–56. London: Hogarth, 1914.

Friendly, Abigail. "The Changing Landscape of Civil Society in Niterói, Brazil." *Latin American Research Review* 51, no. 1 (2016): 218–41.

Gabeira, Fernando. *O que é isso companheiro?* Rio de Janeiro: CODECRI, 1979.

Gadea, Carlos A., and Rogério Ferreira de Souza. "Memória coletiva e social no Brasil contemporâneo." *Revista Brasileira de Sociologia* 5, no. 11 (2017): 199–218.

Gaffey, Adam. "Imagining the Words of Others: Public Memory and Ceremonial Repetition in American Public Discourse." PhD diss., Texas A&M University, 2013.

Gilmore, Leigh. *Tainted Witness: Why We Doubt What Women Say about Their Lives*. New York: Columbia University Press, 2017.

Gonçalves, Danyelle Nilin. *O preço do passado: Anistia e reparação de perseguidos políticos no Brasil*. São Paulo: Editora Expressão Popular, 2009.

Goulart, João. *Discursos selecionados do presidente João Goulart*. Brasília: Fundação Alexandre de Gusmão, 2010.

Green, James N. *Exile within Exiles: Herbert Daniel, Gay Brazilian Revolutionary*. Durham, NC: Duke University Press, 2018.

———. *We Cannot Remain Silent: Opposition to the Brazilian Military Dictatorship in the United States*. Durham, NC: Duke University Press, 2010.

———. "'Who Is the Macho Who Wants to Kill Me?' Male Homosexuality, Revolutionary Masculinity, and the Brazilian Armed Struggle of the 1960s and 1970s." *Hispanic American Historical Review* 92, no. 3 (August 2012): 437–69.

Gül, Altınay Ayşe, ed. *Women Mobilizing Memory*. New York: Columbia University Press, 2019.

Henke, Suzette. *Shattered Subjects: Trauma and Testimony in Women's Life-Writing*. New York: St. Martin's, 1998.

Herler, Thomaz Joezer. "Formação e trajetória do primeiro MR-8: possibilidades e limites de construção de uma vanguarda revolucionária político-militar (1964–1969)." Master's thesis, Universidade Estadual do Oeste do Paraná, 2015.

Huberman, Leo, and Paul M. Sweezy, eds. "Régis Debray and the Latin American Revolution." Special issue, *Monthly Review* 20, no. 3 (July–August 1968).

BIBLIOGRAPHY

Jelín, Elizabeth. *Los trabajos de la memoria*. Madrid: Siglo XXI, 2002.

Kelly, Patrick W. *Sovereign Emergencies: Latin America and the Making of Global Human Rights Politics*. New York: Cambridge University Press, 2018.

Knauss, Paulo, and Eric Maia. "Niterói, 1964—Memórias da prisão esquecida: a Operação Limpeza e o cárcere político do Caio Martins." *Acervo* 27, no. 1 (2014): 99–120.

Knudsen, Britta Timm, and Casper Andersen. "Affective Politics and Colonial Heritage, Rhodes Must Fall at UCT and Oxford." *International Journal of Heritage Studies* 25, no. 3 (2019): 239–58.

LaCapra, Dominick. "Trauma, History, Memory, Identity: What Remains?" *History and Theory* 55, no. 3 (2016): 375–400.

Langland, Victoria. *Speaking of Flowers: Student Movements and the Making and Remembering of 1968 in Military Brazil*. Durham, NC: Duke University Press, 2013.

Lima, Umberto Trigueiros. "Encontro com Apolônio." In Ministério da Justiça, *68, a geração que queria mudar o mundo: Relatos*, 292–93. Brasília: Comissão de Anistia, 2011.

Llamojha Mitma, Manuel, and Jaymie Patricia Heilman. *Now Peru Is Mine: The Life and Times of a Campesino Activist*. Durham, NC: Duke University Press, 2016.

Machado, Juliana. *O mel e o sangue: oito histórias sobre a Declaração Universal dos Direitos Humanos*. Self-published, n.d.

Machin, Amanda. "Hunger Power: The Embodied Protest of the Political Hunger Strike." *Interface: A Journal for and about Social Movements* 8, no. 1 (2016): 157–80.

Martins, Roberto Ribeiro, Paulo Ribeiro Martins, and Luís Antonio Palmeira. *Liberdade para os Brasileiros: Anistia ontem e hoje*. Rio de Janeiro: Civilizacão Brasileira, 1978.

Mazzarollo, Juvêncio. *A taipa da injustiça: Itaipu x agricultores expropriados*. Curitiba: Comissão Pastoral da Terra, 1980.

Mezarobba, Glenda. *Um acerto de contas com o futuro: a Anistia e suas conseqüências, um estudo do caso brasileiro*. São Paulo: Editora Humanitas, 2006.

Moreira Alves, Maria. *State and Opposition in Military Brazil*. Austin: University of Texas Press, 1988.

Nunes, Edson. *A revolta das barcas: populismo, violência e conflito político*. São Paulo: Garamond, 2000.

O'Connell, Heather A. "Monuments Outlive History: Confederate Monuments, the Legacy of Slavery, and Black-White Inequality." *Ethnic and Racial Studies* 43, no. 3 (2020): 460–78.

Office of the High Commissioner for Human Rights. *Manual on Human Rights Monitoring*. Rev. ed. New York: United Nations, 2011.

Oriana Bernasconi, Jefferson Jaramillo, and Marisol López. "The Number of Disappearance: Trajectories in the Tally of Victims of Forced Disappearance in Latin America." *Tapuya: Latin American Science, Technology and Society* 5, no. 1 (2022). https://doi.org/10.1080/25729861.2022.209048.

Palmar, Aluízio. "As marquises de Niterói." In Ministério da Justiça, *68, a geração que queria mudar o mundo: Relatos*, 133–39. Brasília: Comissão de Anistia, 2011.

———. *Onde foi que vocês enterraram nossos mortos*, 4th ed. Curitiba: Travessa dos Editores, 2012.

Payne, Leigh A. *Unsettling Accounts: Neither Truth nor Reconciliation in Confessions of State Violence*. Durham, NC: Duke University Press, 2008.

Pericás, Luiz Bernardo. *Caio Prado Júnior: Uma biografia política.* São Paulo: Boitempo, 2017.

Portelli, Alessandro. *The Death of Luigi Trastulli, and Other Stories: Form and Meaning in Oral History.* Albany: SUNY Press, 1991.

Pozzi, Pablo A. "La guerrilla argentina y las masas: El ERP y su inserción." *Revista Tempo e Argumento* 7, no. 16 (2015): 108–28.

Puga, Ana Elena, and Víctor M. Espinosa. *Performances of Suffering in Latin American Migration: Heroes, Martyrs, Saints.* Basingstoke, UK: Palgrave Macmillan, 2020.

Ramos, Marco Antonio. "Making Disappearance Visible: The Realities of Cold War Violence." *American Historical Review* 127, no. 2 (2022): 664–90.

Reis, Daniel Aarão. *A revolução faltou ao encontro: os comunistas no Brasil.* São Paulo: Brasiliense, 1990.

———. *Luís Carlos Prestes: Um revolucionário entre dois mundos.* São Paulo: Companhia das Letras, 2014.

Reis, Daniel Aarão, and Jair Ferreira de Sá. *Imagens da revolução: documentos políticos das organizações clandestinas de esquerda dos anos 1961–1971.* Rio de Janeiro: Marco Zero, 1985.

Reuque Paillalef, Rosa Isolde, and Florencia E. Mallon. *When a Flower Is Reborn: The Life and Times of a Mapuche Feminist.* Durham, NC: Duke University Press, 2002.

Reyes, G. Mitchell, ed. *Public Memory, Race, and Ethnicity.* Newcastle upon Tyne, UK: Cambridge Scholars, 2010.

Ridenti, Marcelo. *O fantasma da revolução brasileira.* São Paulo: UNESP, 1993.

Rippel, Leomar. "Operação Três Passos (1965): movimento de insurreição e resistência contra a ditadura militar brasileira." Master's thesis, Universidade Estadual do Oeste do Paraná, 2020.

Rodeghero, Carla Simone, Gabriel Dienstmann, and Tatiana Trindade. *Anistia ampla, geral e irrestrita: história de uma luta inconclusa.* Santa Cruz do Sul: Edunisc, 2011.

Rollemberg, Denise. "Memória, opinião e cultura política: a Ordem dos Advogados do Brasil sob a ditadura (1964–1974)." *Modernidades alternativas* 1 (2008): 57–96.

Santos, Cecília MacDowell. "Transnational Legal Activism and the State: Reflections on Cases against Brazil in the Inter-American Commission on Human Rights." *Sur: Revista Internacional de Direitos Humanos* 4 (2007): 26–57.

Scelza, Maria Fernanda Magalhães. "Companheiros, camaradas e amigos: memórias de ex-militantes políticos e a formação do Partido da Ilha das Flores (1968–1973)." Master's thesis, Universidade do Estado do Rio de Janeiro, 2009.

Schippert, Ana Carla S. P., Ellen Karine Grov, and Ann Kristin Bjørnnes. "Uncovering Re-traumatization Experiences of Torture Survivors in Somatic Health Care: A Qualitative Systematic Review." *PLoS ONE* 16, no. 2 (2021): e0246074.

Schneider, Ann M. *Amnesty in Brazil: Recompense after Repression, 1895–2010.* Pittsburgh: University of Pittsburgh Press, 2021.

Schneider, Nina. "'Too Little Too Late' or 'Premature'? The Brazilian Truth Commission and the Question of 'Best Timing.'" *Journal of Iberian and Latin American Research* 19, no. 1 (2013): 149–62.

Schneider Marques, Teresa Cristina. "Frágeis e perigosos: a repercussão internacional da violência contra estrangeiros durante o golpe de 1973 no Chile." *Civitas* 13, no. 1 (January–April 2013): 182–98.

Secretaria Especial dos Direitos Humanos. *Direito à verdade e à memória: Comissão Especial sobre Mortes e Desaparecidos Políticos*. Brasília: Secretaria Especial dos Direitos Humanos.

———. *Luta, substantivo feminino: mulheres torturadas, desaparecidas e mortas na resistência à ditadura*. São Paulo: Caros Amigos, 2010.

Sepúlveda dos Santos, Myrian. "O retorno do pesadelo: um estudo sobre a luta da memória contra o esquecimento." *Revista Crítica de Ciências Sociais* 121 (2020): 103–22.

Shirts, Matthew. "Playing Soccer in Brazil: Socrates, Corinthians, and Democracy." *Wilson Quarterly* 13, no. 2 (1989): 119–23.

Sikkink, Kathryn. *The Justice Cascade: How Human Rights Prosecutions Are Changing World Politics*. New York: W. W. Norton, 2011.

Silva, Carla Luciana. *A revolução da VPR: a Vanguarda Popular Revolucionária*. Uberlândia: Navegando, 2021.

———. "Sequestros e terrorismo de Estado no Brasil: casos de resistência revolucionária." *Izquierdas* 49 (2020): 1646–69.

Smyth, Joshua, and Melanie Greenberg. "Scriptotherapy: The Effects of Writing about Traumatic Events." In *Psychodynamic Perspectives on Sickness and Health*, edited by Paul Raphael Duberstein and Joseph M. Masling, 121–60. Washington, DC: American Psychological Association, 2020.

Sontag, Ricardo, Tainá Emília Queiroz Ferreira, and Vitória Mendes Jacob. "Banimento 'em sua forma extra-constitucional' e cultura jurídica no Brasil (1969–1978)." *Revista Culturas Jurídicas* 4, no. 7 (2017): 190–220.

Stern, Steve J. *The Memory Box of Pinochet's Chile*. 3 vols. Durham, NC: Duke University Press, 2004–10.

Sunstein, Cass R. "Unleashed." *Social Research: An International Quarterly* 85, no. 1 (Spring 2018): 73–92.

Taylor, Diana. "Performing Gender: Las Madres de la Plaza de Mayo." In *Negotiating Performance: Gender, Sexuality, and Theatricality in Latin/o America*, edited by Diana Taylor and Juan Villegas, 275–395. Durham, NC: Duke University Press, 1994.

Torelly, Marcelo. "Assessing a Late Truth Commission: Challenges and Achievements of the Brazilian National Truth Commission." *International Journal of Transitional Justice* 12, no. 2 (2018): 194–215.

Van Alphen, Ernst. *Caught by History: Holocaust Effects in Contemporary Art, Literature, and Theory*. Redwood City, CA: Stanford University Press, 1997.

Vieira, Liszt. *A busca: memórias da resistência*. São Paulo: Hucitec, 2008.

Visser, Irene. "Trauma Theory and Postcolonial Literary Studies." *Journal of Postcolonial Writing* 47, no. 3 (2011): 270–82.

Walkowitz, Daniel J., and Lisa Maya Knauer. *Contested Histories in Public Space: Memory, Race, and Nation*. Durham, NC: Duke University Press, 2009.

Weschler, Lawrence. *A Miracle, a Universe: Settling Accounts with Torturers*. Chicago: University of Chicago Press, 1998.

Willis, Graham Denyer. *Keep the Bones Alive: Missing People and the Search for Life in Brazil*. Berkeley: University of California Press, 2022.

INDEX

Page numbers in italics refer to illustrations.

AAA (Argentine Anticommunist Alliance), 155, 163
abertura, 113, 185, 186, 230
academic directorates, 39
Acebey Delgadillo, David, 145, 146, 147–49
activism. *See* Palmar, Aluízio: activism
AESI (Special Committee for Security and Information), 183
agrarian reform, 32–33
Ahú prison, 97, 105, 158
alcohol, 6, 164, 166, 207
Alderete farm, 149, 151–53
aliases: José Augusto, 144–45; José de Augusto Lima, 83, 85–86
Allende, Salvador, 7, 130, 132, 134, 136, 142, 156
Almeida, Adão, 205, 206, 217
Almeida, Eunice. *See* Palmar, Eunice (née Almeida)
ALN. *See* National Liberation Action (ALN)
Alvarez, Marta, 110, *110*, 112
amnesty, for Aluízio Palmar, 179, 180
Amnesty Law (1979): debates over, 173, 215, 239; impunity and, 197, 201, 208; passage of, 3, 175, 177, 178
amnesty movement, in Brazil, 168, 172–73, 175, 176
Anselmo, Cabo, 154, 155, 194, 195
Argentine Anticommunist Alliance (AAA), 155, 163
Argentine People's Revolutionary Army (ERP), 142
armed struggle, 50–51, 52–53, 55–57, 134. *See also* guerrilla warfare

Astica, Sara, 144
Augusto, José (alias), 144–45
Augusto Lima, José de (alias), 83, 85–86
autobiographical memory, 6–7
Avá-Guarani Indigenous community, 182

Bachelet, Michelle, 232
Baixada Fluminense, 31–32
Banhadão farm, 78, 82
banishment, policy of, 127, 169
bank robberies, 54, 63, 72–75
biography, methodology of, 14–17, 235–36, 237, 243, 246n21
Boi-Piquá farm, 63–64, 72
Bolivia, 147
Bolsonaro, Jair: candidacy and election of, 59, 215, 230; legacies of dictatorship and, 221, 238–39; presidency of, 2, 223–24, 232–33, 234–35; prodictatorship views of, 2–3, 215, 221
Borba, Marco Aurélio, 195
Branco, Humberto de Alencar Castelo, 36
Brasil: nunca mais (1985 report), 86, 214, 234
Brazil: A Report on Torture (film), 132–33, 137
Brazilian Amnesty Committee (CBA), 172–73, 176
Brazilian Communist Party (PCB): leaders of, 30; 1964 military coup and, 34–35, 36; Aluízio Palmar's membership in, 17, 28–29; schism within, 43–47, 49–51; student activism within, 27, 42–43
Brazilian Labor Party (PTB), 24, 26, 27, 188
Brazilian Miracle, 117
Brazilian Socialist Party, 27
Bucher, Giovanni Enrico, 125, 126, 127, 128

INDEX

Cabral, César: imprisonment and torture of, 112; marriage to Adelaide Almeida, 76, 77; MR-8 activities of, 63–64, 75; relationship with Aluízio Palmar, 16, 53–54, 174, 209; testimony of Otávio Rainolfo and, 205–6, 207, 211, 217

Campana, Fábio, 185

Cândido Mendes prison, 123

Canudos settlement, 254n71

Cardoso, Fernando Henrique, 193, 197

Caribe, Ivete, 216, 218

Carvalho, Apolônio de, 30–31

CBA (Brazilian Amnesty Committee), 172–73, 176

CDHMP. *See* Center for Human Rights and Popular Memory (CDHMP)

CEMDP (Special Commission on Political Deaths and Disappearances), 197, 200, 202, 208, 214, 230

Cenimar (Centro de Informações da Marinha), 94–95, 108

Center for Human Rights and Popular Memory (CDHMP), 2, 5, 18–19, 215, 224–25, 241

Chaves, Marival Dias, 195, 196

Chilean Revolutionary Left Movement (MIR), 141–42

clandestinity, 48–49, 159, 171–76, 178, 180–81

class prejudice, 123–24

CNV. *See* National Truth Commission (CNV)

codenames, 31, 65, 70, 75, 91–92, 145; of Aluízio Palmar, 77, 153, 157

Coimbra, Cecília, 196, 197

Colby, William, 229

Cold War, 1

COLINA (National Liberation Command), 40, 49, 75, 79, 82, 103, 116, 140

Comício da Central, 32–33, 61

Comissão Estadual da Verdade do Paraná–Teresa Urban, 216–17

Committee for Amnesty in Brazil, 169

Congress of Latin American Solidarity for Cuba (1963), 29–30

Conselheiro, Antônio, 254n71

Correio da Manhã (newspaper), 37, 102–3, 120

Costa, Adolfo Mariano da, 181

coup d'état, Brazil (1964), 17, 23, 28, 33, 34–38

coup d'état, Chile (1973), 156

Cuban Revolution, 63–64

Debray, Régis, 44–45, 51; *Revolution within the Revolution*, 44–45

decompression, political, 113, 172

democracy, return to, 113, 173, 184, 185–86, 188, 230

Democratic Labor Party (PDT), 187, 188–89

Denardin, Valmir, 198

Department of Political and Social Order (DOPS), 48, 69, 79–80, 86, 87, 88, 99, 100, 222, 241

dictatorship, Argentine, 155–56, 164

dictatorship, Brazilian: apologists for, 232–33; arrests by, 81–82, 103; bureaucracy of, 91, 118; end of, 188, 262n16; hardening of, 65; legacies of, 2–4, 238–39; repression by, 58–59, 61, 69, 70, 79–80, 97; surveillance of exiles by, 142, 143; torture by, 85–88, 93–94, 119

dictatorship, Chilean, 156–57

dictatorships, Cold War-era, 33

diretórios acadêmicos, 39

DI-RJ. *See* Dissidência–Rio de Janeiro (DI-RJ)

disappearance, study of, 197–98, 264n14

disappeared, the: 1974 deaths of VPR militants, 203–4, 206–7; memory and, 198; Aluízio Palmar's search for, 199, 201–2, 203, 205, 207–8, 210–12; search for, 3, 4, 18, 193, 194, 196, 230–31. *See also* Medianeira Massacre; National Truth Commission (CNV); Special Commission on Political Deaths and Disappearances (CEMDP)

Dissidência-Guanabara (DI-GB), 45, 49, 50, 104

Dissidência–Rio de Janeiro (DI-RJ), 45, 46, 47–48, 49–50, 51, 52, 63. *See also* October 8 Revolutionary Movement (MR-8)

distensão (political decompression), 113, 172

Documentos Revelados (website), 13, 222–24, 241

DOPS. *See* Department of Political and Social Order (DOPS)

double agents, 194, 196, 218

INDEX

education: access to, 21, 24; of Aluízio Palmar, 26–27, 39–40; and PNA, 31–32
Elbrick, Charles Burke, 75, 104–5, 125
episodic memory, 6
ERP (Argentine People's Revolutionary Army), 142
Estrada do Colono (Settler's Road), 204, *204*, 211
exiles, 117, 180, 196, 225; in Allende's Chile, 130, 134, 136, 142, 156; return of, 3, 141, 168–69, 172–73, 177, 179; surveillance of, 142–43; work of, 7, 111, 113, 133, 140, 209. *See also* Amnesty Law (1979); Palmar, Aluízio: exile; Palmar Aluízio: exile, in Argentina

Fávero, Izabel, 101–2, 234
Fazenda da Casa Branca, 21
Federal Fluminense University (UFF), 39–40, 41, 47, 48, 54, 59
Fernandes, João Manoel, 68–70, 78–79, 95, 102–3, 114, 127
Fernandes, Nielse, 46, 47, 54, 65
Ferreira Netto, Luzia Pires, 21–22, *22*, 23, 35–36
Figueiredo, João Baptista, 173, 177, 188, 229–30
Fleury, Sérgio, 88–89, 91, 137
foco strategy, 7, 49–50, 63, 65, 81. *See also* guerrilla warfare
Foz do Iguaçu Battalion, 87, 91, 93
Fuchs, Werner, 184

Gabeira, Fernando, 125, 209; *Four Days in September*, 46
Gaia Leite, Milton, 36, 46, 64, 65, 75, 81, 102, 112
Garcia Silveira, Antônio Rogério, 46, 93
generation of 1968, 28, 31, 61–62
Gonzaga, Eugênia Augusta, 230
Goulart, João, 30, 32–33, 35, 61
Gralha, Marion Joel, 91
grêmio estudantil (student association), 27, 30, 41
guerrilla warfare: debates regarding, 49; reality of, 65–68; theories of, 44–45, 51; training for, 53–54, 58, 62–64, 70, 72. *See also* foco strategy

Haddad, Fernando, 10
Hélio Gomes prison, 122
hijacking, 120
Hogar Modelo Pedro Aguirre Cerda (building), 136
Hoje Foz (newspaper), 181, 182
Holleben, Ehrenfried von, 125
human rights, 2, 3, 245n5
human rights activism. *See under* Palmar, Aluízio: activism
hunger strikes, 114–15

Iguaçu National Park: guerrilla training in, 64, 80; interrogation of Aluízio Palmar in, 100–101; search for bodies in, 204, *204*, 206–7, 210–12, 230–31, 232
Ilha das Cobras, 113–14, 115–16, 117
Ilha das Flores, 94–96, 109–11
Ilha Grande, 123, 124
impunity, 197, 201, 208, 214, 218, 234
imprisonment, 69–70, 93–94, 111–12. *See also* Palmar, Aluízio: imprisonment
Indigenist Missionary Council, 184
inquérito policial militar. *See* IPM (military police investigation)
Institutional Act 5, 65, 105, 168
Institutional Act 13, 127
insurgency. *See* armed struggle; guerrilla warfare
Inter-American Court of Human Rights (IACtHR), 215, 265n8
interrogation, 46, 80, 81, 93, 119, 150. *See also under* Palmar, Aluízio: imprisonment
IPM (military police investigation), 90–92, 94, 97, 107–8
Itaipu Binational, 224
Itaipu hydroelectric dam, 181–82

Johnson, Lyndon, 33
Jornal do Brasil, 103–4, *104*
Justice and Peace Commission, 184

kidnappings, 104–5, 118, 120, 125–26, 127
Kissinger, Henry, 229

Lacerda, Carlos, 33
Lamarca, Carlos, 140

279

INDEX

Landau, Saul, 132, 133
Law of the Disappeared, 197, 214
lawsuit, against Aluízio Palmar, 1–2, 9, 12, 19, 233–35
life history, 3–4, 5, 8, 9–10, 12–14
Lima, Umberto Trigueiros, 30–31, 41–42, 45, 79, 81
Lisboa, Suzana, 200, 201
LSN (National Security Act), 185, 186

Magalhães, Alfredo, 95
Malhães, Paulo, 203, 217, 218
Manchete (magazine), 76, 77
March for Family with God for Liberty, 33
March of the 100,000, 58–60, 61, 62, 97
Marins, Tânia, *110*
masculinity, 28, 54, 152–53
Mauá Plaza, 94, 113, 119, 121
Mazzarollo, Juvêncio, 182, 183, 185–86, 187
Mazzini (codename). *See* Lima, Umberto Trigueiros
Mazzini Bueno School of Medicine, 31
media coverage, 76, 77, 103, *104*
Medianeira Massacre, 204–7, *204*, 208, 210–12, 216, 230–31
Meireles de Souza, Iná, 75, 102
Meirelles, Iná, 32, 46, 71, 110, *110*, 120, 175, 247n42, 249n41
Mello, Fernando Collor de, 193
memoirs, militant, 54–55, 209; of Aluízio Palmar, 208–10, 212
Memória, Verdade e Justiça, 222
Memorial de Resistência de São Paulo, 241
memory: the disappeared and, 198; food triggers and, 114–15; of perpetrators, 217; struggles of, 239–40; trauma and, 4, 5–7, 61–62, 138–39, 159, 245n7. *See also under* Palmar, Aluízio: activism
memory box, concept of, 4
memory entrepreneur, concept of, 4
memory script: concept of, 4–7, 14, 235; creation of, 89, 158, 194; discrepancies in, 16, 60–61, 62; examples of, 19, 147–48, 236–39, 240, 241–43; of perpetrators, 217, 218–19; repetition in, 175, 178–79, 210; tropes of, 28, 46, 48–49, 54–55
memory vignettes, 146–47, 159

MFPA (Women's Amnesty Movement), 172
Mendes, José Carlos, 150–51, 157, 199
methodology: challenges of, 160, 161; description of, 146, 147–48, 219–20; life history and, 9–10, 12–14
military police investigation (IPM), 90–92, 94, 97, 107–8
MIR (Chilean Revolutionary Left Movement), 141–42
Miranda, Nilmário, 199, 201
Monteiro, Clemente José, 95
Mourão Filho, Olímpio, 34
MR-8. *See* October 8 Revolutionary Movement (MR-8)
MR-8 (second), 46, 103–5, 125, 128, 140
Müller, Ana Maria, 176–77, 227
music, Aluízio Palmar's relationship with, 11, 37–38, 242

National Literacy Plan (PNA), 31–32
National Liberation Action (ALN), 49, 50, 71, 81, 103, 104, 120, 123, 156, 200; kidnappings by, 75, 125
National Liberation Command (COLINA), 40, 49, 75, 79, 82, 103, 116, 140
National Security Act (LSN), 185, 186
National Security Law (1967), 108, 118, 121
National Student Union (UNE), 39, 44, 97–98
National Truth Commission (CNV), 3, 109–10, 213–16, 217, 219, 220–21, 234
Night and Fog Decree, 197
1974 massacre. *See* Medianeira Massacre
Niterói, Brazil, 25–26, 29–30
Nogueira, Afonso Celso, 34–35
Nosso Tempo (newspaper), 9, 182–87, 191–92
Nova Aurora, 199, 200, 201

October 8 Revolutionary Movement (MR-8): armed struggle of, 7, 17–18, 52–58, 61, 62–64; dissolution of, 80–82, 102–3; founding of, 36, 40, 45–47, 249n41; imprisonment and torture of members of, 69–70, 93–94, 111–12; media coverage of, *104*; military trial against, 118–19, 121–22; overview of, 70–76, 77; politics of, 124. *See also* Dissidência-Rio de Janeiro (DI-RJ)

INDEX

Okushi, Nobuo, 125
Onde foi que vocês enterraram nossos mortos? (Palmar), 4–5, 208–10, *210*, 212
Operation Cleanup, 35
Operation Condor, 199, 266n19
Operation Heart of Stone, 264n42
Operation Três Passos, 99
Ostrovski, Mário Espedito, 1–2, 3, 101–2, 216, 219, 233–35

Palmar, Alexandre, 190, 191, 202, 228–29
Palmar, Aluízio
—activism: chronology of, 2, 8, 187–89; human rights, 3, 6, 158, 194, 218, 233; with PDT, 188, *189*; search for the disappeared, 199, 201–2, 203, 205, 207–8, 210–12; on social media, 10–11; under democracy, 191–92
—early life and background: adolescence, 26–27, 28–29; childhood, 22–26, *22*; education, 26–27, 39–40; ideas of masculinity, 28, 54, 152–53
—exile, 7–8, 18, 62, 134; in Chile, 130–31, *135*, 136–37, *138*, 139, *140*, 143
—exile, in Argentina, *135*; clandestinity in, 144–45, 146; family life in, 156, 161–62; isolation of, 165–66; political work during, 149–50, 151–52, 153–54, 157–58, 163–65; return to Brazil from, 168–69, 170
—family life: in Argentina, 156, 162, 166–67; armed struggle and, 141, 142–43; in Chile, *140*; fatherhood and, 107, 116–17, 227–28; courtship and marriage to Eunice Almeida, 76–79; memory script and, 241; return to Brazil, 168, 170–71, 189–90; tensions in, 138–39, 159–61, 178–80, 190–91
—imprisonment: arrest, 82–84; end of, 126–27, 128–29, *129*; family life during, 105–6, 107–8; in Foz do Iguaçu, 86–90, 92–94; at Hélio Gomes prison, 122–23; at Ilha das Cobras, 113–17; at Ilha das Flores, 94–95, 96–97; interrogation, 79, 89–90, 91–92, 95–96, 100–101; punishment during, 124–25; in Río de Janeiro and Curitiba, 97, 98–99
—legal system: amnesty, 179, 180; lawsuit, 1–2, 9, 12, 19, 233–35; trial, 120–22

—militancy: chronology of, 2, 7–8; location of, 20; impact on family of, 6, 79, 190–91; and memoir, 208–10, 212; memory of, 4–5, 18–19, 209–10, 222, 224–27; and music, 11, 37–38, 242; as student, 27, 30–31, 40–43, 44–47, 48; surveillance during, 48, 79–80, 183, 185, 187; and trauma, 87, 114–15, 138–39, 159
—torture: denunciation of, 128; description of, 85–88, 95–96, 99–102; effects of, 97–98, 137; narration of, 10–11; use of, 1–2
—working life: in adolescence, 26–27, 31–32; archival work, 221–23; on environment, 182; in government, 192; in journalism, 181–82, 185; *Onde foi que vocês enterraram nossos mortos?*, 4–5, 208–10, *210*, 212; on truth commissions, 216–17; in university, 41, 42
Palmar, Amanda, 228
Palmar, Andrea, 167, 170–71
Palmar, Anízio, 21–22, *22*, 23, 24, 25, 92
Palmar, Eunice (née Almeida): correspondence with Aluízio Palmar, 88, 90, 96–97, 105–6, 107, 191; courtship and marriage, 76–79, 143, 178–79, 239; experience during Aluízio Palmar's imprisonment, 92–93, 99, 116; life in Argentina, 156, 159, 167–68; life in Chile, 137–38, *138*, *140*
Palmar, Florita, *138*, 159–61, 166–67, 170, 171, 190–91, 229
Palmar, Ivan, 79–80
Palmar, Janaína, 228
Palmar, José Amaro, 22
parrot's perch, 86–87
Party Reform Act, 262n16
PCB. *See* Brazilian Communist Party (PCB)
PDT (Democratic Labor Party), 187, 188–89
People's Revolutionary Vanguard (VPR), 40, 223; activities of, 118, 125, 141–42, 147, 149, 150, 194, 225, 246n16; and COLINA, 103, 116; death of militants, 203, 209, 215–16, 221, 230, 241; dissolution of, 154, 155, 156, 157, 158; and MR-8, 75, 81; Aluízio Palmar's membership in, 18, 139, 140–41, 143, 144–45, 151–52, 162, 163, 195; role of, in Aluízio Palmar's release, 126–30
Pepe (codename), 145, 146, 147–49
Pimenta, Reinaldo Silveira, 102

INDEX

Pinho, João Roberto Castro de, 158
Pinochet, Augusto, 156
Pinto, Helinho Ribeiro, 27
Pinto, Onofre, 158, 193, 194, 195, 198, 204, 263n1
PNA (National Literacy Plan), 31–32
political prisoners, 70, 126–27, 129–30, *129*. *See also* Palmar, Aluízio: imprisonment
POLOP (Revolutionary Marxist Organization-Workers Politics), 27, 40, 45, 49, 51, 140
Ponta dos Oitis, 95–96, 109–11
Popular Colorado Movement, 63
Portelli, Alessandro, 60
Posadas, J., 27
Prestes, Luís Carlos, 44
preventative detention, 91, 92
Prisão Provisória. *See* Ahú prison
prisoner exchange, 126–27, 128, *129*
prisoners, 70, 126–27, 129–30
PT. *See* Workers' Party (PT)
PTB (Brazilian Labor Party), 24, 26, 27, 188

Quadros, Jânio, 30

race, 73–74, 123–24
Rainolfo, Otávio: anonymity and, 209; testimony of, 203, 204–5, 206–7, 208, 211–12, 217–19
Rego, Augusto Sussekind de Moraes, 121
Reis, Daniel Aarão, 28, 104
Resistência (newsletter), 41
Revolta das Barcas (1959), 26
Revolutionary Armed Vanguard–Palmares (VAR-Palmares), 103, 116, 133, 140, 246n16, 249n54
Revolutionary Marxist Organization-Workers Politics (POLOP), 27, 40, 45, 49, 51, 140
Revolution of 1964. *See* coup d'état, Brazil (1964)
Revolution within the Revolution? (Debray), 44–45
Reznik, Rosane, 112
Reznik, Ziléa, 40, 46, 93, 96, 110, *110*, 112, 249n41
Rousseff, Dilma, 27, 221
Ruggia, Liliane, 196, 200, 201

rural life, observations of, 57–58
rural-to-urban migration, 25–26

Santa Cruz, Felipe, 232–33
Santos, Alberi Vieira dos, 99, 158–59, 194–95, 196, 204, 217
São Bento massacre, 154, 194, 195
Secondary Students Union, 28–29
self-narration, 4–5, 8, 139, 160, 175. *See also* memory script
Silva, Luiz Inácio "Lula" da, 59, 203, 213, 223, 239
Silveira, Roberto, 26
social media, 9–11, 12–13; and lawsuit, 2, 9, 233–35; as memory script, 54–55
Souto, Edson Luís de Lima, 58
Souza, João Adelino de, 181, 182, 183, 184, 185, 186
Special Commission on Political Deaths and Disappearances (CEMDP), 197, 200, 202, 208, 214, 230
Special Committee for Security and Information (AESI), 183
Special Secretariat of Human Rights, 199
Spektor, Matias, 229–30
state repression, perpetrators of, 173, 177
Stroessner, Alfredo, 63
student activism, 38–39, 58–59, 97–98
suicidal ideation, 87, 88–89
suicide, 24, 102, 137; as cover-up for murder, 102, 112, 116
Suplicy Law (1964), 38–39
surveillance: of exiles, 142, 143; of Aluízio Palmar, 48, 79–80, 183, 185, 187

Temer, Michel, 230
Terror in Brazil: A Dossier (pamphlet), 111
testimonio, 246n21
Tortura Nunca Mais, 196, 226
torture, 112–13, 119, 132–33, 183–84. *See also* Palmar, Aluízio: torture
Tradition, Family, and Property movement, 23
trauma: food triggers and, 114–15; memory and, 4, 5–7, 61–62, 138–39, 159, 245n7; suicide and, 89, 137
trauma theory, 246n12

trials: against MR-8 militants, 118–19, 121–22; against Aluízio Palmar, 120–22
Tribuna do Paraná (newspaper), 92
Trotskyist Revolutionary Workers Party (PORT), 27, 28
Truth Commission, Brazilian. *See* National Truth Commission (CNV)
Truth Commission, Paraná, 216–17
truth commissions, Latin American, 245n1

UFF (Federal Fluminense University), 39–40, 41, 47, 48, 54, 59
UNE (National Student Union), 39, 44, 97–98
urban guerrillas, 103–4
urbanization, 25–26
Ustra, Carlos Alberto Brilhante, 221
"utopia impasse," 28

Valle, Jorge Medeiros, 75–76, 103
Vannuchi, Paulo, 210, 211

Vargas, Getúlio, 24, 30, 50
VAR-Palmares (Revolutionary Armed Vanguard-Palmares), 103, 116, 133, 140, 246n16, 249n54
Veja (magazine), 177–78, 195
Velho, Bernardino Jorge, 55–56
Vieira, Liszt, 40, 82, 116, 248n17
Vietnam War, 48, 58
Villalba, Rodolfo Ramírez, 63–64
visitation rights, 114–15
VPR. *See* People's Revolutionary Vanguard (VPR)

Wexler, Haskell, 132, 133
women insurgents, 32, 70–72, 96, 103; torture of, 110–12
Women's Amnesty Movement (MFPA), 172
Workers' Party (PT), 10, 203, 213, 215, 221, 239, 247n42, 248n17
World Cup (1970), 117–18